COMBINED WORDS EDITION

KINGSWAY MUSIC
EASTBOURNE

IMPORTANT NOTE

This *Words Edition* is compatible with the two *Songs of Fellowship Music Editions* (ISBN 0 86065 935 6 and 0 85476 770 3). The songs are numbered sequentially, and ordered alphabetically by first line in **two** sections. An **integrated index** is included for reference at the back of this book.

Compilation copyright © 1998 Kingsway Music,
26-28 Lottbridge Drove, Eastbourne, East Sussex, BN23 6NT, UK.
First published 1998.

The words of most of the songs in this publication
are covered by the Church Copyright Licence

United Kingdom
CCL UK Limited, P.O. Box 1339, Eastbourne, East Sussex, BN21 4YF.

United States
CCL Inc., 17201 NE Sacramento Street, Portland, Oregon 97230

Australasia
CCL Asia Pacific Pty Ltd, P.O. Box 26405, Epsom, Auckland 3, New Zealand

Africa
CCL Africa Pty Ltd, P.O. Box 2347, Durbanville 7551, Republic of South Africa

ISBN 0 85476 771 1

Designed and produced by Bookprint Creative Services
P.O. Box 827, BN21 3YJ, England for
KINGSWAY COMMUNICATIONS LTD
Lottbridge Drove, Eastbourne, East Sussex, BN23 6NT, UK.
Printed in Great Britain.

1 Dave Bilbrough.
Copyright © 1977 Kingsway's
Thankyou Music.

ABBA FATHER, let me be
Yours and Yours alone.
May my will forever be
Ever more Your own.
Never let my heart grow cold,
Never let me go.
Abba Father, let me be
Yours and Yours alone.

2 W. H. Monk.

ABIDE WITH ME, fast falls the eventide;
The darkness deepens, Lord, with me abide;
When other helpers fail and comforts flee,
Help of the helpless, O abide with me.

Swift to its close ebbs out life's little day;
Earth's joys grow dim, its glories pass away;
Change and decay in all around I see;
O Thou who changest not, abide with me.

I need Thy presence every passing hour;
What but Thy grace can foil the tempter's
    power?
Who like Thyself my guide and stay can be?
Through cloud and sunshine, O abide with me.

I fear no foe, with Thee at hand to bless;
Ills have no weight, and tears no bitterness.
Where is death's sting? Where, grave, thy
    victory?
I triumph still, if Thou abide with me.

Reveal Thyself before my closing eyes;
Shine through the gloom, and point me to
    the skies,
Heaven's morning breaks, and earth's vain
    shadows flee;
In life, in death, O Lord, abide with me.

3 Kay Chance.
Copyright © 1976 Kay Chance.

AH LORD GOD, Thou hast made the heavens
And the earth by Thy great power.
Ah Lord God, Thou hast made the heavens
And the earth by Thine outstretched arm.

Nothing is too difficult for Thee,
Nothing is too difficult for Thee.
O great and mighty God,
Great in counsel and mighty in deed,
Nothing, nothing, absolutely nothing,
Nothing is too difficult for Thee.

4 Jerry Sinclair.
Copyright © 1972,1978 Manna Music Inc/
Kingsway's Thankyou Music.

ALLELUIA, alleluia,
Alleluia, alleluia.
Alleluia, alleluia,
Alleluia, alleluia.

He's my Saviour...

He is worthy...

I will praise Him...

5 Sherrell Prebble and Howard Clark.
Copyright © 1978 Celebration/
Kingsway's Thankyou Music.

  ALLELUIA! ALLELUIA!
  Opening our hearts to Him,
  Singing alleluia! alleluia!
  Jesus is our King!

Create in us, O God
A humble heart that sets us free
To proclaim the wondrous majesty
Of our Father in heaven.

We bear the name of Christ,
Justified, we meet with Him.
His words and presence calm our fear,
Revealing God our Father here.

Let kindred voices join,
Honouring the Lamb of God
Who teaches us by bread and wine
The mystery of His body.

Pour out Your Spirit on us,
Empowering us to live as one,
To carry Your redeeming love
To a world enslaved by sin.

6 Donald Fishel.
Copyright © 1973 The Word of God Music/Adm
by CopyCare

  ALLELUIA, ALLELUIA,
  Give thanks to the risen Lord,
  Alleluia, alleluia, give praise to His name.

Jesus is Lord of all the earth,
He is the King of creation.

Spread the good news o'er all the earth,
Jesus has died and has risen.

We have been crucified with Christ,
Now we shall live forever.

God has proclaimed the just reward,
Life for all men, alleluia!

Come let us praise the living God,
Joyfully sing to our Saviour.

7 Dave Moody.
Copyright © 1984 Glory Alleluia Music/
Tempo Music Publications/Adm. by CopyCare.

ALL HAIL KING JESUS! All hail Emmanuel!
King of kings, Lord of lords,
Bright Morning Star.
And throughout eternity I'll sing Your praises,
And I'll reign with You throughout eternity.

8 Dave Bilbrough.
Copyright © 1987 Kingsway's
Thankyou Music.

ALL HAIL THE LAMB, enthroned on high;
His praise shall be our battle cry.
He reigns victorious, forever glorious,
His name is Jesus, He is the Lord.

9 Edward Perronet.
Revised John Rippon.

ALL HAIL THE POWER OF JESUS' NAME!
Let angels prostrate fall;
Bring forth the royal diadem,
And crown Him Lord of all.

Crown Him, ye martyrs of your God,
Who from His altar call;
Extol Him in whose path ye trod,
And crown Him Lord of all.

Ye seed of Israel's chosen race,
Ye ransomed of the fall,
Hail Him who saves you by His grace,
And crown Him Lord of all.

Sinners, whose love can ne'er forget
The wormwood and the gall,
Go, spread your trophies at His feet,
And crown Him Lord of all.

Let every kindred, every tribe
On this terrestrial ball,
To Him all majesty ascribe,
And crown Him Lord of all.

O that, with yonder sacred throng,
We at His feet may fall,
Join in the everlasting song,
And crown Him Lord of all!

10 Noel and Tricia Richards.
Copyright © 1987 Kingsway's
Thankyou Music.

ALL HEAVEN DECLARES
The glory of the risen Lord.
Who can compare
With the beauty of the Lord?
Forever He will be
The Lamb upon the throne.
I gladly bow the knee
And worship Him alone.

I will proclaim
The glory of the risen Lord,
Who once was slain
To reconcile man to God.
Forever You will be
The Lamb upon the throne.
I gladly bow the knee
And worship You alone.

11 Graham Kendrick & Chris Rolinson.
Copyright © 1986 Kingsway's
Thankyou Music.

ALL HEAVEN WAITS with bated breath,
For saints on earth to pray.
Majestic angels ready stand
With swords of fiery blade.
Astounding power awaits a word
From God's resplendent throne.
But God awaits our prayer of faith
That cries 'Your will be done.'

Awake, O church, arise and pray;
Complaining words discard.
The Spirit comes to fill your mouth
With truth, His mighty sword.
Go place your feet on Satan's ground
And there proclaim Christ's name,
In step with heaven's armies march
To conquer and to reign!

Now in our hearts and on our lips
The word of faith is near,
Let heaven's will on earth be done,
Let heaven flow from here.
Come blend your prayers with Jesus' own
Before the Father's throne,
And as the incense clouds ascend
God's holy fire rains down.

Soon comes the day when with a shout
King Jesus shall appear,
And with Him all the church,
From every age, shall fill the air.
The brightness of His coming shall
Consume the lawless one,
As with a word the breath of God
Tears down his rebel throne.

One body here, by heaven inspired,
We seek prophetic power;
In Christ agreed, one heart and voice,
To speak this day, this hour,
In every place where chaos rules
And evil forces brood;
Let Jesus' voice speak like the roar
Of a great multitude.

12 Roy Turner.
Copyright © 1984 Kingsway's
Thankyou Music.

ALL OVER THE WORLD THE SPIRIT IS MOVING,
All over the world as the prophet said it
    would be;
All over the world there's a mighty revelation
Of the glory of the Lord, as the waters cover
    the sea.

All over His church God's Spirit is moving,
All over His church as the prophet said it
    would be;
All over His church there's a mighty
    revelation
Of the glory of the Lord, as the waters cover
    the sea.

Right here in this place the Spirit is moving,
Right here in this place as the prophet said it
    would be;
Right here in this place there's a mighty
    revelation
Of the glory of the Lord, as the waters cover
    the sea.

13 William Kethe.

ALL PEOPLE THAT ON EARTH DO DWELL,
Sing to the Lord with cheerful voice;
Him serve with mirth, His praise forthtell,
Come ye before Him and rejoice.

Know that the Lord is God indeed,
Without our aid He did us make:
We are His flock, He doth us feed,
And for His sheep He doth us take.

O enter then His gates with praise,
Approach with joy His courts unto:
Praise, laud, and bless His name always,
For it is seemly so to do.

For why, the Lord our God is good;
His mercy is forever sure;
His truth at all times firmly stood,
And shall from age to age endure.

Praise God from whom all blessings flow,
Praise Him all creatures here below,
Praise Him above, ye heavenly hosts;
Praise Father, Son and Holy Ghost.

14 Cecil F. Alexander.

ALL THINGS BRIGHT AND BEAUTIFUL,
All creatures great and small,
All things wise and wonderful,
The Lord God made them all.

Each little flower that opens,
Each little bird that sings,
He made their glowing colours,
He made their tiny wings.

The purple-headed mountain,
The river running by,
The sunset, and the morning
That brightens up the sky.

The cold wind in the winter,
The pleasant summer sun,
The ripe fruits in the garden,
He made them every one.

He gave us eyes to see them,
And lips that we might tell
How great is God Almighty,
Who has made all things well.

15 Marc Nelson.
Copyright © 1989 Mercy/Vineyard Publishing/
Adm. by CopyCare.

ALL YOU ANGELS ROUND HIS THRONE,
    praise Him!
All you people on earth below, praise Him!
Mountains high and oceans wide, praise
    Him!
Beasts of the field and birds of the sky, praise
    Him!

Give Him praise, give Him praise,
Give Him praise from your hearts.
Give Him praise, give Him praise,
Give Him praise for He is God.

All the angels round Your throne praise You!
All the people on earth below praise You!
Mountains high and oceans wide praise You!
Beasts of the field and birds of the sky praise
    You!

We give You praise, we give You praise,
We give You praise from our hearts.
We give You praise, we give You praise,
We give You praise for You are God.

16 Austin Martin.
Copyright © 1983 Kingsway's
Thankyou Music.

ALMIGHTY GOD, we bring You praise
For Your Son, the Word of God,
By whose power the world was made,
By whose blood we are redeemed.
Morning Star, the Father's glory,
We now worship and adore You.
In our hearts Your light has risen;
Jesus, Lord, we worship You.

17 Copyright © 1980 Central Board of Finance

ALMIGHTY GOD, OUR HEAVENLY FATHER,
We have sinned against You,
And against our fellow men,
In thought and word and deed,
Through negligence, through weakness,
Through our own deliberate fault.
We are truly sorry
And repent of all our sins.
For the sake of Your Son Jesus Christ,
Who died for us,
Who died for us,
Who died for us,
Forgive us all that is past;
And grant that we may serve You
In newness of life.
To the glory of Your name, *(Men)*
To the glory of Your name, *(Women)*
To the glory of Your name, *(Men)*
To the glory of Your name, *(Women)*
To the glory of Your name. *(All)*
Amen, amen.

18 Phil Lawson Johnston.
Copyright © 1987 Kingsway's
Thankyou Music.

ALMIGHTY SOVEREIGN LORD, Creator God,
You made the heavens and the earth.
You've spoken to the world,
Yourself the living Word,
You give us eyes to see Your kingdom.

So stretch out Your hand, O God,
In signs and wonders,
We rest our faith on Your almighty power.
Stretch out Your hand, O God,
To heal and deliver. We declare,
We declare Your kingdom is here.

Stir up Your people like a mighty wind,
Come shake us, wake us from our sleep.
Give us compassion, Lord,
Love for Your holy word,
Give us the courage of Your kingdom.

Why do so many stand against You now,
Bringing dishonour to Your name?
Consider how they mock,
But we will never stop
Speaking with boldness of Your kingdom.

19 John Newton.

AMAZING GRACE! how sweet the sound
That saved a wretch like me;
I once was lost, but now am found,
Was blind, but now I see.

'Twas grace that taught my heart to fear,
And grace my fears relieved;
How precious did that grace appear,
The hour I first believed!

Through many dangers, toils and snares
I have already come;
'Tis grace that brought me safe thus far,
And grace will lead me home.

The Lord has promised good to me,
His word my hope secures;
He will my shield and portion be
As long as life endures.

Yes, when this heart and flesh shall fail,
And mortal life shall cease,
I shall possess within the veil
A life of joy and peace.

When we've been there a thousand years,
Bright shining as the sun,
We've no less days to sing God's praise
Than when we first begun.

20 Dave Bilbrough.
Copyright © 1983 Kingsway's
Thankyou Music.

AN ARMY OF ORDINARY PEOPLE,
A kingdom where love is the key,
A city, a light to the nations,
Heirs to the promise are we.
A people whose life is in Jesus,
A nation together we stand.
Only through grace are we worthy,
Inheritors of the land.

A new day is dawning,
A new age to come,
When the children of promise
Shall flow together as one.
A truth long neglected,
But the time has now come
When the children of promise
Shall flow together as one.

A people without recognition,
But with Him a destiny sealed,
Called to a heavenly vision,
His purpose shall be fulfilled.
Come, let us stand strong together,
Abandon ourselves to the King,
His love shall be ours forever,
This victory song we shall sing.

21 Charles Wesley.

AND CAN IT BE that I should gain
An interest in the Saviour's blood?
Died He for me, who caused His pain?
For me, who Him to death pursued?
Amazing love! how can it be
That Thou, my God, shouldst die for me?

'Tis mystery all! The Immortal dies:
Who can explore His strange design?
In vain the first-born seraph tries
To sound the depths of love divine!
'Tis mercy all! let earth adore,
Let angel minds inquire no more.

He left His Father's throne above,
So free, so infinite His grace;
Emptied Himself of all but love,
And bled for Adam's helpless race.
'Tis mercy all, immense and free;
For, O my God, it found out me.

Long my imprisoned spirit lay
Fast bound in sin and nature's night;
Thine eye diffused a quickening ray,
I woke, the dungeon flamed with light;
My chains fell off, my heart was free;
I rose, went forth, and followed Thee.

No condemnation now I dread;
Jesus, and all in Him, is mine!
Alive in Him, my living Head,
And clothed in righteousness divine,
Bold I approach the eternal throne,
And claim the crown, through Christ my own.

22 Author unknown.

A NEW COMMANDMENT
I give unto you,
That you love one another
As I have loved you,
That you love one another
As I have loved you.
By this shall all men know
That you are My disciples,
If you have love one for another.
By this shall all men know
That you are My disciples,
If you have love one for another.

23 James Montgomery.

ANGELS, FROM THE REALMS OF GLORY,
Wing your flight o'er all the earth;
Ye who sang creation's story,
Now proclaim Messiah's birth:

> *Come and worship*
> *Christ, the new-born King.*
> *Come and worship*
> *Worship Christ, the new-born King.*

Shepherds, in the field abiding,
Watching o'er your flocks by night,
God with man is now residing,
Yonder shines the infant-light:

Sages, leave your contemplations,
Brighter visions beam afar;
Seek the great desire of nations,
Ye have seen His natal star:

Saints, before the altar bending,
Watching long in hope and fear,
Suddenly the Lord descending
In His temple shall appear:

24 Francis Pott.

ANGEL VOICES EVER SINGING
Round Thy throne of light,
Angel harps forever ringing,
Rest not day nor night;
Thousands only live to bless Thee,
And confess Thee
Lord of might.

Thou who art beyond the farthest
Mortal eye can scan,
Can it be that Thou regardest
Songs of sinful man?
Can we know that Thou art near us
And wilt hear us?
Yes, we can.

Yes, we know that Thou rejoicest
O'er each work of Thine;
Thou didst ears and hands and voices
For Thy praise design;
Craftsman's art and music's measure
For Thy pleasure
All combine.

In Thy house, great God, we offer
Of Thine own to Thee,
And for Thine acceptance proffer,
All unworthily,
Hearts and minds and hands and voices
In our choicest
Psalmody.

Honour, glory, might, and merit
Thine shall ever be,
Father, Son, and Holy Spirit,
Blessèd Trinity.
Of the best that Thou hast given
Earth and heaven
Render Thee.

25 Martin Luther.
Tr. Thomas Carlyle.

A SAFE STRONGHOLD OUR GOD IS STILL,
A trusty shield and weapon;
He'll help us clear from all the ill
That hath us now o'ertaken.
The ancient prince of hell
Hath risen with purpose fell;
Strong mail of craft and power
He weareth in this hour;
On earth is not His fellow.

With force of arms we nothing can,
Full soon were we down-ridden;
But for us fights the proper Man,
Whom God Himself hath bidden.
Ask ye: Who is this same?
Christ Jesus is His name,
The Lord Sabaoth's Son;
He, and no other one,
Shall conquer in the battle.

And were this world all devils o'er,
And watching to devour us,
We lay it not to heart so sore;
Not they can overpower us.
And let the prince of ill
Look grim as e'er he will,
He harms us not a whit;
For why? his doom is writ;
A word shall quickly slay him.

God's word, for all their craft and force,
One moment will not linger,
But, spite of hell, shall have its course;
'Tis written by His finger.
And though they take our life,
Goods, honour, children, wife,
Yet is their profit small:
These things shall vanish all;
The city of God remaineth.

26 Mary Lou King and Mary Kirkbride Barthow.
Copyright © 1979 Peter West/
Integrity's Hosanna! Music/
Adm. by Kingsway's Thankyou Music.

ASCRIBE GREATNESS to our God, the Rock,
His work is perfect and all His ways are just.
Ascribe greatness to our God, the Rock,
His work is perfect and all His ways are just.
A God of faithfulness and without injustice,
Good and upright is He;
A God of faithfulness and without injustice,
Good and upright is He.

27 Martin J. Nystrom.
Copyright © 1983 Restoration Music Ltd./
Adm. by Sovereign Music UK.

AS THE DEER pants for the water,
So my soul longs after You.
You alone are my heart's desire
And I long to worship You.

> *You alone are my strength, my shield,*
> *To You alone may my spirit yield.*
> *You alone are my heart's desire*
> *And I long to worship You.*

I want You more than gold or silver,
Only You can satisfy.
You alone are the real joy-giver
And the apple of my eye.

You're my Friend and You are my Brother,
Even though You are a King.
I love You more than any other,
So much more than anything.

28 John Daniels.
Copyright © 1979 Word's Spirit of Praise Music/
Adm. by CopyCare.

AS WE ARE GATHERED Jesus is here;
One with each other, Jesus is here.
Joined by the Spirit, washed in the blood,
Part of the body, the church of God.
As we are gathered Jesus is here,
One with each other, Jesus is here.

29 Dale Garratt.
Copyright © 1982 Scripture in Song, a division
of Integrity Music/Adm. by Kingsway's
Thankyou Music.

> **AS WE COME WITH PRAISE** *before His*
>   *majesty,*
> *We will celebrate with joy and victory,*
> *For the Lord has come and set His people*
>   *free,*
> *We are marching on with Him,*
> *He's our deliverer.*
>   (Repeat)

The two-edgèd sword is sharpened in our
    hand.
We come with vengeance to possess our
    land.
We bind the kings because of God's right
    hand,
And carry out the sentence that our God has
    planned.

    (Last time)
    As we come with praise before His
      majesty,
    We will celebrate with joy and victory,
    For the Lord has come and set His people
      free,
    We are marching on with Him,
    He's our deliverer,
    He's our deliverer,
    He's our deliverer,
    He's our deliverer.

30 Dave Bilbrough.
Copyright © 1990 Kingsway's
Thankyou Music.

AS WE SEEK YOUR FACE,
May we know Your heart,
Feel Your presence, acceptance,
As we seek Your face.

Move among us now,
Come reveal Your power,
Show Your presence, acceptance,
Move among us now.

At Your feet we fall,
Sovereign Lord,
We cry 'holy, holy',
At Your feet we fall.

31 W. C. Dix.

AS WITH GLADNESS men of old
Did the guiding star behold;
As with joy they hailed its light,
Leading onward, beaming bright,
So, most gracious God, may we
Evermore be led by Thee.

As with joyful steps they sped,
Saviour, to Thy lowly bed,
There to bend the knee before
Thee whom heaven and earth adore,
So may we with willing feet
Ever seek Thy mercy-seat.

As they offered gifts most rare
At Thy cradle rude and bare,
So may we with holy joy,
Pure, and free from sin's alloy,
All our costliest treasures bring,
Christ, to Thee, our heavenly King.

Holy Jesus, every day
Keep us in the narrow way;
And, when earthly things are past,
Bring our ransomed souls at last
Where they need no star to guide,
Where no clouds Thy glory hide.

In the heavenly country bright
Need they no created light;
Thou its light, its joy, its crown,
Thou its sun, which goes not down.
There forever may we sing
Hallelujahs to our King.

32 Caroline Maria Noel.

AT THE NAME OF JESUS
Every knee shall bow,
Every tongue confess Him
King of glory now;
'Tis the Father's pleasure
We should call Him Lord,
Who from the beginning
Was the mighty Word.

Humbled for a season,
To receive a name
From the lips of sinners
Unto whom He came;
Faithfully He bore it
Spotless to the last,
Brought it back victorious,
When from death He passed.

Bore it up triumphant
With its human light,
Through all ranks of creatures
To the central height,
To the throne of Godhead,
To the Father's breast,
Filled it with the glory
Of that perfect rest.

In your hearts enthrone Him;
There let Him subdue
All that is not holy,
All that is not true;
Crown Him as your Captain
In temptation's hour,
Let His will enfold you
In its light and power.

Brothers, this Lord Jesus
Shall return again,
With His Father's glory,
With His angel-train;
For all wreaths of empire
Meet upon His brow,
And our hearts confess Him
King of glory now.

33 Graham Kendrick.
Copyright © 1988 Make Way Music.

AT THIS TIME OF GIVING,
Gladly now we bring
Gifts of goodness and mercy
From a heavenly King.

Earth could not contain the treasures
Heaven holds for you,
Perfect joy and lasting pleasures,
Love so strong and true.

May His tender love surround you
At this Christmastime;
May you see His smiling face
That in the darkness shines.

But the many gifts He gives
Are all poured out from one;
Come receive the greatest gift,
The gift of God's own Son.

Lai, lai, lai … (*etc.*)

34 David Fellingham.
Copyright © 1982 Kingsway's
Thankyou Music.

AT YOUR FEET WE FALL, mighty risen
Lord,
As we come before Your throne to worship
You.
By Your Spirit's power You now draw our
hearts,
And we hear Your voice in triumph ringing
clear.

I am He that liveth, that liveth and was
dead,
Behold I am alive forever more.

There we see You stand, mighty risen Lord,
Clothed in garments pure and holy, shining
bright.
Eyes of flashing fire, feet like burnished
bronze,
And the sound of many waters is Your
voice.

Like the shining sun in its noonday strength,
We now see the glory of Your wondrous face.
Once that face was marred, but now You're
glorified,
And Your words like a two-edged sword have
mighty power.

35 David J. Hadden.
Copyright © 1982 Word's Spirit of Praise
Music/Adm. by CopyCare.

AWAKE, AWAKE, O ZION,
Come clothe yourself with strength.
Awake, awake, O Zion,
Come clothe yourself with strength.

Put on your garments of splendour,
O Jerusalem.
Come sing your songs of joy and triumph,
See that your God reigns.

Burst into songs of joy together,
O Jerusalem.
The Lord has comforted His people,
The redeemed Jerusalem.

36 Verses 1 & 2 unknown.
Verse 3 J. T. McFarland.

AWAY IN A MANGER, no crib for a bed,
The little Lord Jesus laid down His sweet
head;
The stars in the bright sky looked down
where He lay;
The little Lord Jesus asleep on the hay.

The cattle are lowing, the Baby awakes,
But little Lord Jesus, no crying He makes:
I love You, Lord Jesus! Look down from the sky
And stay by my side until morning is nigh.

Be near me, Lord Jesus: I ask You to stay
Close by me forever and love me, I pray;
Bless all the dear children in Your tender care,
And fit us for heaven to live with You there.

37 Morris Chapman.
Copyright © 1983 Word Music/Adm. by CopyCare.

BE BOLD, BE STRONG,
For the Lord your God is with you.
Be bold, be strong,
For the Lord your God is with you.
I am not afraid,
I am not dismayed,
Because I'm walking in faith and victory,
Come on and walk in faith and victory,
For the Lord your God is with you.

38

BEHOLD THE DARKNESS shall cover the
  earth,
And gross darkness the people,
But the Lord shall arise upon thee
And His glory shall be seen upon thee.

So arise, shine, for thy light is come
And the glory of the Lord is risen;
So arise, shine, for thy light is come
And the glory of the Lord is upon thee.

The Gentiles shall come to thy light,
And kings to the brightness of thy rising,
And they shall call thee the city of the Lord,
The Zion of the Holy One of Israel.

Lift up thine eyes round about and see,
They gather themselves together;
And they shall come, thy sons from afar,
And thy daughters shall be nursed at thy
  side.

Then shalt thou see and flow together,
And thy heart shall be enlarged.
The abundance of the sea is converted unto
  thee,
And the nations shall come unto thee.

The sun shall no more go down,
Neither shall the moon withdraw itself;
But the Lord shall be thine everlasting light,
And the days of thy mourning shall be
  ended.

39

BENEATH THE CROSS OF JESUS
I fain would take my stand,
The shadow of a mighty rock
Within a weary land;
A home within the wilderness,
A rest upon the way,
From the burning of the noontide heat,
And the burden of the day.

O safe and happy shelter!
O refuge tried and sweet!
O trysting place where heaven's love
And heaven's justice meet!
As to the holy patriarch
That wondrous dream was given,
So seems my Saviour's cross to me
A ladder up to heaven.

There lies, beneath its shadow,
But on the farther side,
The darkness of an awful grave
That gapes both deep and wide;
And there between us stands the cross,
Two arms outstretched to save;
Like a watchman set to guard the way
From that eternal grave.

Upon that cross of Jesus
Mine eye at times can see
The very dying form of One
Who suffered there for me;
And from my smitten heart, with tears,
Two wonders I confess—
The wonders of His glorious love,
And my own worthlessness.

I take, O cross, thy shadow,
For my abiding place;
I ask no other sunshine than
The sunshine of His face;
Content to let the world go by,
To know no gain nor loss—
My sinful self my only shame,
My glory all the cross.

40

BE STILL, for the presence of the Lord, the
  Holy One is here;
Come bow before Him now with reverence
  and fear.
In Him no sin is found, we stand on holy
  ground;
Be still, for the presence of the Lord, the Holy
  One is here.

Be still, for the glory of the Lord is shining all
  around;
He burns with holy fire, with splendour He is
  crowned.
How awesome is the sight, our radiant King
  of light!
Be still, for the glory of the Lord is shining all
  around.

Be still, for the power of the Lord is moving in
  this place;
He comes to cleanse and heal, to minister His
  grace.
No work too hard for Him, in faith receive
  from Him;
Be still, for the power of the Lord is moving in
  this place.

41 Author unknown.

BE STILL AND KNOW that I am God,
Be still and know that I am God,
Be still and know that I am God.

I am the Lord that healeth thee ... *(etc.)*

In Thee, O Lord, do I put my trust ... *(etc.)*

42 Tr. Mary E. Byrne & Eleanor H. Hull.

BE THOU MY VISION, O Lord of my heart,
Be all else but naught to me, save that Thou
art;
Be Thou my best thought in the day and the
night,
Both waking and sleeping, Thy presence my
light.

Be Thou my wisdom, be Thou my true word,
Be Thou ever with me, and I with Thee, Lord;
Be Thou my great Father, and I Thy true son;
Be Thou in me dwelling, and I with Thee one.

Be Thou my breastplate, my sword for the
fight;
Be Thou my whole armour, be Thou my true
might;
Be Thou my soul's shelter, be Thou my
strong tower:
O raise Thou me heavenward, great Power of
my power.

Riches I need not, nor man's empty praise:
Be Thou mine inheritance now and always;
Be Thou and Thou only the first in my heart:
O Sovereign of heaven, my treasure Thou art.

High King of heaven, Thou heaven's bright
Sun,
O grant me its joys after victory is won;
Great Heart of my own heart, whatever befall,
Still be Thou my vision, O Ruler of all.

43 Bob Gillman.
Copyright © 1977 Kingsway's
Thankyou Music.

   BIND US TOGETHER, *Lord,*
   Bind us together
   With cords that cannot be broken.
   Bind us together, Lord,
   Bind us together,
   Bind us together with love.

There is only one God,
There is only one King;
There is only one Body,
That is why we sing:

Made for the glory of God,
Purchased by His precious Son;
Born with the right to be clean,
For Jesus the victory has won.

You are the family of God,
You are the promise divine;
You are God's chosen desire,
You are the glorious new wine.

44 Fanny J. Crosby.

BLESSÈD ASSURANCE, Jesus is mine:
O what a foretaste of glory divine!
Heir of salvation, purchase of God;
Born of His Spirit, washed in His blood.

   This is my story, this is my song,
   Praising my Saviour all the day long.
   This is my story, this is my song,
   Praising my Saviour all the day long.

Perfect submission, perfect delight,
Visions of rapture burst on my sight;
Angels descending bring from above
Echoes of mercy, whispers of love.

Perfect submission, all is at rest,
I in my Saviour am happy and blessed;
Watching and waiting, looking above,
Filled with His goodness, lost in His love.

45 David Fellingham.
Copyright © 1983 Kingsway's
Thankyou Music.

BLESSÈD BE the God and Father
Of our Lord Jesus Christ,
Who has blessed us with every spiritual
blessing
In heavenly places in Christ.

And He has chosen us
Before the world was formed
To be holy and blameless before Him.
In His love He has predestined us
To be adopted as sons
Through Jesus Christ to Himself.

46
Kevin Prosch & Danny Daniels.
Copyright © 1989 Mercy/Vineyard
Publishing/Adm. by CopyCare.

BLESSED BE THE NAME OF THE LORD.
Blessed be the name of the Lord.
Blessed be the name of the Lord.
Blessed be the name of the Lord.
For He is our Rock, for He is our Rock,
He is the Lord.
For He is our Rock, for He is our Rock,
He is the Lord.

Jesus reigns on high in all the earth.
Jesus reigns on high in all the earth.
Jesus reigns on high in all the earth.
Jesus reigns on high in all the earth.
The universe is in the hands
Of the Lord.
The universe is in the hands
Of the Lord.

47
Phil Rogers.
Copyright © 1989 Kingsway's
Thankyou Music.

BLESS THE LORD, O MY SOUL,
And let all that is within me bless His
   name.
O Lord my God, You are so great,
For You are clothed with splendour and
   with majesty.

How can I forget all Your benefits to me?
You forgive my sin in its entirety.
You heal me when I'm sick, from the pit
   You set me free!
You crown my life with Your love.

48
Author unknown.

BLESS THE LORD, O MY SOUL,
Bless the Lord, O my soul,
And all that is within me
Bless His holy name.
Bless the Lord, O my soul,
Bless the Lord, O my soul,
And all that is within me
Bless His holy name.

King of kings, (for ever and ever,)
Lord of lords, (for ever and ever,)
King of kings, (for ever and ever,)
King of kings and Lord of lords.

49
John Fawcett.

BLEST BE THE TIE that binds
Our hearts in Christian love;
The fellowship of kindred minds
Is like to that above.

Before our Father's throne
We pour our ardent prayers;
Our fears, our hopes, our aims are one,
Our comforts and our cares.

We share our mutual woes,
Our mutual burdens bear,
And often for each other flows
The sympathising tear.

When for a while we part,
This thought will soothe our pain,
That we shall still be joined in heart,
And hope to meet again.

This glorious hope revives
Our courage by the way,
While each in expectation lives,
And longs to see the day.

From sorrow, toil and pain,
And sin we shall be free;
And perfect love and friendship reign
Through all eternity.

50
Verses 1 & 4 Mary A. Lathbury.
Verses 2 & 3 Alexander Groves.

BREAK THOU THE BREAD OF LIFE,
Dear Lord, to me,
As Thou didst break the bread
Beside the sea;
Beyond the sacred page
I seek Thee, Lord;
My spirit longs for Thee,
Thou Living Word.

Thou art the Bread of Life,
O Lord, to me,
Thy holy Word the truth
That saveth me;
Give me to eat and live
With Thee above;
Teach me to love Thy truth,
For Thou art love.

O send Thy Spirit, Lord,
Now unto me,
That He may touch my eyes
And make me see;
Show me the truth concealed
Within Thy Word,
And in Thy Book revealed,
I see Thee, Lord.

Bless Thou the Bread of Life
To me, to me,
As Thou didst bless the loaves
By Galilee;
Then shall all bondage cease,
All fetters fall,
And I shall find my peace,
My all in all.

51 Edwin Hatch.

BREATHE ON ME, BREATH OF GOD,
Fill me with life anew;
That I may love what Thou dost love
And do what Thou wouldst do.

Breathe on me, Breath of God,
Until my heart is pure;
Until my will is one with Thine
To do and to endure.

Breathe on me, Breath of God,
Till I am wholly Thine;
Until this earthly part of me
Glows with Thy fire divine.

Breathe on me, Breath of God,
So shall I never die,
But live with Thee the perfect life
Of Thine eternity.

52 Brent Chambers.

BRING A PSALM to the Lord,
From the Spirit and from His word.
Lift your voice and rejoice,
For our God is a mighty King,
So come and clap your hands,
Raise a shout, as we stand before the Lord,
For the Lord is He who has the power to free,
Who by His mighty arm gives strength and
    victory.
So as we hail the King
Then let His praises ring,
And bring a psalm of joy before the Lord.

53 Janet Lunt.

BROKEN FOR ME, broken for you,
The body of Jesus, broken for you.

He offered His body, He poured out His soul;
Jesus was broken, that we might be whole:

Come to My table and with Me dine;
Eat of My bread and drink of My wine.

This is My body given for you;
Eat it remembering I died for you.

This is My blood I shed for you;
For your forgiveness, making you new.

54 Richard Gillard.

BROTHER, LET ME BE YOUR SERVANT,
Let me be as Christ to you;
Pray that I may have the grace
To let you be my servant, too.

We are pilgrims on a journey,
We are brothers on the road;
We are here to help each other
Walk the mile and bear the load.

I will hold the Christlight for you
In the night-time of your fear;
I will hold my hand out to you,
Speak the peace you long to hear.

I will weep when you are weeping,
When you laugh I'll laugh with you;
I will share your joy and sorrow
Till we've seen this journey through.

When we sing to God in heaven
We shall find such harmony,
Born of all we've known together
Of Christ's love and agony.

Brother, let me be your servant,
Let me be as Christ to you;
Pray that I may have the grace
To let you be my servant, too.

55 Noel & Tricia Richards.

BY YOUR SIDE I would stay;
In Your arms I would lay.
Jesus, lover of my soul,
Nothing from You I withhold.

Lord, I love You, and adore You;
What more can I say?
You cause my love to grow stronger
With every passing day.
(Repeat)

56 Edward R. Miller.
Copyright © 1974 Maranatha! Music/
Adm. by CopyCare.

CAUSE ME TO COME to Thy river, O Lord,
Cause me to come to Thy river, O Lord,
Cause me to come to Thy river, O Lord,
Cause me to come,
Cause me to drink,
Cause me to live.

Cause me to drink from Thy river, O Lord,
Cause me to drink from Thy river, O Lord,
Cause me to drink from Thy river, O Lord,
Cause me to come,
Cause me to drink,
Cause me to live.

Cause me to live by Thy river, O Lord,
Cause me to live by Thy river, O Lord,
Cause me to live by Thy river, O Lord,
Cause me to come,
Cause me to drink,
Cause me to live.

57 Gary Oliver.
Copyright © 1988 Integrity's Hosanna! Music.
Adm. Kingsway's Thankyou Music.

CELEBRATE JESUS, celebrate!
Celebrate Jesus, celebrate!
Celebrate Jesus, celebrate!
Celebrate Jesus, celebrate!

He is risen, He is risen,
And He lives forever more.
He is risen, He is risen,
Come on and celebrate
The resurrection of our Lord.

58 Eddie Espinosa.
Copyright © 1982 Mercy/Vineyard
Publishing/Adm. by CopyCare.

CHANGE MY HEART, O GOD,
Make it ever true;
Change my heart, O God,
May I be like You.

You are the potter,
I am the clay;
Mould me and make me,
This is what I pray.

59 J. Byrom, altd.

CHRISTIANS AWAKE! Salute the happy
  morn,
Whereon the Saviour of mankind was born;
Rise to adore the mystery of love
Which hosts of angels chanted from above;
With them the joyful tidings first begun
Of God Incarnate and the Virgin's Son.

Then to the watchful shepherds it was told,
Who heard the angelic herald's voice 'Behold,
I bring good tidings of a Saviour's birth
To you and all the nations upon earth:
This day hath God fulfilled His promised
  word,
This day is born a Saviour, Christ the Lord.'

He spake; and straightway the celestial choir
In hymns of joy unknown before conspire;
High praise of God's redeeming love they
  sang,
And heaven's whole orb with hallelujahs
  rang;
God's highest glory was their anthem still,
'On earth be peace, and unto men goodwill.'

O may we keep and ponder in our mind
God's wondrous love in saving lost mankind;
Trace we the Babe who hath retrieved our
  loss,
From His poor manger to His bitter cross;
Tread in His steps, assisted by His grace,
Till man's first heavenly state again takes
  place.

Then may we hope, the angelic hosts among,
To sing, redeemed, a glad triumphant song:
He that was born upon this joyful day
Around us all His glory shall display;
Saved by His love, incessant we shall sing
Eternal praise to heaven's almighty King.

60 Chris Rolinson.
Copyright © 1989 Kingsway's
Thankyou Music.

CHRIST IS RISEN!
Hallelujah, hallelujah!
Christ is risen!
Risen indeed, hallelujah!

Love's work is done,
The battle is won:
Where now, O death, is your sting?
He rose again
To rule and to reign,
Jesus our conquering King.

Lord over sin,
Lord over death,
At His feet Satan must fall!
Every knee bow,
All will confess
Jesus is Lord over all!

Tell it abroad
'Jesus is Lord!'
Shout it and let your praise ring!
Gladly we raise
Our songs of praise,
Worship is our offering.

61 Charles Wesley.

CHRIST THE LORD IS RISEN TODAY:
    Hallelujah!
Sons of men and angels say: Hallelujah!
Raise your joys and triumphs high:
    Hallelujah!
Sing, ye heavens, and earth reply: Hallelujah!

Love's redeeming work is done: Hallelujah!
Fought the fight, the battle won: Hallelujah!
Vain the stone, the watch, the seal:
    Hallelujah!
Christ hath burst the gates of hell: Hallelujah!

Lives again our glorious King: Hallelujah!
Where, O death, is now thy sting? Hallelujah!
Once He died, our souls to save: Hallelujah!
Where thy victory, O grave? Hallelujah!

Soar we now where Christ hath led:
    Hallelujah!
Following our exalted Head: Hallelujah!
Made like Him, like Him we rise: Hallelujah!
Ours the cross, the grave, the skies:
    Hallelujah!

Hail the Lord of earth and heaven: Hallelujah!
Praise to Thee by both be given: Hallelujah!
Thee we greet, in triumph sing: Hallelujah!
Hail our resurrected King: Hallelujah!

62 Michael Saward.
Words Copyright © Michael Saward/
Jubilate Hymns.

CHRIST TRIUMPHANT, ever reigning,
Saviour, Master, King,
Lord of heaven, our lives sustaining,
Hear us as we sing:

    Yours the glory and the crown,
    The high renown, the eternal name.

Word incarnate, truth revealing,
Son of Man on earth!
Power and majesty concealing
By your humble birth:

Suffering Servant, scorned, ill-treated,
Victim crucified!
Death is through the cross defeated,
Sinners justified:

Priestly King, enthroned forever
High in heaven above!
Sin and death and hell shall never
Stifle hymns of love:

So, our hearts and voices raising
Through the ages long,
Ceaselessly upon You gazing,
This shall be our song:

63 Graham Kendrick.
Copyright © 1988 Make Way Music.

CLEAR THE ROAD, make wide the way. *(echo)*
Welcome now the God who saves.   *(echo)*
Fill the streets with shouts of joy.   *(echo)*
(Cheers, etc.)

    Prepare the way of the Lord!   *(echo)*
    Prepare the way of the Lord!   *(echo)*

Raise your voice and join the song,   *(echo)*
God made flesh to us has come.   *(echo)*
Welcome Him, your banners wave.   *(echo)*
(Cheers, shouts, wave banners, etc.)

For all sin the price is paid,   *(echo)*
All our sins on Jesus laid.   *(echo)*
By His blood we are made clean.   *(echo)*
(Cheers, shouts of thanksgiving)

At His feet come humbly bow,   *(echo)*
In your lives enthrone Him now.   *(echo)*
See, your great Deliverer comes.   *(echo)*
(Cheers, shouts welcoming Jesus)

64 Sue McClellan, John Pac, Keith Ryecroft.
Copyright © 1974 Kingsway's Thankyou Music.

COLOURS OF DAY dawn into the mind,
The sun has come up, the night is behind.
Go down in the city, into the street,
And let's give the message to the people we
    meet.

    So light up the fire and let the flame burn,
    Open the door, let Jesus return.
    Take seeds of His Spirit, let the fruit grow,
    Tell the people of Jesus, let His love show.

Go through the park, on into the town;
The sun still shines on, it never goes down.
The light of the world is risen again;
The people of darkness are needing a friend.

Open your eyes, look into the sky,
The darkness has come, the sun came to
   die.
The evening draws on, the sun disappears,
But Jesus is living, His Spirit is near.

65 Andy Carter.
Copyright © 1977 Kingsway's
Thankyou Music.

**COME AND PRAISE HIM, ROYAL
   PRIESTHOOD,**
Come and worship, holy nation.
Worship Jesus, our Redeemer,
He is precious, King of glory.

66 Mike Kerry.
Copyright © 1982 Kingsway's
Thankyou Music.

COME AND PRAISE THE LIVING GOD,
*Come and worship, come and worship.
He has made you priest and king,
Come and worship the living God.*

We come not to a mountain of fire and
   smoke,
Not to gloom and darkness or trumpet
   sound;
We come to the new Jerusalem,
The holy city of God.

By His voice He shakes the earth,
His judgements known throughout the
   world.
But we have a city that forever stands,
The holy city of God.

67 Graham Kendrick.
Copyright © 1989 Make Way Music.

COME AND SEE, come and see,
Come and see the King of love;
See the purple robe and crown of thorns He
   wears.
Soldiers mock, rulers sneer,
As He lifts the cruel cross;
Lone and friendless now He climbs towards
   the hill.

*We worship at Your feet,
Where wrath and mercy meet,
And a guilty world is washed
By love's pure stream.
For us He was made sin—
Oh, help me take it in.
Deep wounds of love cry out
'Father, forgive.'
I worship, I worship,
The Lamb who was slain.*

Come and weep, come and mourn
For your sin that pierced Him there;
So much deeper than the wounds of thorn
   and nail.
All our pride, all our greed,
All our fallenness and shame;
And the Lord has laid the punishment on
   Him.

Man of heaven, born to earth
To restore us to Your heaven,
Here we bow in awe beneath Your searching
   eyes.
From Your tears comes our joy,
From Your death our life shall spring;
By Your resurrection power we shall rise.

68 Author unknown.

COME BLESS THE LORD,
All ye servants of the Lord,
Who stand by night in the house of the Lord.
Lift up your hands in the holy place,
Come bless the Lord,
Come bless the Lord.

69 John Sellers.
Copyright © 1984 Integrity's Hosanna! Music.
Adm. Kingsway's Thankyou Music.

COME INTO THE HOLY OF HOLIES,
Enter by the blood of the Lamb;
Come into His presence with singing,
Worship at the throne of God.
(Repeat)

Lifting holy hands
To the King of kings,
Worship Jesus.

70 Isaac Watts.

**COME, LET US JOIN OUR CHEERFUL
   SONGS**
With angels round the throne;
Ten thousand thousand are their tongues,
But all their joys are one.

'Worthy the Lamb that died,' they cry,
'To be exalted thus.'
'Worthy the Lamb,' our lips reply,
'For He was slain for us.'

Jesus is worthy to receive
Honour and power divine:
And blessings, more than we can give,
Be, Lord, forever Thine.

Let all that dwell above the sky,
And air, and earth, and seas,
Conspire to lift Thy glories high,
And speak Thine endless praise.

The whole creation join in one
To bless the sacred name
Of Him that sits upon the throne
And to adore the Lamb.

71 Brent Chambers.
Copyright © 1985 Scripture in Song,
a division of Integrity Music/Adm. by
Kingsway's Thankyou Music.

COME, LET US SING for joy to the Lord,
Come let us sing for joy to the Lord,
Come let us sing for joy to the Lord,
Come let us sing for joy to the Lord!

> *Come let us sing for joy to the Lord,*
> *Let us shout aloud to the Rock of our*
> *salvation!*
> (Repeat)

Let us come before Him with thanksgiving,
And extol Him with music and song;
For the Lord, our Lord, is a great God,
The great King above all gods.

Let us bow before Him in our worship,
Let us kneel before God, our great King;
For He is our God, and we are His people,
That's why we shout and sing!

72 Robert Walmsley.

**COME, LET US SING OF A WONDERFUL
LOVE,**
Tender and true;
Out of the heart of the Father above,
Streaming to me and to you:
Wonderful love
Dwells in the heart of the Father above.

Jesus, the Saviour, this gospel to tell,
Joyfully came;
Came with the helpless and hopeless to
dwell,
Sharing their sorrow and shame;
Seeking the lost,
Saving, redeeming at measureless cost.

Jesus is seeking the wanderers yet;
Why do they roam?
Love only waits to forgive and forget;
Home, weary wanderer, home!
Wonderful love
Dwells in the heart of the Father above.

Come to my heart, O Thou wonderful love,
Come and abide,
Lifting my life, till it rises above
Envy and falsehood and pride,
Seeking to be
Lowly and humble, a learner of Thee.

73 Patricia Morgan & Dave Bankhead.
Copyright © 1984 Kingsway's
Thankyou Music.

COME ON AND CELEBRATE
His gift of love, we will celebrate
The Son of God who loved us
And gave us life.
We'll shout Your praise, O King,
You give us joy nothing else can bring,
We'll give to You our offering
In celebration praise.

Come on and celebrate,
Celebrate,
Celebrate and sing,
Celebrate and sing to the King.
Come on and celebrate,
Celebrate,
Celebrate and sing,
Celebrate and sing to the King.

74 Graham Kendrick.
Copyright © 1985 Kingsway's
Thankyou Music.

COME SEE THE BEAUTY OF THE LORD,
Come see the beauty of His face.
See the Lamb that once was slain,
See on His palms is carved your name.
See how our pain has pierced His heart,
And on His brow He bears our pride;
A crown of thorns.

But only love pours from His heart
As silently He takes the blame.
He has my name upon His lips,
My condemnation falls on Him.
This love is marvellous to me,
His sacrifice has set me free
And now I live.

Come see the beauty of the Lord,
Come see the beauty of His face.

75 Henry Alford.

COME, YE THANKFUL PEOPLE, COME,
Raise the song of harvest home!
All is safely gathered in
Ere the winter storms begin;
God, our Maker, doth provide
For our needs to be supplied;
Come to God's own temple, come,
Raise the song of harvest-home.

All the world is God's own field,
Fruit unto His praise to yield;
Wheat and tares together sown,
Unto joy or sorrow grown;
First the blade, and then the ear,
Then the full corn shall appear:
Lord of harvest, grant that we
Wholesome grain and pure may be.

For the Lord our God shall come
And shall take His harvest home,
From His field shall in that day
All offences purge away,
Give His angels charge at last
In the fire the tares to cast,
But the fruitful ears to store
In His garner evermore.

Even so, Lord, quickly come,
Bring Thy final harvest home;
Gather Thou Thy people in,
Free from sorrow, free from sin;
There, forever purified,
In Thy garner to abide:
Come, with all Thine angels, come,
Raise the glorious harvest-home.

76 David Fellingham.
Copyright © 1983 Kingsway's
Thankyou Music.

CREATE IN ME a clean heart, O God,
And renew a right spirit in me.
Create in me a clean heart, O God,
And renew a right spirit in me.
Wash me, cleanse me, purify me;
Make my heart as white as snow.
Create in me a clean heart, O God,
And renew a right spirit in me.

77 Matthew Bridges & Godfrey Thring.

CROWN HIM WITH MANY CROWNS,
The Lamb upon His throne;
Hark, how the heavenly anthem drowns
All music but its own!
Awake, my soul, and sing
Of Him who died for thee,
And hail Him as thy matchless King
Through all eternity.

Crown Him the Lord of life,
Who triumphed o'er the grave
And rose victorious in the strife
For those He came to save:
His glories now we sing,
Who died and rose on high,
Who died eternal life to bring
And lives that death may die.

Crown Him the Lord of love;
Behold His hands and side,
Those wounds yet visible above
In beauty glorified:
No angel in the sky
Can fully bear that sight,
But downward bends His burning eye
At mysteries so bright.

Crown Him the Lord of peace,
Whose power a sceptre sways
From pole to pole, that wars may cease,
And all be prayer and praise:
His reign shall know no end,
And round His piercèd feet
Fair flowers of paradise extend
Their fragrance ever sweet.

Crown Him the Lord of years,
The Potentate of time,
Creator of the rolling spheres,
Ineffably sublime!
All hail, Redeemer, hail!
For Thou hast died for me;
Thy praise shall never, never fail
Throughout eternity.

78 Graham Kendrick.
Copyright © 1985 Kingsway's
Thankyou Music.

DARKNESS LIKE A SHROUD covers the
earth;
Evil like a cloud covers the people.
But the Lord will rise upon you,
And His glory will appear on you—
Nations will come to your light.

Arise, shine, your light has come,
The glory of the Lord has risen on you!
Arise, shine, your light has come,
Jesus the Light of the world has come.

Children of the light, be clean and pure.
Rise, you sleepers, Christ will shine on
    you.
Take the Spirit's flashing two-edged s
    word
And with faith declare God's mighty
    word;
Stand up and in His strength be strong.

Here among us now, Christ the light
Kindles brighter flames in our trembling
    hearts.
Living Word, our lamp, come guide our
    feet
As we walk as one in light and peace,
Till justice and truth shine like the sun.

Like a city bright so let us blaze;
Lights in every street turning night to day.
And the darkness shall not overcome
Till the fulness of Christ's kingdom comes,
Dawning to God's eternal day.

79   John G. Whittier.

DEAR LORD AND FATHER OF MANKIND,
Forgive our foolish ways;
Reclothe us in our rightful mind;
In purer lives Thy service find,
In deeper reverence, praise,
In deeper reverence, praise.

In simple trust like theirs who heard,
Beside the Syrian sea,
The gracious calling of the Lord,
Let us, like them, without a word
Rise up and follow Thee,
Rise up and follow Thee.

O sabbath rest by Galilee!
O calm of hills above,
Where Jesus knelt to share with Thee
The silence of eternity,
Interpreted by love,
Interpreted by love.

With that deep hush subduing all
Our words and works that drown
The tender whisper of Thy call,
As noiseless let Thy blessing fall
As fell Thy manna down,
As fell Thy manna down.

Drop Thy still dews of quietness,
Till all our strivings cease;
Take from our souls the strain and stress,
And let our ordered lives confess
The beauty of Thy peace,
The beauty of Thy peace.

Breathe through the heats of our desire
Thy coolness and Thy balm;
Let sense be dumb, let flesh retire;
Speak through the earthquake, wind and fire,
O still small voice of calm,
O still small voice of calm!

80   Chris Bowater.
       Copyright © 1986 Sovereign Lifestyle Music.

DO SOMETHING NEW, LORD,
In my heart, make a start;
Do something new, Lord,
Do something new.

I open up my heart,
As much as can be known;
I open up my will
To conform to Yours alone.

I lay before Your feet
All my hopes and desires;
Unreservedly submit
To what Your Spirit may require.

I only want to live
For Your pleasure now;
I long to please You, Father—
Will You show me how?

81   Stuart DeVane & Glenn Gore.
       Copyright © 1987 Mercy/Vineyard
       Publishing/Adm. by CopyCare.

DRAW ME CLOSER, Lord,
Draw me closer, dear Lord,
So that I might touch You,
So that I might touch You,
Lord, I want to touch You.

Touch my eyes, Lord,
Touch my eyes, dear Lord,
So that I might see You,
So that I might see You,
Lord, I want to see You:

    Your glory and Your love,
    Your glory and Your love,
    Your glory and Your love,
    And Your majesty.

82

EL-SHADDAI, El-Shaddai,
El-Elyon na Adonai,
Age to age You're still the same
By the power of the Name.
El-Shaddai, El-Shaddai,
Erkamka na Adonai,
We will praise and lift You high.
El-Shaddai.

Through Your love and through the ram
You saved the son of Abraham;
Through the power of Your hand,
Turned the sea into dry land.
To the outcast on her knees
You were the God who really sees,
And by Your might You set Your children free.

Through the years You made it clear
That the time of Christ was near,
Though the people couldn't see
What Messiah ought to be.
Though Your word contained the plan,
They just could not understand
Your most awesome work was done
Through the frailty of Your Son.

83

EMMANUEL, Emmanuel,
We call Your name, Emmanuel.
God with us, revealed in us,
We call Your name, Emmanuel.

84

ENTER IN to His great love,
Kneel before His throne;
For His blood has washed away your sin,
So enter in and worship Him.

85

ETERNAL GOD, we come to You,
We come before Your throne;
We enter by a new and living way,
With confidence we come.
We declare Your faithfulness,
Your promises are true;
We will now draw near to worship You.

(Men)
O holy God, we come to You,
O holy God, we see Your faithfulness and
love;
Your mighty power, Your majesty,
Are now revealed to us in Jesus who has
died,
Jesus who was raised,
Jesus now exalted on high.

(Women)
O holy God, full of justice,
Wisdom and righteousness, faithfulness and
love;
Your mighty power and Your majesty
Are now revealed to us in Jesus who has
died for our sin,
Jesus who was raised from the dead,
Jesus now exalted on high.

86

EXALTED, YOU ARE EXALTED,
Lord of heaven and the earth.
Exalted, You are exalted,
Ruler of the universe.
For at the name of Jesus
Every knee shall bow,
Honour and praise to Jesus,
We give You glory now.
Lord, we come before You,
Worship and adore You.

87

EXALT THE LORD OUR GOD,
Exalt the Lord our God,
And worship at His footstool,
Worship at His footstool;
Holy is He, holy is He.

88

FACING A TASK UNFINISHED,
That drives us to our knees,
A need that, undiminished,
Rebukes our slothful ease:
We, who rejoice to know Thee,
Renew before Thy throne
The solemn pledge we owe Thee
To go and make Thee known.

Where other lords beside Thee
Hold their unhindered sway,
Where forces that defied Thee
Defy Thee still today;
With none to heed their crying
For life, and love, and light,
Unnumbered souls are dying,
And pass into the night.

We bear the torch that flaming
Fell from the hands of those
Who gave their lives proclaiming
That Jesus died and rose.
Ours is the same commission,
The same glad message ours;
Fired by the same ambition,
To Thee we yield our powers.

O Father who sustained them,
O Spirit who inspired,
Saviour, whose love constrained them
To toil with zeal untired,
From cowardice defend us,
From lethargy awake!
Forth on Thine errands send us
To labour for Thy sake.

89 Brian Doerksen.
Copyright © 1989 Mercy/Vineyard
Publishing/Adm. by CopyCare.

FAITHFUL ONE, so unchanging,
Ageless One, You're my Rock of peace.
Lord of all, I depend on You,
I call out to You again and again.
I call out to You again and again.
You are my rock in times of trouble.
You lift me up when I fall down.
All through the storm Your love is the anchor,
My hope is in You alone.

90 Danny Daniels.
Copyright © 1989 Mercy/Vineyard
Publishing/Adm. by CopyCare.

FATHER, I can call You Father,
For I am Your child today,
Tomorrow and always,
You are my Father.

Father, how I love You, Father,
I will sing Your praise today,
Tomorrow and always,
For You're my Father.

Father, Father,
Father to me.
Father, holy Father,
Father to me.

Father, I will serve You, Father,
I will seek Your face today,
Tomorrow and always,
You are my Father.

91 Jack Hayford.
Copyright © 1981 Rocksmith Music/
Leosong Copyright Service.

FATHER GOD,
I give all thanks and praise to Thee,
Father God,
My hands I humbly raise to Thee;
For Your mighty power and love
Amazes me, amazes me,
And I stand in awe and worship, Father God.

92 Ian Smale.
Copyright © 1984 Kingsway's
Thankyou Music.

FATHER GOD, I WONDER how I managed to
exist
Without the knowledge of Your parenthood
and Your loving care.
But now I am Your son, I am adopted in Your
family,
And I can never be alone,
'Cause Father God, You're there beside me.

I will sing Your praises,
I will sing Your praises,
I will sing Your praises,
Forever more.
I will sing Your praises,
I will sing Your praises,
I will sing Your praises,
Forever more.

93 Graham Kendrick.
Copyright © 1981 Kingsway's
Thankyou Music.

FATHER GOD, we worship You,
Make us part of all You do.
As You move among us now
We worship You.

Jesus King, we worship You,
Help us listen now to You.
As You move among us now
We worship You.

Spirit pure, we worship You,
With Your fire our zeal renew.
As You move among us now
We worship You.

94
Danny Daniels.
Copyright © 1989 Mercy/Vineyard
Publishing/Adm. by CopyCare.

FATHER HERE I AM again,
In need of mercy, hurt from sin,
So by the blood and Jesus' love,
Let forgiveness flow.

To me, from me,
So my heart will know;
Fully and sweetly,
Let forgiveness flow.

In my heart and in my mind,
In word and deed, I've been so blind,
So by the blood and Jesus' love,
Let forgiveness flow.

95
Dave Bilbrough.
Copyright © 1985 Kingsway's
Thankyou Music.

FATHER IN HEAVEN,
Our voices we raise;
Receive our devotion,
Receive now our praise,
As we sing of the glory
Of all that You've done,
The greatest love story
That's ever been sung.

And we will crown You Lord of all, ·
Yes, we will crown You Lord of all,
For You have won the victory,
Yes, we will crown You Lord of all.

Father in heaven,
Our lives are Your own;
We've been caught by a vision
Of Jesus alone,
Who came as a servant
To free us from sin.
Father in heaven,
Our worship we bring:

We will sing 'Hallelujah,'
We will sing to the King,
To our Mighty Deliverer
Our hallelujahs will ring.
Yes, our praise is resounding
To the Lamb on the throne;
He alone is exalted
Through the love He has shown.

96
Bob Fitts.
Copyright © 1985 Scripture in Song,
a division of Integrity Music/Adm.
by Kingsway's Thankyou Music.

FATHER IN HEAVEN, HOW WE LOVE YOU,
We lift Your name in all the earth.
May Your kingdom be established in our
  praises
As Your people declare Your mighty works.

Blessèd be the Lord God Almighty,
Who was and is and is to come;
Blessèd be the Lord God Almighty,
Who reigns forever more.

97
Jenny Hewer.
Copyright © 1975 Kingsway's
Thankyou Music.

FATHER, I PLACE INTO YOUR HANDS
The things I cannot do.
Father, I place into Your hands
The things that I've been through.
Father, I place into Your hands
The way that I should go,
For I know I always can trust You.

Father, I place into Your hands
My friends and family.
Father, I place into Your hands
The things that trouble me.
Father, I place into Your hands
The person I would be,
For I know I always can trust You.

Father, we love to see Your face,
We love to hear Your voice.
Father, we love to sing Your praise
And in Your name rejoice.
Father, we love to walk with You
And in Your presence rest,
For we know we always can trust You.

Father, I want to be with You
And do the things You do.
Father, I want to speak the words
That You are speaking too.
Father, I want to love the ones
That You will draw to You,
For I know that I am one with You.

98
Rick Ridings.
Copyright © 1976 Scripture in Song,
a division of Integrity Music/Adm. by
Kingsway's Thankyou Music.

FATHER, MAKE US ONE,
Father, make us one,
That the world may know
Thou hast sent the Son,
Father, make us one.

Behold how pleasant and how good it is
For brethren to dwell in unity,
For there the Lord commands the blessing,
Life forever more.

99 Terry Coelho.
Copyright © 1972 Maranatha! Music/
Adm. by CopyCare.

FATHER, WE ADORE YOU,
Lay our lives before You,
How we love You.

Jesus, we adore You ... *(etc.)*

Spirit, we adore You ... *(etc.)*

100 Philip Lawson Johnston.
Copyright © 1989 Kingsway's
Thankyou Music.

FATHER, WE ADORE YOU,
We are Your children gathered here;
To be with You is our delight,
A feast beyond compare.

Father, in Your presence
There is such freedom to enjoy.
We find in You a lasting peace
That nothing can destroy.

You are the Fountain of life,
You are the Fountain of life,
And as we drink, we are more than
satisfied
By You, O Fountain of life.

101 Carl Tuttle.
Copyright © 1982 Mercy/Vineyard
Publishing/Adm. by CopyCare.

FATHER, WE ADORE YOU,
You've drawn us to this place.
We bow down before You,
Humbly on our face.

All the earth shall worship
At the throne of the King.
Of His great and awesome power,
We shall sing!
(Repeat)

Jesus, we love You,
Because You first loved us;
You reached out and healed us
With Your mighty touch.

Spirit, we need You
To lift us from this mire;
Consume and empower us
With Your holy fire.

Faithful is He;
Awesome is He;
Saviour is He;
Master is He;
Mighty is He;
Have mercy on me.

102 Donna Adkins.
Copyright © 1976 Maranatha! Music/
Adm. by CopyCare.

FATHER, WE LOVE YOU,
We worship and adore You,
Glorify Your name in all the earth.
Glorify Your name,
Glorify Your name,
Glorify Your name in all the earth.

Jesus, we love You ... *(etc.)*

Spirit, we love You ... *(etc.)*

103 Andy Park.
Copyright © 1987 Mercy/Vineyard
Publishing/Adm. by CopyCare.

FATHER, YOU ARE MY PORTION in this life,
And You are my hope and my delight,
And I love You, yes, I love You,
Lord, I love You, my delight.

Jesus, You are my treasure in this life,
And You are so pure and so kind,
And I love You, yes, I love You,
Lord, I love You, my delight.

104 Everett Perry.
Copyright © 1983 Kingsway's
Thankyou Music.

FATHER, YOUR LOVE IS PRECIOUS beyond
all loves,
Father, Your love overwhelms me.
Father, Your love is precious beyond all
loves,
Father, Your love overwhelms me.

So I lift up my hands, an expression of my
love,
And I give You my heart in joyful obedience.
Father, Your love is precious beyond all
loves,
Father, Your love overwhelms me.

105 Phil Pringle.
Copyright © 1987 Seam of Gold/
Kingsway's Thankyou Music.

FEAR NOT, for I am with you,
Fear not, for I am with you,
Fear not, for I am with you,
Says the Lord.
(Repeat)

I have redeemed you,
I've called you by name;
Child, you are Mine.
When you walk through the waters,
I will be there,
And through the flame.
You'll not be drowned,
You'll not be burned,
For I am with you.

106 Priscilla Wright Porter.
Copyright © 1971, 1975 Celebration/
Kingsway's Thankyou Music.

FEAR NOT, REJOICE AND BE GLAD,
The Lord hath done a great thing;
Hath poured out His Spirit on all mankind,
On those who confess His name.

The fig tree is budding, the vine beareth fruit,
The wheat fields are golden with grain.
Thrust in the sickle, the harvest is ripe,
The Lord has given us rain.

Ye shall eat in plenty and be satisfied,
The mountains will drip with sweet wine.
My children shall drink of the fountain of life,
My children will know they are Mine.

My children shall dwell in a Body of love,
A light to the world they will be.
Life shall come forth from the Father above,
My Body will set mankind free.

107 John S. B. Monsell.

FIGHT THE GOOD FIGHT with all thy might,
Christ is thy strength, and Christ thy right;
Lay hold on life, and it shall be
Thy joy and crown eternally.

Run the straight race through God's good grace,
Lift up thine eyes and seek His face;
Life with its way before thee lies,
Christ is the path, and Christ the prize.

Cast care aside, lean on thy Guide;
His boundless mercy will provide;
Lean, and the trusting soul shall prove
Christ is its life, and Christ its love.

Faint not, nor fear, His arms are near,
He changeth not, and thou art dear;
Only believe, and thou shalt see
That Christ is all in all to thee.

108 Horatius Bonar.

FILL THOU MY LIFE, O Lord my God,
In every part with praise,
That my whole being may proclaim
Thy being and Thy ways.

Not for the lip of praise alone,
Nor e'en the praising heart
I ask, but for a life made up
Of praise in every part:

Praise in the common things of life,
Its goings out and in;
Praise in each duty and each deed,
However small and mean.

Fill every part of me with praise;
Let all my being speak
Of Thee and of Thy love, O Lord,
Poor though I be and weak.

So shall Thou, gracious Lord, from me
Receive the glory due;
And so shall I begin on earth
The song forever new.

So shall no part of day or night
From sacredness be free;
But all my life, in every step,
Be fellowship with Thee.

109 W. W. How.

FOR ALL THE SAINTS, who from their
labours rest,
Who Thee by faith before the world
confessed,
Thy name, O Jesus, be forever blest.
Hallelujah! Hallelujah!

Thou wast their Rock, their fortress, and their
might;
Thou, Lord, their Captain in the well-fought
fight;
Thou in the darkness drear their one true
light.
Hallelujah! Hallelujah!

O may Thy soldiers, faithful, true and bold,
Fight as the saints who nobly fought of old,
And win, with them, the victor's crown of gold!
Hallelujah! Hallelujah!

O blest communion, fellowship divine!
We feebly struggle, they in glory shine;
Yet all are one in Thee, for all are Thine.
Hallelujah! Hallelujah!

And when the strife is fierce, the warfare
    long,
Steals on the ear the distant triumph song,
And hearts are brave again, and arms are
    strong.
Hallelujah! Hallelujah!

The golden evening brightens in the west;
Soon, soon to faithful warriors cometh rest;
Sweet is the calm of paradise the blest.
Hallelujah! Hallelujah!

But lo! there breaks a yet more glorious day;
The saints triumphant rise in bright array;
The King of glory passes on His way.
Hallelujah! Hallelujah!

From earth's wide bounds, from ocean's
    farthest coast,
Through gates of pearl streams in the
    countless host,
Singing to Father, Son and Holy Ghost.
Hallelujah! Hallelujah!

110 Dale Garratt.
Copyright © 1972 Scripture in Song,
a division of Integrity Music/Adm.
by Kingsway's Thankyou Music.

FOR HIS NAME IS EXALTED,
His glory above heaven and earth.
Holy is the Lord God Almighty,
Who was and who is and who is to come.
For His name is exalted,
His glory above heaven and earth.
Holy is the Lord God Almighty,
Who sitteth on the throne
And who lives forever more.

111 Dave Richards.
Copyright © 1977 Kingsway's
Thankyou Music.

FOR I'M BUILDING A PEOPLE OF POWER,
And I'm making a people of praise
That will move through this land by My Spirit,
And will glorify My precious name.

Build Your church, Lord,
Make us strong, Lord,
Join our hearts, Lord, through Your Son.
Make us one, Lord,
In Your Body,
In the kingdom of Your Son.

112 Folliot S. Pierpoint.

FOR THE BEAUTY OF THE EARTH,
For the beauty of the skies,
For the love which from our birth
Over and around us lies:
Father, unto Thee we raise
This our sacrifice of praise.

For the beauty of each hour
Of the day and of the night,
Hill and vale, and tree and flower,
Sun and moon, and stars of light:
Father, unto Thee we raise
This our sacrifice of praise.

For the joy of human love,
Brother, sister, parent, child,
Friends on earth, and friends above;
For all gentle thoughts and mild:
Father, unto Thee we raise
This our sacrifice of praise.

For each perfect gift of Thine
To our race so freely given,
Graces, human and divine,
Flowers of earth, and buds of heaven:
Father, unto Thee we raise
This our sacrifice of praise.

113 Bonnie Low.
Copyright © 1977 Scripture in Song,
a division of Integrity Music/Adm.
by Kingsway's Thankyou Music.

FOR THE LORD IS MARCHING ON,
And His army is ever strong;
And His glory shall be seen upon our land.
Raise the anthem, sing the victor's song;
Praise the Lord for the battle's won.
No weapon formed against us shall stand.

For the Captain of the host is Jesus;
We're following in His footsteps.
No foe can stand against us in the fray.
(Repeat)

We are marching in Messiah's band,
The keys of victory in His mighty hand;
Let us march on to take our promised land!
For the Lord is marching on,
And His army is ever strong;
And His glory shall be seen upon our land.

114 Graham Kendrick.
Copyright © 1985 Kingsway's
Thankyou Music.

FOR THIS PURPOSE Christ was revealed,
To destroy all the works
Of the Evil One.
Christ in us has overcome,
So with gladness we sing
And welcome His kingdom in.

(Men)
Over sin He has conquered,
(Women)
Hallelujah, He has conquered.
(Men)
Over death victorious,
(Women)
Hallelujah, victorious.
(Men)
Over sickness He has triumphed,
(Women)
Hallelujah, He has triumphed.
(All)
Jesus reigns over all!

In the name of Jesus we stand,
By the power of His blood
We now claim this ground.
Satan has no authority here;
Powers of darkness must flee,
For Christ has the victory.

115 Pete Sanchez Jnr.
Copyright © 1977 Pete Sanchez Jnr/
Gabriel Music.

FOR THOU O LORD ART HIGH above all the
earth,
Thou art exalted far above all gods.
For Thou O Lord art high above all the earth,
Thou art exalted far above all gods.

I exalt Thee, I exalt Thee,
I exalt Thee, O Lord.
I exalt Thee, I exalt Thee,
I exalt Thee, O Lord.

116 Author unknown.

FOR UNTO US A CHILD IS BORN,
Unto us a Son is given.
And the government shall be upon His
shoulder,
And His name shall be called
Wonderful Counsellor, the Mighty God,
The Everlasting Father,
And the Prince of Peace is He.

117 Susan Hutchinson.
Copyright © 1979 Word's Spirit of
Praise Music/Adm. by CopyCare.

FOR WE SEE JESUS enthroned on high,
Clothed in His righteousness, we worship
Him.
Glory and honour we give unto You,
We see You in Your holiness
And bow before Your throne;
You are the Lord,
Your name endures forever,
Jesus the Name high over all.

118 David J. Hadden.
Copyright © 1990 Restoration Music Ltd./
Adm. by Sovereign Music UK.

FOR YOUR WONDERFUL DEEDS we give You
thanks, Lord,
For Your marvellous acts on behalf of the
people You love.
We honour You, we honour You,
For Your wonderful deeds we honour You.

For Your bountiful grace we give You thanks,
Lord,
For the peace and the joy You bestow on the
people You love.
We honour You, we honour You,
For Your bountiful grace we honour You.

119 Isaac Watts.

**FROM ALL THAT DWELL BELOW THE
SKIES**
Let the Creator's praise arise:
Alleluia! Alleluia!
Let the Redeemer's name be sung
Through every land, by every tongue.

Alleluia! Alleluia!
Alleluia! Alleluia!
Alleluia!

Eternal are Thy mercies, Lord;
Eternal truth attends Thy word:
Alleluia! Alleluia!
Thy praise shall sound from shore to
shore,
Till suns shall rise and set no more.

Your lofty themes, ye mortals, bring,
In songs of praise divinely sing:
Alleluia! Alleluia!
The great salvation loud proclaim,
And shout for joy the Saviour's name.

In every land begin the song;
To every land the strains belong.
Alleluia! Alleluia!
In cheerful sounds all voices raise,
And fill the world with loudest praise.

120 Graham Kendrick.
Copyright © 1983 Kingsway's
Thankyou Music.

FROM HEAVEN YOU CAME,
Helpless babe,
Entered our world,
Your glory veiled;
Not to be served
But to serve,
And give Your life
That we might live.

This is our God,
The Servant King,
He calls us now
To follow Him,
To bring our lives
As a daily offering
Of worship to
The Servant King.

There in the garden
Of tears,
My heavy load
He chose to bear;
His heart with sorrow
Was torn,
'Yet not My will
But Yours,' He said.

Come see His hands
And His feet,
The scars that speak
Of sacrifice;
Hands that flung stars
Into space
To cruel nails
Surrendered.

So let us learn
How to serve,
And in our lives
Enthrone Him;
Each other's needs
To prefer,
For it is Christ
We're serving.

121 Paul S. Deming.
Copyright © 1976 Integrity's Hosanna! Music.
Adm. Kingsway's Thankyou Music.

FROM THE RISING OF THE SUN
To the going down of the same,
The Lord's name
Is to be praised.
From the rising of the sun
To the going down of the same
The Lord's name
Is to be praised.

Praise ye the Lord,
Praise Him all ye servants of the Lord,
Praise the name of the Lord.
Blessèd be the name of the Lord
From this time forth and forever more.

122 Graham Kendrick.
Copyright © 1987 Make Way Music.

FROM THE SUN'S RISING
Unto the sun's setting,
Jesus our Lord
Shall be great in the earth;
And all earth's kingdoms
Shall be His dominion,
All of creation
Shall sing of His worth.

Let every heart, every voice,
Every tongue join with spirits ablaze;
One in His love, we will circle the world
With the song of His praise.
O, let all His people rejoice,
And let all the earth hear His voice!

To every tongue, tribe
And nation He sends us,
To make disciples,
To teach and baptise.
For all authority
To Him is given;
Now as His witnesses
We shall arise.

Come let us join with
The church from all nations,
Cross every border,
Throw wide every door;
Workers with Him
As He gathers His harvest,
Till earth's far corners
Our Saviour adore.

123

GIVE ME LIFE, HOLY SPIRIT,
Guide my steps in Your sight;
Help me always give You pleasure,
Keep me walking in Your light.
Give me life, Holy Spirit,
Fill me now, make us one;
I will dwell with You forever,
In the Father and the Son.

I will dwell with You,
I will dwell with You.
I will dwell with You
In the Father and the Son.

124

GIVE THANKS with a grateful heart.
Give thanks to the Holy One.
Give thanks because He's given
Jesus Christ, His Son.
(Repeat)

And now let the weak say 'I am strong,'
Let the poor say 'I am rich,'
Because of what the Lord has done for us.
(Repeat)

(Last time)
Give thanks.

125

GIVE THANKS TO THE LORD,
Call upon His name,
Make known among the nations
What He has done.
(Repeat)

Sing to Him,
Sing praise to Him,
Tell of all His wonderful acts.
Glory in His holy name,
Let the hearts of those
Who seek the Lord rejoice.

126

GLORIOUS FATHER, we exalt You,
We worship, honour and adore You.
We delight to be in Your presence, O Lord,
We magnify Your holy name.

And we sing, 'Come, Lord Jesus,
Glorify Your name.'
And we sing, 'Come, Lord Jesus,
Glorify Your name.'

127

GLORIOUS THINGS OF THEE ARE SPOKEN,
Zion, city of our God!
He whose word cannot be broken
Formed thee for His own abode.
On the Rock of Ages founded,
What can shake thy sure repose?
With salvation's walls surrounded,
Thou mayest smile at all thy foes.

See! The streams of living waters,
Springing from eternal love,
Well supply thy sons and daughters,
And all fear of want remove;
Who can faint, whilst such a river
Ever flows their thirst to assuage?
Grace which, like the Lord, the Giver,
Never fails from age to age.

Round each habitation hovering,
See the cloud and fire appear!
For a glory and a covering,
Showing that the Lord is near.
He who gives them daily manna,
He who listens when they cry:
Let Him hear the loud hosanna
Rising to His throne on high.

Saviour, if of Zion's city
I, through grace, a member am,
Let the world deride or pity,
I will glory in Thy name.
Fading is the worldling's pleasure,
All his boasted pomp and show,
Solid joys and lasting treasure
None but Zion's children know.

128

GLORY, glory in the highest;
Glory, to the Almighty;
Glory to the Lamb of God,
And glory to the living Word;
Glory to the Lamb!

I give glory, (glory)
Glory, (glory)
Glory, glory to the Lamb!
I give glory, (glory)
Glory, (glory)
Glory, glory to the Lamb!
I give glory to the Lamb!

129

GOD FORGAVE MY SIN in Jesus' name,
I've been born again in Jesus' name;
And in Jesus' name I come to you
To share His love as He told me to.

He said: 'Freely, freely, you have received,
Freely, freely give;
Go in My name, and because you believe
Others will know that I live.'

All power is given in Jesus' name,
In earth and heaven in Jesus' name;
And in Jesus' name I come to you
To share His power as He told me to.

130

GOD HAS EXALTED HIM
To the highest place,
Given Him the name
That is above every name.

And every knee shall bow,
And every tongue confess
That Jesus Christ is Lord
To the glory of God the Father.

131

GOD HAS SPOKEN TO HIS PEOPLE,
Through His prophets long ago,
Of the days in which we're living,
And the things His church should know.
Listen then, you sons of Zion,
Lend your ears to what God says,
Then respond in full obedience,
Gladly walk in all His ways.

These are times of great refreshing
Coming from the throne in heaven,
Times of building and of shaking,
When God rids His church of leaven.
Not a patching up of wineskins
Or of garments that are old,
But a glorious restoration
Just exactly as foretold.

Reign on, O God victorious,
Fulfil Your promises.
Seed of Abraham, remember
You will see all nations blessed.

Powers of darkness, we remind you
Of Christ's victory on the cross.
Hear the truth we are declaring,
Jesus won and you have lost.

132

GOD IS GOOD, *we sing and shout it.*
God is good, we celebrate.
God is good, no more we doubt it.
God is good, we know it's true.

And when I think of His love for me,
My heart fills with praise
And I feel like dancing.
For in His heart there is room for me,
And I run with arms open wide.

(Last time)
We know it's true.
Hey!

133

GOD IS HERE, GOD IS PRESENT,
God is moving by His Spirit;
Can you hear what He is saying,
Are you willing to respond?
God is here, God is present,
God is moving by His Spirit;
Lord, I open up my life to You,
Please do just what You will.

Lord, I won't stop loving You,
You mean more to me than anything else.
Lord, I won't stop loving You,
You mean more to me than life itself.

134

GOD IS OUR FATHER,
For He has made us His own,
Made Jesus our brother
And hand in hand we'll grow together as one.
Sing praise to the Lord with the tambourine,
Sing praise to the Lord with clapping hands,
Sing praise to the Lord with dancing feet,
Sing praise to the Lord with our voice.

La, la, la … *(etc.)*

135 Arthur C. Ainger.

GOD IS WORKING HIS PURPOSE OUT,
As year succeeds to year;
God is working His purpose out,
And the time is drawing near;
Nearer and nearer draws the time,
The time that shall surely be,
When the earth shall be filled
With the glory of God,
As the waters cover the sea.

From utmost East to utmost West,
Where'er man's foot hath trod,
By the mouth of many messengers
Goes forth the voice of God;
Give ear to Me, ye continents,
Ye isles, give ear to Me,
That the earth may be filled
With the glory of God,
As the waters cover the sea.

March we forth in the strength of God
With the banner of Christ unfurled,
That the light of the glorious gospel of truth
May shine throughout the world:
Fight we the fight with sorrow and sin,
To set their captives free,
That the earth may be filled
With the glory of God,
As the waters cover the sea.

All we can do is nothing worth,
Unless God blesses the deed;
Vainly we hope for the harvest-tide
Till God gives life to the seed;
Yet nearer and nearer draws the time,
The time that shall surely be,
When the earth shall be filled
With the glory of God,
As the waters cover the sea.

136 John Wimber.

GOD OF ALL COMFORT,
God of all grace,
Oh, we have come to seek You,
We have come to seek Your face.

Because You have called us,
We're gathered in this place.
Oh, we have come to seek You,
We have come to seek Your face.

137 David Fellingham.

GOD OF GLORY, we exalt Your name,
You who reign in majesty.
We lift our hearts to You
And we will worship, praise and magnify
Your holy name.

In power resplendent
You reign in glory,
Eternal King, You reign forever.
Your word is mighty,
Releasing captives,
Your love is gracious,
You are my God.

138 Chris Bowater.

GOD OF GRACE, I turn my face
To You, I cannot hide;
My nakedness, my shame, my guilt,
Are all before Your eyes.

Strivings and all anguished dreams
In rags lie at my feet,
And only grace provides the way
For me to stand complete.

And Your grace clothes me in
righteousness,
And Your mercy covers me in love.
Your life adorns and beautifies,
I stand complete in You.

139 H. E. Fosdick.

GOD OF GRACE AND GOD OF GLORY,
On Thy people pour Thy power;
Crown Thine ancient church's story;
Bring her bud to glorious flower.
Grant us wisdom,
Grant us courage,
For the facing of this hour.

Lo! the hosts of evil round us
Scorn Thy Christ, assail His ways!
Fears and doubts too long have bound us;
Free our hearts to work and praise.
Grant us wisdom,
Grant us courage,
For the living of these days.

Heal Thy children's warring madness;
Bend our pride to Thy control;
Shame our wanton, selfish gladness,
Rich in things and poor in soul.
Grant us wisdom,
Grant us courage,
Lest we miss Thy kingdom's goal.

Set our feet on lofty places;
Gird our lives that they may be
Armoured with all Christlike graces
In the fight to set men free.
Grant us wisdom,
Grant us courage,
That we fail not man nor Thee.

Save us from weak resignation
To the evils we deplore;
Let the search for Thy salvation
Be our glory ever more.
Grant us wisdom,
Grant us courage,
Serving Thee whom we adore.

140 John Mason Neale, altd.

GOOD CHRISTIAN MEN, REJOICE
With heart and soul and voice;
Give ye heed to what we say,
Jesus Christ is born today;
Ox and ass before Him bow,
And He is in the manger now.
Christ is born today;
Christ is born today!

Good Christian men, rejoice
With heart and soul and voice;
Now ye hear of endless bliss,
Jesus Christ was born for this:
He hath opened heaven's door
And man is blessed forever more.
Christ was born for this;
Christ was born for this!

Good Christian men, rejoice
With heart and soul and voice;
Now ye need not fear the grave,
Jesus Christ was born to save;
Calls you one and calls you all
To gain His everlasting hall.
Christ was born to save;
Christ was born to save!

141 Bob Pitcher.
Copyright © 1980 Kingsway's
Thankyou Music.

GREAT AND MARVELLOUS are Thy works,
O Lord God the Almighty.
Righteous and true are Thy ways,
O Thou King of the nations.
Who will not fear, O Lord,
And glorify Thy name?
For Thou alone art holy,
And all the nations will come before Thee
And worship, worship, worship before Thee,
And worship, worship, worship before Thee.

142 Kevin Prosch.
Copyright © 1987 Mercy/Vineyard
Publishing/Adm. by CopyCare.

GREAT AND MARVELLOUS ARE THY
WORKS,
Lord God Almighty;
Just and true are Thy ways, O Lord,
For You are the King of saints.

Who shall not fear Thee,
Who shall not glorify Thy name, O Lord?
For only Thou art holy.
All the nations shall come and worship
before Thee,
For Thy judgements are made manifest.
For Thy judgements are made manifest.

Hallelujah, (hallelujah)
Hallelujah to the King of saints.
Glory hallelujah, (glory hallelujah)
Glory hallelujah to the King of saints.

143 Stuart Dauermann.
Copyright © 1975 Lillenas Publishing Co./
Adm. by CopyCare.

GREAT AND WONDERFUL are Thy wondrous
deeds,
O Lord God the Almighty.
Just and true are all Thy ways, O Lord,
King of the ages art Thou.
Who shall not fear and glorify
Thy name, O Lord?
For Thou alone art holy,
Thou alone.
All the nations shall come and worship Thee,
For Thy glory shall be revealed.
Hallelujah, hallelujah, hallelujah, Amen.

Lai, lai, lai ... *(etc.)*

144 Author unknown.

GREAT IS THE LORD and greatly to be
  praised,
In the city of our God,
In the mountain of His holiness.
Beautiful for situation, the joy of the whole
  earth
Is Mount Zion on the sides of the north,
The city of the great King,
Is Mount Zion on the sides of the north,
The city of the great King.

One body, one Spirit, one faith, one Lord,
One people, one nation, praise ye the Lord.

145 Steve McEwan.
Copyright © 1985 Body Songs/Adm. by
CopyCare.

GREAT IS THE LORD and most worthy of
  praise,
The city of our God, the holy place,
The joy of the whole earth.
Great is the Lord in whom we have the
  victory,
He aids us against the enemy,
We bow down on our knees.

  *And Lord, we want to lift Your name on
    high,
  And Lord, we want to thank You,
  For the works You've done in our lives;
  And Lord, we trust in Your unfailing love,
  For You alone are God eternal,
  Throughout earth and heaven above.*

146 Dale Garratt.
Copyright © 1980 Scripture in Song,
a division of Integrity Music/
Adm. by Kingsway's Thankyou Music.

**GREAT IS THE LORD AND MIGHTY IN
  POWER,**
His understanding has no limit;
The Lord delights in those who fear Him,
Who put their hope in His unfailing love.

He strengthens the bars of your gates,
He grants you peace in your borders,
He reveals His word to His people;
He has done this for no other nation.

Great is the Lord and mighty in power,
His understanding has no limit;
Extol the Lord, O Jerusalem,
Praise your God, O people of Zion.

147 Thomas O. Chisholm (1866–1960)
William M. Runyan (1870–1957)
Copyright © 1951 Hope Publishing Co/
Adm. by CopyCare.

GREAT IS THY FAITHFULNESS, O God my
  Father,
There is no shadow of turning with Thee;
Thou changest not, Thy compassions, they
  fail not;
As Thou hast been Thou forever wilt be.

  *Great is Thy faithfulness!
  Great is Thy faithfulness!
  Morning by morning new mercies I see;
  All I have needed Thy hand hath provided,
  Great is Thy faithfulness, Lord, unto me!*

Summer and winter, and springtime and
  harvest,
Sun, moon and stars in their courses above,
Join with all nature in manifold witness
To Thy great faithfulness, mercy and love.

Pardon for sin and a peace that endureth,
Thine own dear presence to cheer and to
  guide;
Strength for today and bright hope for
  tomorrow,
Blessings all mine, with ten thousand beside!

148 William Williams.
Tr. Peter Williams.

GUIDE ME, O THOU GREAT JEHOVAH,
Pilgrim through this barren land;
I am weak, but Thou art mighty,
Hold me with Thy powerful hand:
Bread of heaven, Bread of heaven,
Feed me now and ever more,
Feed me now and ever more.

Open Thou the crystal fountain
Whence the healing stream doth flow;
Let the fiery, cloudy pillar
Lead me all my journey through:
Strong Deliverer, strong Deliverer,
Be Thou still my strength and shield,
Be Thou still my strength and shield.

When I tread the verge of Jordan
Bid my anxious fears subside;
Death of death, and hell's destruction,
Land me safe on Canaan's side:
Songs of praises, songs of praises,
I will ever give to Thee,
I will ever give to Thee.

149

John Bakewell.

HAIL, THOU ONCE DESPISÈD JESUS,
Hail, Thou Galilean King!
Thou didst suffer to release us,
Thou didst free salvation bring.
Hail, Thou agonising Saviour,
Bearer of our sin and shame;
By Thy merits we find favour,
Life is given through Thy name.

Paschal Lamb, by God appointed,
All our sins on Thee were laid.
With almighty love anointed
Thou hast full atonement made.
All Thy people are forgiven
Through the virtue of Thy blood:
Opened is the gate of heaven,
Man is reconciled to God.

Jesus, hail! enthroned in glory,
There forever to abide;
All the heavenly hosts adore Thee,
Seated at Thy Father's side:
There for sinners Thou art pleading,
There Thou dost our place prepare,
Ever for us interceding,
Till in glory we appear.

Worship, honour, power, and blessing
Thou art worthy to receive:
Loudest praises, without ceasing,
Right it is for us to give:
Come, O mighty Holy Spirit,
As our hearts and hands we raise,
Help us sing our Saviour's merits,
Help us sing Immanuel's praise.

150

James Montgomery.

HAIL TO THE LORD'S ANOINTED,
Great David's greater Son!
Hail, in the time appointed,
His reign on earth begun!
He comes to break oppression,
To set the captive free,
To take away transgression,
And rule in equity.

He comes, with succour speedy,
To those who suffer wrong;
To help the poor and needy,
And bid the weak be strong;
To give them songs for sighing,
Their darkness turn to light,
Whose souls, condemned and dying,
Were precious in His sight.

He shall come down like showers
Upon the fruitful earth;
Love, joy and hope, like flowers,
Spring in His path to birth;
Before Him, on the mountains,
Shall peace, the herald, go;
And righteousness, in fountains,
From hill to valley flow.

Kings shall fall down before Him,
And gold and incense bring;
All nations shall adore Him,
His praise all people sing;
To Him shall prayer unceasing
And daily vows ascend,
His kingdom still increasing,
A kingdom without end.

O'er every foe victorious,
He on His throne shall rest;
From age to age more glorious,
All-blessing and all-blessed.
The tide of time shall never
His covenant remove;
His name shall stand forever,
His changeless name of Love.

151

Dale Garratt.

HALLELUJAH, FOR THE LORD OUR GOD
The Almighty reigns.
Hallelujah, for the Lord our God
The Almighty reigns.
Let us rejoice and be glad
And give the glory unto Him.
Hallelujah, for the Lord our God
The Almighty reigns.

152

Tim Cullen.

HALLELUJAH, MY FATHER,
For giving us Your Son;
Sending Him into the world,
To be given up for men.
Knowing we would bruise Him
And smite Him from the earth.
Hallelujah, my Father,
In His death is my birth;
Hallelujah, my Father,
In His life is my life.

153 William C. Dix.

HALLELUJAH! SING TO JESUS;
His the sceptre, His the throne;
Hallelujah! His the triumph,
His the victory alone.
Hark, the songs of holy Zion
Thunder like a mighty flood:
'Jesus out of every nation
Hath redeemed us by His blood.'

Hallelujah! not as orphans
Are we left in sorrow now;
Hallelujah! He is near us,
Faith believes, nor questions how.
Though the clouds from sight received
  Him
When the forty days were o'er,
Shall our hearts forget His promise,
'I am with you ever more'?

Hallelujah! Bread of heaven,
Thou on earth our food, our stay;
Hallelujah! here the sinful
Flee to Thee from day to day.
Intercessor, Friend of sinners,
Earth's Redeemer, plead for me
Where the songs of all the sinless
Sweep across the crystal sea.

Hallelujah! sing to Jesus;
His the sceptre, His the throne;
Hallelujah! His the triumph,
His the victory alone.
Hark, the songs of holy Zion
Thunder like a mighty flood:
'Jesus out of every nation
Hath redeemed us by His blood.'

154 Philip Doddridge, altd.

HARK THE GLAD SOUND! The Saviour
  comes,
The Saviour promised long;
Let every heart prepare a throne,
And every voice a song.

He comes the prisoners to release,
In Satan's bondage held;
The gates of brass before Him burst,
The iron fetters yield.

He comes the broken heart to bind,
The bleeding soul to cure,
And with the treasures of His grace
To enrich the humble poor.

Our glad hosannas, Prince of Peace,
Thy welcome shall proclaim;
And heaven's eternal arches ring
With Thy belovèd name.

155 Charles Wesley, altd.

HARK! THE HERALD ANGELS SING:
'Glory to the new-born King!
Peace on earth, and mercy mild,
God and sinners reconciled!'
Joyful, all ye nations rise,
Join the triumph of the skies,
With the angelic host proclaim,
'Christ is born in Bethlehem.'
Hark! the herald angels sing:
'Glory to the new-born King!'

Christ, by highest heaven adored,
Christ, the everlasting Lord,
Late in time behold Him come,
Offspring of a virgin's womb.
Veiled in flesh the Godhead see!
Hail the incarnate Deity!
Pleased as man with man to dwell,
Jesus, our Immanuel.
Hark! the herald angels sing:
'Glory to the new-born King.'

Hail the heaven-born Prince of Peace!
Hail, the Sun of righteousness!
Light and life to all He brings,
Risen with healing in His wings,
Mild, He lays His glory by;
Born that men no more may die;
Born to raise the sons of earth;
Born to give them second birth.
Hark! the herald angels sing:
'Glory to the new-born King.'

156 A. A. Pollard.
Copyright © HarperCollins
Religious/Adm. by CopyCare

HAVE THINE OWN WAY, LORD,
Have Thine own way;
Thou art the Potter,
I am the clay.
Mould me and make me,
After Thy will,
While I am waiting
Yielded and still.

Have Thine own way, Lord,
Have Thine own way;
Search me and try me,
Master today.
Whiter than snow, Lord,
Wash me just now,
As in Thy presence
Humbly I bow.

Have Thine own way, Lord,
Have Thine own way;
Wounded and weary,
Help me, I pray.
Power, all power,
Surely is Thine;
Touch me and heal me,
Saviour divine.

Have Thine own way, Lord,
Have Thine own way;
Hold o'er my being
Absolute sway.
Fill with Thy Spirit
Till all shall see
Christ only, always,
Living in me.

157 Dave Bilbrough.
Copyright © 1990 Kingsway's
Thankyou Music.

HEALING GRACE, *healing grace,*
Show me more of Your healing grace.
Fill my life anew as I worship You,
For Your healing grace to me.

My eyes have been opened,
And now I can see
The love of the Father
Given to me.

My Saviour, Deliverer,
The reason I sing,
To You I surrender,
For You are my King.

158 Graham Kendrick.
Copyright © 1989 Make Way Music.

HEAR, O LORD, OUR CRY,
Revive us, revive us again.
For the sake of Your glory,
Revive us, revive us again.
Lord, hear our cry.
Lord, hear our cry.

Hear, O Lord, our cry,
Revive us, revive us again.
For the sake of the children,
Revive us, revive us again.
Lord, hear our cry.
Lord, hear our cry.

159 David Fellingham.
Copyright © 1988 Kingsway's
Thankyou Music.

HEAR, O SHEPHERD of Your people,
Let Your face shine and we will be saved.
Shine forth, O God, in this pagan darkness.
Awaken Your power, and come to restore.

O Lord of hosts, turn again now,
Make Your church strong to speak out
Your word.
We'll not turn back from our great
commission
To reach the lost and save this land.

Let Your power fall upon us,
Give strength unto the sons of Your right hand.
We now hear the call to seek You,
Awaken Your power, and come to restore.

160 Author unknown.

HEAVENLY FATHER, I APPRECIATE YOU.
Heavenly Father, I appreciate You.
I love You, adore You,
I bow down before You.
Heavenly Father, I appreciate You.

Son of God, what a wonder You are.
Son of God, what a wonder You are.
You cleansed my soul from sin,
You set the Holy Ghost within.
Son of God, what a wonder You are.

Holy Ghost, what a comfort You are.
Holy Ghost, what a comfort You are.
You lead us, You guide us,
You live right inside us.
Holy Ghost, what a comfort You are.

161 John Pantry.
Copyright © 1990 Kingsway's
Thankyou Music.

HE CAME TO EARTH, not to be served,
But gave His life to be a ransom for many;
The Son of God, the Son of man,
He shared our pain and bore our sins in His
body.

King of kings and Lord of lords,
I lift my voice in praise;
Such amazing love, but I do believe
This King has died for me.

And so I stand, a broken soul,
To see the pain that I have brought to Jesus;
And yet each heart will be consoled,
To be made new, the joy of all believers.

And from now on, through all my days,
I vow to live each moment here for Jesus;
Not looking back, but giving praise
For all my Lord has done for this believer.

162 Robert Whitney Manzano.
Copyright © 1984 Kingsway's
Thankyou Music.

HE GAVE ME BEAUTY for ashes,
The oil of joy for mourning,
The garment of praise
For the spirit of heaviness.
That we might be trees of righteousness,
The planting of the Lord,
That He might be glorified.

163 Joan Parsons.
Copyright © 1978 Kingsway's
Thankyou Music.

HE HOLDS THE KEY to salvation,
Jesus is over all.
He is the Lord of creation:

Allelu, alleluia.
Allelu, alleluia, Lord.

He is the Rock ever standing,
No man could break Him down.
He is the Truth everlasting:

He is a Light in the darkness,
All men shall see His face.
He breaks all chains to redeem us:

All power to Him who is mighty,
All praise to Him who is God.
All glory now and for ever:

164 Twila Paris.
Copyright © 1985 Straightway Music/
Mountain Spring/EMI Christian Music
Publishing/Adm. by CopyCare.

HE IS EXALTED,
The King is exalted on high,
I will praise Him.
He is exalted,
Forever exalted
And I will praise His name!

He is the Lord,
Forever His truth shall reign.
Heaven and earth
Rejoice in His holy name.
He is exalted,
The King is exalted on high!

165 Author unknown.

HE IS LORD, He is Lord,
He is risen from the dead
And He is Lord.
Every knee shall bow,
Every tongue confess
That Jesus Christ is Lord.

166 Kandela Groves.
Copyright © 1985 Maranatha! Music/
Adm. by CopyCare.

HE IS OUR PEACE,
Who has broken down every wall;
He is our peace.
He is our peace.
He is our peace,
Who has broken down every wall;
He is our peace.
He is our peace.

Cast all your cares on Him,
For He cares for you;
He is our peace,
He is our peace.
Cast all your cares on Him,
For He cares for you;
He is our peace,
He is our peace.

167 Chris Bowater.
Copyright © 1981 Sovereign Lifestyle Music.

HERE I AM, *wholly available;*
As for me, I will serve the Lord.
Here I am, wholly available;
As for me, I will serve the Lord.

The fields are white unto harvest,
But O, the labourers are so few;
So Lord, I give myself to help the reaping,
To gather precious souls unto You.

The time is right in the nation
For works of power and authority;
God's looking for a people who are willing
To be counted in His glorious victory.

As salt are we ready to savour?
In darkness are we ready to be light?
God's seeking out a very special people
To manifest His truth and His might.

168 William Rees.

HERE IS LOVE vast as the ocean,
Loving kindness as the flood,
When the Prince of life, our ransom
Shed for us His precious blood.
Who His love will not remember?
Who can cease to sing His praise?
He can never be forgotten
Throughout heaven's eternal days.

On the Mount of Crucifixion
Fountains opened deep and wide;
Through the floodgates of God's mercy
Flowed a vast and gracious tide.
Grace and love, like mighty rivers,
Poured incessant from above,
And heaven's peace and perfect justice
Kissed a guilty world in love.

169 Steve Hampton.
Copyright © 1978 Scripture in Song,
a division of Integrity Music/Adm.
by Kingsway's Thankyou Music.

HERE WE ARE,
Gathered together as a family;
Bound as one,
Lifting up our voices
To the King of kings.
We cry:

Abba, Father, worthy is Your name.
Abba, Father, worthy is Your name.

Here we are,
Singing together as a family;
Bound as one,
Lifting up our voices
To the King of kings.
We sing:

Abba, Father, holy is Your name.
Abba, Father, holy is Your name.

170 John Watson & Stuart Townend.
Copyright © 1991 Ampelos Music/
Adm. by CopyCare/Kingsway's
Thankyou Music.

HE SHALL REIGN as King of kings,
He shall reign as Lord of lords;
Messiah God, the living Word,
Hallelujah, hallelujah,
Let earth declare Him King!

171 Graham Kendrick.
Copyright © 1986 Kingsway's
Thankyou Music.

HE THAT IS IN US *is greater than he*
That is in the world.
He that is in us is greater than he
That is in the world.

Therefore I will sing and I will rejoice
For His Spirit lives in me.
Christ the Living One has overcome
And we share in His victory.

All the powers of death and hell and sin
Lie crushed beneath His feet;
Jesus owns the Name above all names,
Crowned with honour and majesty.

172 Graham Kendrick.
Copyright © 1988 Make Way Music.

HE WALKED WHERE I WALK, *(echo)*
He stood where I stand, *(echo)*
He felt what I feel, *(echo)*
He understands. *(echo)*
He knows my frailty, *(echo)*
Shared my humanity, *(echo)*
Tempted in every way, *(echo)*
Yet without sin. *(echo)*

God with us, so close to us. (all)
God with us, Immanuel!
(Repeat)

One of a hated race, *(echo)*
Stung by the prejudice, *(echo)*
Suffering injustice, *(echo)*
Yet He forgives. *(echo)*
Wept for my wasted years, *(echo)*
Paid for my wickedness, *(echo)*
He died in my place *(echo)*
That I might live. *(echo)*

173 Maggi Dawn.
Copyright © 1987 Kingsway's
Thankyou Music.

HE WAS PIERCED for our transgressions,
And bruised for our iniquities;
And to bring us peace He was punished,
And by His stripes we are healed.

He was led like a lamb to the slaughter,
Although He was innocent of crime;
And cut off from the land of the living,
He paid for the guilt that was mine.

We like sheep have gone astray,
Turned each one to his own way,
And the Lord has laid on Him
The iniquity of us all.

(Descant)
Like a lamb, like a lamb
To the slaughter He came.
And the Lord laid on Him
The iniquity of us all.

174 John Bunyan.

HE WHO WOULD VALIANT BE
'Gainst all disaster,
Let him in constancy
Follow the Master.
There's no discouragement
Shall make him once relent
His first avowed intent
To be a pilgrim.

Who so beset him round
With dismal stories,
Do but themselves confound—
His strength the more is.
No foes shall stay his might,
Though he with giants fight;
He will make good his right
To be a pilgrim.

Since, Lord, Thou dost defend
Us with Thy Spirit,
We know we at the end
Shall life inherit.
Then fancies flee away!
I'll fear not what men say,
I'll labour night and day
To be a pilgrim.

175 Issac Balinda.
Copyright © 1990 Integrity's Hosanna!
Music/Adm. by Kingsway's Thankyou Music.

HIGHER, HIGHER,
Higher, higher, higher,
Higher, higher, lift up Jesus higher.
Higher, higher,
Higher, higher, higher,
Higher, higher, lift up Jesus higher.

Cast your burdens onto Jesus,
He cares for you.
Cast your burdens onto Jesus,
He cares for you.

Lower, lower,
Lower, lower, lower,
Lower, lower, lower Satan lower.
Lower, lower,
Lower, lower, lower,
Lower, lower, lower Satan lower.

176 Author unknown.

HIS NAME IS HIGHER than any other,
His name is Jesus, His name is Lord.
His name is Wonderful,
His name is Counsellor,
His name is Prince of Peace,
The mighty God.
His name is higher than any other,
His name is Jesus, His name is Lord.

177 Audrey Mieir.
Copyright © 1959/1987 Manna Music Inc/
Kingsway's Thankyou Music.

HIS NAME IS WONDERFUL,
His name is Wonderful,
His name is Wonderful,
Jesus my Lord.
He is the mighty King,
Master of everything,
His name is Wonderful,
Jesus my Lord.

He's the great Shepherd,
The Rock of all ages,
Almighty God is He.
Bow down before Him,
Love and adore Him,
His name is Wonderful,
Jesus my Lord.

178 Bill Anderson.
Copyright © 1985 Kingsway's
Thankyou Music.

HIS VOICE IS THE SEA
And the sounding of the trumpets;
And the calling of the Shepherd is so sweet.
His face is the sun,
Brighter than the morning;
And all creation bows down at His feet.

Jesus is Lord, and all the earth adores
Him.
Jesus is Lord, He sits upon the throne.
When all men stand before Him,
Then every knee shall bow,
And every tongue cry 'Jesus is Lord.'

His mouth is a sword
That rules o'er the nations,
And His sword will draw His children to His
side.
His eyes are a fire
That burns throughout the kingdom,
And the burning purifies the Master's bride.

179 Danny Daniels.
Copyright © 1982 Mercy/Vineyard
Publishing/Adm. by CopyCare.

(Men and women in canon)
HOLD ME LORD, in Your arms,
Fill me Lord, with Your Spirit.
Touch my heart with Your love,
Let my life
Glorify Your name. *(All)*

Singing, Alleluia,
Singing, Alleluia,
Singing, Alleluia,
Singing, Alleluia.

Alleluia, (Alleluia,)
Allelu, (Allelu,)
Alleluia, (Alleluia,)
Allelu, (Allelu.)

180 Danny Daniels.
Copyright © 1989 Mercy/Vineyard
Publishing/Adm. by CopyCare.

HOLINESS UNTO THE LORD,
Unto the King.
Holiness unto Your name
I will sing.

Holiness unto Jesus,
Holiness unto You, Lord.
Holiness unto Jesus,
Holiness unto You, Lord.

I love You, I love Your ways,
I love Your name.
I love You, and all my days
I'll proclaim:

181 Andy Park.
Copyright © 1990 Mercy/Vineyard
Publishing/Adm. by CopyCare.

HOLY, HOLY, HOLY is the Lord God
Almighty.
Holy, holy, holy is the Lord God Almighty.
All the angels cry out holy;
All the angels exalt Your name,
Crying holy, holy, holy,
Holy is the Lord.

Holy, holy, holy is the Lord God Almighty.
Holy, holy, holy is the Lord God Almighty.
All Your people cry out holy;
All Your people exalt Your name,
Crying holy, holy, holy,
Holy is the Lord.

Glory, glory, glory to the Lord God
Almighty.
Glory, glory, glory to the Lord God
Almighty.
The whole earth is filled with Your glory;
The whole earth will exalt Your name,
Crying holy, holy, holy,
Holy is the Lord.

182 Author unknown.

HOLY, HOLY, HOLY IS THE LORD,
Holy is the Lord God Almighty.
Holy, holy, holy is the Lord,
Holy is the Lord God Almighty,
Who was and is and is to come,
Holy, holy, holy is the Lord.

Worthy, worthy, worthy is ... *(etc.)*

Jesus, Jesus, Jesus is ... *(etc.)*

Glory, glory, glory to ... *(etc.)*

183 Reginald Heber.

HOLY, HOLY, HOLY, LORD GOD ALMIGHTY!
Early in the morning
Our song shall rise to Thee:
Holy, holy, holy, merciful and mighty,
God in three Persons, blessèd Trinity!

Holy, holy, holy! all the saints adore Thee,
Casting down their golden crowns
Around the glassy sea;
Cherubim and seraphim falling down before
Thee,
Who were, and are, and ever more shall be.

Holy, holy, holy! though the darkness hide
Thee,
Though the eye of sinful man
Thy glory may not see;
Only Thou art holy, there is none beside
Thee,
Perfect in power, in love and purity.

Holy, holy, holy, Lord God Almighty!
All Thy works shall praise Thy name
In earth, and sky, and sea;
Holy, holy, holy, merciful and mighty,
God in three Persons, blessèd Trinity!

184 Author unknown.

HOLY, HOLY, HOLY LORD,
God of power and might,
Heaven and earth are filled with Your glory.
Holy, holy, holy Lord,
God of power and might,
Heaven and earth are filled with Your glory.
Hosanna, hosanna in the highest!
Hosanna, hosanna in the highest!

185 Kelly Green.
Copyright © 1982 Mercy/Vineyard
Publishing/Adm. by CopyCare.

(Men and women in canon)
HOLY IS THE LORD,
Holy is the Lord.
Holy is the Lord,
Holy is the Lord.
Righteousness and mercy,
Judgement and grace.
Faithfulness and sovereignty;
Holy is the Lord,
Holy is the Lord.

186 Chris Bowater.
Copyright © 1991 Sovereign Music UK.

HOLY ONE, Holy One,
Blessèd be the Holy One,
Almighty ever-living God,
I worship only You.

(Last time)
Holy One.

187 Alan Leppitt.
Copyright © 1991 Kingsway's
Thankyou Music.

HOLY SPIRIT, LEAD ME TO MY FATHER,
To bow before Him, and worship at His throne,
For He's my refuge, my strength and
    deliverer,
I will dwell in the shadow of Almighty God.

188 Chris Bowater.
Copyright © 1986 Sovereign Lifestyle Music.

HOLY SPIRIT, WE WELCOME YOU.
Holy Spirit, we welcome You.
Move among us with holy fire,
As we lay aside all earthly desires,
Hands reach out and our hearts aspire.
Holy Spirit, Holy Spirit,
Holy Spirit, we welcome You.

Holy Spirit, we welcome You.
Holy Spirit, we welcome You.
Let the breeze of Your presence blow,
That Your children here might truly know
How to move in the Spirit's flow.
Holy Spirit, Holy Spirit,
Holy Spirit, we welcome You.

Holy Spirit, we welcome You.
Holy Spirit, we welcome You.
Please accomplish in me today
Some new work of loving grace, I pray;
Unreservedly have Your way.
Holy Spirit, Holy Spirit,
Holy Spirit, we welcome You.

189 Carl Tuttle.
Copyright © 1985 Mercy/Vineyard
Publishing/Adm. by CopyCare.

HOSANNA, hosanna, hosanna in the
    highest.
Hosanna, hosanna, hosanna in the highest.
Lord we lift up Your name, with hearts full of
    praise,
Be exalted, O Lord, my God,
Hosanna in the highest.

Glory, glory, glory to the King of kings.
Glory, glory, glory to the King of kings.
Lord, we lift up Your name, with hearts full of
    praise,
Be exalted, O Lord, my God,
Glory to the King of kings.

190 Keith & Melody Green.
Copyright © 1982 BMG Songs Inc/Birdwing
Music/Ears to Hear Music/EMI Christian
Music Publishing/Adm. by CopyCare.

HOW I LOVE YOU,
You are the One,
You are the One.
How I love You,
You are the One for me.

I was so lost,
But You showed the way,
'Cause You are the Way.
I was so lost,
But You showed the way to me!

I was lied to,
But You told the truth,
'Cause You are the Truth.
I was lied to,
But You showed the truth to me!

I was dying,
But You gave me life,
'Cause You are the Life.
I was dying,
And You gave Your life for me!

How I love You,
You are the One,
You are the One.
How I love You,
You are the One,
God's risen Son.
You are the One for me!

Hallelujah!
You are the One,
You are the One.
Hallelujah!
You are the One for me!

191 Author unknown.

HOW LOVELY IS THY DWELLING PLACE,
O Lord of hosts,
My soul longs and yearns for Your courts,
And my heart and flesh sing for joy
To the living God.
One day in Your presence
Is far better to me than gold,
Or to live my whole life somewhere else;
And I would rather be
A doorkeeper in Your house
Than to take my fate upon myself.
You are my sun and my shield,
You are my lover from the start,
And the highway to Your city
Runs through my heart.

192 Leonard E. Smith Jnr.
Copyright © 1974, 1978 Kingsway's
Thankyou Music.

Popular version

HOW LOVELY ON THE MOUNTAINS are the
feet of Him
Who brings good news, good news,
Proclaiming peace, announcing news of
happiness,
Our God reigns, our God reigns.

Our God reigns, our God reigns,
Our God reigns, our God reigns.

You watchmen lift your voices joyfully as
one,
Shout for your King, your King.
See eye to eye the Lord restoring Zion:
Your God reigns, your God reigns!

Waste places of Jerusalem break forth with
joy,
We are redeemed, redeemed.
The Lord has saved and comforted His
people:
Your God reigns, your God reigns!

Ends of the earth, see the salvation of your
God,
Jesus is Lord, is Lord.
Before the nations He has bared His holy
arm:
Your God reigns, your God reigns!

Original version

HOW LOVELY ON THE MOUNTAINS are the
feet of Him
Who brings good news, good news,
Announcing peace, proclaiming news of
happiness,
Saying to Zion: Your God reigns.
Your God reigns, your God reigns,
Your God reigns, your God reigns.

He had no stately form, He had no majesty,
That we should be drawn to Him.
He was despised and we took no account of
Him,
Yet now He reigns with the Most High.
Now He reigns, now He reigns,
Now He reigns with the Most High!

It was our sin and guilt that bruised and
wounded Him,
It was our sin that brought Him down.
When we like sheep had gone astray, our
Shepherd came
And on His shoulders bore our shame.
On His shoulders, on His shoulders,
On His shoulders He bore our shame.

Meek as a lamb that's led out to the
slaughterhouse,
Dumb as a sheep before its shearer,
His life ran down upon the ground like
pouring rain,
That we might be born again.
That we might be, that we might be,
That we might be born again.

Out from the tomb He came with grace and
majesty,
He is alive, He is alive.
God loves us so, see here His hands, His feet,
His side,
Yes, we know He is alive.
He is alive, He is alive,
He is alive, He is alive.

How lovely on the mountains are the feet of
  Him
Who brings good news, good news,
Announcing peace, proclaiming news of
  happiness:
Our God reigns, our God reigns.
Our God reigns, our God reigns,
Our God reigns, our God reigns.

193 Phil Rogers.
Copyright © 1982 Kingsway's
Thankyou Music.

HOW PRECIOUS, O LORD,
Is Your unfailing love,
We find refuge in the shadow of Your wings.
We feast, Lord Jesus, on the abundance of
  Your house
And drink from Your river of delights.
With You is the fountain of life,
In Your light we see light.
With You is the fountain of life,
In Your light we see light.

194 John Newton.

**HOW SWEET THE NAME OF JESUS
  SOUNDS**
In a believer's ear!
It soothes his sorrows, heals his wounds,
And drives away his fear.

It makes the wounded spirit whole,
And calms the troubled breast;
'Tis manna to the hungry soul,
And to the weary, rest.

Dear name, the rock on which I build,
My shield and hiding place,
My never-failing treasury, filled
With boundless stores of grace!

Jesus! My Shepherd, Saviour, Friend,
My Prophet, Priest and King,
My Lord, my Life, my Way, my End,
Accept the praise I bring.

Weak is the effort of my heart,
And cold my warmest thought;
But when I see Thee as Thou art,
I'll praise Thee as I ought.

Till then I would Thy love proclaim
With every fleeting breath;
And may the music of Thy name
Refresh my soul in death.

195 Chris Welch.
Copyright © 1987 Kingsway's
Thankyou Music.

HOW YOU BLESS OUR LIVES, Lord God!
How You fill our lives, Lord God!
I simply want to say I love You, Lord.
I simply want to say I bless You,
I simply want to say I adore You,
And I want to lift Your name even higher.

196 Graham Kendrick.
Copyright © 1986 Kingsway's
Thankyou Music.

I AM A LIGHTHOUSE, a shining and bright
  house,
Out in the waves of a stormy sea.
The oil of the Spirit keeps my lamp burning;
Jesus, my Lord, is the light in me.
And when people see the good things that I
  do,
They'll give praises to God who has sent us
  Jesus.
We'll send out a lifeboat of love and
  forgiveness
And give them a hand to get in.
(Repeat)

While the storm is raging, whoosh, whoosh,
And the wind is blowing, ooo, ooo,
And the waves are crashing,
Crash! crash! crash! crash!

197 Dave Bilbrough.
Copyright © 1983 Kingsway's
Thankyou Music.

I AM A NEW CREATION,
No more in condemnation,
Here in the grace of God I stand.
My heart is overflowing,
My love just keeps on growing,
Here in the grace of God I stand.

And I will praise You Lord,
Yes, I will praise You Lord,
And I will sing of all that You have done.

A joy that knows no limit,
A lightness in my spirit,
Here in the grace of God I stand.

198
Danny Daniels.
Copyright © 1985 Mercy/Vineyard
Publishing/Adm. by CopyCare.

I AM A WOUNDED SOLDIER but I will not
  leave the fight,
Because the Great Physician is healing me.
So I'm standing in the battle, in the armour of
  His light,
Because His mighty power is real in me.

I am loved, I am accepted,
By the Saviour of my soul.
I am loved, I am accepted
And my wounds will be made whole.

199
John Pantry.
Copyright © 1990 Kingsway's
Thankyou Music.

I AM NOT ASHAMED *to belong to Jesus;*
I am not afraid to stand my ground,
For there is no higher cause
Than working for the King.
To Him I lift my praise,
For I am not ashamed.

Whom then shall I fear?
What shall daunt my spirit?
Sure and steadfast, anchored firm to the
  cross,
Standing with my brothers,
Serving God and others.
Though the world may ridicule, I'll still say:

At the King's returning,
Every soul will know Him,
All creation shall bow down to His name;
Brothers all, together
Serving Him forever,
He who gave His life for me, I will praise:

(Last chorus)
We are not ashamed to belong to Jesus,
We are not afraid to stand our ground,
For there is no higher cause
Than working for the King.
To Him we lift our praise,
For we are not ashamed.

200
S. Suzanne Toolan.
Copyright © 1971 G. I. A. Publications/
Adm. by Calamus.

I AM THE BREAD OF LIFE,
He who comes to Me shall not hunger,
He who believes in Me shall not thirst.
No one can come to Me
Unless the Father draw him.

And I will raise him up,
And I will raise him up,
And I will raise him up on the last day.

The bread that I will give
Is My flesh for the life of the world,
And he who eats of this bread,
He shall live for ever,
He shall live for ever.

Unless you eat
Of the flesh of the Son of Man
And drink of His blood,
And drink of His blood,
You shall not have life within you.

I am the resurrection,
I am the life,
He who believes in Me
Even if he die,
He shall live for ever.

Yes, Lord, we believe
That You are the Christ,
The Son of God
Who has come
Into the world.

201
Don Moen.
Copyright © 1985 Integrity's Hosanna! Music.
Adm. Kingsway's Thankyou Music.

I AM THE GOD THAT HEALETH THEE,
I am the Lord, your healer.
I sent My word and healed your disease,
I am the Lord, your healer.

You are the God that healeth me,
You are the Lord, my healer.
You sent Your word and healed my disease,
You are the Lord, my healer.

202
Frances Ridley Havergal.

I AM TRUSTING THEE, LORD JESUS,
Trusting only Thee!
Trusting Thee for full salvation,
Great and free.

I am trusting Thee for pardon,
At Thy feet I bow;
For Thy grace and tender mercy,
Trusting now.

I am trusting Thee for cleansing
In the crimson flood;
Trusting Thee to make me holy,
By Thy blood.

I am trusting Thee for power,
Thine can never fail;
Words which Thou Thyself shalt give me
Must prevail.

I am trusting Thee to guide me,
Thou alone shalt lead;
Every day and hour supplying
All my need.

I am trusting Thee, Lord Jesus;
Never let me fall;
I am trusting Thee for ever,
And for all.

203 Marc Nelson.
Copyright © 1987 Mercy/Vineyard
Publishing/Adm. by CopyCare.

I BELIEVE IN JESUS:
I believe He is the Son of God.
I believe He died and rose again,
I believe He paid for us all.

(Men)	And I believe He's here now,
(Women)	I believe that He is here,
(All)	Standing in our midst.
(Men)	Here with the power to heal now,
(Women)	With the power to heal,
(All)	And the grace to forgive.

I believe in You, Lord;
I believe You are the Son of God.
I believe You died and rose again,
I believe You paid for us all.

(Men)	And I believe You're here now,
(Women)	I believe that You're here,
(All)	Standing in our midst.
(Men)	Here with the power to heal now,
(Women)	With the power to heal,
(All)	And the grace to forgive.

204 Peter & Hanneke Jacobs.
Copyright © 1985 Maranatha! Music/
Adm. by CopyCare.

I CAN ALMOST SEE Your holiness,
As I look around this place;
With my hands stretched out,
To receive Your love,
I can see You on each face.

Spirit of God, lift me up,
Spirit of God, lift me up,
Fill me again with Your love,
Sweet Spirit of God.
    (Repeat)

205 William Y. Fullerton.

I CANNOT TELL why He, whom angels
    worship,
Should set His love upon the sons of men,
Or why, as Shepherd, He should seek the
    wanderers,
To bring them back, they know not how or
    when.
But this I know, that He was born of Mary,
When Bethlehem's manger was His only
    home,
And that He lived at Nazareth and laboured,
And so the Saviour, Saviour of the world, is
    come.

I cannot tell how silently He suffered,
As with His peace He graced this place of
    tears,
Or how His heart upon the cross was
    broken,
The crown of pain to three-and-thirty years.
But this I know, He heals the broken-
    hearted,
And stays our sin, and calms our lurking
    fear,
And lifts the burden from the heavy-laden,
For yet the Saviour, Saviour of the world, is
    here.

I cannot tell how He will win the nations,
How He will claim His earthly heritage,
How satisfy the needs and aspirations
Of east and west, of sinner and of sage.
But this I know, all flesh shall see His glory,
And He shall reap the harvest He has sown,
And some glad day His sun shall shine in
    splendour,
When He the Saviour, Saviour of the world, is
    known.

I cannot tell how all the lands shall worship,
When, at his bidding, every storm is stilled,
Or who can say how great the jubilation
When all the hearts of men with love are
    filled.
But this I know, the skies will thrill with
    rapture,
And myriad, myriad human voices sing,
And earth to heaven, and heaven to earth,
    will answer:
'At last the Saviour, Saviour of the world, is
    King!'

206
Chris Bowater.
Copyright © 1981 Sovereign Lifestyle Music.

I DELIGHT GREATLY IN THE LORD,
My soul rejoices in my God.
I delight greatly in the Lord,
My soul rejoices in my God.
For He has clothed me with garments of
  salvation,
And arrayed me in a robe of righteousness.
He has clothed me with garments of
  salvation,
And arrayed me in a robe of righteousness.

207
Cecily Feldman.
Copyright © 1989 Cecily Feldman/
Kingsway's Thankyou Music.

I EXALT YOU,
Just and true are all Your ways.
I exalt You,
And glorify Your name.
(Repeat)

For You are resplendent in Your majesty,
There is no other god beside You;
Magnificent in power and in glory,
You are Jehovah God Almighty.
Holy is the Lord of hosts,
Holy is the Lord.
Holy is the Lord of hosts,
Holy is the Lord!

208
Brian Howard.
Copyright © 1974 Mission Hills/
Adm. by Kingsway's Thankyou Music.

IF I WERE A BUTTERFLY,
I'd thank You, Lord, for giving me wings.
And if I were a robin in a tree,
I'd thank You, Lord, that I could sing.
And if I were a fish in the sea,
I'd wiggle my tail and I'd giggle with glee;
But I just thank You, Father,
For making me 'me'.

> *For You gave me a heart*
> *And You gave me a smile,*
> *You gave me Jesus*
> *And You made me Your child,*
> *And I just thank You, Father,*
> *For making me 'me'.*

If I were an elephant,
I'd thank You, Lord, by raising my trunk.
And if I were a kangaroo,
You know I'd hop right up to You.
And if I were an octopus,
I'd thank You, Lord, for my fine looks;
But I just thank You, Father,
For making me 'me'.

If I were a wiggily worm,
I'd thank You, Lord, that I could squirm.
And if I were a billy goat,
I'd thank You, Lord, for my strong throat.
And if I were a fuzzy-wuzzy bear,
I'd thank You, Lord, for my fuzzy-wuzzy hair;
But I just thank You, Father,
For making me 'me'.

209
Mick Ray.
Copyright © 1978 Kingsway's
Thankyou Music.

I GET SO EXCITED, LORD,
Every time I realise
I'm forgiven, I'm forgiven.
Jesus, Lord, You've done it all,
You've paid the price:
I'm forgiven, I'm forgiven.

> *Hallelujah, Lord,*
> *My heart just fills with praise;*
> *My feet start dancing, my hands rise up,*
> *And my lips they bless Your name.*
> *I'm forgiven, I'm forgiven, I'm forgiven.*
> *I'm forgiven, I'm forgiven, I'm forgiven.*

Living in Your presence, Lord,
Is life itself:
I'm forgiven, I'm forgiven.
With the past behind, grace for today
And a hope to come,
I'm forgiven, I'm forgiven.

210
Carl Tuttle.
Copyright © 1982 Mercy/Vineyard
Publishing/Adm. by CopyCare.

I GIVE YOU ALL THE HONOUR
And praise that's due Your name,
For You are the King of glory,
The Creator of all things.

> *And I worship You,*
> *I give my life to You,*
> *I fall down on my knees.*
> *Yes, I worship You,*
> *I give my life to You,*
> *I fall down on my knees.*

As Your Spirit moves upon me now
You meet my deepest need,
And I lift my hands up to Your throne,
Your mercy I've received.

You have broken chains that bound me,
You've set this captive free;
I will lift my voice to praise Your name
For all eternity.

211
Amy Rose.
Copyright © 1988 Samsongs/Coronation/
Kingsway's Thankyou Music.

I GIVE YOU NOW all I have;
I give to you My everything.
You have the power inside of you
To overcome all the hosts of darkness.

Go, go into the world,
Tell them I'm alive,
Go into the streets,
Tell them that I live,
Ooh, that I live in you.
Go, go into the world,
Claim it for your King,
Go into the streets,
Dry those people's tears,
Ooh, make the old things new.

212
Mark Altrogge.
Copyright © 1986 People of Destiny International/
Word Music/Adm. by CopyCare.

I HAVE A DESTINY *I know I shall fulfil,*
I have a destiny in that city on a hill.
I have a destiny and it's not an empty
wish,
For I know I was born for such a time as
this.

Long before the ages You predestined me
To walk in all the works You have prepared
for me.
You've given me a part to play in history
To help prepare a bride for eternity.

I did not choose You but You have chosen
me
And appointed me for bearing fruit
abundantly.
I know You will complete the work begun in
me,
By the power of Your Spirit working mightily.

213
Marc Nelson.
Copyright © 1987 Mercy/Vineyard
Publishing/Adm. by CopyCare.

I HAVE FOUND such joy in my salvation
Since I gave my heart to You,
I have found the reason I'm living,
So in love, so near to You.

I worship You, my Lord,
With all my life, praise Your name.
I worship You, worship You, my Lord.

Oh my Lord, my life I'm giving,
A living sacrifice to You.
Oh my Lord, the reason I'm living
Is to serve and worship You.

214
Karen Barrie.
Copyright © 1973 Karen Barrie.

I HAVE MADE A COVENANT with My chosen,
Given My servant My word.
I have made Your name to last forever,
Built to outlast all time.

I will celebrate Your love forever, Yahweh,
Age on age my words proclaim Your love.
For I claim that love is built to last forever,
Founded firm Your faithfulness.

Yahweh, that assembly of those who love
You
Applaud Your marvellous word.
Who in the skies can compare with Yahweh?
Who can rival Him?

Happy the people who learn to acclaim You,
They rejoice in Your light.
You are our glory and You are our courage,
Our hope belongs to You.

I have revealed My chosen servant
And He can rely on Me,
Given Him My love to last forever,
He shall rise in My name.

He will call to Me, 'My Father, My God!'
For I make Him My firstborn Son.
I cannot take back My given promise,
I've called Him to shine like the sun.

215 Horatius Bonar.

I HEARD THE VOICE OF JESUS SAY:
'Come unto Me and rest;
Lay down, thou weary one, lay down
Thy head upon My breast.'
I came to Jesus as I was,
Weary and worn and sad;
I found in Him a resting place,
And He has made me glad.

I heard the voice of Jesus say:
'Behold I freely give
The living water, thirsty one,
Stoop down and drink and live.'
I came to Jesus, and I drank
Of that life-giving stream;
My thirst was quenched, my soul revived,
And now I live in Him.

I heard the voice of Jesus say:
'I am this dark world's light;
Look unto Me, thy morn shall rise,
And all thy day be bright.'
I looked to Jesus, and I found
In Him my Star, my Sun;
And in that light of life I'll walk,
Till travelling days are done.

216

I HEAR THE SOUND OF RUSTLING in the
   leaves of the trees,
The Spirit of the Lord has come down on the
   earth.
The church that seemed in slumber has now
   risen from its knees,
And dry bones are responding with the fruits
   of new birth.
Oh, this is now a time for declaration,
The word will go to all men everywhere;
The church is here for healing of the nations,
Behold the day of Jesus drawing near.

   *My tongue will be the pen of a ready
      writer,
   And what the Father gives to me I'll sing;
   I only want to be His breath,
   I only want to glorify the King.*

And all around the world the body waits
   expectantly,
The promise of the Father is now ready to
   fall.
The watchmen on the tower all exhort us to
   prepare,
And the church responds—a people who will
   answer the call.
And this is not a phase which is passing;
It's the start of an age that is to come.
And where is the wise man and the scoffer?
Before the face of Jesus they are dumb.

A body now prepared by God and ready for
   war,
The prompting of the Spirit is our word of
   command.
We rise, a mighty army, at the bidding of the
   Lord,
The devils see and fear, for their time is at
   hand.
And children of the Lord hear our
   commission
That we should love and serve our God as
   one.
The Spirit won't be hindered by division
In the perfect work that Jesus has begun.

217

I HEAR THE SOUND OF THE ARMY OF THE LORD,
I hear the sound of the army of the Lord.
It's the sound of praise,
It's the sound of war,
The army of the Lord,
The army of the Lord,
The army of the Lord is marching on.

218

I JUST WANT TO PRAISE YOU,
Lift my hands and say: 'I love You.'
You are everything to me,
And I exalt Your holy name on high.
I just want to praise You,
Lift my hands and say: 'I love You.'
You are everything to me,
And I exalt Your holy name,
I exalt Your holy name,
I exalt Your holy name on high.

219

I JUST WANT TO PRAISE YOU, I just want to
   sing.
I just want to give You, Lord, my everything,
In every situation, in everything I do,
To give You my devotion, for my delight is
   You.

   *Lord, I lift You high.
   Your love will never die.*

220

I KNOW NOT WHY GOD'S WONDROUS GRACE
To me hath been made known;
Nor why, unworthy as I am,
He claimed me for His own.

   *But I know whom I have believèd;
   And am persuaded that He is able
   To keep that which I've committed
   Unto Him against that day.*

I know not how this saving faith
To me He did impart;
Or how believing in His word
Wrought peace within my heart.

I know not how the Spirit moves,
Convincing men of sin;
Revealing Jesus through the word,
Creating faith in Him.

I know not what of good or ill
May be reserved for me,
Of weary ways or golden days
Before His face I see.

I know not when my Lord may come;
I know not how, nor where;
If I shall pass the vale of death,
Or 'meet Him in the air'.

221

I LIFT MY EYES UP to the mountains,
Where does my help come from?
My help comes from You, Maker of
    heaven,
Creator of the earth.

O, how I need You, Lord,
You are my only hope;
You're my only prayer.
So I will wait for You
To come and rescue me,
Come and give me life.

222

I LIFT MY HANDS,
I raise my voice,
I give my heart to You, my Lord,
And I rejoice.
There are many, many reasons why I do the
    things I do,
O, but most of all I praise You,
Most of all I praise You,
Jesus, most of all I praise You because You're
    You.

I lift my hands,
I raise my voice,
I give my life to You, my Lord,
And I rejoice.
There are many, many reasons why I do the
    things I do,
O, but most of all I love You,
Most of all I love You,
Jesus, most of all I love You because You're
    You.

I lift my hands,
I raise my voice,
I give my love to You, my Lord,
And I rejoice.
There are many, many reasons why I do the
    things I do,
O, but most of all I love You,
Most of all I love You,
Jesus, most of all I love You because You're
    You.

223

I LIFT MY HANDS *(echo)*
To the coming King, *(echo)*
To the great I AM, *(echo)*
To You I sing, *(echo)*
For You're the One *(echo)*
Who reigns within my heart. *(all)*

And I will serve no foreign god,
Or any other treasure;
You are my heart's desire,
Spirit without measure.
Unto Your name
I will bring my sacrifice.

224

I LIFT MY VOICE to praise Your name,
That through my life I might proclaim
The praises of the One who reigns:
Jesus, my Lord.

Like a mighty flame that burns so bright,
I am a bearer of His light.
No longer I, for He is my life:
Jesus, my Lord.

Jesus, Jesus, alive in me.
Jesus, Jesus, setting me free.

225

I LIVE, I live because He is risen,
I live, I live with power over sin;
I live, I live because He is risen,
I live, I live to worship Him.

Thank You Jesus, thank You Jesus,
Because You're alive,
Because You're alive,
Because You're alive I live.

226
Laurie Klein.
Copyright © 1978 Maranatha! Music/
Adm. by CopyCare.

I LOVE YOU, LORD, and I lift my voice
To worship You, O my soul rejoice.
Take joy, my King, in what You hear,
May it be a sweet, sweet sound in Your ear.
(Let me)

227
David Fellingham.
Copyright © Kingsway's
Thankyou Music.

I LOVE YOU, MY LORD,
For giving to me Your great salvation,
Setting me free from sin and death
And the kingdom of Satan's destruction.
There's power in the blood
To cleanse all my sin, I know I'm forgiven;
I'm reigning in life, I'm living by faith,
I'm now united with Christ.

(1st part)
I confess with my mouth that Jesus is Lord,
Jesus is Lord, and believe in my heart
He's been raised from the dead.
I confess with my mouth that Jesus is Lord,
Jesus is Lord, and now I have life,
Now I have life by the Spirit of God.

(2nd part)
I confess with my mouth that Jesus is Lord,
And believe in my heart
He's been raised from the dead.
I confess with my mouth that Jesus is my Lord,
And now I have life by the Spirit of God.

228
James Gilbert.
Copyright © 1975 Bud John Songs/
EMI Christian Music Publishing/
Adm. by CopyCare.

I LOVE YOU WITH THE LOVE OF THE LORD,
Yes, I love you with the love of the Lord.
I can see in you the glory of my King,
And I love you with the love of the Lord.

229
Rob Hayward.
Copyright © 1985 Kingsway's
Thankyou Music.

I'M ACCEPTED, I'm forgiven,
I am fathered by the true and living God.
I'm accepted, no condemnation,
I am loved by the true and living God.
There's no guilt or fear as I draw near
To the Saviour and Creator of the world.
There is joy and peace
As I release my worship to You, O Lord.

230
Dave Bilbrough.
Copyright © 1977 Kingsway's
Thankyou Music.

I'M GONNA THANK THE LORD, He set me
free.
I'm gonna thank the Lord, He set me free,
For my Saviour He redeemed me,
For my Saviour rescued me.
Yes, I'm gonna thank the Lord, He set me
free.

I'm gonna clap my hands and stamp my feet
… *(etc.)*

I'm gonna sing and shout aloud for joy …
(etc.)

I'm gonna raise my hands in victory … *(etc.)*

231
Danny Daniels.
Copyright © 1987 Mercy/Vineyard
Publishing/Adm. by CopyCare.

I'M IN LOVE WITH YOU,
For You have called me child.
I'm in love with You,
For You have called me child.
You reached out and touched me,
You heard my lonely cry;
I will praise Your name forever,
And give You all my life.

232
Graham Kendrick.
Copyright © 1979 Kingsway's
Thankyou Music.

IMMANUEL,
God is with us,
Immanuel,
He is here.
Immanuel,
He is among us,
Immanuel,
His kingdom is here.

Wonderful Counsellor, they laughed at His
wisdom,
The Mighty God on a dusty road.
Everlasting Father, a friend of sinners,
The Prince of Peace in a cattle stall.

He was despised and rejected,
A man of sorrows acquainted with grief.
From Him we turned and hid our faces;
He was despised, Him we did not esteem.

But He was wounded for our transgressions,
He was bruised for our iniquities.
On Him was the punishment that made us
whole,
And by His stripes we are healed.

He was oppressed, He was afflicted,
And yet He opened not His mouth.
Like a lamb that is led to the slaughter,
Like a sheep before his shearers He did not
speak.

233 Graham Kendrick.
Copyright © 1988 Make Way Music.

IMMANUEL, O IMMANUEL,
Bowed in awe I worship at Your feet,
And sing Immanuel, God is with us;
Sharing my humanness, my shame,
Feeling my weaknesses, my pain,
Taking the punishment, the blame,
Immanuel.
And now my words cannot explain,
All that my heart cannot contain,
How great are the glories of Your name,
Immanuel.

234 Walter Chalmers Smith.

IMMORTAL, INVISIBLE, God only wise,
In light inaccessible hid from our eyes,
Most blessèd, most glorious, the Ancient of
Days,
Almighty, victorious, Thy great name we
praise.

Unresting, unhasting, and silent as light,
Nor wanting, nor wasting, Thou rulest in
might;
Thy justice like mountains high soaring
above
Thy clouds which are fountains of goodness
and love.

To all life Thou givest, to both great and
small;
In all life Thou livest, the true life of all;
We blossom and flourish as leaves on the
tree,
And wither and perish; but naught changeth
Thee.

Great Father of glory, pure Father of light,
Thine angels adore Thee, all veiling their
sight;
All laud we would render: O help us to see
'Tis only the splendour of light hideth Thee.

Immortal, invisible, God only wise,
In light inaccessible hid from our eyes,
Most blessèd, most glorious, the Ancient of
Days,
Almighty, victorious, Thy great name we
praise.

235 Diane Davis Andrew.
Copyright © 1971, 1975 Celebration/
Kingsway's Thankyou Music.

I'M NOT ALONE *for my Father is with me,*
With me wherever I go.
Speaking words of faith, of courage and of
love,
He's with me, He loves me, wherever I go.

Waking in the morning,
Getting ready for school,
Walking down the road;
In class, at work, or at play,
He's with me, He loves me, wherever I go.

And when I find myself in a mess,
I can trust in Him;
Call on His name and watch Him move,
He's with me, He loves me, wherever I go.

All of my life, everywhere that I go,
I will walk with Him;
Praising Him and blessing His name,
He's with me, He loves me, wherever I go.

236 Graham Kendrick.
Copyright © 1986 Kingsway's
Thankyou Music.

I'M SPECIAL because God has loved me,
For He gave the best thing that He had to
save me;
His own Son Jesus, crucified to take the
blame
For all the bad things I have done.
Thank You Jesus, thank You Lord,
For loving me so much.
I know I don't deserve anything.
Help me feel Your love right now,
To know deep in my heart
That I'm Your special friend.

237 Jamie Owens-Collins.
Copyright © 1984 Fairhill Music/
Adm. by CopyCare.

IN HEAVENLY ARMOUR we'll enter the land,
The battle belongs to the Lord.
No weapon that's fashioned against us will
stand,
The battle belongs to the Lord.

And we sing glory, honour,
Power and strength to the Lord.
We sing glory, honour,
Power and strength to the Lord.

When the power of darkness comes in like a
    flood,
The battle belongs to the Lord.
He's raised up a standard, the power of His
    blood,
The battle belongs to the Lord.

When your enemy presses in hard, do not
    fear,
The battle belongs to the Lord.
Take courage, my friend, your redemption is
    near.
The battle belongs to the Lord.

238   Anna L. Waring.

IN HEAVENLY LOVE ABIDING,
No change my heart shall fear;
And safe is such confiding,
For nothing changes here:
The storm may roar without me,
My heart may low be laid;
But God is round about me,
And can I be dismayed?

Wherever He may guide me,
No want shall turn me back;
My Shepherd is beside me,
And nothing can I lack:
His wisdom ever waketh,
His sight is never dim;
He knows the way He taketh,
And I will walk with Him.

Green pastures are before me,
Which yet I have not seen;
Bright skies will soon be o'er me,
Where darkest clouds have been;
My hope I cannot measure,
My path to life is free;
My Saviour has my treasure,
And He will walk with me.

239   Randy Speir.

IN HIM WE LIVE AND MOVE
And have our being,
In Him we live and move
And have our being.

Make a joyful noise,
Sing unto the Lord,
Tell Him of your love,
Dance before Him.
Make a joyful noise,
Sing unto the Lord,
Tell Him of your love:
Hallelujah!

240   David Fellingham.

IN MAJESTY HE COMES,
The Lamb who once was slain;
Riding in majesty, faithful and true,
Eyes ablaze, crowns on His head,
Robe dipped in blood from His suffering,
He is the Word of God,
Coming again, King of kings.

We shall rise,
We shall meet Him in the air
When He comes again,
And we will worship Him, worship Him,
Give Him praise forever more,
King of kings and Lord of lords.

241   David Graham.

IN MOMENTS LIKE THESE I sing out a song,
I sing out a love song to Jesus.
In moments like these I lift up my hands,
I lift up my hands to the Lord.

Singing, I love You, Lord,
Singing, I love You, Lord,
Singing, I love You, Lord,
I love You.

242   Bob Kilpatrick.

IN MY LIFE, LORD, be glorified, be glorified.
In my life, Lord, be glorified today.

In Your church, Lord, be glorified, be
    glorified.
In Your church, Lord, be glorified today.

243 Christina G. Rossetti.

IN THE BLEAK MIDWINTER,
Frosty wind made moan;
Earth stood hard as iron,
Water like a stone.
Snow had fallen, snow on snow,
Snow on snow;
In the bleak midwinter,
Long ago.

Our God, heaven cannot hold Him,
Nor earth sustain,
Heaven and earth shall flee away
When He comes to reign.
In the bleak midwinter
A stable-place sufficed
The Lord God Almighty,
Jesus Christ.

Angels and archangels
May have gathered there,
Cherubim and seraphim
Thronged the air.
But His mother only,
In her maiden bliss,
Worshipped the Belovèd
With a kiss.

What can I give Him,
Poor as I am?
If I were a shepherd,
I would bring a lamb.
If I were a wise man,
I would do my part;
Yet what I can I give Him—
Give my heart.

244 Brent Chambers.
Copyright © 1977 Scripture in Song,
a division of Integrity Music/Adm.
by Kingsway's Thankyou Music.

IN THE PRESENCE OF YOUR PEOPLE
I will praise Your name,
For alone You are holy,
Enthroned in the praises of Israel.
Let us celebrate Your goodness
And Your steadfast love,
May Your name be exalted
Here on earth and in heaven above.

Lai, lai, lai-lai-lai-lai-lai-lai … *(etc.)*

245 Graham Kendrick.
Copyright © 1986 Kingsway's
Thankyou Music.

IN THE TOMB SO COLD they laid Him,
Death its victim claimed.
Powers of hell, they could not hold Him;
Back to life He came!

Christ is risen! (Christ is risen!)
Death has been conquered. (Death has
been conquered.)
Christ is risen! (Christ is risen!)
He shall reign for ever.

Hell had spent its fury on Him,
Left Him crucified.
Yet, by blood, He boldly conquered,
Sin and death defied.

Now the fear of death is broken,
Love has won the crown.
Prisoners of the darkness listen,
Walls are tumbling down.

Raised from death to heaven ascending,
Love's exalted King.
Let His song of joy, unending,
Through the nations ring!

246 Bruce Clewett.
Copyright © 1983 Kingsway's
Thankyou Music.

IN THROUGH THE VEIL now we enter,
Boldly approaching Your throne,
Bearing a sacrifice of fragrance sweet;
The fruit of some seeds You have sown.
From our lips we offer these praises,
May You be blessed as we sing.
Lord, we adore You, like incense before You
Our worship ascends to the King.
Welling up within our hearts
Is a song of praise to You,
We lift up our hands with our voice.
Blessings and honour,
Glory and power be unto You,
Let us rejoice, rejoice.
Blessings and honour,
Glory and power be unto You,
Let us rejoice.

247 Mike Kerry.
Copyright © 1982 Kingsway's
Thankyou Music.

IN THY PRESENCE there's fulness of joy,
Fulness of joy, fulness of joy.
At Thy right hand are pleasures forever,
Pleasures forever more.

I keep the Lord before me,
I shall not be moved.
My heart is glad and my soul rejoices;
I shall dwell in safety.

And in Thy presence there's fulness of joy,
Fulness of joy, fulness of joy.
At Thy right hand are pleasures forever,
Pleasures forever more.

248 Paul Armstrong.
Copyright © 1980 Word's Spirit of
Praise Music/Adm. by CopyCare.

I RECEIVE YOUR LOVE,
I receive Your love,
In my heart I receive Your love, O Lord.
I receive Your love
By Your Spirit within me,
I receive, I receive Your love.

I confess Your love,
I confess Your love,
From my heart I confess Your love, O Lord.
I confess Your love
By Your Spirit within me,
I confess, I confess Your love.

249 Author unknown.

I SEE THE LORD, I see the Lord,
He is high and lifted up
And His train fills the temple.
He is high and lifted up
And His train fills the temple.
The angels cry, Holy,
The angels cry, Holy,
The angels cry, Holy is the Lord.

250 John Wimber.
Copyright © 1980 Mercy/Vineyard
Publishing/Adm. by CopyCare.

ISN'T HE BEAUTIFUL, beautiful isn't He?
Prince of Peace, Son of God, isn't He?
Isn't He wonderful, wonderful isn't He?
Counsellor, Almighty God, isn't He, isn't He,
isn't He?

Yes, You are beautiful...

251 E. H. Sears.

IT CAME UPON THE MIDNIGHT CLEAR,
That glorious song of old,
From angels bending near the earth
To touch their harps of gold:
'Peace on the earth, goodwill to men
From heaven's all gracious King!'
The world in solemn stillness lay
To hear the angels sing.

Still through the cloven skies they come,
With peaceful wings unfurled,
And still their heavenly music floats
O'er all the weary world:
Above its sad and lowly plains
They bend on hovering wing,
And ever o'er its Babel sounds
The blessèd angels sing.

Yet with woes of sin and strife
The world has suffered long,
Beneath the angel-strain have rolled
Two thousand years of wrong;
And man, at war with man, hears not
The love-song which they bring:
O hush the noise, ye men of strife,
And hear the angels sing.

For lo! the days are hastening on,
By prophet bards foretold,
When with the ever-circling years
Comes round the age of gold;
When peace shall over all the earth
Its ancient splendours fling,
And all the world send back the song
Which now the angels sing.

252 W. W. How.

IT IS A THING MOST WONDERFUL,
Almost too wonderful to be,
That God's own Son should come from
heaven
And die to save a child like me.

And yet I know that it is true;
He came to this poor world below,
And wept, and toiled, and mourned, and
died,
Only because He loved us so.

I cannot tell how He could love
A child so weak and full of sin;
His love must be most wonderful,
If He could die my love to win.

It is most wonderful to know
His love for me so free and sure;
But 'tis more wonderful to see
My love for Him so faint and poor.

And yet I want to love Thee, Lord;
O light the flame within my heart,
And I will love Thee more and more,
Until I see Thee as Thou art.

253 Tim Blomdahl.
Copyright © 1976 Bible Temple Music/
Music Services/Adm. by CopyCare.

IT IS GOOD FOR ME to draw near unto God;
Lord, I put my trust in Thee,
That I may declare all Thy works, O my God,
Lord, I put my trust in Thee.
My flesh and my heart they fail me,
But God is the strength of my life;
You are my portion both now and ever more,
There is none that I desire but Thee.

254 Sally Ellis.
Copyright © 1980 Kingsway's
Thankyou Music.

IT IS NO LONGER I THAT LIVETH
But Christ that liveth in me,
It is no longer I that liveth
But Christ that liveth in me.
He lives, He lives,
Jesus is alive in me.
It is no longer I that liveth
But Christ that liveth in me.

The life that I live in the body
I live by faith in the Son.
The life that I live in the body
I live by faith in the Son.
He loves, He loves,
Jesus gave Himself for me.
The life that I live in the body
I live by faith in the Son.

255 Gary Pfeiffer.
Copyright © 1973 Fred Bock Music/
Kingsway's Thankyou Music.

IT'S A HAPPY DAY, and I thank God for the
  weather.
It's a happy day, living it for my Lord.
It's a happy day, things are gonna get better,
Living each day by the promises in God's
  word.

It's a grumpy day, and I can't stand the
  weather.
It's a grumpy day, living it for myself.
It's a grumpy day, and things aren't gonna get
  better
Living each day with my Bible up on my
  shelf.

256 Len Magee.
Copyright © 1977 Len Magee Music.

**IT'S THE PRESENCE OF YOUR SPIRIT, LORD,
WE NEED,**
It's the presence of Your Spirit, Lord, we
  need,
So help us, Lord, to worship You,
It's the presence of Your Spirit, Lord, we
  need.

It's the presence of Your Spirit, Lord, we love,
It's the presence of Your Spirit, Lord, we love,
So help us, Lord, to worship You,
It's the presence of Your Spirit, Lord, we love.

For the moving of Your Spirit, Lord,
  we pray … *(etc.)*

257 Michael Christ.
Copyright © 1985 Mercy/Vineyard
Publishing/Adm. by CopyCare.

IT'S YOUR BLOOD that cleanses me,
It's Your blood that gives me life.
It's Your blood that took my place
In redeeming sacrifice,
And washes me whiter than the snow, than
  the snow.
My Jesus, God's precious sacrifice.

258 Dave Renehan.
Copyright © 1982 Kingsway's
Thankyou Music.

I WANNA SING, wanna sing.
I wanna sing, wanna sing
For Jesus, for Jesus, for Jesus.
Oh, I wanna sing for Him.

I wanna clap, wanna clap.
I wanna clap, wanna clap
For Jesus, for Jesus, for Jesus.
Oh, I wanna clap for Him.

I wanna dance, praise, work,
  love, live … *(etc.)*

259 Graham Kendrick.
Copyright © 1988 Make Way Music.

I WANT TO BE A HISTORY MAKER, *(echo)*
I want to be a world shaker, *(echo)*
To be a pen on history's pages, *(echo)*
Faithful to the end of the ages. *(echo)*

I want to see Your kingdom come,
I want to see Your will be done
On the earth.
I want to see Your kingdom come,
I want to see Your will be done
On the earth as it is in heaven.

I believe I was called and chosen *(echo)*
Long before the world's creation, *(echo)*
Called to be a holy person, *(echo)*
Called to bear good fruit for heaven. *(echo)*

We want to be the generation *(echo)*
Taking the news to every nation, *(echo)*
Filled with the Spirit without measure, *(echo)*
Working for a heavenly treasure. *(echo)*

260 Mark Altrogge.
Copyright © 1982 People of Destiny
International/Word Music/Adm. by
CopyCare.

I WANT TO SERVE THE PURPOSE OF GOD
In my generation.
I want to serve the purpose of God
While I am alive.
I want to give my life
For something that will last forever.
Oh, I delight, I delight to do Your will.

I want to build with silver and gold
In my generation.
I want to build with silver and gold
While I am alive.
I want to give my life
For something that will last forever.
Oh, I delight, I delight to do Your will.

What is on Your heart?
Tell me what to do;
Let me know Your will
And I will follow You.
(Repeat)

I want to see the kingdom of God
In my generation.
I want to see the kingdom of God
While I am alive.
I want to live my life
For something that will last forever.
Oh, I delight, I delight to do Your will.

I want to see the Lord come again
In my generation.
I want to see the Lord come again
While I am alive.
I want to give my life
For something that will last forever.
Oh I delight, I delight to do Your will.

261 C. Simmonds.
Copyright © 1964 C. Simmonds.

I WANT TO WALK WITH JESUS CHRIST
All the days I live of this life on earth;
To give to Him complete control
Of body and of soul.

Follow Him, follow Him, yield your life to
Him,
He has conquered death, He is King of
kings;
Accept the joy which He gives to those
Who yield their lives to Him.

I want to learn to speak to Him,
To pray to Him, confess my sin;
To open my life and let Him in,
For joy will then be mine:

I want to learn to speak of Him,
My life must show that He lives in me;
My deeds, my thoughts, my words must
speak
All of His love for me:

I want to learn to read His word,
For this is how I know the way
To live my life as pleases Him,
In holiness and joy:

O Holy Spirit of the Lord,
Enter now into this heart of mine;
Take full control of my selfish will,
And make me wholly Thine:

262 Chris Christensen.
Copyright © 1986 Integrity's Hosanna! Music.
Adm. Kingsway's Thankyou Music.

I WAS MADE TO PRAISE YOU,
I was made to glorify Your name,
In every circumstance
To find a chance to thank You.
I was made to love You
I was made to worship at Your feet,
And to obey You, Lord.
I was made for You.

I will always praise You,
I will always glorify Your name.
In every circumstance
I'll find a chance to thank You.
I will always love You,
I will always worship at Your feet,
And I'll obey You, Lord.
I was made for You.

263

I WAS ONCE IN DARKNESS, now my eyes
    can see,
I was lost but Jesus sought and found me.
O what love He offers, O what peace He
    gives,
I will sing forever more, He lives.

Hallelujah Jesus! Hallelujah Lord!
Hallelujah Father, I am shielded by His
    word.
I will live forever, I will never die,
I will rise up to meet Him in the sky.

264

I WILL BUILD MY CHURCH, (Men)
I will build My church, (Women)
And the gates of hell (Men)
And the gates of hell (Women)
Shall not prevail (Men)
Shall not prevail (Women)
Against it. (All)
(Repeat)

So you powers in the heavens above, bow
    down!
And you powers on the earth below, bow
    down!
And acknowledge that Jesus,
Jesus, Jesus is Lord, is Lord.

265

(Men and women in canon)
I WILL CALL upon the Lord,
Who is worthy to be praised.
I will call upon the Lord,
Who is worthy to be praised.

(Together)
So shall I be saved,
So shall I be saved from my enemies.

266

I WILL CALL UPON THE LORD, (echo)
Who is worthy to be praised, (echo)
So shall I be saved from mine enemies. (echo)

The Lord liveth, and blessèd be my Rock,
And may the God of my salvation be
    exalted.
The Lord liveth, and blessèd be my Rock,
And may the God of my salvation be
    exalted.

267

I WILL CHANGE YOUR NAME,
You shall no longer be called
Wounded, outcast, lonely or afraid.
I will change your name,
Your new name shall be,
Confidence, joyfulness, overcoming one;
Faithfulness, friend of God,
One who seeks My face.

268

I WILL ENTER HIS GATES with thanksgiving
    in my heart,
I will enter His courts with praise;
I will say this is the day that the Lord has
    made,
I will rejoice for He has made me glad.

He has made me glad,
He has made me glad,
I will rejoice for He has made me glad.
He has made me glad,
He has made me glad,
I will rejoice for He has made me glad.

269

I WILL GIVE THANKS TO THEE,
O Lord, among the people,
I will sing praises to Thee
Among the nations.
For Thy steadfast love is great,
Is great to the heavens,
And Thy faithfulness,
Thy faithfulness to the clouds.

Be exalted, O God,
Above the heavens.
Let Thy glory be over all the earth.
Be exalted, O God,
Above the heavens.
Let Thy glory be over all the earth.

(Last time only)
Be exalted, O God,
Above the heavens.
Let Thy glory be over all the earth.
Be exalted, O God,
Above the heavens.
Let Thy glory, let Thy glory,
Let Thy glory be over all the earth.

270

I WILL GIVE YOU PRAISE,
I will sing Your song,
I will bless Your holy name;
For there is no other god
Who is like unto You,
You're the only way.

Only You are the Author of life,
Only You can bring the blind their sight,
Only You are called Prince of Peace,
Only You promised You'd never leave.
Only You are God.

271

I WILL MAGNIFY Thy name
Above all the earth.
I will magnify Thy name
Above all the earth.

I will sing unto Thee
The praises in my heart.
I will sing unto Thee
The praises in my heart.

272

I WILL PRAISE YOU ALL MY LIFE;
I will sing to You with my whole heart.
I will trust in You, my hope and my help,
My Maker and my faithful God.

> *O faithful God, O faithful God,*
> *You lift me up and You uphold my cause;*
> *You give me life, You dry my eyes,*
> *You're always near, You're a faithful God.*

273 Author unknown.

I WILL REJOICE IN YOU AND BE GLAD,
I will extol Your love more than wine.
Draw me after You and let us run together,
I will rejoice in You and be glad.

274

I WILL REJOICE, I WILL REJOICE,
I will rejoice in the Lord with my whole
 heart.
I will rejoice, I will rejoice,
I will rejoice in the Lord.
You anoint my head with oil,
And my cup surely overflows,
Goodness and love shall follow me
All the days that I dwell in Your house.

275

I WILL RISE AND BLESS YOU, LORD,
Lift my hands and shout Your praise,
I will tell of the marvellous things You have
 done
And declare Your faithfulness.
I will rise and bless You, Lord,
Lift You high and dance for joy.
Oh, nothing can separate me
From Your wonderful, wonderful love.

276

> **I WILL SEEK YOUR FACE,** *O Lord;*
> *I will seek Your face, O Lord.*
> *I will seek Your face, O Lord;*
> *I will seek Your face, O Lord.*

Lord, how awesome is Your presence;
Who can stand in Your light?
Those who by Your grace and mercy
Are made holy in Your sight.

I will dwell in Your presence
All the days of my life;
There to gaze upon Your glory,
And to worship only You.

277 J. H. Fillmore.

I WILL SING OF THE MERCIES of the Lord for
 ever,
I will sing, I will sing.
I will sing of the mercies of the Lord for ever,
I will sing of the mercies of the Lord.

With my mouth will I make known
Thy faithfulness, Thy faithfulness.
With my mouth will I make known
Thy faithfulness to all generations.

278
Francis Rawley (1854–1952).
Words Copyright © 1952 HarperCollins
Religious/Adm. by CopyCare.

I WILL SING THE WONDROUS STORY
Of the Christ who died for me;
How He left His home in glory
For the cross on Calvary.
I was lost but Jesus found me,
Found the sheep that went astray;
Threw His loving arms around me,
Drew me back into His way.

I was bruised but Jesus healed me,
Faint was I from many a fall;
Sight was gone, and fears possessed me,
But He freed me from them all.
Days of darkness still come o'er me;
Sorrow's paths I often tread,
But the Saviour still is with me,
By His hand I'm safely led.

He will keep me till the river
Rolls its waters at my feet,
Then He'll bear me safely over,
All my joys in Him complete.
Yes, I'll sing the wondrous story
Of the Christ who died for me;
Sing it with the saints in glory,
Gathered by the crystal sea.

279
Donya Brockway.
Copyright © 1972 His Eye Music/
Multisongs/EMI Christian Music
Publ./Adm. by CopyCare.

I WILL SING UNTO THE LORD as long as I
  live,
I will sing praise to my God while I have my
  being.
My meditation of Him shall be sweet,
I will be glad, I will be glad in the Lord.

Bless thou the Lord, O my soul,
Praise ye the Lord.
Bless thou the Lord, O my soul,
Praise ye the Lord.
Bless thou the Lord, O my soul,
Praise ye the Lord.
Bless thou the Lord, O my soul,
Praise ye the Lord.

280
Dave Bankhead, Sue Rinaldi, Ray Goudie &
Steve Bassett.
Copyright © 1990 Word's Spirit of Praise
Music/Adm. by CopyCare.

I WILL SPEAK OUT for those who have no
  voices,
I will stand up for the rights of all the
  oppressed;
I will speak truth and justice,
I'll defend the poor and the needy,
I will lift up the weak in Jesus' name.

I will speak out for those who have no choices,
I will cry out for those who live without love;
I will show God's compassion
To the crushed and broken in spirit,
I will lift up the weak in Jesus' name.

281
Daniel Gardner.
Copyright © 1981 Integrity's Hosanna! Music/
Adm. by Kingsway's Thankyou Music.

I WILL WORSHIP YOU, LORD, with all of my
  might,
I will praise You with a psalm.
I will worship You, Lord, with all of my might,
I will praise You all day long.

For Thou, O Lord, art glorious,
And Thy name is greatly to be praised;
May my heart be pure and holy in Thy sight,
As I worship You with all of my might.

282
Sondra Corbett.
Copyright © 1986 Integrity's Hosanna! Music.
Adm. Kingsway's Thankyou Music.

I WORSHIP YOU, ALMIGHTY GOD,
There is none like You.
I worship You, O Prince of Peace,
That is what I love to do.
I give You praise,
For You are my righteousness.
I worship You, Almighty God,
There is none like You.

283
Ian Smale.
Copyright © 1987 Kingsway's
Thankyou Music.

JEHOVAH JIREH, God will provide,
Jehovah Rophe, God heals;
Jehovah M'keddesh, God who sanctifies,
Jehovah Nissi, God is my banner.

Jehovah Rohi, God my Shepherd,
Jehovah Shalom, God is peace;
Jehovah Tsidkenu, God our righteousness,
Jehovah Shammah, God who is there.

284 Merla Watson.
Copyright © 1974 Tempo Music
Publications/Adm. by CopyCare.

JEHOVAH JIREH, MY PROVIDER,
His grace is sufficient for me, for me, for me.
Jehovah Jireh, my Provider,
His grace is sufficient for me.

My God shall supply all my needs
According to His riches in glory;
He will give His angels charge over me,
Jehovah Jireh cares for me, for me, for me,
Jehovah Jireh cares for me.

285 Lyra Davidica.

JESUS CHRIST IS RISEN TODAY; Hallelujah!
Our triumphant holy day; Hallelujah!
Who did once upon the cross; Hallelujah!
Suffer to redeem our loss; Hallelujah!

Hymns of praise then let us sing; Hallelujah!
Unto Christ our heavenly King; Hallelujah!
Who endured the cross and grave; Hallelujah!
Sinners to redeem and save: Hallelujah!

But the pains which He endured; Hallelujah!
Our salvation have procured; Hallelujah!
Now in heaven above He's King; Hallelujah!
Where the angels ever sing: Hallelujah!

286 Jonathan Wallis.
Copyright © 1983 Kingsway's
Thankyou Music.

JESUS HAS SAT DOWN at God's right hand,
He is reigning now on David's throne.
God has placed all things beneath His feet,
His enemies will be His footstool.

*For the government is now upon His
    shoulder,
For the government is now upon His
    shoulder,
And of the increase of His government
    and peace
There will be no end, there will be no end,
There will be no end.*

God has now exalted Him on high,
Given Him a name above all names.
Every knee will bow and tongue confess
That Jesus Christ is Lord.

Jesus is now living in His church,
Men who have been purchased by His blood.
They will serve their God, a royal priesthood,
And they will reign on earth.

Sound the trumpets, good news to the poor,
Captives will go free, the blind will see;
The kingdom of this world will soon become
The kingdom of our God.

287 Dave Bolton.
Copyright © 1975 Kingsway's
Thankyou Music.

JESUS, HOW LOVELY YOU ARE,
*You are so gentle, so pure and kind.
You shine as the morning star,
Jesus, how lovely You are.*

Hallelujah, Jesus is my Lord and King;
Hallelujah, Jesus is my everything.

Hallelujah, Jesus died and rose again;
Hallelujah, Jesus forgave all my sin.

Hallelujah, Jesus is meek and lowly;
Hallelujah, Jesus is pure and holy.

Hallelujah, Jesus is the Bridegroom;
Hallelujah, Jesus will take His Bride soon.

288 Jude Del Hierro.
Copyright © 1985 Mercy/Vineyard
Publishing/Adm. by CopyCare.

JESUS, I LOVE YOU;
I bow down before You.
Praises and worship
To our King.

Alleluia, alleluia;
Alleluia, allelu.

289 Wendy Churchill.
Copyright © 1982 Word's Spirit of Praise
Music/Adm. by CopyCare.

JESUS IS KING and I will extol Him,
Give Him the glory, and honour His name.
He reigns on high, enthroned in the
    heavens,
Word of the Father, exalted for us.

We have a hope that is steadfast and certain,
Gone through the curtain and touching the
    throne.
We have a Priest who is there interceding,
Pouring His grace on our lives day by day.

We come to Him, our Priest and Apostle,
Clothed in His glory and bearing His name,
Laying our lives with gladness before Him;
Filled with His Spirit we worship the King.

O Holy One, our hearts do adore You;
Thrilled with Your goodness we give You our
 praise.
Angels in light with worship surround Him,
Jesus, our Saviour, forever the same.

290 David J. Mansell.
Copyright © 1982 Word's Spirit of Praise
Music/Adm. by CopyCare.

JESUS IS LORD! Creation's voice proclaims it,
For by His power each tree and flower
Was planned and made.
Jesus is Lord! The universe declares it,
Sun, moon and stars in heaven
Cry, 'Jesus is Lord!'

Jesus is Lord! Jesus is Lord!
Praise Him with hallelujahs
For Jesus is Lord!

Jesus is Lord! Yet from His throne eternal
In flesh He came to die in pain
On Calvary's tree.
Jesus is Lord! From Him all life proceeding,
Yet gave His life a ransom
Thus setting us free.

Jesus is Lord! O'er sin the mighty conqueror,
From death He rose, and all His foes
Shall own His name.
Jesus is Lord! God sent His Holy Spirit
To show by works of power
That Jesus is Lord.

291 Marilyn Baker.
Copyright © 1986 Word's Spirit of Praise
Music/Adm. by CopyCare.

JESUS IS LORD OF ALL,
Satan is under His feet,
Jesus is reigning on high
And all power is given to Him
In heaven and earth.

We are joined to Him,
Satan is under our feet,
We are seated on high
And all authority is given
To us through Him.

One day we'll be like Him,
Perfect in every way,
Chosen to be His bride,
Ruling and reigning with Him
Forever more.

292 Chris Bowater.
Copyright © 1982 Sovereign Lifestyle Music.

JESUS, I WORSHIP YOU,
Worship, honour and adore Your lovely
 name.
Jesus, I worship You,
Lord of lords and King of kings, I worship
 You,
From a thankful heart I sing;
I worship You.

293 John Barnett.
Copyright © 1988 Mercy/Vineyard
Publishing/Adm. by CopyCare.

JESUS, JESUS,
Holy and anointed One,
Jesus.
Jesus, Jesus,
Risen and exalted One,
Jesus.

Your name is like honey on my lips,
Your Spirit like water to my soul.
Your word is a lamp unto my feet;
Jesus I love You, I love You.

294 Chris Bowater.
Copyright © 1979 Sovereign Music UK.

JESUS, JESUS, JESUS,
Your love has melted my heart.
Jesus, Jesus, Jesus,
Your love has melted my heart.

295 Chris Rolinson.
Copyright © 1988 Kingsway's
Thankyou Music.

JESUS, KING OF KINGS,
We worship and adore You.
Jesus, Lord of heaven and earth,
We bow down at Your feet.
Father, we bring to You our worship;
Your sovereign will be done,
On earth Your kingdom come,
Through Jesus Christ, Your only Son.

Jesus, Sovereign Lord,
We worship and adore You.
Jesus, Name above all names,
We bow down at Your feet.
Father, we offer You our worship;
Your sovereign will be done,
On earth Your kingdom come,
Through Jesus Christ, Your only Son.

Jesus, Light of the world,
We worship and adore You.
Jesus, Lord Emmanuel,
We bow down at Your feet.
Father, for Your delight we worship;
Your sovereign will be done,
On earth Your kingdom come,
Through Jesus Christ, Your only Son.

296 Christian F. Gellert.
Tr. Frances E. Cox.

JESUS LIVES! thy terrors now
Can, O death, no more appal us;
Jesus lives! by this we know,
Thou, O grave, canst not enthral us.
Hallelujah!

Jesus lives! henceforth is death
But the gate of life immortal;
This shall calm our trembling breath,
When we pass its gloomy portal.
Hallelujah!

Jesus lives! for us He died;
Then, alone to Jesus living,
Pure in heart may we abide,
Glory to our Saviour giving.
Hallelujah!

Jesus lives! our hearts know well,
Naught from us His love shall sever;
Life, nor death, nor powers of hell,
Tear us from His keeping ever.
Hallelujah!

Jesus lives! to Him the throne
Over all the world is given:
May we go where He is gone,
Rest and reign with Him in heaven.
Hallelujah!

297 Charles Wesley.

JESUS, LOVER OF MY SOUL,
Let me to Thy bosom fly,
While the nearer waters roll,
While the tempest still is high;
Hide me, O my Saviour, hide,
Till the storm of life is past;
Safe into the haven guide,
O receive my soul at last.

Other refuge have I none,
Hangs my helpless soul on Thee;
Leave, ah, leave me not alone,
Still support and comfort me.
All my trust on Thee is stayed,
All my help from Thee I bring;
Cover my defenceless head
With the shadow of Thy wing.

Thou, O Christ, art all I want;
More than all in Thee I find;
Raise the fallen, cheer the faint,
Heal the sick, and lead the blind.
Just and holy is Thy name,
I am all unrighteousness;
False and full of sin I am,
Thou art full of truth and grace.

Plenteous grace with Thee is found,
Grace to cover all my sin;
Let the healing streams abound,
Make and keep me pure within.
Thou of life the fountain art,
Freely let me take of Thee;
Spring Thou up within my heart,
Rise to all eternity.

298 Naida Hearn.
Copyright © 1974 Scripture in Song,
a division of Integrity Music/Adm.
by Kingsway's Thankyou Music.

JESUS, NAME ABOVE ALL NAMES,
Beautiful Saviour, Glorious Lord;
Emmanuel, God is with us,
Blessèd Redeemer, Living Word.

299 Graham Kendrick.
Copyright © 1986 Kingsway's
Thankyou Music.

**JESUS PUT THIS SONG INTO OUR
HEARTS,**
Jesus put this song into our hearts,
It's a song of joy no one can take away,
Jesus put this song into our hearts.

Jesus taught us how to live in harmony,
Jesus taught us how to live in harmony,
Different faces, different races, He made us
one,
Jesus taught us how to live in harmony.

Jesus taught us how to be a family,
Jesus taught us how to be a family,
Loving one another with the love that He
gives,
Jesus taught us how to be a family.

Jesus turned our sorrow into dancing,
Jesus turned our sorrow into dancing,
Changed our tears of sadness into rivers of joy,
Jesus turned our sorrow into a dance.

300 Chris Rolinson.
Copyright © 1988 Kingsway's
Thankyou Music.

JESUS, SEND MORE LABOURERS,
For, Lord, we see the need;
The land is ready for harvest,
The fields are ripe indeed.

Oh Lord, but start with me,
Jesus, begin with me.
Who will go for You, Lord?
Who will go for You, Lord?
Here I am, Lord,
Send me,
Send me, Lord,
Send me.

Lord, we love our country,
Countless lives to be won;
Jesus, bring revival,
That through us Your will be done.

Lord, we sense Your moving,
Touching our lives with power;
We are ready to serve You,
To go this day, this hour.

301 Isaac Watts.

JESUS SHALL REIGN where'er the sun
Doth his successive journeys run;
His kingdom stretch from shore to shore,
Till moons shall wax and wane no more.

For Him shall endless prayer be made,
And praises throng to crown His head;
His name like sweet perfume shall rise
With every morning sacrifice.

People and realms of every tongue
Dwell on His love with sweetest song,
And infant voices shall proclaim
Their early blessings on His name.

Blessings abound where'er He reigns;
The prisoner leaps to lose his chains;
The weary find eternal rest,
And all the sons of want are blessed.

Let every creature rise and bring
Peculiar honours to our King;
Angels descend with songs again,
And earth repeat the loud Amen!

302 Chris Bowater.
Copyright © 1988 Sovereign Lifestyle Music.

JESUS SHALL TAKE THE HIGHEST HONOUR,
Jesus shall take the highest praise.
Let all earth join heaven in exalting
The Name which is above all other names.
Let's bow the knee in humble adoration,
For at His name every knee must bow.
Let every tongue confess He is Christ, God's
    only Son;
Sovereign Lord, we give You glory now.

For all honour and blessing and power
Belongs to You, belongs to You.
All honour and blessing and power
Belongs to You, belongs to You,
Lord Jesus Christ, Son of the living God.

303 Graham Kendrick.
Copyright © 1977 Kingsway's
Thankyou Music.

JESUS, STAND AMONG US
At the meeting of our lives;
Be our sweet agreement
At the meeting of our eyes.
O Jesus, we love You, so we gather here;
Join our hearts in unity and take away our
    fear.

So to You we're gathering
Out of each and every land;
Christ the love between us
At the joining of our hands.
O Jesus, we love You, so we gather here;
Join our hearts in unity and take away our
    fear.

(Optional verse for Communion:)
Jesus, stand among us
At the breaking of the bread;
Join us as one body
As we worship You, our Head.
O Jesus, we love You, so we gather here;
Join our hearts in unity and take away our
    fear.

304 William Pennefather.

JESUS, STAND AMONG US,
IN THY RISEN POWER,
Let this time of worship
Be a hallowed hour.

Breathe Thy Holy Spirit
Into every heart,
Bid the fears and sorrows
From each soul depart.

Thus with quickened footsteps
We'll pursue our way,
Watching for the dawning
Of eternal day.

305 Dave Bryant.
Copyright © 1978 Kingsway's
Thankyou Music.

JESUS TAKE ME AS I AM,
I can come no other way.
Take me deeper into You,
Make my flesh life melt away.
Make me like a precious stone,
Crystal clear and finely honed,
Life of Jesus shining through,
Giving glory back to You.

306 Hilary Davies.
Copyright © 1988 Samsongs/Coronation
Music/Kingsway's Thankyou Music.

JESUS, THE NAME ABOVE ALL NAMES,
Forever more the same,
And lifting up our hands we exalt You;
Come among us once again,
And glorify Your name,
So everyone will know
You are Emmanuel.

*Emmanuel, Emmanuel,
Emmanuel, God is with us.*

307 Charles Wesley.

JESUS! THE NAME HIGH OVER ALL,
In hell, or earth, or sky;
Angels and men before it fall,
And devils fear and fly,
And devils fear and fly.

Jesus! the name to sinners dear,
The name to sinners given;
It scatters all their guilty fear,
It turns their hell to heaven,
It turns their hell to heaven.

Jesus! the prisoners' fetters breaks,
And bruises Satan's head;
Power into strengthless souls it speaks,
And life into the dead,
And life into the dead.

O that the world might taste and see
The riches of His grace!
The arms of love that compass me
Would all mankind embrace,
Would all mankind embrace.

His only righteousness I show,
His saving grace proclaim;
'Tis all my business here below
To cry: 'Behold the Lamb!'
To cry: 'Behold the Lamb!'

Happy if with my latest breath
I might but gasp His name;
Preach Him to all, and cry in death:
'Behold, behold the Lamb!'
'Behold, behold the Lamb!'

308 St Bernard of Clairvaux.
Tr. Edward Caswall.

JESUS, THE VERY THOUGHT OF THEE
With sweetness fills the breast;
But sweeter far Thy face to see,
And in Thy presence rest.

Nor voice can sing, nor heart can frame,
Nor can the memory find
A sweeter sound than Thy blessed name,
O Saviour of mankind!

O hope of every contrite heart,
O joy of all the meek,
To those who fall how kind Thou art,
How good to those who seek!

But what to those who find? Ah, this
Nor tongue nor pen can show:
The love of Jesus, what it is
None but His loved ones know.

Jesus, Thy mercies are untold
Through each returning day;
Thy love exceeds a thousandfold
Whatever we can say.

Jesus, our only joy be Thou,
As Thou our prize wilt be;
Jesus, be Thou our glory now,
And through eternity.

309 John Gibson.
Copyright © 1987 Kingsway's
Thankyou Music.

JESUS, WE CELEBRATE YOUR VICTORY:
*Jesus, we revel in Your love.
Jesus, we rejoice, You've set us free;
Jesus, Your death has brought us life.*

It was for freedom that Christ has set us free,
No longer to be subject to a yoke of slavery;
So we're rejoicing in God's victory,
Our hearts responding to His love.

His Spirit in us releases us from fear,
The way to Him is open, with boldness we
    draw near;
And in His presence our problems
    disappear,
Our hearts responding to His love.

310 Paul Kyle.
Copyright © 1980 Kingsway's
Thankyou Music.

JESUS, WE ENTHRONE YOU,
We proclaim You our King.
Standing here in the midst of us,
We raise You up with our praise.
And as we worship, build a throne,
And as we worship, build a throne,
And as we worship, build a throne:
Come, Lord Jesus, and take Your place.

311 Marilyn Baker.
Copyright © 1981 Word's Spirit of
Praise Music/Adm. by CopyCare.

JESUS, YOU ARE CHANGING ME,
By Your Spirit You're making me like You.
Jesus, You're transforming me,
That Your loveliness may be seen in all I do.
You are the potter and I am the clay,
Help me to be willing to let You have Your
    way.
Jesus, You are changing me,
As I let You reign supreme within my heart.

312 David Fellingham.
Copyright © 1985 Kingsway's
Thankyou Music.

JESUS, YOU ARE THE RADIANCE of the
Father's glory,
You are the Son, the appointed heir,
Through whom all things are made.
You are the One who sustains all things by
    Your powerful word.
You have purified us from sin,
You are exalted, O Lord,
Exalted, O Lord,
To the right hand of God.

(Last time)
Crowned with glory,
Crowned with honour,
We worship You.

313 Isaac Watts.

JOIN ALL THE GLORIOUS NAMES
Of wisdom, love, and power,
That ever mortals knew,
That angels ever bore:
All are too mean to speak His worth,
Too mean to set my Saviour forth.

Great Prophet of my God,
My tongue would bless Thy name:
By Thee the joyful news
Of our salvation came:
The joyful news of sins forgiven,
Of hell subdued and peace with heaven.

Jesus, my great High Priest,
Offered His blood, and died;
My guilty conscience seeks
No sacrifice beside:
His powerful blood did once atone,
And now it pleads before the throne.

My Saviour and my Lord,
My Conqueror and my King,
Thy sceptre and Thy sword,
Thy reigning grace I sing:
Thine is the power; behold, I sit
In willing bonds beneath Thy feet.

Now let my soul arise,
And tread the tempter down:
My Captain leads me forth
To conquest and a crown.
March on, nor fear to win the day,
Though death and hell obstruct the way.

Should all the hosts of death,
And powers of hell unknown,
Put their most dreadful forms
Of rage and malice on,
I shall be safe; for Christ displays
Superior power and guardian grace.

314 Isaac Watts.

JOY TO THE WORLD! the Lord has come;
Let earth receive her King.
Let every heart prepare Him room,
And heaven and nature sing,
And heaven and nature sing,
And heaven, and heaven and nature sing!

Joy to the earth! the Saviour reigns;
Your sweetest songs employ.
While fields and streams and hills and plains
Repeat the sounding joy,
Repeat the sounding joy,
Repeat, repeat the sounding joy!

He rules the world with truth and grace,
And makes the nations prove
The glories of His righteousness,
The wonders of His love,
The wonders of His love,
The wonders, the wonders of His love.

315 Fred Dunn.
Copyright © 1977, 1980 Kingsway's
Thankyou Music.

JUBILATE, EVERYBODY,
Serve the Lord in all your ways,
And come before His presence singing,
Enter now His courts with praise.
For the Lord our God is gracious,
And His mercy's everlasting.
Jubilate, Jubilate, Jubilate Deo.

316 Charlotte Elliot.

JUST AS I AM, without one plea
But that Thy blood was shed for me,
And that Thou bid'st me come to Thee,
O Lamb of God, I come.

Just as I am, and waiting not
To rid my soul of one dark blot,
To Thee, whose blood can cleanse each spot,
O Lamb of God, I come.

Just as I am, though tossed about
With many a conflict, many a doubt,
Fightings and fears within, without,
O Lamb of God, I come.

Just as I am, poor, wretched, blind;
Sight, riches, healing of the mind,
Yea, all I need in Thee to find,
O Lamb of God, I come.

Just as I am, Thou wilt receive,
Wilt welcome, pardon, cleanse, relieve,
Because Thy promise I believe,
O Lamb of God, I come.

Just as I am, Thy love unknown
Has broken every barrier down;
Now to be Thine, yea, Thine alone,
O Lamb of God, I come.

Just as I am, of that free love
The breadth, length, depth and height to
prove,
Here for a season, then above,
O Lamb of God, I come.

317 Patty Kennedy.
Copyright © 1982 Mercy/Vineyard
Publishing/Adm. by CopyCare.

JUST LIKE YOU PROMISED, You've come;
Just like You told us, You're here,
And our desire is that You know
We love You, we worship You,
We welcome You here.

318 Jane Norton.
Copyright © 1986 Kingsway's
Thankyou Music.

KING FOREVER, Lord Messiah,
He who was, and is, and is to come;
Prince of glory, name of Jesus,
Be Your praise and worship ever sung.

And we will sing hosanna to Jesus,
We exalt and raise Your name above;
And we proclaim the glory of Jesus,
Prince of Peace, and worthy King of love.

Lord anointed, our salvation,
He whom angels call the Word of God;
True and faithful, Lamb of mercy,
Now receive our worship and our love.

319 Graham Kendrick.
Copyright © 1988 Make Way Music.

KING OF KINGS, Lord of lords,
Lion of Judah, Word of God.
King of kings, Lord of lords,
Lion of Judah, Word of God.

And here He comes, the King of glory comes!
In righteousness He comes to judge the
earth.
And here He comes, the King of glory comes!
With justice He'll rule the earth.

320 Chris Bowater.
Copyright © 1988 Sovereign Lifestyle Music.

LAMB OF GOD, Holy One,
Jesus Christ, Son of God,
Lifted up willingly to die,
That I the guilty one may know
The blood once shed, still freely flowing,
Still cleansing, still healing.

I exalt You, Jesus my sacrifice;
I exalt You, my Redeemer and my Lord.
I exalt You, worthy Lamb of God,
And in honour I bow down before Your
throne.

321 James Edmeston, altd.

LEAD US, HEAVENLY FATHER, LEAD US
O'er the world's tempestuous sea;
Guard us, guide us, keep us, feed us,
For we have no help but Thee;
Yet possessing every blessing
If our God our Father be.

Saviour, breathe forgiveness o'er us;
All our weakness Thou dost know,
Thou didst tread this earth before us,
Thou didst feel its keenest woe;
Tempted, taunted, yet undaunted,
Through the desert Thou didst go.

Spirit of our God, descending,
Fill our hearts with heavenly joy,
Love with every passion blending,
Pleasure that can never cloy;
Thus provided, pardoned, guided,
Nothing can our peace destroy.

322 Graham Kendrick.
Copyright © 1983 Kingsway's
Thankyou Music.

LED LIKE A LAMB to the slaughter
In silence and shame,
There on Your back You carried a world
Of violence and pain.
Bleeding, dying, bleeding, dying.

You're alive, You're alive,
You have risen, Alleluia!
And the power and the glory is given,
Alleluia, Jesus, to You.

At break of dawn, poor Mary,
Still weeping she came,
When through her grief she heard Your
voice
Now speaking her name.
Mary, Master, Mary, Master!

At the right hand of the Father
Now seated on high
You have begun Your eternal reign
Of justice and joy.
Glory, glory, glory, glory.

323 Graham Kendrick.
Copyright © 1984 Kingsway's
Thankyou Music.

LET GOD ARISE
And let His enemies
Be scattered;
And let those who hate Him
Flee before Him.
Let God arise,
And let His enemies
Be scattered;
And let those who hate Him
Flee away.

(Men)
But let the righteous be glad,
Let them exult before God,
Let them rejoice with gladness,
Building up a highway for the King.
We go in the name of the Lord,
Let the shout go up
In the name of the Lord.

(Women)
The righteous be glad,
Let them exult before God,
O let them rejoice
For the King,
In the name of the Lord.

324 Ian Smale.
Copyright © 1982 Kingsway's
Thankyou Music.

LET GOD SPEAK *and I will listen,*
Let God speak, there's things I'm needing
to put right.
Let God speak and I will obey what He
says,
Please God, I want to hear Your voice
tonight.

Lord I want to hear Your voice,
Lord I want to hear Your voice,
Lord I want to hear Your voice
Tonight, tonight.

325 Graham Kendrick.
Copyright © 1977 Kingsway's
Thankyou Music.

LET ME HAVE MY WAY AMONG YOU,
Do not strive, do not strive.
Let Me have My way among you,
Do not strive, do not strive.
For Mine is the power and the glory
For ever and ever the same.
Let Me have My way among you,
Do not strive, do not strive.

We'll let You have Your way among us,
We'll not strive, we'll not strive.
We'll let You have Your way among us,
We'll not strive, we'll not strive.
For Yours is the power and the glory
For ever and ever the same.
We'll let You have Your way among us,
We'll not strive, we'll not strive.

Let My peace rule within your hearts,
Do not strive, do not strive.
Let My peace rule within your hearts,
Do not strive, do not strive.
For Mine is the power and the glory,
For ever and ever the same.
Let My peace rule within your hearts,
Do not strive, do not strive.

We'll let Your peace rule within our hearts,
We'll not strive, we'll not strive.
We'll let Your peace rule within our hearts,
We'll not strive, we'll not strive.
For Yours is the power and the glory,
For ever and ever the same.
We'll let Your peace rule within our hearts,
We'll not strive, we'll not strive.

326 Brent Chambers.
Copyright © 1979 Scripture in Song,
a division of Integrity Music/Adm.
by Kingsway's Thankyou Music.

LET OUR PRAISE TO YOU BE AS INCENSE,
Let our praise to You be as pillars of Your
    throne.
Let our praise to You be as incense,
As we come before You and worship You
    alone.
As we see You in Your splendour,
As we gaze upon Your majesty,
As we join the hosts of angels
And proclaim together Your holiness.

Holy, holy, holy,
Holy is the Lord.
Holy, holy, holy,
Holy is the Lord.

327 Mike & Claire McIntosh.
Copyright © 1982 Mike and Claire McIntosh.

LET PRAISES RING, let praises ring,
Lift voices up to love Him,
Lift hearts and hands to touch Him,
O let praises ring.
And fill the skies with anthems high
That tell His excellencies,
As priests and kings who rule with Him
Through all eternity;

Let praises ring, let praises ring
To our glorious King.

Let praises ring, let praises ring,
Bow down in adoration,
Cry out His exaltation,
O let praises ring.
And lift the Name above all names
Till every nation knows
The love of God has come to men,
His mercies overflow.

328 James & Elizabeth Greenelsh.
Copyright © Integrity's Hosanna! Music.
Adm. Kingsway's Thankyou Music 1978.

    (1st part)
LET THERE BE GLORY AND HONOUR and
    praises,
Glory and honour to Jesus,
Glory, honour, glory and honour to Him.

    (2nd part)
Glory, glory and honour to Jesus,
Glory, honour, glory and honour to Him.

    (1st and 2nd parts)
Keep your light shining brightly
As the darkness covers the earth;
For a people that walk in darkness,
They shall see, they shall see a great light.

329 Dave Bilbrough.
Copyright © 1979 Kingsway's
Thankyou Music.

LET THERE BE LOVE shared among us,
Let there be love in our eyes;
May now Your love sweep this nation,
Cause us, O Lord, to arise.
Give us a fresh understanding
Of brotherly love that is real;
Let there be love shared among us,
Let there be love.

330 Author unknown.

LET US BREAK BREAD TOGETHER, WE ARE
    ONE.
Let us break bread together, we are one.
We are one as we stand
With our face to the risen Son.
O Lord, have mercy on us.

Let us drink wine together, we are one ...
(etc.)

Let us praise God together, we are one ...
(etc.)

331 Ian White.
Copyright © 1985 Little Misty Music/
Kingsway's Thankyou Music.

LET US GO TO THE HOUSE OF THE LORD.

I rejoiced with those who said to me,
'Let us go to the house of the Lord.'
Our feet are standing in your gates,
   Jerusalem;
Like a city built together,
Where the people of God go up
To praise the name of the Lord.

For peace for all Jerusalem
And loved ones this we pray;
May all men be secure where they must
   live.
And to all my friends and brothers,
May the peace be within you
For the sake of the house of the Lord.

332 Pale Sauni.
Copyright © 1983 Scripture in Song,
a division of Integrity Music/Adm.
by Kingsway's Thankyou Music.

LET US PRAISE HIS NAME WITH DANCING

And with the tambourine.
Let us praise His name with dancing,
Make a joyful noise and sing.

> *Dance, dance, dance before the King.*
> *Dance, dance, celebrate and sing.*

Let us celebrate with dancing;
The King has set us free.
Let us celebrate with dancing,
Rejoice in victory.

333 John Milton.

LET US WITH A GLADSOME MIND

Praise the Lord, for He is kind:

> *For His mercies shall endure,*
> *Ever faithful, ever sure.*

Let us blaze His name abroad,
For of gods He is the God:

He, with all-commanding might,
Filled the new-made world with light:

He the golden-tressèd sun
Caused all day his course to run:

And the silver moon by night,
'Mid her spangled sisters bright:

He His chosen race did bless
In the wasteful wilderness:

All things living He doth feed,
His full hand supplies their need:

Let us with a gladsome mind
Praise the Lord, for He is kind:

334 John Watson.
Copyright © 1986 Ampelos Music/
Adm. by CopyCare.

LET YOUR LIVING WATER FLOW over my soul.

Let Your Holy Spirit come and take control
Of every situation that has troubled my mind.
All my cares and burdens on to You I roll.

> *Jesus, Jesus, Jesus.*
> *Father, Father, Father.*
> *Spirit, Spirit, Spirit.*

Come now, Holy Spirit, and take control.
Hold me in Your loving arms and make me
   whole.
Wipe away all doubt and fear and take my
   pride,
Draw me to Your love and keep me by Your
   side.

Give your life to Jesus, let Him fill your soul.
Let Him take you in His arms and make you
   whole.
As you give your life to Him He'll set you free.
You will live and reign with Him eternally.

335 Graham Kendrick.
Copyright © 1989 Make Way Music.

LIFT HIGH THE CROSS.
Lift high the cross.
In majesty,
In victory.

Here raged the fight, *(Women echo)*
Darkness and light. *(Women echo)*
All heaven and hell *(Women echo)*
Battled here. *(All)*

Here once for all *(Women echo)*
Was sacrificed *(Women echo)*
The Lamb of God, *(Women echo)*
Jesus Christ. *(All)*

Raise now your voices give glory and praise
    Him, *(Leader – All echo)*
For He has poured out His blood as a
    ransom. *(Leader – All echo)*
Hell's power is broken and heaven stands
    open, *(Leader – All echo)*
Lift high the cross. *(All)*

336 Steven Fry.
Copyright © 1974 BMG Songs Inc/
Birdwing Music/EMI Christian Music Publishing/
Adm. by CopyCare.

LIFT UP YOUR HEADS to the coming King;
Bow before Him and adore Him, sing
To His majesty, let your praises be
Pure and holy, giving glory
To the King of kings.

337 Graham Kendrick.
Copyright © 1991 Make Way Music.

LIFT UP YOUR HEADS, O you gates,
Swing wide you everlasting doors.
Lift up your heads, O ye gates,
Swing wide you everlasting doors.

> *That the King of glory may come in,*
> *That the King of glory may come in.*
> *That the King of glory may come in,*
> *That the King of glory may come in.*

Up from the dead He ascends,
Through every rank of heavenly power.
Let heaven prepare the highest place,
Throw wide the everlasting doors:

With trumpet blast and shouts of joy,
All heaven greets the risen King.
With angel choirs come line the way,
Throw wide the gates and welcome Him.

338 Terry Manship.
Copyright © 1986 Kingsway's
Thankyou Music.

LIFT UP YOUR HEADS, O YE GATES,
And be ye lifted up, ye everlasting doors.
Lift up your heads, O ye gates,
And be ye lifted up, ye everlasting doors;
And the King of glory shall come in,
The King of glory shall come in,
The King of glory shall come in.

(Women)
Who is the King of glory?
What is His name?
    (Men)
The Lord strong and mighty,
The Lord, mighty in battle, strong to save.

    (Women)
Who shall ascend the hill,
The hill of the Lord?
    (Men)
Even he that hath clean hands
And a pure heart with which to praise his
    God.

339 Mick Gisbey.
Copyright © 1987 Kingsway's
Thankyou Music.

> **LIGHT A FLAME** *within my heart*
> *That's burning bright;*
> *Fan the fire of joy in me*
> *To set the world alight.*
> *Let my flame begin to spread,*
> *My life to glow;*
> *God of light may I reflect*
> *Your love to all I know.*

From heaven's splendour
He comes to earth,
While all the angels celebrate
The goodness of His birth.

We too exalt You,
Our glorious King;
Jesus our Saviour
Paid the price to take away our sin.

340 Copyright © Central Board of Finance.

LIGHTEN OUR DARKNESS, Lord we
    pray; *(echo)*
And in Your mercy defend us *(echo)*
From all perils and dangers of this
    night, *(echo)*
For the love of Your only Son, *(all)*
Our Saviour Jesus Christ.
Amen, Amen.
Amen, Amen.

341 Graham Kendrick.
Copyright © 1988 Make Way Music.

LIGHT HAS DAWNED that ever shall blaze;
Darkness flees away.
Christ the light has shone in our hearts,
Turning night to day.

We proclaim Him King of kings,
We lift high His name.
Heaven and earth shall bow at His feet
When He comes to reign.

Saviour of the world is He,
Heaven's King come down.
Judgement, love and mercy meet
At His thorny crown.

Life has sprung from hearts of stone,
By the Spirit's breath.
Hell shall let her captives go,
Life has conquered death.

Blood has flowed that cleanses from sin,
God His love has proved.
Men may mock and demons may rage,
We shall not be moved!

342

LIGHT OF THE WORLD, shine Your light
Into my heart.
God of love, pierce my soul
With Your mercy.

So we might see Your glory,
So we might see Your face.
So we can feel Your heartbeat,
And hear You call our name.

Fire of God, burn away
What is not holy.
Jesus, take our hearts
And make them new.

343

LIKE A GENTLE BREEZE, like a mighty wind,
Like a roaring fire,
You will visit us, you will cleanse our souls,
And our hearts inspire,
Bringing peace to us, like a healing balm,
Or a gentle dove;
O come to us, O bring to us
God's gifts of love.

Come with holy fire,
Melt these hearts of clay.
Let them beat with love
That will never fade.
Holy Spirit come,
Holy Spirit come,
Holy Spirit come again.

344

LIKE A RIVER GLORIOUS is God's perfect
peace,
Over all victorious, in its bright increase:
Perfect, yet it floweth fuller every day;
Perfect, yet it groweth deeper all the way.

Stayed upon Jehovah, hearts are fully
blest;
Finding, as He promised, perfect peace
and rest.

Hidden in the hollow of His blessèd hand,
Never foe can follow, never traitor stand;
Not a surge of worry, not a shade of care,
Not a blast of hurry touched the Spirit there.

Every joy or trial falleth from above,
Traced upon our dial by the sun of love.
We may trust Him fully, all for us to do;
They who trust Him wholly find Him wholly
true.

345

LION OF JUDAH on the throne,
I shout Your name, let it be known
That You are the King of kings,
You are the Prince of Peace,
May Your kingdom's reign never cease.
Hail to the King!
Hail to the King!

Lion of Judah come to earth,
I want to thank You for Your birth,
For the living Word,
For Your death on the tree,
For Your resurrection victory.
Hallelujah! Hallelujah!

Lion of Judah, come again,
Take up Your throne Jerusalem,
Bring release to this earth
And the consummation
Of Your kingdom's reign, let it come.
Maranatha! Maranatha!

Lion of Judah on the throne,
I shout Your name, let it be known
That You are the King of kings,
You are the Prince of Peace,
May Your kingdom's reign never cease.
Hail to the King!
Hail to the King!
You are my King!

346

LIVING UNDER THE SHADOW OF HIS WING
We find security.
Standing in His presence we will bring
Our worship, worship, worship to the King.

Bowed in adoration at His feet
We dwell in harmony.
Voices joined together that repeat,
Worthy, worthy, worthy is the Lamb.

Heart to heart embracing in His love
Reveals His purity.
Soaring in my spirit like a dove,
Holy, holy, holy is the Lord.

347

**LO, HE COMES WITH CLOUDS
DESCENDING,**
Once for favoured sinners slain;
Thousand thousand saints attending
Swell the triumph of His train:
Alleluia!
Alleluia!
Alleluia!
God appears on earth to reign.

Every eye shall now behold Him
Robed in glorious majesty;
Those who set at naught and sold Him,
Pierced and nailed Him to the tree,
Deeply wailing,
Deeply wailing,
Deeply wailing,
Shall their true Messiah see.

Those dear tokens of His passion
Still His dazzling body bears;
Cause of endless exultation
To His ransomed worshippers:
With what rapture,
With what rapture,
With what rapture,
Gaze we on those glorious scars.

Yea, Amen, let all adore Thee,
High on Thine eternal throne;
Saviour, take the power and glory,
Claim the kingdom for Thine own:
Come, Lord Jesus!
Come, Lord Jesus!
Come, Lord Jesus!
Everlasting God, come down!

348

**LOOK AND SEE THE GLORY OF THE
KING,**
*Sense the presence of the Lord amongst
His people.*
*Feel Him fill the temple of our lives
As He sits upon the throne of our
praise.*

We are His church,
We are all God's own people.
We all proclaim that He is King, He is King.

At God's right hand
Jesus Christ is exalted.
His rule is now, and shall be forever more.

349

**LOOK, YE SAINTS, THE SIGHT IS
GLORIOUS;**
See the Man of Sorrows now,
From the fight returned victorious;
Every knee to Him shall bow:
Crown Him! Crown Him!
Crown Him! Crown Him!
Crowns become the Victor's brow.

Crown the Saviour, angels, crown Him;
Rich the trophies Jesus brings;
In the seat of power enthrone Him,
While the vault of heaven rings:
Crown Him! Crown Him!
Crown Him! Crown Him!
Crown the Saviour, King of kings!

Sinners in derision crowned Him,
Mocking thus the Saviour's claim;
Saints and angels throng around Him,
Own His title, praise His name:
Crown Him! Crown Him!
Crown Him! Crown Him!
Spread abroad the Victor's fame.

Hark, those bursts of acclamation!
Hark, those loud triumphant chords!
Jesus takes the highest station:
O what joy the sight affords!
Crown Him! Crown Him!
Crown Him! Crown Him!
King of kings, and Lord of lords!

350
Noel Richards.
Copyright © 1982 Kingsway's
Thankyou Music.

LORD AND FATHER, KING FOR EVER,
Throned with majesty and power,
We adore You, we exalt You,
Worship we bring, our offering,
Worship we bring to You our King.

351
Chris Rolinson.
Copyright © 1988 Kingsway's
Thankyou Music.

LORD, COME AND HEAL YOUR CHURCH,
Take our lives and cleanse with Your fire.
Let Your deliverance flow,
As we lift Your name up higher.

We will draw near,
And surrender our fear;
Lift our hands to proclaim
Holy Father, You are here.

Spirit of God, come in
And release our hearts to praise You.
Make us whole, for
Holy we'll become, and serve You.

Show us Your power, we pray,
That we might share in Your glory.
We shall arise and go
To proclaim Your works most holy.

352 G. H. Bourne.

**LORD, ENTHRONED IN HEAVENLY
  SPLENDOUR,**
First-begotten from the dead,
Thou alone, our strong Defender,
Liftest up Thy people's head.
Alleluia! Alleluia!
Jesus, true and living Bread.

Here our humblest homage pay we,
Here in loving reverence bow;
Here for faith's discernment pray we,
Lest we fail to know Thee now.
Alleluia! Alleluia!
Thou art here, we ask not how.

Though the lowliest form doth veil Thee
As of old in Bethlehem,
Here as there Thine angels hail Thee
Branch and Flower of Jesse's stem.
Alleluia! Alleluia!
We in worship join with them.

Paschal Lamb, Thine offering, finished
Once for all when Thou wast slain,
In its fulness undiminished
Shall forever more remain,
Alleluia! Alleluia!
Cleansing souls from every stain.

Life-imparting, heavenly Manna,
Stricken Rock with streaming side,
Heaven and earth with loud hosanna
Worship Thee, the Lamb who died,
Alleluia! Alleluia!
Risen, ascended, glorified!

353
Susan Hutchinson.
Copyright © 1979 Word's Spirit of
Praise Music/Adm. by CopyCare.

LORD GOD, HEAVENLY KING,
You are our God, to You we sing;
Receive the worship of our hearts,
The adoration of our lips;
How we love You,
Lord God, heavenly King.

354
Graham Kendrick.
Copyright © 1986 Kingsway's
Thankyou Music.

LORD HAVE MERCY on us,
Come and heal our land.
Cleanse with Your fire, heal with Your touch,
Humbly we bow and call upon You now.
O Lord, have mercy on us,
O Lord, have mercy on us.

355
Stuart Townend.
Copyright © 1990 Kingsway's
Thankyou Music.

LORD HOW MAJESTIC YOU ARE,
My eyes meet Your gaze
And my burden is lifted.
Your word is a lamp to my feet,
Your hand swift to bless
And Your banner a shield.

You are my everything,
You who made earth and sky and sea,
All that You've placed inside of me
Calls out Your name.
To You I bow,
The King who commands my every breath,
The Man who has conquered sin and
* death,*
My Lord and my King,
My everything!

Lord, how resplendent You are,
When I think of Your heavens,
The work of Your fingers—
What is man, that You are mindful of him?
Yet You've crowned him with glory
And caused him to reign!

356 Dave Bilbrough.
Copyright © 1987 Kingsway's
Thankyou Music.

LORD, I WILL CELEBRATE YOUR LOVE,
From deep within my heart,
I celebrate Your love;
I celebrate Your love given to me.

You are the one that I adore;
Lord, in Your presence is life forever more;
The one that I adore.
You are my Lord.

Healing me, releasing me,
More and more reveal Yourself in me,
My Lord, my Lord!

357 Patrick Appleford.
Copyright © 1960 Josef Weinberger Ltd.

LORD JESUS CHRIST,
You have come to us,
You are one with us,
Mary's son.
Cleansing our souls from all their sin,
Pouring Your love and goodness in;
Jesus, our love for You we sing,
Living Lord.

(Optional communion verse:)
Lord Jesus Christ,
Now and every day,
Teach us how to pray,
Son of God.
You have commanded us to do
This in remembrance, Lord, of You:
Into our lives Your power breaks through,
Living Lord.

Lord Jesus Christ,
You have come to us,
Born as one of us,
Mary's son.
Led out to die on Calvary,
Risen from death to set us free,
Living Lord Jesus, help us see
You are Lord.

Lord Jesus Christ,
We would come to You,
Live our lives for You,
Son of God.
All Your commands we know are true,
Your many gifts will make us new,
Into our lives Your power breaks through,
Living Lord.

358 Rae Ranford.
Copyright © 1990 Kingsway's
Thankyou Music.

LORD JESUS, HERE I STAND before You,
To worship You, glorify Your name,
I humbly bow the knee before Your majesty,
Give You the glory, give You the praise.
I love You, lay my life before You,
I trust You for my every need;
I lift my hands to You, surrender everything,
You are my Saviour, My Lord and King.

359 Jesus Fellowship Church.
Copyright © 1990 Jesus Fellowship Church/
Adm. by CopyCare.

LORD, KEEP MY HEART TENDER,
Reaching with outstretched hands
To Jesus Christ;
Feeling my hardness melt,
Knowing how Jesus felt,
Possessed by love,
Warm Calvary love.

Lord, keep my heart tender,
Reaching with outstretched hands
For healing grace;
Believe the word revealed—
'By His stripes we are healed'—
Possessed by love,
Whole Calvary love.

Lord, keep my heart tender,
Reaching with outstretched hands
To those in need;
Finding, as tears I weep,
Compassion's well is deep,
Possessed by love,
Fresh Calvary love.

Lord, keep my heart tender,
Reaching with outstretched hands
To God most high;
Worshipping with desire,
My heart consumed by fire,
Possessed by love,
Strong Calvary love.

360

LORD MAKE ME AN INSTRUMENT,
An instrument of worship;
I lift up my hands in Your name.
Lord make me an instrument,
An instrument of worship;
I lift up my hands in Your name.

I'll sing You a love song,
A love song of worship,
I'll lift up my hands in Your name.
I'll sing You a love song,
A love song to Jesus,
I'll lift up my hands in Your name.

For we are a symphony,
A symphony of worship;
We lift up our hands in Your name.
For we are a symphony,
A symphony of worship;
We lift up our hands in Your name.

We'll sing You a love song,
A love song of worship,
We'll lift up our hands in Your name.
We'll sing you a love song,
A love song to Jesus,
We'll lift up our hands in Your name.

361

LORD OF LORDS, King of kings,
Maker of heaven and earth and all good
    things,
We give You glory.
Lord Jehovah, Son of Man,
Precious Prince of Peace and the great I AM,
We give You glory.

Glory to God!
Glory to God!
Glory to God Almighty,
In the highest!

Lord, You're righteous in all Your ways.
We bless Your holy name and we will give
    You praise,
We give You glory.
You reign forever in majesty,
We praise You and lift You up for eternity,
We give You glory.

362

LORD, THE LIGHT OF YOUR LOVE is shining,
In the midst of the darkness, shining;
Jesus, Light of the world, shine upon us,
Set us free by the truth You now bring us,
Shine on me, shine on me.

Shine, Jesus, shine,
Fill this land with the Father's glory;
Blaze, Spirit, blaze,
Set our hearts on fire.
Flow, river, flow,
Flood the nations with grace and mercy;
Send forth Your word,
Lord, and let there be light.

Lord, I come to Your awesome presence,
From the shadows into Your radiance;
By the blood I may enter Your brightness,
Search me, try me, consume all my darkness.
Shine on me, shine on me.

As we gaze on Your kingly brightness
So our faces display Your likeness.
Ever changing from glory to glory,
Mirrored here may our lives tell Your story.
Shine on me, shine on me.

363

LORD WE COME in Your name,
Gathered here to worship You.
Join us all in harmony,
Spirit, come.

And join our hearts together in love,
    (men)
Join our hearts together in love, (women)
Join our hearts together in love, (men)
Join our hearts, (women)
And come like the dew on the mountains
    descending. (all)
Join our hearts together in love, (men)
Join our hearts together in love, (women)
Join our hearts together in love, (men)
Join our hearts, (women)
For there the Lord has commanded the
    blessing. (all)

O how good, how beautiful
When we live in unity;   *(women)*
Flowing like anointing oil
On Jesus' head.   *(men)*

So join our hearts ... (etc.)

So let us all agree
To make strong our bonds of peace.
Here is life forever more,
Spirit, come.

And join our hearts ... (etc.)

364 Mick Ray.
Copyright © 1987 Kingsway's
Thankyou Music.

LORD, WE GIVE YOU PRAISE;
Our prayer of thanks to You we bring.
We sing our songs to You,
For praise belongs to You;
Lord, we give You praise.

Your love goes on and on;
You never change, You never turn.
Our hands we raise to You,
And bring our praise to You;
Lord, we give You praise.

365 Trish Morgan, Ray Goudie,
Ian Townend, Dave Bankhead.
Copyright © 1986 Kingsway's
Thankyou Music.

LORD, WE LONG FOR YOU to move in
power;
There's a hunger deep within our hearts,
To see healing in our nation.
Send Your Spirit to revive us:

Heal our nation,
Heal our nation,
Heal our nation,
Pour out Your Spirit on this land.

Lord we hear Your Spirit, coming closer,
A mighty wave to break upon our land,
Bringing justice, and forgiveness.
God we cry to You, 'Revive us':

366 Dave Bilbrough.
Copyright © 1984 Kingsway's
Thankyou Music.

LORD, WE WORSHIP YOU,
Lord, we worship You,
Lord, we worship You,
Lord, we worship You.

In humble adoration
We lift our voices to You,
And sing in acclamation
Our song of praise to You.

367 Simon and Lorraine Fenner.
Copyright © 1989 Kingsway's
Thankyou Music.

LORD, YOU ARE CALLING the people of Your
kingdom
To battle in Your name against the enemy;
To stand before You, a people who will serve
You,
Till Your kingdom is released throughout the
earth.

Let Your kingdom come,
Let Your will be done
On earth as it is in heaven.
(Repeat)

At the name of Jesus every knee must bow;
The darkness of this age must flee away.
Release Your power to flow throughout the
land;
Let Your glory be revealed as we praise.

368 Lynn DeShazo.
Copyright © 1985 Integrity's Hosanna! Music.
Adm. Kingsway's Thankyou Music.

LORD, YOU ARE MORE PRECIOUS than
silver,
Lord, You are more costly than gold.
Lord, You are more beautiful than diamonds,
And nothing I desire compares with You.

369 Graham Kendrick.
Copyright © 1986 Kingsway's
Thankyou Music.

LORD, YOU ARE SO PRECIOUS TO ME,
Lord, You are so precious to me,
And I love You,
Yes, I love You,
Because You first loved me.

Lord, You are so gracious to me,
Lord, You are so gracious to me,
And I love You,
Yes, I love You,
Because You first loved me.

370 Ian Smale.
Copyright © 1983 Kingsway's
Thankyou Music.

LORD, YOU PUT A TONGUE IN MY MOUTH
And I want to sing to You.
Lord, You put a tongue in my mouth
And I want to sing to You.
Lord, You put a tongue in my mouth
And I want to sing only to You.
Lord Jesus, free us in our praise;
Lord Jesus, free us in our praise.

Lord, You put some hands on my arms
Which I want to raise to You ... *(etc.)*

Lord, You put some feet on my legs
And I want to dance to You ... *(etc.)*

371 Don Moen.
Copyright © 1986 Integrity's Hosanna! Music.
Adm. Kingsway's Thankyou Music.

LORD, YOU'RE FAITHFUL AND JUST,
In You I put my trust, mighty God,
Everlasting Father.
Your word is faithful and true,
What You promised You will do, oh Lord.
Your word endures for ever.

> *You're faithful, faithful, and Your mercy
>   never ends;*
> *The world will pass away, but Your words
>   are here to stay.*
> *You're wonderful, Counsellor, Mighty
>   God.*
> *Lord Jehovah, You are the great I AM.*

372 Craig Musseau.
Copyright © 1990 Mercy/Vineyard
Publishing/Adm. by CopyCare.

LORD, YOUR GLORY FILLS MY HEART,
Your presence deep within me stirs my
    soul.
O Lord, how awesome are Your ways,
Your majesty surrounding all the earth.

> *All wisdom and honour and glory forever,*
> *All power and greatness and splendour,*
> *They are Yours above all others, my Lord.*

Lord, Your Spirit moves me now,
I see a picture of Your holiness.
O Lord, I look into Your eyes,
And feel a fire burn into my heart.

373 Tom Shirey.
Copyright © 1987 Mercy Publishing/
Kingsway's Thankyou Music.

LORD, YOUR NAME IS HOLY,
Lord, Your name is holy,
Holy, Lord,
You are holy,
Lord, You are holy,
Holy, Lord.

> *I love You, Lord,*
> *I glorify and praise Your holy name.*
> *Lord, I love You, Lord,*
> *I glorify and praise Your holy name.*

Lord, Your name is mighty,
Lord, Your name is mighty,
Mighty, Lord,
You are mighty,
Lord, You are mighty,
Mighty, Lord.

374 Barry Taylor.
Copyright © 1990 Kingsway's
Thankyou Music.

LORD, YOUR NAME IS WONDERFUL,
At Your name the captives shall go free.
We declare the mighty name of Jesus,
And proclaim Your holy victory.

At Your name the kingdoms fall;
We declare You Lord of all.
At Your name the enemy shall flee,
You are mighty,
You are mighty Lord of all.
Mighty Lord of all.

(Last time)
Mighty Lord of all!

375 Dave Bilbrough.
Copyright © 1984 Kingsway's
Thankyou Music.

LOVE BEYOND MEASURE, mercy so free,
Your endless resources given to me.
Strength to the weary, healing our lives,
Your love beyond measure has opened my
    eyes,
Opened my eyes.

376 Christina Rossetti (1830–94).

LOVE CAME DOWN AT CHRISTMAS,
Love all lovely, Love divine;
Love was born at Christmas,
Star and angels gave the sign.

Worship we the Godhead,
Love Incarnate, Love divine;
Worship we our Jesus:
But wherewith for sacred sign?

Love shall be our token,
Love be yours and love be mine,
Love to God and all men,
Love for plea and gift and sign.

377 Charles Wesley.

LOVE DIVINE, all loves excelling,
Joy of heaven to earth come down!
Fix in us Thy humble dwelling,
All Thy faithful mercies crown.
Jesus, Thou art all compassion,
Pure unbounded love Thou art;
Visit us with Thy salvation,
Enter every trembling heart.

Breathe, O breathe Thy loving Spirit
Into every troubled breast!
Let us all in Thee inherit,
Let us find Thy promised rest.
Take away the love of sinning;
Alpha and Omega be;
End of faith, as its beginning,
Set our hearts at liberty.

Come, Almighty to deliver,
Let us all Thy grace receive;
Suddenly return, and never,
Never more Thy temples leave.
Thee we would be always blessing,
Serve Thee as Thy hosts above,
Pray, and praise Thee without ceasing,
Glory in Thy perfect love.

Finish then Thy new creation,
Pure and spotless let us be;
Let us see Thy great salvation
Perfectly restored in Thee;
Changed from glory into glory,
Till in heaven we take our place;
Till we cast our crowns before Thee,
Lost in wonder, love and praise.

378 Robert Lowry.

LOW IN THE GRAVE HE LAY,
Jesus, my Saviour,
Waiting the coming day,
Jesus, my Lord:

> *Up from the grave He arose,*
> *With a mighty triumph o'er His foes;*
> *He arose a Victor from the dark domain,*
> *And He lives for ever with His saints to*
>   *reign:*
> *He arose! He arose!*
> *Alleluia! Christ arose!*

Vainly they watch His bed,
Jesus, my Saviour,
Vainly they seal the dead,
Jesus, my Lord:

Death cannot keep his prey,
Jesus, my Saviour;
He tore the bars away,
Jesus, my Lord:

379 Jack W. Hayford.
Copyright © 1976 Rocksmith Music/
Leosong Copyright Service.

MAJESTY, worship His majesty,
Unto Jesus be glory, honour and praise.
Majesty, kingdom authority,
Flow from His throne unto His own,
His anthem raise.

So exalt, lift up on high the name of Jesus,
Magnify, come glorify Christ Jesus the King.
Majesty, worship His majesty,
Jesus who died, now glorified,
King of all kings.

380 Dave Bilbrough.
Copyright © 1988 Kingsway's
Thankyou Music.

MAKE A JOYFUL MELODY,
Join together in harmony,
We are a part of a family,
The family of God.

His Spirit is our guarantee
That He lives in you and me,
We are a part of a family,
The family of God.

> *Lord, we praise You, praise You,*
> *Your love is great!*
> *Lord, we praise You, praise You,*
> *We celebrate!*

381 Sebastian Temple.
Copyright © 1967 Sebastian Temple/
OCP Publications/Adm. by Calamus.

MAKE ME A CHANNEL OF YOUR PEACE.
Where there is hatred let me bring Your love;
Where there is injury, Your pardon, Lord;
And where there's doubt, true faith in You.

> *Oh, Master, grant that I may never seek*
> *So much to be consoled as to console;*
> *To be understood as to understand;*
> *To be loved as to love with all my soul.*

Make me a channel of Your peace.
Where there's despair in life let me bring
   hope;
Where there is darkness, only light;
And where there's sadness, ever joy.

Make me a channel of Your peace.
It is in pardoning that we are pardoned,
In giving to all men that we receive,
And in dying that we're born to eternal life.

382 Chris Bowater.
Copyright © 1983 Sovereign Lifestyle Music.

MAKE ME, LORD, A DREAMER for Your
kingdom;
Plant in my heart heavenly desires.
Grant faith that can say, impossibilities shall
be,
And vision lest a world should perish not
knowing Thee.

Make me, Lord, a dreamer for Your kingdom;
I would aspire to greater goals in God.
So cause faith to rise, to motivate each word
and deed,
A faith that's well convinced that Jesus meets
every need.

Make me, Lord, a dreamer for Your kingdom,
Dreams that will change a world that's lost its
way.
May dreams that first found their birth in
Your omnipotence,
Come alive in me, becoming reality.

383 Maldwyn Pope.
Copyright © 1988 Samsongs/Coronation Music/
Kingsway's Thankyou Music.

MAKE US ONE, LORD, *make us one, Lord,*
By Your Spirit, make us one, Lord.
We are members of one body,
Make us one, Lord, we pray.

Every tribe and nation
Is represented here,
Watching with each other
As the day of Christ draws near;
Worshipping the Saviour
Who died to set us free,
We belong together;
We are family.

384 Graham Kendrick.
Copyright © 1986 Kingsway's
Thankyou Music.

MAKE WAY, make way, for Christ the King
In splendour arrives.
Fling wide the gates and welcome Him
Into your lives.

Make way! (Make way!)
Make way! (Make way!)
For the King of kings.
(For the King of kings.)
Make way! (Make way!)
Make way! (Make way!)
And let His kingdom in.

He comes the broken hearts to heal,
The prisoners to free.
The deaf shall hear, the lame shall dance,
The blind shall see.

And those who mourn with heavy hearts,
Who weep and sigh;
With laughter, joy and royal crown
He'll beautify.

We call you now to worship Him
As Lord of all.
To have no gods before Him,
Their thrones must fall!

385 Philipp Bliss.

MAN OF SORROWS! what a name
For the Son of God, who came
Ruined sinners to reclaim!
Hallelujah! what a Saviour!

Bearing shame and scoffing rude,
In my place condemned He stood;
Sealed my pardon with His blood:
Hallelujah! what a Saviour!

Guilty, vile, and helpless, we;
Spotless Lamb of God was He:
Full atonement—can it be?
Hallelujah! what a Saviour!

Lifted up was He to die,
'It is finished!' was His cry:
Now in heaven exalted high:
Hallelujah! what a Saviour!

When He comes, our glorious King,
All His ransomed home to bring,
Then anew this song we'll sing:
'Hallelujah! what a Saviour!'

386 Frances Ridley Havergal.

MASTER, SPEAK! THY SERVANT HEARETH,
Longing for Thy gracious word,
Longing for Thy voice that cheereth;
Master, let it now be heard.
I am listening, Lord, for Thee;
What hast Thou to say to me?

Speak to me by name, O Master,
Let me know it is to me;
Speak, that I may follow faster,
With a step more firm and free,
Where the Shepherd leads the flock
In the shadow of the rock.

Master, speak! though least and lowest,
Let me not unheard depart;
Master, speak! for O Thou knowest
All the yearning of my heart,
Knowest all its truest need;
Speak and make me blessed indeed.

Master, speak! and make me ready,
When Thy voice is truly heard,
With obedience glad and steady
Still to follow every word.
I am listening, Lord, for Thee;
Master, speak! O speak to me!

387

MAY MY LIFE declare the honour of Your
   name,
Reveal the heart of Christ who came
To light the darkest place
With sacrificial love.
(Last time)
Sacrificial love.

Cause me, Lord, to reach out in the Father's
   name,
To glorify the Lamb once slain,
To light the darkest place
With sacrificial love.

   *Teach me, Lord, to make my life as an
      offering,
   To tell the world that Jesus Christ is King,
   For the glory of God.*

388

MAY THE FRAGRANCE of Jesus fill this
   place. *(Men)*
May the fragrance of Jesus fill this
   place. *(Women)*
May the fragrance of Jesus fill this
   place. *(Men)*
Lovely fragrance of Jesus, *(Women)*
Rising from the sacrifice *(All)*
Of lives laid down in adoration.

May the glory of Jesus fill His church. *(Men)*
May the glory of Jesus fill His
   church. *(Women)*
May the glory of Jesus fill His church. *(Men)*
Radiant glory of Jesus, *(Women)*
Shining from our faces *(All)*
As we gaze in adoration.

May the beauty of Jesus fill my life. *(Men)*
May the beauty of Jesus fill my life. *(Women)*
May the beauty of Jesus fill my life. *(Men)*
Perfect beauty of Jesus, *(Women)*
Fill my thoughts, my words, my deeds, *(All)*
My all I give in adoration.

389

MAY WE BE A SHINING LIGHT to the nations,
A shining light to the peoples of the earth;
Till the whole world sees the glory of Your
   name,
May Your pure light shine through us.

May we bring a word of hope to the
   nations,
A word of life to the peoples of the earth;
Till the whole world knows there's salvation
   through Your name,
May Your mercy flow through us.

May we be a healing balm to the nations,
A healing balm to the peoples of the earth;
Till the whole world knows the power of Your
   name,
May Your healing flow through us.

May we sing a song of joy to the nations,
A song of praise to the peoples of the earth;
Till the whole world rings with the praises of
   Your name,
May Your song be sung through us.

May Your kingdom come to the nations,
Your will be done in the peoples of the
   earth;
Till the whole world knows that Jesus Christ
   is Lord,
May Your kingdom come in us,
May Your kingdom come in us,
May Your kingdom come on earth.

390 Graham Kendrick.
Copyright © 1986 Kingsway's
Thankyou Music.

MEEKNESS AND MAJESTY,
Manhood and Deity,
In perfect harmony,
The Man who is God.
Lord of eternity
Dwells in humanity,
Kneels in humility
And washes our feet.

> O what a mystery,
> Meekness and majesty.
> Bow down and worship
> For this is your God,
> This is your God.

Father's pure radiance,
Perfect in innocence,
Yet learns obedience
To death on a cross.
Suffering to give us life,
Conquering through sacrifice,
And as they crucify
Prays: 'Father forgive.'

Wisdom unsearchable,
God the invisible,
Love indestructible
In frailty appears.
Lord of infinity,
Stooping so tenderly,
Lifts our humanity
To the heights of His throne.

391 Maggi Dawn.
Copyright © 1987 Kingsway's
Thankyou Music.

MIGHTY GOD, gracious King, strong
  Deliverer;
You have heard all our prayers, and You've
  answered;
So we give to You our deep appreciation,
You're the living God, You are Lord;
You're the living God, You are Lord.

392 Jude Del Hierro.
Copyright © 1987 Mercy/Vineyard
Publishing/Adm. by CopyCare.

MORE LOVE (more love),
MORE POWER (more power),
More of You in my life.
More love (more love),
More power (more power),
More of You in my life.

And I will worship You with all of my
  heart,
And I will worship You with all of my
  mind,
And I will worship You with all of my
  strength,
For You are my Lord.

(Last time)
> And I will seek Your face with all of my
>   heart,
> And I will seek Your face with all of my
>   mind,
> And I will seek Your face with all of my
>   strength,
> For You are my Lord,
> You are my Lord.

393 Eleanor Farjeon.
Copyright © David Higham Associates Ltd.

MORNING HAS BROKEN
Like the first morning;
Blackbird has spoken
Like the first bird.
Praise for the singing!
Praise for the morning!
Praise for them, springing
Fresh from the Word!

Sweet the rain's new fall
Sunlit from heaven,
Like the first dewfall
On the first grass.
Praise for the sweetness
Of the wet garden,
Sprung in completeness
Where His feet pass.

Mine is the sunlight!
Mine is the morning
Born of the one light
Eden saw play!
Praise with elation,
Praise every morning,
God's re-creation
Of the new day!

394 Patricia Morgan.
Copyright © 1984 Kingsway's
Thankyou Music.

MOVE HOLY SPIRIT,
We ask You to
Fill us afresh.
We receive You.

395

Frederick W. Faber.

MY GOD, HOW WONDERFUL THOU ART,
Thy majesty how bright!
How beautiful Thy mercy-seat,
In depths of burning light!

How dread are Thine eternal years,
O everlasting Lord,
By prostrate spirits day and night
Incessantly adored!

How wonderful, how beautiful
The sight of Thee must be,
Thine endless wisdom, boundless power,
And awesome purity!

O how I fear Thee, living God,
With deepest, tenderest fears,
And worship Thee with trembling hope
And penitential tears!

Yet I may love Thee too, O Lord,
Almighty as Thou art,
For Thou hast stooped to ask of me
The love of my poor heart.

No earthly father loves like Thee;
No mother e'er so mild
Bears and forbears as Thou hast done
With me, Thy sinful child.

Father of Jesus, love's reward,
What rapture will it be
Prostrate before Thy throne to lie,
And gaze, and gaze on Thee.

396

Graham Kendrick.
Copyright © 1991 Make Way Music.

MY HEART IS FULL of admiration
For You, my Lord, my God and King.
Your excellence my inspiration,
Your words of grace have made my spirit
　sing.

　　All the glory, honour and power
　　Belong to You, belong to You.
　　Jesus, Saviour, Anointed One,
　　I worship You, I worship You.

You love what's right and hate what's evil,
Therefore Your God sets You on high,
And on Your head pours oil of gladness,
While fragrance fills Your royal palaces.

Your throne, O God, will last forever,
Justice will be Your royal decree.
In majesty, ride out victorious,
For righteousness, truth and humility.

397

Joan Parsons.
Copyright © 1978 Kingsway's
Thankyou Music.

MY LORD, HE IS THE FAIREST OF THE FAIR,
He is the lily of the valley,
The bright and morning star.
His love is written deep within my heart,
He is the never-ending fountain
Of everlasting life.

And He lives, He lives,
He lives, He lives in me.

398

Graham Kendrick.
Copyright © 1989 Make Way Music.

MY LORD, WHAT LOVE IS THIS
That pays so dearly,
That I, the guilty one,
May go free!

　　Amazing love, O what sacrifice,
　　The Son of God given for me.
　　My debt He pays, and my death He
　　　dies,
　　That I might live, that I might live.
　　　(Last time only)
　　That I might live!

And so they watched Him die,
Despised, rejected;
But oh, the blood He shed
Flowed for me!

And now, this love of Christ
Shall flow like rivers;
Come wash your guilt away,
Live again!

399

Keith Routledge.
Copyright © 1975 Sovereign Music UK.

MY PEACE I give unto you,
It's a peace that the world cannot give,
It's a peace that the world cannot
　understand:
Peace to know, peace to live,
My peace I give unto you.

My joy...*(etc.)*
My love...*(etc)*

400
Samuel Crossman.

MY SONG IS LOVE UNKNOWN,
My Saviour's love to me:
Love to the loveless shown,
That they might lovely be.
O who am I, that for my sake
My Lord should take frail flesh and die?

He came from His blessed throne,
Salvation to bestow;
But men made strange, and none
The longed-for Christ would know:
But O! my Friend, my Friend indeed,
Who at my need His life did spend.

Sometimes they strew His way,
And His sweet praises sing;
Resounding all the day
Hosannas to their King:
Then 'Crucify!' is all their breath,
And for His death they thirst and cry.

They rise and needs will have
My dear Lord made away;
A murderer they save,
The Prince of life they slay,
Yet cheerful He to suffering goes,
That He His foes from thence might free.

In life no house, no home
My Lord on earth might have;
In death, no friendly tomb,
But what a stranger gave.
What may I say? Heaven was His home;
And mine the tomb wherein He lay.

Here might I stay and sing,
No story so divine;
Never was love, dear King!
Never was grief like Thine.
This is my Friend, in whose sweet praise
I all my days could gladly spend.

401
David Fellingham.
Copyright © 1988 Kingsway's
Thankyou Music.

MY SOUL LONGS FOR YOU, O my God;
I seek You with all of my heart.
In this dry and thirsty land
My voice cries out to You;
Only Your presence can satisfy my need.

And so I enter into Your sanctuary,
To behold Your glory.
I'll give You my praise as long as I live,
Raise my hands, my life I'll give
To You, O I love You, Lord.

402
Andy Park.
Copyright © 1988 Mercy/Vineyard
Publishing/Adm. by CopyCare.

NO-ONE BUT YOU, LORD,
Can satisfy the longing in my heart.
Nothing I do, Lord,
Can take the place of drawing near to You.

*Only You can fill my deepest longing,
Only You can breathe in me new life;
Only You can fill my heart with laughter,
Only You can answer my heart's cry.*

Father, I love You,
Come satisfy the longing in my heart.
Fill me, overwhelm me,
Until I know Your love deep in my heart.

403
Philip Lawson Johnston.
Copyright © 1989 Kingsway's
Thankyou Music.

NOT UNTO US, *but unto Your name*
Be glory, honour and praise.
Not unto us, but unto Your name
Be glory, honour and praise.

Yours is the greatness and power.
You alone deserve all the fame.
Yours is the splendour and majesty.
From everlasting You're the same.

Yours is the glorious kingdom.
You alone are the King over all.
The earth is under Your dominion now.
You say when nations rise or fall.

404
Bill Anderson.
Copyright © 1985 Kingsway's
Thankyou Music.

NOT WITHOUT A CAUSE do we go marching
forth to war,
Not without a cause that we'll see
righteousness restored.
Clean your weapons, stir your hearts, shed all
fears before we start,
When we stand to do our part we shall say:

*'Not without a right do we unsheath our
silent swords,
Not without a fight but we will crown Him
Lord of lords.
Lift your banner, lift it high, Jesus is our
battle cry.
As we've lived, so we shall die, by His
side.'*

Not without a foe do we prepare ourselves to
fight,
Not without a shout will we scale hell's
unconquered height.
Let the hosts of Satan pray, when we rise as
one that day,
Let them run in disarray, when we say:

Not without a cheer will we hear bells and
trumpets ring,
Not without a tear we'll set Him on the throne
of kings.
Eyes on fire and faces grim, we will free
Jerusalem,
Through the gates we'll follow Him, as we
say:

405 Martin Rinkart.
Tr. Catherine Winkworth.

NOW THANK WE ALL OUR GOD,
With hearts and hands and voices;
Who wondrous things has done,
In whom His world rejoices;
Who from our mother's arms
Has blessed us on our way
With countless gifts of love,
And still is ours today.

O may this bounteous God
Through all our life be near us,
With ever joyful hearts
And blessèd peace to cheer us;
And keep us in His grace,
And guide us when perplexed,
And free us from all ills
In this world and the next.

All praise and thanks to God
The Father now be given,
The Son, and Him who reigns
With them in highest heaven,
The one eternal God,
Whom earth and heaven adore;
For thus it was, is now,
And shall be ever more.

406 Joey Holder.
Copyright © 1984 Far Lane Music Publishing/
Kingsway's Thankyou Music.

NOW UNTO THE KING eternal,
Unto the King immortal,
Unto the King invisible,
The only wise God,
The only wise God.
(Repeat)

Unto the King be glory and honour,
Unto the King for ever,
Unto the King be glory and honour for ever
And ever, Amen, Amen.

407 Elizabeth Porter Head.

**O BREATH OF LIFE, COME SWEEPING
THROUGH US,**
Revive Thy church with life and power.
O Breath of Life, come, cleanse, renew us,
And fit Thy church to meet this hour.

O Wind of God, come, bend us, break us,
Till humbly we confess our need;
Then in Thy tenderness remake us,
Revive, restore; for this we plead.

O Breath of Love, come, breathe within us,
Renewing thought and will and heart:
Come, love of Christ, afresh to win us,
Revive Thy church in every part.

Revive us, Lord! is zeal abating
While harvest fields are vast and white?
Revive us, Lord, the world is waiting,
Equip Thy church to spread the light.

408 Tr. Frederick Oakeley, altd.

O COME, ALL YE FAITHFUL,
Joyful and triumphant,
O come ye, O come ye to Bethlehem;
Come and behold Him,
Born the King of angels;

O come, let us adore Him,
O come, let us adore Him,
O come, let us adore Him,
Christ the Lord!

God of God,
Light of light,
Lo, He abhors not the virgin's womb;
Very God,
Begotten, not created:

Sing, choirs of angels,
Sing in exultation,
Sing, all ye citizens of heaven above;
Glory to God
In the highest:

Yea, Lord, we greet Thee,
Born this happy morning,
Jesus, to Thee be glory given;
Word of the Father
Now in flesh appearing:

409 Author unknown.

O COME LET US ADORE HIM,
O come let us adore Him,
O come let us adore Him,
Christ the Lord.

For He alone is worthy... *(etc.)*

We'll give Him all the glory... *(etc.)*

410 Tr. John Mason Neale, altd.

O COME, O COME, IMMANUEL,
And ransom captive Israel,
That mourns in lonely exile here
Until the Son of God appear.

> *Rejoice, rejoice! Immanuel*
> *Shall come to thee, O Israel.*

O come, O come, Thou Lord of might
Who to Thy tribes on Sinai's height
In ancient times didst give the law
In cloud, and majesty, and awe.

O come, Thou Rod of Jesse, free
Thine own from Satan's tyranny;
From depths of hell Thy people save
And give them victory o'er the grave.

O come, Thou Dayspring, come and cheer
Our spirits by Thine advent here;
Disperse the gloomy clouds of night,
And death's dark shadows put to flight.

O come, Thou Key of David, come
And open wide our heavenly home;
Make safe the way that leads on high,
And close the path to misery.

411 Charles Wesley.

O FOR A HEART TO PRAISE MY GOD,
A heart from sin set free;
A heart that always feels Thy blood
So freely shed for me;

A heart resigned, submissive, meek,
My great Redeemer's throne,
Where only Christ is heard to speak,
Where Jesus reigns alone;

A humble, lowly, contrite heart,
Believing, true, and clean;
Which neither life nor death can part
From Him who dwells within;

A heart in every thought renewed,
And full of love divine;
Perfect and right, and pure, and good:
A copy, Lord, of Thine.

Thy nature, gracious Lord, impart;
Come quickly from above;
Write Thy new name upon my heart,
Thy new best name of love.

412 Charles Wesley.

O FOR A THOUSAND TONGUES to sing
My great Redeemer's praise,
My great Redeemer's praise!
The glories of my God and King,
The triumphs of His grace!

Jesus! the name that charms our fears,
That bids our sorrows cease,
That bids our sorrows cease;
'Tis music in the sinner's ears,
'Tis life, and health, and peace.

See all your sins on Jesus laid;
The Lamb of God was slain,
The Lamb of God was slain;
His soul was once an offering made
For every soul of man.

He breaks the power of cancelled sin,
He sets the prisoner free,
He sets the prisoner free;
His blood can make the foulest clean,
His blood availed for me.

He speaks and, listening to His voice,
New life the dead receive,
New life the dead receive;
The mournful, broken hearts rejoice,
The humble poor believe.

Hear Him, ye deaf; His praise, ye dumb,
Your loosened tongues employ,
Your loosened tongues employ;
Ye blind, behold your Saviour come;
And leap, ye lame, for joy!

My gracious Master and my God,
Assist me to proclaim,
Assist me to proclaim,
To spread through all the earth abroad
The honours of Thy name.

413 Joanne Pond.
Copyright © 1980 Kingsway's
Thankyou Music.

O GIVE THANKS to the Lord,
All you His people.
O give thanks to the Lord for He is good.
Let us praise, let us thank,
Let us celebrate and dance,
O give thanks to the Lord for He is good.

414 Graham Kendrick.
Copyright © 1979 Kingsway's
Thankyou Music.

O GOD MY CREATOR, create in me
That river of water that flows full and free.
Let it bring life to the dead and stagnant sea;
Spring up, O well, and flow on out of me.

*We come to the throne
Where flows the living stream,
And drink from the water,
And drink from the water,
And drink from the water that flows from
    Thee.*

O God my Creator, create in me
That new way of living that flows full and
    free.
Let it bring life to the wilderness of man;
Spring up, O well, and flood this thirsty land.

415 Isaac Watts.

O GOD, OUR HELP IN AGES PAST,
Our hope for years to come,
Our shelter from the stormy blast,
And our eternal home.

Under the shadow of Thy throne
Thy saints have dwelt secure;
Sufficient is Thine arm alone,
And our defence is sure.

Before the hills in order stood,
Or earth received her frame,
From everlasting Thou art God,
To endless years the same.

A thousand ages in Thy sight
Are like an evening gone,
Short as the watch that ends the night
Before the rising sun.

Time, like an ever-rolling stream,
Bears all its sons away;
They fly forgotten, as a dream
Dies at the opening day.

O God, our help in ages past,
Our hope for years to come,
Be Thou our guard while troubles last,
And our eternal home.

416 Graham Kendrick.
Copyright © 1991 Make Way Music.

O HEAVEN, IS IN MY HEART.
O, heaven is in my heart.

The kingdom of our God is here, *(Leader)*
Heaven is in my heart. *(All)*
The presence of His majesty, *(Leader)*
Heaven is in my heart. *(All)*
And in His presence joy abounds, *(Leader)*
Heaven is in my heart. *(All)*
The light of holiness surrounds, *(Leader)*
Heaven is in my heart. *(All)*

His precious life on me He spent, *(All)*
Heaven is in my heart.
To give me life without an end,
Heaven is in my heart.
In Christ is all my confidence,
Heaven is in my heart.
The hope of my inheritance,
Heaven is in my heart.

We are a temple for His throne, *(Women)*
Heaven is in my heart. *(All)*
And Christ is the foundation stone, *(Women)*
Heaven is in my heart. *(All)*
He will return to take us home, *(Women)*
Heaven is in my heart. *(All)*
The Spirit and the Bride say 'Come!'
    (Women)
Heaven is in my heart.

417 Shona Sauni.
Copyright © 1982 Scripture in Song,
a division of Integrity Music/Adm.
by Kingsway's Thankyou Music.

O I WILL SING UNTO YOU WITH JOY, O Lord,
For You're the rock of my salvation,
Come before You with thanksgiving
And extol You with a song.
For You're the greatest King above all else,
You hold the depths of the earth in Your
    hand.
O I will sing unto You with joy, O Lord,
For You're the rock of my salvation.

418
John Ernest Bode.

O JESUS, I HAVE PROMISED
To serve Thee to the end;
Be Thou forever near me,
My Master and my Friend;
I shall not fear the battle
If Thou art by my side,
Nor wander from the pathway
If Thou wilt be my Guide.

O let me feel Thee near me;
The world is ever near;
I see the sights that dazzle,
The tempting sounds I hear;
My foes are ever near me,
Around me and within;
But Jesus, draw Thou nearer,
And shield my soul from sin.

O let me hear Thee speaking
In accents clear and still,
Above the storms of passion,
The murmurs of self-will;
O speak to reassure me,
To hasten, or control;
O speak, and make me listen,
Thou Guardian of my soul.

O Jesus, Thou hast promised
To all who follow Thee
That where Thou art in glory
There shall Thy servants be;
And, Jesus, I have promised
To serve Thee to the end;
O give me grace to follow
My Master and my Friend.

O let me see Thy footmarks,
And in them plant mine own;
My hope to follow duly
Is in Thy strength alone.
O guide me, call me, draw me,
Uphold me to the end;
And then in heaven receive me,
My Saviour and my Friend.

419
John Wimber.

O LET THE SON OF GOD ENFOLD YOU
With His Spirit and His love,
Let Him fill your heart and satisfy your soul.
O let Him have the things that hold you,
And His Spirit like a dove
Will descend upon your life and make you
  whole.

Jesus, O Jesus,
Come and fill Your lambs.
Jesus, O Jesus,
Come and fill Your lambs.

O come and sing this song with gladness
As your hearts are filled with joy,
Lift your hands in sweet surrender to His name.
O give Him all your tears and sadness,
Give Him all your years of pain,
And you'll enter into life in Jesus' name.

420
Philips Brooks.

O LITTLE TOWN OF BETHLEHEM,
How still we see thee lie!
Above thy deep and dreamless sleep
The silent stars go by.
Yet in thy dark streets shineth
The everlasting Light;
The hopes and fears of all the years
Are met in thee tonight.

O morning stars, together
Proclaim the holy birth,
And praises sing to God the King,
And peace to men on earth;
For Christ is born of Mary,
And gathered all above,
While mortals sleep, the angels keep
Their watch of wondering love.

How silently, how silently
The wondrous gift is given!
So God imparts to human hearts
The blessings of His heaven.
No ear may hear His coming;
But in this world of sin,
Where meek souls will receive Him, still
The dear Christ enters in.

O holy Child of Bethlehem,
Descend to us, we pray;
Cast out our sin, and enter in;
Be born in us today.
We hear the Christmas angels
The great glad tidings tell;
O come to us, abide with us,
Our Lord Immanuel!

421
Chris Roe/Dave Markee.

O LORD, GIVE ME AN UNDIVIDED HEART
To follow You.
O Lord, give me an undiminished love,
To see what You see, to do what You do,
O Lord, give me an undivided heart.

O Lord, give me an unrelenting mind
To seek Your face.
O Lord, give me an undefeated faith,
To see victory in all that I do,
To worship in spirit and truth.
To see less of me, and much more of You,
O Lord, give me an undivided heart.
O Lord, give me an undivided heart.

422 Carl Tuttle.
Copyright © 1985 Mercy/Vineyard
Publishing/Adm. by CopyCare.

O LORD, HAVE MERCY ON ME, and heal me;
O Lord, have mercy on me, and free me.
Place my feet upon a rock,
Put a new song in my heart, in my heart;
O Lord, have mercy on me.

O Lord, may Your love and Your grace protect
me;
O Lord, may Your ways and Your truth direct
me.
Place my feet upon a rock,
Put a new song in my heart, in my heart;
O Lord, have mercy on me.

423 Jacques Berthier/Taizé.
Copyright © 1982 Ateliers et Presses
de Taize (France).

O LORD, HEAR MY PRAYER,
O Lord, hear my prayer:
When I call answer me.
O Lord, hear my prayer,
O Lord, hear my prayer:
Come and listen to me.

424 Wendy Churchill.
Copyright © 1980 Word's Spirit of Praise
Music/Adm. by CopyCare.

O LORD, MOST HOLY GOD,
Great are Your purposes,
Great is Your will for us,
Great is Your love.
And we rejoice in You,
And we will sing to You,
O Father, have Your way,
Your will be done.

For You are building
A temple without hands,
A city without walls
Enclosed by fire.
A place for You to dwell,
Built out of living stones,
Shaped by a Father's hand
And joined in love.

425 Stuart K. Hine.
Copyright © 1953 Stuart K. Hine/
Kingsway's Thankyou Music.

O LORD MY GOD! when I in awesome
wonder
Consider all the works Thy hand hath made,
I see the stars, I hear the mighty thunder,
Thy power throughout the universe displayed:

Then sings my soul, my Saviour God to
Thee,
How great Thou art! How great Thou art!
Then sings my soul, my Saviour God, to
Thee,
How great Thou art! How great Thou art!

When through the woods and forest glades I
wander
And hear the birds sing sweetly in the trees;
When I look down from lofty mountain
grandeur,
And hear the brook, and feel the gentle
breeze;

And when I think that God His Son not
sparing,
Sent Him to die—I scarce can take it in.
That on the cross my burden gladly bearing,
He bled and died to take away my sin:

When Christ shall come with shout of
acclamation
And take me home—what joy shall fill my
heart!
Then shall I bow in humble adoration
And there proclaim, my God, how great Thou
art!

426 Phil Lawson Johnston.
Copyright © 1982 Kingsway's
Thankyou Music.

O LORD OUR GOD, how majestic is Your
name,
The earth is filled with Your glory.
O Lord our God, You are robed in majesty,
You've set Your glory above the heavens.

We will magnify, we will magnify
The Lord enthroned in Zion.
We will magnify, we will magnify
The Lord enthroned in Zion.

O Lord our God, You have established a
throne,
You reign in righteousness and splendour.
O Lord our God, the skies are ringing with
Your praise,
Soon those on earth will come to worship.

O Lord our God, the world was made at Your
    command,
In You all things now hold together.
Now to Him who sits on the throne and to the
    Lamb,
Be praise and glory and power forever.

427 Mike Kerry.
Copyright © 1982 Kingsway's
Thankyou Music.

O LORD OUR GOD, YOU ARE A GREAT GOD,
Your majesty beyond compare.
Who is a God like unto You,
And who like me could know Your care?

It's good, dear Lord, to know Your
    greatness,
It's good, dear Lord, to know Your care.
It's good just to be in Your presence,
It's good just to know that You are there.

428 Hilary Davies.
Copyright © 1988 Samsongs/Coronation Music/
Kingsway's Thankyou Music.

  O LORD, OUR LORD, *how excellent is*
    Your name in all the earth.
  O Lord, our Lord, how excellent is Your
    name in all the earth.

You have set Your glory above the
    heavens,
From children's lips You have ordained
    praise;
You have set the moon and the stars in
    place,
And You still remember me.

What is man that You are mindful of him;
The son of man that You take care of him?
You have put everything beneath his feet,
And made him ruler of Your works.

429 Graham Kendrick.
Copyright © 1987 Make Way Music.

O LORD, THE CLOUDS ARE GATHERING,
The fire of judgement burns,
How we have fallen!
O Lord, You stand appalled to see
Your laws of love so scorned,
And lives so broken.

Have mercy, Lord, (Men)
Have mercy, Lord, (Women)
Forgive us, Lord, (Men)
Forgive us, Lord, (Women)
Restore us, Lord, (All)
Revive Your church again.
Let justice flow (Men)
Let justice flow (Women)
Like rivers, (Men)
Like rivers, (Women)
And righteousness like a (All)
Never failing stream.

O Lord, over the nations now
Where is the dove of peace?
Her wings are broken.
O Lord, while precious children starve
The tools of war increase;
Their bread is stolen.

O Lord, dark powers are poised to flood
Our streets with hate and fear;
We must awaken!
O Lord, let love reclaim the lives
That sin would sweep away
And let Your kingdom come.

Yet, O Lord, Your glorious cross shall tower
Triumphant in this land,
Evil confounding.
Through the fire Your suffering church display
The glories of her Christ:
Praises resounding!

430 David J. Hadden.
Copyright © 1983 Restoration Music Ltd./
Adm. by Sovereign Music UK.

O LORD, YOU ARE MY GOD,
I will exalt You and praise Your name,
I will exalt You and praise Your name.
For in Your perfect faithfulness
You have done marvellous things.
O Lord, You are my God,
I will exalt You and praise Your name.

431 David Fellingham.
Copyright © 1983 Kingsway's
Thankyou Music.

  O LORD, YOU ARE MY LIGHT,
  O Lord, You are my salvation.
  You have delivered me from all my fear,
  For You are the defence of my life.

For my life is hidden with Christ in God,
You have concealed me in Your love,
You've lifted me up, placed my feet on a rock;
I will shout for joy in the house of God.

432 Keith Green.
Copyright © 1980 Birdwing Music/
BMG Songs/EMI Christian Music Publishing/
Adm. by CopyCare.

O LORD, YOU'RE BEAUTIFUL,
Your face is all I seek,
For when Your eyes are on this child,
Your grace abounds to me.

O Lord, please light the fire
That once burned bright and clear,
Replace the lamp of my first love
That burns with holy fear!

I wanna take Your word
And shine it all around,
But first help me just to live it, Lord!
And when I'm doing well,
Help me to never seek a crown,
For my reward is giving glory to You.

433 Graham Kendrick.
Copyright © 1986 Kingsway's
Thankyou Music.

O LORD, YOUR TENDERNESS,
Melting all my bitterness,
O Lord, I receive Your love.
O Lord, Your loveliness,
Changing all my ugliness,
O Lord, I receive Your love,
O Lord, I receive Your love,
O Lord, I receive Your love.

434 George Matheson.

O LOVE THAT WILT NOT LET ME GO,
I rest my weary soul in thee:
I give thee back the life I owe,
That in thine ocean depths its flow
May richer, fuller be.

O light that followest all my way,
I yield my flickering torch to thee:
My heart restores its borrowed ray,
That in thy sunshine's blaze its day
May brighter, fairer be.

O joy that seekest me through pain,
I cannot close my heart to thee:
I trace the rainbow through the rain,
And feel the promise is not vain,
That morn shall tearless be.

O cross that liftest up my head,
I dare not ask to fly from thee:
I lay in dust life's glory dead,
And from the ground there blossoms red
Life that shall endless be.

435 Maggi Dawn.
Copyright © 1986 Kingsway's
Thankyou Music.

O MAGNIFY THE LORD *with me,*
And let us exalt His name together.
O magnify the Lord with me,
And let us exalt His name together.

I called to the Lord and He answered,
Saved me from all of my trouble;
He delivered me from all my fear,
So I'll rejoice, I'll rejoice!

We will boast about the Lord,
Tell of the things He has done;
Let the whole world hear about it,
And they'll rejoice, they'll rejoice!

We will magnify Jesus together;
We will magnify You, O Lord.
We will magnify Jesus together;
We will magnify You, O Lord.

436 Geoff Roberts.
Copyright © 1990 Kingsway's
Thankyou Music.

O MY LORD, YOU ARE MOST GLORIOUS,
King of kings and Prince of Peace.
By Your word this world was created;
By Your love I have been set free.
And I lift my hands in worship up to Your throne,
I will declare how much You mean to me.
You are my Lord, it's You I worship;
Son of God, You reign in majesty.

437 William W. How.

O MY SAVIOUR, LIFTED
From the earth for me,
Draw me, in Thy mercy,
Nearer unto Thee.

Lift my earthbound longings,
Fix them, Lord, above;
Draw me with the magnet
Of Thy mighty love.

And I come, Lord Jesus;
Dare I turn away?
No! Thy love hath conquered,
And I come today.

Bringing all my burdens,
Sorrow, sin, and care;
At Thy feet I lay them,
And I leave them there.

438 Cecil F. Alexander.

ONCE, IN ROYAL DAVID'S CITY,
Stood a lowly cattle shed,
Where a mother laid her baby
In a manger for His bed.
Mary was that mother mild,
Jesus Christ, her little child.

He came down to earth from heaven,
Who is God and Lord of all,
And His shelter was a stable,
And His cradle was a stall:
With the poor and meek and lowly
Lived on earth our Saviour holy.

And through all His wondrous childhood
He would honour and obey,
Love and watch the lowly mother
In whose gentle arms He lay.
Christian children all should be
Mild, obedient, good as He.

For He is our childhood's pattern:
Day by day like us He grew;
He was little, weak and helpless;
Tears and smiles like us He knew:
And He feeleth for our sadness,
And He shareth in our gladness.

And our eyes at last shall see Him
Through His own redeeming love;
For that child, so dear and gentle,
Is our Lord in heaven above;
And He leads His children on
To the place where He is gone.

Not in that poor lowly stable,
With the oxen standing by,
We shall see Him, but in heaven,
Set at God's right hand on high;
When like stars His children crowned,
All in white shall wait around.

439 Graham Kendrick.

ONE SHALL TELL ANOTHER,
And he shall tell his friend,
Husbands, wives and children
Shall come following on.
From house to house in families
Shall more be gathered in,
And lights will shine in every street,
So warm and welcoming.

Come on in and taste the new wine,
The wine of the kingdom,
The wine of the kingdom of God.
Here is healing and forgiveness,
The wine of the kingdom,
The wine of the kingdom of God.

Compassion of the Father
Is ready now to flow,
Through acts of love and mercy
We must let it show.
He turns now from His anger
To show a smiling face,
And longs that men should stand beneath
The fountain of His grace.

He longs to do much more than
Our faith has yet allowed,
To thrill us and surprise us
With His sovereign power.
Where darkness has been darkest
The brightest light will shine,
His invitation comes to us,
It's yours and it is mine.

440 Andy Park.

ONE THING I ASK, one thing I seek,
That I may dwell in Your house, O Lord.
All of my days, all of my life,
That I may see You, Lord.

Hear me, O Lord, hear me when I cry;
Lord, do not hide Your face from me.
You have been my strength,
You have been my shield,
And You will lift me up.

One thing I ask,
One thing I desire
Is to see You,
Is to see You.

441 Gerrit Gustafson.

ONLY BY GRACE can we enter,
Only by grace can we stand;
Not by our human endeavour,
But by the blood of the Lamb.
Into Your presence You call us,
You call us to come.
Into Your presence You draw us,
And now by Your grace we come,
Now by Your grace we come.

Lord, if You mark our transgressions,
Who would stand?
Thanks to Your grace we are cleansed
By the blood of the Lamb.
    (Repeat)

442 Sabine Baring-Gould.

ONWARD, CHRISTIAN SOLDIERS,
Marching as to war,
With the cross of Jesus
Going on before!
Christ, the royal Master,
Leads against the foe;
Forward into battle,
See, His banners go!

> *Onward, Christian soldiers,*
> *Marching as to war,*
> *With the cross of Jesus*
> *Going on before.*

At the name of Jesus
Satan's host doth flee;
On then, Christian soldiers,
On to victory!
Hell's foundations quiver
At the shout of praise;
Brothers, lift your voices;
Loud your anthems raise:

Like a mighty army
Moves the church of God:
Brothers we are treading
Where the saints have trod.
We are not divided,
All one body we,
One in hope and doctrine,
One in charity.

Crowns and thrones may perish,
Kingdoms rise and wane,
But the church of Jesus
Constant will remain;
Gates of hell can never
'Gainst that church prevail;
We have Christ's own promise,
And that cannot fail:

Onward, then, ye people!
Join our happy throng;
Blend with ours your voices
In the triumph-song:
Glory, laud, and honour
Unto Christ the King!
This through countless ages
Men and angels sing:

443 Robert Cull.
Copyright © 1976 Maranatha! Music/
Adm. by CopyCare.

OPEN OUR EYES, LORD,
We want to see Jesus,
To reach out and touch Him
And say that we love Him.
Open our ears, Lord,
And help us to listen.
Open our eyes, Lord,
We want to see Jesus.

444 Carl Tuttle.
Copyright © 1985 Mercy/Vineyard
Publishing/Adm. by CopyCare.

OPEN YOUR EYES, see the glory of the King.
Lift up your voice and His praises sing.
I love You, Lord, I will proclaim:
Hallelujah, I bless Your name.

445 Henry W. Baker.

O PRAISE YE THE LORD!
Praise Him in the height;
Rejoice in His word,
Ye angels of light;
Ye heavens adore Him
By whom ye were made,
And worship before Him
In brightness arrayed.

O praise ye the Lord!
Praise Him upon earth,
In tuneful accord,
Ye sons of new birth;
Praise Him who hath brought you
His grace from above,
Praise Him who hath taught you
To sing of His love.

O praise ye the Lord,
All things that give sound;
Each jubilant chord,
Re-echo around:
Loud organs, His glory
Forthtell in deep tone,
And sweet harp, the story
Of what He hath done.

O praise ye the Lord!
Thanksgiving and song
To Him be outpoured
All ages along;
For love in creation,
For heaven restored,
For grace of salvation,
O praise ye the Lord!

446

Paulus Gerhardt.
Tr. James W. Alexander.

O SACRED HEAD, ONCE WOUNDED,
With grief and pain weighed down,
How scornfully surrounded
With thorns, Thine only crown!
How pale art Thou with anguish,
With sore abuse and scorn!
How does that visage languish,
Which once was bright as morn!

O Lord of life and glory,
What bliss till now was Thine!
I read the wondrous story,
I joy to call Thee mine.
Thy grief and Thy compassion
Were all for sinners' gain;
Mine, mine was the transgression,
But Thine the deadly pain.

What language shall I borrow
To praise Thee, heavenly Friend,
For this, Thy dying sorrow,
Thy pity without end?
Lord, make me Thine for ever,
Nor let me faithless prove;
O let me never, never
Abuse such dying love!

Be near me, Lord, when dying;
O show Thyself to me;
And for my succour flying,
Come, Lord, to set me free:
These eyes, new faith receiving,
From Jesus shall not move;
For he who dies believing,
Dies safely through Thy love.

447

Phil Rogers.
Copyright © 1984 Kingsway's
Thankyou Music.

O TASTE AND SEE that the Lord is good,
How blessèd is the man who hides himself in
   Him.
I sought the Lord and He answered me
And set me free from all my fears.

I will give thanks to Him, for He is good,
His steadfast love to me will never end.
I will give thanks to Him, for He is good,
His steadfast love to me will never end.

448

Phil Rogers.
Copyright © 1988 Kingsway's
Thankyou Music.

O, THAT YOU WOULD BLESS ME,
And enlarge my borders,
That Your hand would be with me,
O Lord, O Lord.
O, that You would keep me,
Keep me from all evil,
So that I may not be ashamed,
O Lord, O Lord.

   May Your kingdom come,
   May Your will be done
   On earth as it is in heaven;
   May Your kingdom come,
   May Your will be done
   Through me, O Lord, O Lord.

O, that You would fill me,
Fill me with Your Spirit,
So that I may know Your power,
O Lord, O Lord.
O, that You would use me
To fulfil Your purposes,
That through me Your glory would shine,
O Lord, O Lord.

449

Dave Bilbrough.
Copyright © 1988 Kingsway's
Thankyou Music.

O, THE JOY OF YOUR FORGIVENESS,
Slowly sweeping over me;
Now in heartfelt adoration
This praise I'll bring
To You, my King,
I'll worship You, my Lord.

450

Dave Bilbrough.
Copyright © 1980 Kingsway's
Thankyou Music.

O THE VALLEYS SHALL RING
With the sound of praise,
And the lion shall lie with the lamb.
Of His government there shall be no end,
And His glory shall fill the earth.

May Your will be done,
May Your kingdom come,
Let it rule, let it reign in our lives.
There's a shout in the camp as we answer the
   call,
Hail the King, Hail the Lord of lords!

451 Charles Wesley.

O THOU WHO CAMEST FROM ABOVE
The pure celestial fire to impart,
Kindle a flame of sacred love
On the mean altar of my heart.

There let it for Thy glory burn
With inextinguishable blaze,
And trembling to its source return,
In humble prayer and fervent praise.

Jesus, confirm my heart's desire
To work, and speak, and think for Thee;
Still let me guard the holy fire,
And still stir up Thy gift in me.

Ready for all Thy perfect will,
My acts of faith and love repeat,
Till death Thy endless mercies seal,
And make the sacrifice complete.

452 Noel & Tricia Richards.
Copyright © 1989 Kingsway's
Thankyou Music.

OUR CONFIDENCE IS IN THE LORD,
The source of our salvation.
Rest is found in Him alone,
The Author of creation.
We will not fear the evil day,
Because we have a refuge;
In every circumstance we say,
Our hope is built on Jesus.

He is our fortress,
We will never be shaken.
He is our fortress,
We will never be shaken.
(Repeat)

We will put our trust in God.
We will put our trust in God.

453 Rich Mullins.
Copyright © 1989 Edward Grant Inc/
BMG Music Publishing Ltd/Adm. by CopyCare.

OUR GOD IS AN AWESOME GOD,
He reigns from heaven above,
With wisdom, power and love,
Our God is an awesome God!
Our God is an awesome God,
He reigns from heaven above,
With wisdom, power and love,
Our God is an awesome God!

454 Patricia Morgan.
Copyright © 1986 Kingsway's
Thankyou Music.

OUT OF YOUR GREAT LOVE, You have
relented.
Out of Your great love, You have shown us
grace.
Though we've caused You pain, and we have
hurt You,
Out of Your great love, You've turned again.

455 Steven Fry.
Copyright © 1986 Birdwing Music/
Adm. by CopyCare.

O, WE ARE MORE THAN CONQUERORS.
*O, we are more than conquerors,
And who can separate us from
The love, the love of God?
O yes, we are,
We are more than conquerors.
O, we are more than conquerors.*

For He has promised to fulfil His will in us,
He said that He would guide us with His eye;
For He has blessed us with all gifts in Christ,
And we are His delight.

For He's within to finish what's begun in me,
He opens doors that no one can deny;
He makes a way where there's no other way,
And gives me wings to fly.

456 Robert Grant.

O WORSHIP THE KING,
All glorious above;
O gratefully sing
His power and His love:
Our Shield and Defender,
The Ancient of Days,
Pavilioned in splendour
And girded with praise.

O tell of His might,
O sing of His grace,
Whose robe is the light,
Whose canopy space;
His chariots of wrath
The deep thunder-clouds form,
And dark is His path
On the wings of the storm.

The earth, with its store
Of wonders untold,
Almighty, Thy power
Hath founded of old;
Hath 'stablished it fast,
By a changeless decree,
And round it hath cast,
Like a mantle, the sea.

Thy bountiful care
What tongue can recite?
It breathes in the air,
It shines in the light;
It streams from the hills,
It descends to the plain,
And sweetly distils
In the dew and the rain.

Frail children of dust,
And feeble as frail,
In Thee do we trust,
Nor find Thee to fail;
Thy mercies how tender,
How firm to the end,
Our Maker, Defender,
Redeemer, and Friend!

457 John S. B. Monsell.

O WORSHIP THE LORD in the beauty of
    holiness,
Bow down before Him, His glory proclaim;
With gold of obedience and incense of
    lowliness,
Kneel and adore Him; the Lord is His name.

Low at His feet lay thy burden of carefulness,
High on His heart He will bear it for thee,
Comfort thy sorrows, and answer thy
    prayerfulness,
Guiding thy steps as may best for thee be.

Fear not to enter His courts in the
    slenderness
Of the poor wealth thou wouldst reckon as
    thine;
Truth in its beauty, and love in its tenderness,
These are the offerings to lay on His shrine.

These, though we bring them in trembling
    and fearfulness,
He will accept for the name that is dear;
Mornings of joy give for evenings of
    tearfulness,
Trust for our trembling, and hope for our fear.

O worship the Lord in the beauty of holiness,
Bow down before Him, His glory proclaim;
With gold of obedience and incense of
    lowliness,
Kneel and adore Him: the Lord is His name.

458 Author unknown.

PEACE IS FLOWING LIKE A RIVER,
Flowing out through you and me,
Spreading out into the desert,
Setting all the captives free.

Let it flow through me,
Let it flow through me,
Let the mighty peace of God
Flow out through me.
Let it flow through me,
Let it flow through me,
Let the mighty peace of God
Flow out through me.

Love is flowing ... *(etc.)*

Joy is flowing ... *(etc.)*

Faith is flowing ... *(etc.)*

Hope is flowing ... *(etc.)*

459 John Watson.

PEACE LIKE A RIVER,
Love like a mountain,
The wind of Your Spirit
Is blowing everywhere.
Joy like a fountain,
Healing spring of life;
Come, Holy Spirit,
Let Your fire fall.

460 Graham Kendrick.

PEACE TO YOU.
We bless you now in the name of the Lord.
Peace to you.
We bless you now in the name of the Prince
    of Peace.
Peace to you.

461 Anne Ortlund.

PRAISE GOD FOR THE BODY,
Praise God for the Son;
Praise God for the life
That binds our hearts in one.

Joy is the food we share;
Love is our home, brothers.
Praise God for the body;
Shalom, Shalom.

Guard your circle, brothers,
Clasp your hand in hand;
Satan cannot break
The bond in which we stand.

Shed your extra clothing,
Keep your baggage light;
Rough will be the battle,
Long will be the fight, but...

Praise God for the body,
Praise God for the Son;
Praise God for the life
That binds our hearts in one.

462 Ken Thomas.
Copyright © 1972 Bud John Songs/
EMI Christian Music Publishing/
Adm. by CopyCare.

PRAISE GOD FROM WHOM ALL BLESSINGS FLOW,
Praise Him, all creatures here below,
Praise Him above, ye heavenly host;
Praise Father, Son and Holy Ghost.

463 Twila Paris.
Copyright © Singspiration Music/John T.
Benson Publishing Co./Adm. by CopyCare.

PRAISE HIM, praise Him,
Praise Him with your song.
Praise Him, praise Him,
Praise Him all day long!

For the Lord is worthy,
Worthy to receive our praise.
For the Lord is worthy,
Worthy to receive our praise.

Praise Him, praise Him,
Praise Him with your heart.
Praise Him, praise Him,
Give Him all you are.

Praise Him, praise Him,
Praise Him with your life.
Praise Him, praise Him,
Lift His name up high.

464 John Kennett
Copyright © 1981 Kingsway's
Thankyou Music.

PRAISE HIM ON THE TRUMPET,
The psaltery and harp,
Praise Him on the timbrel and the dance,
Praise Him with stringed instruments, too.
Praise Him on the loud cymbals,
Praise Him on the loud cymbals,
Let everything that has breath praise the
Lord.

Hallelujah, praise the Lord,
Hallelujah, praise the Lord,
Let everything that has breath praise the
Lord.
Hallelujah, praise the Lord,
Hallelujah, praise the Lord,
Let everything that has breath praise the
Lord.

465 Fanny J. Crosby.

PRAISE HIM, PRAISE HIM! JESUS, OUR BLESSÈD REDEEMER;
Sing, O earth, His wonderful love proclaim!
Hail Him, hail Him! highest archangels in
glory,
Strength and honour give to His holy name.
Like a shepherd, Jesus will guard His
children,
In His arms He carries them all day long;
O ye saints that dwell in the mountains of
Zion,
Praise Him! praise Him! ever in joyful song.

Praise Him, praise Him! Jesus, our blessèd
Redeemer;
For our sins He suffered and bled and died.
He, our Rock, our hope of eternal salvation,
Hail Him, hail Him! Jesus the Crucified.
Loving Saviour, meekly enduring sorrow,
Crowned with thorns that cruelly pierced His
brow;
Once for us rejected, despised, and forsaken,
Prince of glory, ever triumphant now.

Praise Him, praise Him! Jesus, our blessèd
Redeemer;
Heavenly portals loud with hosannas ring!
Jesus, Saviour, reigneth for ever and ever,
Crown Him, crown Him! Prophet and Priest
and King!
Death is vanquished, tell it with joy, ye
faithful!
Where is now thy victory, boasting grave?
Jesus lives, no longer thy portals are
cheerless;
Jesus lives, the mighty and strong to save.

466 Henry Francis Lyte.

PRAISE, MY SOUL, THE KING OF HEAVEN;
To His feet thy tribute bring.
Ransomed, healed, restored, forgiven,
Who like thee His praise should sing?
Praise Him! Praise Him!
Praise Him! Praise Him!
Praise the everlasting King!

Praise Him for His grace and favour
To our fathers in distress;
Praise Him, still the same forever,
Slow to chide, and swift to bless.
Praise Him! Praise Him!
Praise Him! Praise Him!
Glorious in His faithfulness.

Father-like, He tends and spares us;
Well our feeble frame He knows;
In His hands He gently bears us,
Rescues us from all our foes.
Praise Him! Praise Him!
Praise Him! Praise Him!
Widely as His mercy flows.

Angels in the height, adore Him;
Ye behold Him face to face;
Sun and moon, bow down before Him,
Dwellers all in time and space.
Praise Him! Praise Him!
Praise Him! Praise Him!
Praise with us the God of grace!

467 David Fellingham.
Copyright © 1986 Kingsway's
Thankyou Music.

PRAISE THE LORD, praise Him in His temple,
Praise Him in the sanctuary of His power.
Lift your voices with great rejoicing,
For God is great in all the earth.

Praise Him for His excellence,
Praise Him for His love;
Praise Him for His mercy,
Giving us new life.

468 Roy Hicks Jnr.
Copyright © 1975 Latter Rain Music/
EMI Christian Music Publishing/
Adm. by CopyCare.

PRAISE THE NAME OF JESUS,
Praise the name of Jesus,
He's my rock, He's my fortress,
He's my deliverer, in Him will I trust.
Praise the name of Jesus.

469 John H. Newman.

PRAISE TO THE HOLIEST IN THE HEIGHT,
And in the depth be praise;
In all His words most wonderful,
Most sure in all His ways.

O loving wisdom of our God!
When all was sin and shame,
A second Adam to the fight
And to the rescue came.

O wisest love! that flesh and blood,
Which did in Adam fail,
Should strive afresh against the foe,
Should strive and should prevail;

And that a higher gift than grace
Should flesh and blood refine,
God's presence and His very self,
And essence all-divine.

O generous love! that He, who smote
In Man for man the foe,
The double agony in Man
For man should undergo;

And in the garden secretly,
And on the cross on high,
Should teach His brethren, and inspire
To suffer and to die.

Praise to the Holiest in the height,
And to the depth be praise;
In all His words most wonderful,
Most sure in all His ways.

470 Joachim Neander.
Tr. Catherine Winkworth 1863,
and P. Dearmer 1906.

PRAISE TO THE LORD, THE ALMIGHTY, the
King of creation!
O my soul, praise Him, for He is thy health
and salvation!
All ye who hear,
Brothers and sisters, draw near,
Praise Him in glad adoration.

Praise to the Lord, who doth prosper thy
work and defend thee;
Surely His goodness and mercy here daily
attend thee:
Ponder anew
What the Almighty can do,
Who with His love doth befriend thee.

Praise to the Lord, who doth nourish thy life
and restore thee,
Fitting thee well for the tasks that are ever
before thee,
Then to thy need
He like a mother doth speed,
Spreading the wings of grace o'er thee.

Praise to the Lord, who when tempests their
warfare are waging,
Who, when the elements madly around thee
are raging,
Biddeth them cease,
Turneth their fury to peace,
Whirlwinds and waters assuaging.

Praise to the Lord, who, when darkness of sin
is abounding,
Who, when the godless do triumph, all virtue
confounding,
Sheddeth His light,
Chaseth the horrors of night,
Saints with His mercy surrounding.

Praise to the Lord! O let all that is in me
adore Him!
All that hath life and breath, come now with
praises before Him!
Let the Amen
Sound from His people again:
Gladly for aye we adore Him.

471

PRAISE YE THE LORD, praise ye the Lord,
For He has done marvellous things
Whereof we are glad,
We are glad,
Praise ye the Lord, praise ye the Lord.

472

PRAISE YOU, LORD,
For the wonder of Your healing.
Praise You, Lord,
For Your love so freely given;
Outpouring, anointing,
Flowing in to heal our wounds:
Praise You, Lord, for Your love for me.

Praise You, Lord,
For Your gift of liberation.
Praise You, Lord,
You have set the captives free;
The chains that bind are broken
By the sharpness of Your sword:
Praise You, Lord, You gave Your life for me.

Praise You, Lord,
You have borne the depths of sorrow.
Praise You, Lord,
For Your anguish on the tree;
The nails that tore Your body
And the pain that tore Your soul:
Praise You, Lord, Your tears they fell for me.

Praise You, Lord,
You have turned our thorns to roses.
Glory, Lord,
As they bloom upon Your brow;
The path of pain is hallowed,
For Your love has made it sweet:
Praise You, Lord, and may I love You now.

473

PREPARE THE WAY of the Lord,
Make His paths straight,
Open the gates,
That He may enter freely into our life.
'Hosanna!' we cry to the Lord.

*And we will fill the earth with the sound
of His praise.
Jesus is Lord!
Let Him be adored!
Yes, we will have this Man to reign over
us,
Hosanna! We follow the Lord!*

And He will come to us as He came before,
Clothed in His grace,
To stand in our place.
And we behold Him now our Priest and
King,
'Hosanna!' we sing to the Lord.

His kingdom shall increase,
To fill all the earth
And show forth His worth.
Then every knee shall bow and every tongue
confess
That Jesus Christ is Lord.

474

PRINCE OF PEACE YOU ARE,
You're bright and morning star;
Wondrous royal King,
You have made my heart to sing.
I worship You in spirit and in truth;
Lifting my praise, Your name in song I
raise.
I give to You my life,
I offer up my sacrifice,
I pledge my love to You,
My God and King.

475

PURIFY MY HEART,
Let me be as gold
And precious silver.
Purify my heart,
Let me be as gold,
Pure gold.

Refiner's fire,
My heart's one desire
Is to be holy,
Set apart for You, Lord.
I choose to be holy,
Set apart for You, my Master,
Ready to do Your will.

Purify my heart,
Cleanse me from within
And make me holy.
Purify my heart,
Cleanse me from my sin,
Deep within.

476

RAISE UP AN ARMY, *O God,*
Awake Your people throughout the earth.
Raise up an army, O God,
To proclaim Your kingdom,
To declare Your word,
To declare Your glory, O God.

Our hope, our heart, our vision,
To see in every land
Your chosen people coming forth.
Fulfilling Your holy mission,
United as we stand,
Pledging our lives unto You, Lord.

O God, our glorious Maker,
We marvel at Your grace,
That You would use us in Your plan.
Rejoicing at Your favour,
Delighting in Your ways,
We'll gladly follow Your command!

477

RECONCILED, I'm reconciled,
I'm reconciled to God for ever;
Know He took away my sin,
I know His love will leave me never.
Reconciled, I am His child,
I know it was on me He smiled,
I'm reconciled, I'm reconciled to God.

Hallelujah, I'm justified, I'm justified,
It's just as if I'd never sinned,
And once I knew such guilty fear,
But now I know His peace within me.
Justified, I'm justified,
It's all because my Jesus died,
I'm justified, I'm justified by God.

Hallelujah I'll magnify, I'll magnify,
I'll magnify His name for ever,
Wear the robe of righteousness
And bless the name of Jesus, Saviour.
Magnify the One who died,
The One who reigns for me on high,
I'll magnify, I'll magnify my God.

478

REIGN IN ME, sovereign Lord,
Reign in me.
Reign in me, sovereign Lord,
Reign in me.

Captivate my heart,
Let Your kingdom come,
Establish there Your throne,
Let Your will be done.

479

REIGNING IN ALL SPLENDOUR,
Victorious love,
Christ Jesus the Saviour,
Transcendent above.
All earthly dominions
And kingdoms shall fall,
For His name is Jesus
And He is the Lord.

He is Lord,
He is Lord,
He is Lord,
He is Lord.

480

REJOICE! *Rejoice!*
Christ is in you,
The hope of glory
In our hearts.
He lives! He lives!
His breath is in you,
Arise a mighty army,
We arise.

Now is the time for us
To march upon the land,
Into our hands
He will give the ground we claim.
He rides in majesty
To lead us into victory,
The world shall see
That Christ is Lord!

God is at work in us
His purpose to perform,
Building a kingdom
Of power not of words,
Where things impossible,
By faith shall be made possible;
Let's give the glory
To Him now.

Though we are weak, His grace
Is everything we need;
We're made of clay
But this treasure is within.
He turns our weaknesses
Into His opportunities,
So that the glory
Goes to Him.

481 Chris Bowater.
Copyright © 1986 Sovereign Lifestyle Music.

REJOICE, REJOICE, REJOICE!
Rejoice, rejoice, rejoice!
My soul rejoices in the Lord.
(Repeat)

My soul magnifies the Lord,
And my spirit rejoices in God my
    Saviour;
My soul magnifies the Lord,
And my spirit rejoices in my God.

482 Charles Wesley.

REJOICE, THE LORD IS KING!
Your Lord and King adore;
Mortals, give thanks, and sing,
And triumph ever more:

> *Lift up your heart, lift up your voice;*
> *Rejoice! Again I say: rejoice!*

Jesus the Saviour reigns,
The God of truth and love;
When He had purged our stains,
He took His seat above:

His kingdom cannot fail,
He rules o'er earth and heaven;
The keys of death and hell
Are to our Jesus given:

He sits at God's right hand
Till all His foes submit,
And bow to His command,
And fall beneath His feet:

Rejoice in glorious hope;
Jesus the Judge shall come,
And take His servants up
To their eternal home:

> *We soon shall hear the archangel's voice;*
> *The trump of God shall sound: rejoice!*

483 Graham Kendrick & Chris Rolinson.
Copyright © 1981 Kingsway's
Thankyou Music.

RESTORE, O LORD,
The honour of Your name,
In works of sovereign power
Come shake the earth again;
That men may see
And come with reverent fear
To the living God,
Whose kingdom shall outlast the years.

Restore, O Lord,
In all the earth Your fame,
And in our time revive
The church that bears Your name.
And in Your anger,
Lord, remember mercy,
O living God,
Whose mercy shall outlast the years.

Bend us, O Lord,
Where we are hard and cold,
In Your refiner's fire
Come purify the gold.
Though suffering comes
And evil crouches near,
Still our living God
Is reigning, He is reigning here.

Restore, O Lord,
The honour of Your name,
In works of sovereign power
Come shake the earth again;
That men may see
And come with reverent fear
To the living God,
Whose kingdom shall outlast the years.

484 Doug Horley.
Copyright © 1991 Kingsway's
Thankyou Music.

REVIVAL! *We're praying for revival,*
That Your kingdom may come,
Your will may be done
Throughout this land.
(Repeat)

Send now Your Spirit, Lord, may He come;
Cause us to glorify Jesus Your Son,
That all in this nation might know
He is the Lord.
Send now Your Spirit, let truth arise;
Where darkness has blinded, open closed eyes,
Bring spiritual health to this nation
As we cry to You:
Come heal our land.
Come heal our land.
Come heal our land.
Come heal our land.

485 H. H. Milman.

RIDE ON, RIDE ON IN MAJESTY!
In lowly pomp ride on to die!
O Christ, Thy triumphs now begin
O'er captive death and conquered sin.

Ride on, ride on in majesty!
Hark all the tribes 'hosanna' cry;
Thine humble beast pursues his road
With palms and scattered garments strowed.

Ride on, ride on in majesty!
Thy last and fiercest strife is nigh;
The Father on His sapphire throne
Expects His own anointed Son.

Ride on, ride on in majesty!
In lowly pomp ride on to die!
Bow Thy meek head to mortal pain,
Then take, O God, Thy power, and reign!

486 Mark Altrogge.
Copyright © 1982 People of Destiny
International/Word Music/Adm. by CopyCare.

RISE UP, you champions of God,
Rise up, you royal nation;
Rise up, and bear His light abroad,
We'll reach this generation.
We've got our marching orders,
We've got our marching orders;
Now is the time to carry them forth.

Go forth! Jesus loves them.
Go forth! Take the gospel.
Go forth! The time is now.
The harvest is ripening:
Go forth!

Feel now the burden of the Lord,
Feel how He longs to save them;
Feel now for those who never heard
About the Son He gave them.
We've got our marching orders,
We've got our marching orders;
Now is the time to carry them forth.

487 Dougie Brown.
Copyright © 1980 Kingsway's
Thankyou Music.

RIVER, WASH OVER ME,
Cleanse me and make me new.
Bathe me, refresh me and fill me anew,
River wash over me.

Spirit, watch over me,
Lead me to Jesus' feet.
Cause me to worship and fill me anew,
Spirit, watch over me.

Jesus, rule over me,
Reign over all my heart.
Teach me to praise You and fill me anew,
Jesus, rule over me.

488 Augustus Montague Toplady.

ROCK OF AGES, cleft for me,
Let me hide myself in Thee;
Let the water and the blood,
From Thy riven side which flowed,
Be of sin the double cure,
Cleanse me from its guilt and power.

Not the labour of my hands
Can fulfil Thy law's demands;
Could my zeal no respite know,
Could my tears forever flow,
All for sin could not atone:
Thou must save, and Thou alone.

Nothing in my hand I bring,
Simply to Thy cross I cling;
Naked, come to Thee for dress;
Helpless, look to Thee for grace;
Foul, I to the fountain fly:
Wash me, Saviour, or I die.

While I draw this fleeting breath,
When mine eyes shall close in death,
When I soar to worlds unknown,
See Thee on Thy judgement throne,
Rock of ages, cleft for me,
Let me hide myself in Thee.

489 Edward Caswall.

SEE, AMID THE WINTER'S SNOW,
Born for us on earth below,
See, the Lamb of God appears,
Promised from eternal years.

Hail, thou ever-blessèd morn!
Hail, redemption's happy dawn!
Sing through all Jerusalem:
Christ is born in Bethlehem!

Lo, within a manger lies
He who built the starry skies,
He who throned in height sublime
Sits amid the cherubim.

Say, ye holy shepherds, say,
What your joyful news today;
Wherefore have ye left your sheep
On the lonely mountain steep?

'As we watched at dead of night,
Lo, we saw a wondrous light:
Angels singing, "Peace on earth"
Told us of the Saviour's birth.'

Sacred Infant, all divine,
What a tender love was Thine,
Thus to come from highest bliss
Down to such a world as this!

Teach, O teach us, holy Child,
By Thy face so meek and mild,
Teach us to resemble Thee
In Thy sweet humility.

490

SEE HIM COME, the King upon a donkey.
Where is all His majesty and power?
He who was glorious, yet for my sake
Put away glory to die upon the cross.
His body was broken,
His heart was torn apart for me upon the
    cross.

See the people line His path with palm
    leaves;
Hear the children shouting out His name.
He who was glorious, yet for my sake
Put away power to die upon the cross.
His body was broken,
His heart was torn apart for me upon the
    cross.

491

SEE HIM LYING ON A BED OF STRAW,
A draughty stable with an open door;
Mary cradling the babe she bore;
The Prince of glory is His name.

O now carry me to Bethlehem,
To see the Lord appear to men;
Just as poor as was the stable then,
The Prince of glory when He came.

Star of silver, sweep across the skies,
Show where Jesus in the manger lies;
Shepherds, swiftly from your stupor rise
To see the Saviour of the world.

Angels, sing again the song you sang,
Bring God's glory to the heart of man;
Sing that Bethlehem's little baby can
Be salvation to the soul.

Mine are riches, from Thy poverty,
From Thine innocence, eternity;
Mine, forgiveness by Thy death for me,
Child of sorrow for my joy.

492

SEE HIS GLORY, see His glory,
See His glory now appear.
See His glory, see His glory,
See His glory now appear.
God of light,
Holiness and truth, power and might,
See glory, see it now appear.

Now we declare our God is good
And His mercies endure forever.
Now we declare our God is good,
And His mercies endure forever.

493

SEEK YE FIRST the kingdom of God
And His righteousness,
And all these things shall be added unto you,
Hallelu, hallelujah!

Hallelujah! Hallelujah!
Hallelujah! Hallelu, hallelujah!

Man shall not live by bread alone,
But by every word
That proceeds from the mouth of God,
Hallelu, hallelujah!

Ask and it shall be given unto you,
Seek and ye shall find.
Knock and it shall be opened unto you,
Hallelu, hallelujah!

If the Son shall set you free,
Ye shall be free indeed.
Ye shall know the truth and the truth shall set
    you free,
Hallelu, hallelujah!

Let your light so shine before men
That they may see your good works
And glorify your Father in heaven,
Hallelu, hallelujah!

Trust in the Lord with all thine heart,
He shall direct thy paths,
In all thy ways acknowledge Him,
Hallelu, hallelujah!

494 Author unknown.

SET MY SPIRIT FREE that I might worship
  Thee,
Set my spirit free that I might praise Thy name.
Let all bondage go and let deliverance flow,
Set my spirit free to worship Thee.

495 Dave Bilbrough.
Copyright © 1983 Kingsway's
Thankyou Music.

SHOUT FOR JOY and sing,
Let your praises ring;
See that God is building
A kingdom for a King.
His dwelling place with men,
The new Jerusalem;
Where Jesus is Lord over all.

  And we will worship, worship,
  We will worship Jesus the Lord.
  We will worship, worship,
  We will worship Jesus the Lord.

A work so long concealed,
In time will be revealed,
As the sons of God shall rise and take their
  stand.
Clothed in His righteousness,
The church made manifest,
Where Jesus is Lord over all.

Sovereign over all,
Hail Him risen Lord.
He alone is worthy of our praise.
Reigning in majesty,
Ruling in victory,
Jesus is Lord over all.

496 David Fellingham.
Copyright © 1988 Kingsway's
Thankyou Music.

SHOUT FOR JOY AND SING your praises to
  the King,
Lift your voice and let your hallelujahs ring;
Come before His throne to worship and adore,
Enter joyfully now the presence of the Lord.

You are my Creator, You are my
  Deliverer,
You are my Redeemer, You are Lord,
And You are my Healer.
You are my Provider,
You are now my Shepherd and my
  Guide,
Jesus, Lord and King, I worship You.

497 Graham Kendrick.
Copyright © 1988 Make Way Music.

SHOW YOUR POWER, O LORD,
Demonstrate the justice of Your kingdom.
Prove Your mighty word.
Vindicate Your name
Before a watching world.
Awesome are Your deeds, O Lord;
Renew them for this hour.
Show Your power, O Lord,
Among the people now.

Show Your power, O Lord,
Cause Your church to rise and take action.
Let all fear be gone,
Powers of the age to come
Are breaking through.
We Your people are ready to serve,
To arise and to obey.
Show Your power, O Lord,
And set the people free.

498 Joseph Mohr.
Tr. S. A. Brooke.

SILENT NIGHT, holy night!
Sleeps the world; hid from sight,
Mary and Joseph in stable bare
Watch o'er the Child beloved and
  fair,
Sleeping in heavenly rest,
Sleeping in heavenly rest.

Silent night, holy night!
Shepherds first saw the light,
Heard resounding clear and long,
Far and near, the angel-song:
'Christ the Redeemer is here,
Christ the Redeemer is here.'

Silent night, holy night!
Son of God, O how bright
Love is smiling from Thy face!
Strikes for us now the hour of
  grace,
Saviour, since Thou art born,
Saviour, since Thou art born.

499

(Men)
SING HALLELUJAH TO THE LORD,
Sing Hallelujah to the Lord,
Sing Hallelujah, sing Hallelujah,
Sing Hallelujah to the Lord.

(Women)
Sing Hallelujah to the Lord,
Sing Hallelujah,
Hallelujah,
Sing Hallelujah to the Lord.

Jesus is risen from the dead ... *(etc.)*

Jesus is Lord of heaven and earth ... *(etc.)*

Jesus is living in His church ... *(etc.)*

Jesus is coming for His own ... *(etc.)*

500

SING PRAISES UNTO GOD, *sing praises,*
Sing praises unto God, sing praises,
Sing praises unto God, sing praises,
Hallelujah!
(Repeat)

For God is the King over all the earth,
Sing praises unto Him with understanding.
O clap your hands and shout, all ye people,
For He is to be greatly praised.

501

SING TO THE LORD, be joyful in praise,
Exalt His magnificent ways.
Sing to the Lord again and again,
Forever His glory proclaim.
Let anthems of worship ascend to the King,
Giving all honour to Him.
Great is His name throughout all the earth,
With all of our strength let us sing,
Let us sing:

Glory to the Lord!
Glory to the Lord!
With our voices we shall give
Glory to the Lord!

502

SING UNTO THE LORD A NEW SONG,
Sing unto the Lord, all the earth.
Sing to the Lord, bless His name,
He is greatly to be praised,
Sing unto the Lord a new song.

Tell among the nations the Lord reigns,
The world shall never be moved.
Let the heavens be glad
And the earth rejoice,
Sing unto the Lord a new song.

Then shall all the trees sing for joy
Before the Lord, for He comes.
He will judge the world
With His righteousness,
Sing unto the Lord a new song.

503

SO FREELY,
Flows the endless love You give to me;
So freely,
Not dependent on my part.
As I am reaching out
Reveal the love within Your heart,
As I am reaching out
Reveal the love within Your heart.

Completely,
That's the way You give Your love to me;
Completely,
Not dependent on my part.
As I am reaching out
Reveal the love within Your heart,
As I am reaching out
Reveal the love within Your heart.

So easy,
I receive the love You give to me;
So easy,
Not dependent on my part.
Flowing out to me
The love within Your heart,
Flowing out to me
The love within Your heart.

504 Cindy Gough.
Copyright © 1989 Mercy/Vineyard
Publishing/Adm. by CopyCare.

SOFTEN MY HEART Lord, I want to meet You
here.
Soften my heart Lord, tender me with tears,
For Your presence is beyond anything I could
desire;
Soften my heart Lord, consume me with Your
holy fire.

Soften my heart Lord, I have made a choice.
Soften my heart Lord, I want to hear Your
voice,
For Your presence is beyond anything I could
desire;
Soften my heart Lord, consume me with Your
holy fire.

505 Graham Kendrick.
Copyright © 1988 Make Way Music.

SOFTEN MY HEART, LORD,
Soften my heart.
From all indifference
Set me apart,
To feel Your compassion,
To weep with Your tears;
Come soften my heart, O Lord,
Soften my heart.

506 Charles Wesley.

SOLDIERS OF CHRIST, ARISE,
And put your armour on;
Strong in the strength which God supplies,
Through His eternal Son;

Strong in the Lord of hosts,
And in His mighty power;
Who in the strength of Jesus trusts
Is more than conqueror.

Stand, then, in His great might,
With all His strength endued;
And take, to arm you for the fight,
The panoply of God.

Leave no unguarded place,
No weakness of the soul;
Take every virtue, every grace,
And fortify the whole.

From strength to strength go on,
Wrestle and fight and pray;
Tread all the powers of darkness down,
And win the well-fought day.

That having all things done,
And all your conflicts past,
Ye may o'ercome, through Christ alone,
And stand complete at last.

507 John Wimber.
Copyright © 1979 Mercy/Vineyard
Publishing/Adm. by CopyCare.

SON OF GOD, this is our praise song.
Jesus, my Lord, I sing to You.
Come now, Spirit of God,
Breathe life into these words of love;
Angels join from above
As we sing our praise song.

We praise You, we praise You,
We praise You, we worship You.
We praise You, we worship You.

Son of God, this is our love song.
Jesus, my Lord, I sing to You.
Come now, Spirit of God,
Breathe life into these words of love;
Angels join from above
As we sing our love song.

We love You, we love You,
We love You, we worship You.
We love You, we worship You.

508 Noel & Tricia Richards.
Copyright © 1990 Kingsway's
Thankyou Music.

SOVEREIGN LORD, I am Yours,
Now and ever more.
You're my King, You're the One
I am living for.
I choose to do what pleases You,
Lord, may my life forever be
A living sacrifice.

509 Graham Kendrick & Dave Bilbrough.
Copyright © 1990 Kingsway's Thankyou Music/
Make Way Music.

SPIRIT BREATHE ON US, fall afresh on us,
As we gather in Your name.
Bring Your healing touch, do Your work
in us,
As we gather in Your holy name.
Join us together, one to another,
As we surrender to You,
To You, O Lord.

510
Daniel Iverson.
Copyright © 1935 Birdwing Music/EMI
Christian Music Publishing/Adm. by CopyCare.

SPIRIT OF THE LIVING GOD,
Fall afresh on me;
Spirit of the living God,
Fall afresh on me.
Break me, melt me, mould me, fill me.
Spirit of the living God,
Fall afresh on me.

511
Paul Armstrong.
Copyright © 1984 Restoration Music Ltd./
Adm. by Sovereign Music UK.

SPIRIT OF THE LIVING GOD,
Fall afresh on me;
Spirit of the living God,
Fall afresh on me.
Fill me anew,
Fill me anew.
Spirit of the Lord
Fall afresh on me.

512
James Montgomery.

STAND UP, AND BLESS THE LORD,
Ye people of His choice;
Stand up, and bless the Lord your God
With heart, and soul, and voice.

Though high above all praise,
Above all blessing high,
Who would not fear His holy name,
And laud and magnify?

O for the living flame
From His own altar brought,
To touch our lips, our minds inspire,
And wing to heaven our thought!

God is our strength and song,
And His salvation ours;
Then be His love in Christ proclaimed
With all our ransomed powers.

Stand up, and bless the Lord,
The Lord your God adore;
Stand up, and bless His glorious name
Henceforth forever more.

513
George Duffield.

STAND UP! STAND UP FOR JESUS,
Ye soldiers of the cross!
Lift high His royal banner,
It must not suffer loss.
From victory unto victory
His army He shall lead,
Till every foe is vanquished,
And Christ is Lord indeed.

Stand up, stand up for Jesus!
The trumpet-call obey;
Forth to the mighty conflict
In this His glorious day!
Ye that are His, now serve Him
Against unnumbered foes;
Let courage rise with danger,
And strength to strength oppose.

Stand up, stand up for Jesus!
Stand in His strength alone;
The arm of flesh will fail you,
Ye dare not trust your own.
Put on the gospel armour,
Each piece put on with prayer;
Where duty calls, or danger,
Be never wanting there.

Stand up, stand up for Jesus!
The strife will not be long;
This day the noise of battle,
The next the victor's song.
To him that overcometh
A crown of life shall be;
He with the King of glory
Shall reign eternally.

514
Graham Kendrick.
Copyright © 1988 Make Way Music.

SUCH LOVE, pure as the whitest snow;
Such love, weeps for the shame I know;
Such love, paying the debt I owe;
O Jesus, such love.

Such love, stilling my restlessness;
Such love, filling my emptiness;
Such love, showing me holiness;
O Jesus, such love.

Such love, springs from eternity;
Such love, streaming through history;
Such love, fountain of life to me;
O Jesus, such love.

515
Dave Bryant.
Copyright © 1982 Kingsway's
Thankyou Music.

SUCH LOVE! Such grace!
Makes the pieces come falling into place,
Breaks through the darkness,
Turns on the light,
Making blindness give way to sight.
Your love has conquered,
Has set us free
To become all You've called us to be,
Healing the wounded, making us stand,
Bringing peace and a sword in our hand.

And no power in the universe
Can separate us from the love of God.
We're Yours forever
With nothing to fear,
Willing slaves to the love that brought us here.

516 Ronnie Wilson.
Copyright © 1978 Kingsway's
Thankyou Music.

SWEET FELLOWSHIP, Jesus in the midst,
Life blossoms in the church,
Men by men are blessed
When Jesus is in the midst.

Peace and harmony—Jesus reigning here;
The church moves at His command,
No room for doubt or fear,
For Jesus is reigning here.

I've never known a time like this,
Feel the spirit within me rise.
Come and see what God is doing.
Lord, we love You.

Sweet fellowship, Jesus in the midst,
Life blossoms in the church,
Men by men are blessed
When Jesus is in the midst.

517 Chris Bowater.
Copyright © 1986 Sovereign Lifestyle Music.

SWING WIDE THE GATES,
Let the King come in;
Swing wide the gates,
Make a way for Him.

Here He comes, the King of glory,
Here He comes, mighty in victory,
Here He comes, in splendour and majesty.
Swing wide the gates,
Swing wide the gates,
Let the King come in.

518 Paul Simmons.
Copyright © 1985 Kingsway's
Thankyou Music.

TAKE, EAT, THIS IS MY BODY,
Broken for you,
For I am come that you might have life;
Eat of My flesh and live,
Eat of My flesh and live.

My blood was shed for many,
Taking away your sin,
And if I shall make you free
Then you shall be free indeed,
You shall be free indeed.

Though your sins be as scarlet
They shall be white as snow,
Though they be red like crimson
They shall be as wool,
They shall be as wool.

For God so loved the world
He gave His only Son,
That whosoever believeth on Him
Might have everlasting life,
Might have everlasting life.

519 Frances Ridley Havergal.

TAKE MY LIFE, AND LET IT BE
Consecrated, Lord, to Thee;
Take my moments and my days,
Let them flow in ceaseless praise.

Take my hands, and let them move
At the impulse of Thy love;
Take my feet, and let them be
Swift and beautiful for Thee.

Take my voice, and let me sing
Always, only, for my King;
Take my lips, and let them be
Filled with messages from Thee.

Take my silver and my gold,
Not a mite would I withhold;
Take my intellect, and use
Every power as Thou shalt choose.

Take my will, and make it Thine;
It shall be no longer mine:
Take my heart, it is Thine own;
It shall be Thy royal throne.

Take my love; my Lord, I pour
At Thy feet its treasure store:
Take myself, and I will be
Ever, only, all for Thee.

520 Timothy Dudley-Smith.
Copyright © 1961 Timothy Dudley-Smith.

TELL OUT, MY SOUL, the greatness of the
Lord!
Unnumbered blessings give my spirit voice;
Tender to me the promise of His word;
In God my Saviour shall my heart rejoice.

Tell out, my soul, the greatness of His name!
Make known His might, the deeds His arm
has done;
His mercy sure, from age to age the same;
His holy name—the Lord, the mighty One.

Tell out, my soul, the greatness of His
    might!
Powers and dominions lay their glory by;
Proud hearts and stubborn wills are put to
    flight,
The hungry fed, the humble lifted high.

Tell out, my soul, the glories of His word!
Firm is His promise, and His mercy sure:
Tell out, my soul, the greatness of the Lord
To children's children and forever more!

521 Robert Stoodley.
Copyright © 1978 Sovereign Music UK.

THANKS BE TO GOD
Who gives us the victory,
Gives us the victory,
Through our Lord Jesus Christ.
Thanks be to God
Who gives us the victory,
Gives us the victory
Through our Lord Jesus Christ.

He is able to keep us from falling,
And to set us free from sin;
So let us each live up to our calling,
And commit our way to Him.

Jesus knows all about our temptations,
He has had to bear them too;
He will show us how to escape them,
If we trust Him He will lead us through.

He has led us from the power of darkness
To the kingdom of His blessed Son.
So let us join in praise together
And rejoice in what the Lord has done.

Praise the Lord for sending Jesus
To the cross of Calvary;
Now He's risen, reigns in power,
And death is swallowed up in victory.

522 Graham Kendrick.
Copyright © 1985 Kingsway's
Thankyou Music.

THANK YOU FOR THE CROSS,
The price You paid for us,
How You gave Yourself,
So completely,
Precious Lord (precious Lord).
Now our sins are gone,
All forgiven,
Covered by Your blood,
All forgotten,
Thank You, Lord (thank You, Lord).

Oh, I love You, Lord,
Really love You, Lord.
I will never understand
Why You love me.
You're my deepest joy,
You're my heart's desire,
And the greatest thing of all, O Lord, I see:
You delight in me!

For our healing there,
Lord, You suffered,
And to take our fear
You poured out Your love,
Precious Lord (precious Lord).
Calvary's work is done,
You have conquered,
Able now to save
So completely,
Thank You, Lord (thank You, Lord).

523 Alison Huntley.
Copyright © 1978 Kingsway's
Thankyou Music.

THANK YOU, JESUS, *thank You, Jesus,*
Thank You, Lord, for loving me.
Thank You, Jesus, thank You, Jesus,
Thank You, Lord, for loving me.

You went to Calvary,
And there You died for me,
Thank You, Lord, for loving me.
You went to Calvary,
And there You died for me,
Thank You, Lord, for loving me.

You rose up from the grave,
To me new life You gave,
Thank You, Lord, for loving me.
You rose up from the grave,
To me new life You gave,
Thank You, Lord, for loving me.

524 Diane Davis Andrew.
Copyright © 1971, 1975 Celebration/
Kingsway's Thankyou Music.

THANK YOU, LORD, FOR THIS FINE DAY,
Thank You, Lord, for this fine day,
Thank You, Lord, for this fine day,
Right where we are.

Alleluia, praise the Lord!
Alleluia, praise the Lord!
Alleluia, praise the Lord,
Right where we are.

Thank You, Lord, for loving us ... *(etc.)*

Thank You, Lord, for giving us peace ... *(etc.)*

Thank You, Lord, for setting us free ... *(etc.)*

525 Samuel John Stone.

THE CHURCH'S ONE FOUNDATION
Is Jesus Christ, her Lord;
She is His new creation
By water and the word;
From heaven He came and sought her
To be His holy bride,
With His own blood He bought her,
And for her life He died.

Elect from every nation,
Yet one o'er all the earth,
Her charter of salvation—
One Lord, one faith, one birth;
One holy name she blesses,
Partakes one holy food,
And to one hope she presses
With every grace endued.

Though with a scornful wonder
Men see her sore oppressed,
By schisms rent asunder,
By heresies distressed,
Yet saints their watch are keeping,
Their cry goes up, 'How long?'
And soon the night of weeping
Shall be the morn of song.

'Mid toil, and tribulation,
And tumult of her war,
She waits the consummation
Of peace forever more;
Till with the vision glorious
Her longing eyes are blessed,
And the great church victorious
Shall be the church at rest.

Yet she on earth hath union
With God the Three in One,
And mystic sweet communion
With those whose rest is won:
O happy ones and holy!
Lord, give us grace that we,
Like them, the meek and lowly,
On high may dwell with Thee.

526 Dave Bilbrough.
Copyright © 1986 Kingsway's
Thankyou Music.

THE CHURCH'S ONE FOUNDATION
Is Jesus Christ the Lord,
And on that revelation
Each one of us is called
To taste His full salvation,
To know His life within;
A pure and holy nation
To glorify the King.

Hallelujah, how great You are,
Reigning in glory, enthroned in power;
Bright Morning Star, how great You are;
Reigning in glory, enthroned in power.

This time of preparation
Eventually will yield
The fruit of all His labours;
His heart will be fulfilled.
From every tribe and nation
His people shall be known;
Drawn to be His kingdom,
Made out of living stones.

See Him and be radiant,
Taste the Lord and know
He wants to take us deeper,
For what we are we sow;
With streams of living water
He longs to overflow,
That out to all creation
His glory He will show.

527 John Ellerton.

THE DAY THOU GAVEST, LORD, IS ENDED,
The darkness falls at Thy behest;
To Thee our morning hymns ascended,
Thy praise shall sanctify our rest.

We thank Thee that Thy church unsleeping,
While earth rolls onward into light,
Through all the world her watch is keeping,
And rests not now by day or night.

As o'er each continent and island
The dawn leads on another day,
The voice of prayer is never silent,
Nor dies the strain of praise away.

The sun that bids us rest is waking
Our brethren 'neath the western sky,
And hour by hour fresh lips are making
Thy wondrous doings heard on high.

So be it, Lord! Thy throne shall never,
Like earth's proud empires, pass away;
Thy kingdom stands, and grows for ever,
Till all Thy creatures own Thy sway.

528 Graham Kendrick.
Copyright © 1986 Kingsway's
Thankyou Music.

THE EARTH IS THE LORD'S (Men)
And everything in it, (Women)
The earth is the Lord's, (Men)
The work of His hands. (Women)
The earth is the Lord's (Men)
And everything in it; (Women)
And all things were made (All)
For His glory.

(Last time)
And all things were made,
Yes, all things were made,
And all things were made
For His glory.

The mountains are His,
The seas and the islands,
The cities and towns,
The houses and streets.
Let rebels bow down
And worship before Him,
For all things were made
For His glory.

529 Author unknown.

THE FIRST NOWELL the angel did say
Was to certain poor shepherds in fields as
    they lay;
In fields where they lay keeping their sheep,
On a cold winter's night that was so deep.

    Nowell, nowell, nowell, nowell,
    Born is the King of Israel!

They lookèd up and saw a star
Shining in the east, beyond them far,
And to the earth it gave great light,
And so it continued both day and night.

And by the light of that same star
Three wise men came from country far;
To seek for a King was their intent,
And to follow the star wherever it went.

This star drew nigh to the north-west;
Over Bethlehem it took its rest,
And there it did both stop and stay
Right over the place where Jesus lay.

Then entered in those wise men three
Full reverently upon their knee,
And offered there in His presence
Their gold, and myrrh, and frankincense.

Then let us all with one accord
Sing praises to our heavenly Lord,
That hath made heaven and earth of nought,
And with His blood mankind hath bought.

530 Thomas Olivers.

THE GOD OF ABRAHAM PRAISE,
Who reigns enthroned above,
Ancient of everlasting days,
And God of love.
Jehovah! Great I AM!
By earth and heaven confessed;
I bow and bless the sacred name
Forever blessed.

The God of Abraham praise,
At whose supreme command
From earth I rise, and seek the joys
At His right hand.
I all on earth forsake—
Its wisdom, fame, and power—
And Him my only portion make,
My shield and tower.

The God of Abraham praise,
Whose all-sufficient grace
Shall guide me all my happy days
In all my ways.
He calls a worm His friend,
He calls Himself my God;
And He shall save me to the end
Through Jesu's blood.

He by Himself hath sworn,
I on His oath depend:
I shall, on eagles' wings upborne,
To heaven ascend;
I shall behold His face,
I shall His power adore,
And sing the wonders of His grace
Forever more.

There dwells the Lord our King,
The Lord our Righteousness,
Triumphant o'er the world and sin,
The Prince of Peace;
On Zion's sacred height
His kingdom still maintains,
And glorious with His saints in light
Forever reigns.

The God who reigns on high
The great archangels sing;
And, holy, holy, holy, cry,
Almighty King.
Who was and is the same,
And ever more shall be;
Jehovah, Father, Great I AM,
We worship Thee.

Before the Saviour's face
The ransomed nations bow;
O'erwhelmed at His almighty grace,
Forever new:
He shows His prints of love,
They kindle to a flame,
And sound through all the worlds above
The slaughtered Lamb.

The whole triumphant host
Give thanks to God on high;
Hail, Father, Son, and Holy Ghost!
They ever cry.
Hail, Abraham's God, and mine!
I join the heavenly lays;
All might and majesty are Thine,
And endless praise.

531 Thomas Kelly.

THE HEAD THAT ONCE WAS CROWNED WITH THORNS
Is crowned with glory now;
A royal diadem adorns
The mighty Victor's brow.

The highest place that heaven affords
Is His by sovereign right,
The King of kings, the Lord of lords,
And heaven's eternal light.

The joy of all who dwell above,
The joy of all below,
To whom He manifests His love,
And grants His name to know.

To them the cross, with all its shame,
With all its grace, is given;
Their name an everlasting name,
Their joy the joy of heaven.

They suffer with their Lord below,
They reign with Him above;
Their profit and their joy to know
The mystery of His love.

The cross He bore is life and health,
Though shame and death to Him;
His people's hope, His people's wealth,
Their everlasting theme.

532 Graham Kendrick.
Copyright © 1981 Kingsway's
Thankyou Music.

THE KING IS AMONG US,
His Spirit is here,
Let's draw near and worship,
Let songs fill the air.

He looks down upon us,
Delight in His face,
Enjoying His children's love,
Enthralled by our praise.

For each child is special,
Accepted and loved,
A love gift from Jesus
To His Father above.

And now He is giving
His gifts to us all,
For no one is worthless
And each one is called.

The Spirit's anointing
On all flesh comes down,
And we shall be channels
For works like His own.

We come now believing
Your promise of power,
For we are Your people
And this is Your hour.

The King is among us,
His Spirit is here,
Let's draw near and worship,
Let songs fill the air.

533 Henry Williams Baker.

THE KING OF LOVE my Shepherd is,
Whose goodness faileth never;
I nothing lack if I am His
And He is mine forever.

Where streams of living water flow
My ransomed soul He leadeth,
And where the verdant pastures grow
With food celestial feedeth.

Perverse and foolish oft I strayed,
But yet in love He sought me,
And on His shoulder gently laid,
And home rejoicing brought me.

In death's dark vale I fear no ill
With Thee, dear Lord, beside me;
Thy rod and staff my comfort still,
Thy cross before to guide me.

Thou spread'st a table in my sight;
Thy unction grace bestoweth:
And O what transport of delight
From Thy pure chalice floweth!

And so through all the length of days
Thy goodness faileth never;
Good Shepherd, may I sing Thy praise
Within Thy house forever.

534 Author unknown.

THE LORD HAS GIVEN a land of good things,
I will press in and make them mine.
I'll know His power, I'll know His glory,
And in His kingdom I will shine.

With the high praises of God in our mouth
And a two-edged sword in our hand,
We'll march right on to the victory side,
Right into Canaan's land.

Gird up your armour, ye sons of Zion,
Gird up your armour, let's go to war.
We'll win the battle with great rejoicing,
And so we'll praise Him more and more.

We'll bind their kings in chains and fetters,
We'll bind their nobles tight in iron,
To execute God's written judgement;
March on to glory, sons of Zion!

535 Chris Bowater.
Copyright © 1982 Sovereign Lifestyle Music.

THE LORD HAS LED FORTH *His people
    with joy,
And His chosen ones with singing,
    singing.
The Lord has led forth His people with joy,
And His chosen ones with singing.*

He has given to them the lands of the
    nations,
To possess the fruit and keep His laws,
And praise, praise His name.

536 Graham Kendrick.
Copyright © 1986 Kingsway's
Thankyou Music.

THE LORD IS MARCHING OUT in splendour,
In awesome majesty He rides,
For truth, humility and justice,
His mighty army fills the skies.

> *O give thanks to the Lord for His love
>   endures,
> O give thanks to the Lord for His love
>   endures,
> O give thanks to the Lord for His love
>   endures,
> For ever, for ever.*

His army marches out with dancing
For He has filled our hearts with joy.
Be glad the kingdom is advancing,
The love of God our battle cry!

537 Scottish Psalter.

THE LORD'S MY SHEPHERD, I'll not want;
He makes me down to lie
In pastures green; He leadeth me
The quiet waters by.

My soul He doth restore again;
And me to walk doth make
Within the paths of righteousness,
E'en for His own name's sake.

Yea, though I walk in death's dark vale,
Yet will I fear no ill;
For Thou art with me; and Thy rod
And staff me comfort still.

My table Thou hast furnishèd
In presence of my foes;
My head Thou dost with oil anoint,
And my cup overflows.

Goodness and mercy all my life
Shall surely follow me;
And in God's house forever more
My dwelling place shall be.

538 Author unknown.

THE LORD YOUR GOD IS IN YOUR MIDST,
The Lord of lords His name;
He will exult over you with joy,
He will renew you in His love,
He will rejoice over you
With shouts of joy, shouts of joy.
Shouts of joy, shouts of joy,
Shouts of joy.

539 Mark Altrogge.
Copyright © 1986 People of Destiny
International/Word Music/Adm. by CopyCare.

THE NATIONS ARE WAITING for us,
They're dying to hear the song we sing.
The nations are waiting for us,
Waiting for the gospel we will bring,
That in each nation men might come to know
    the King.

Jesus, You lead us,
Calling us onward,
A glorious army
With banners unfurled.
It's our decision
To follow Your vision,
We're on a mission,
A mission to the world.
And the nations are waiting,
The nations are waiting,
Waiting.

540 Graham Kendrick.
Copyright © 1983 Kingsway's
Thankyou Music.

THE PRICE IS PAID,
Come let us enter in
To all that Jesus died
To make our own.
For every sin
More than enough He gave,
And bought our freedom
From each guilty stain.

The price is paid,
Alleluia,
Amazing grace,
So strong and sure;
And so with all my heart,
My life in every part,
I live to thank You for
The price You paid.

The price is paid,
See Satan flee away;
For Jesus crucified
Destroys his power.
No more to pay,
Let accusation cease,
In Christ there is
No condemnation now.

The price is paid,
And by that scourging cruel
He took our sicknesses
As if His own.
And by His wounds,
His body broken there,
His healing touch may now
By faith be known.

The price is paid,
'Worthy the Lamb' we cry,
Eternity shall never
Cease His praise.
The church of Christ
Shall rule upon the earth,
In Jesus' name we have
Authority.

541 Ruth Lake.
Copyright © 1972 Scripture in Song,
a division of Integrity Music/Adm.
by Kingsway's Thankyou Music.

THEREFORE THE REDEEMED of the Lord
    shall return
And come with singing unto Zion,
And everlasting joy shall be upon their head.
(Repeat)

They shall obtain gladness and joy,
And sorrow and mourning shall flee away.

Therefore the redeemed of the Lord shall
    return
And come with singing unto Zion,
And everlasting joy shall be upon their head.

542 Cecil Frances Alexander.

THERE IS A GREEN HILL FAR AWAY,
Outside a city wall,
Where the dear Lord was crucified,
Who died to save us all.

We may not know, we cannot tell,
What pains He had to bear;
But we believe it was for us
He hung and suffered there.

He died that we might be forgiven,
He died to make us good,
That we might go at last to heaven,
Saved by His precious blood.

There was no other good enough
To pay the price of sin;
He only could unlock the gate
Of heaven, and let us in.

O dearly, dearly has He loved!
And we must love Him too,
And trust in His redeeming blood,
And try His works to do.

543 Frederick Whitfield.

THERE IS A NAME I LOVE TO HEAR,
I love to speak its worth;
It sounds like music in my ear,
The sweetest name on earth.

    O, how I love the Saviour's name,
    O, how I love the Saviour's name,
    O, how I love the Saviour's name,
    The sweetest name on earth.

It tells me of a Saviour's love,
Who died to set me free;
It tells me of His precious blood,
The sinner's perfect plea.

It tells of One whose loving heart
Can feel my deepest woe;
Who in my sorrow bears a part
That none can bear below.

It bids my trembling heart rejoice,
It dries each rising tear;
It tells me in a still, small voice
To trust and never fear.

Jesus, the name I love so well,
The name I love to hear!
No saint on earth its worth can tell,
No heart conceive how dear!

544

THERE IS A REDEEMER,
Jesus, God's own Son,
Precious Lamb of God, Messiah,
Holy One.

Thank You, O my Father,
For giving us Your Son,
And leaving Your Spirit—
Till the work on earth is done.

Jesus my Redeemer,
Name above all names,
Precious Lamb of God, Messiah,
O for sinners slain.

When I stand in glory
I will see His face,
And there I'll serve my King forever
In that holy place.

545

THERE IS POWER IN THE NAME OF JESUS;
We believe in His name.
We have called on the name of Jesus;
We are saved! We are saved!
At His name the demons flee.
At His name captives are freed.
For there is no other name that is higher
Than Jesus!

There is power in the name of Jesus,
Like a sword in our hands.
We declare in the name of Jesus,
We shall stand! We shall stand!
At His name God's enemies
Shall be crushed beneath our feet.
For there is no other name that is higher
Than Jesus!

546

THERE'S A QUIET UNDERSTANDING
When we're gathered in the Spirit,
It's a promise that He gives us
When we gather in His name.
There's a love we feel in Jesus,
There's a manna that He feeds us,
It's a promise that He gives us
When we gather in His name.

And we know when we're together,
Sharing love and understanding,
That our brothers and our sisters
Feel the oneness that He brings.
Thank You, thank You, thank You, Jesus,
For the way You love and feed us,
For the many ways You lead us;
Thank You, thank You, Lord.

547

THERE'S A SOUND ON THE WIND like a
victory song,
Listen now, let it rest on your soul.
It's a song that I learned from a heavenly
King,
It's the song of a battle royal.

There's a loud shout of victory that leaps
from our hearts
As we wait for our conquering King.
There's a triumph resounding from dark ages
past
To the victory song we now sing.

Come on heaven's children,
The city is in sight.
There will be no sadness
On the other side.

There'll be crowns for the conquerors and
white robes to wear,
There will be no more sorrow or pain.
And the battles of earth shall be lost in the
sight
Of the glorious Lamb that was slain.

Now the King of the ages approaches the
earth,
He will burst through the gates of the sky,
And all men shall bow down to His beautiful
name,
We shall rise with a shout, we shall fly!

Come on, heaven's children,
The city is in sight.
There will be no sadness
On the other side.

Now the King of the ages approaches the
earth,
He will burst through the gates of the sky,
And all men shall bow down to His beautiful
name
We shall rise with a shout, we shall fly!

548

THE SPIRIT OF THE LORD,
The sovereign Lord, is on me,
Because He has anointed me
To preach good news to the poor:

Proclaiming Jesus, only Jesus—
It is Jesus, Saviour, healer and baptiser,
And the mighty King,
The victor and deliverer—
He is Lord, He is Lord, He is Lord!

And He has called on me
To bind up all the broken hearts,
To minister release
To every captivated soul:

Let righteousness arise
And blossom as a garden;
Let praise begin to spring
In every tongue and nation:

549

THE STEADFAST LOVE OF THE LORD never
    ceases,
His mercies never come to an end;
They are new every morning,
New every morning,
Great is Thy faithfulness, O Lord,
Great is Thy faithfulness.

550

THE TRUMPETS SOUND, the angels sing,
The feast is ready to begin;
The gates of heaven are open wide,
And Jesus welcomes you inside.

Tables are laden with good things,
O taste the peace and joy He brings;
He'll fill you up with love divine,
He'll turn your water into wine.

Sing with thankfulness songs of pure
    delight.
Come and revel in heaven's love and light;
Take your place at the table of the King.
The feast is ready to begin.
The feast is ready to begin.

The hungry heart He satisfies,
Offers the poor His paradise;
Now hear all heaven and earth applaud
The amazing goodness of the Lord.

Ldr: Jesus,   *(All echo each line)*
    We thank You
    For Your love,
    For Your joy.
    Jesus,
    We thank You
    For the good things
    You give to us.

551

THINE BE THE GLORY,
Risen, conquering Son;
Endless is the victory
Thou o'er death hast won.
Angels in bright raiment
Rolled the stone away,
Kept the folded grave-clothes
Where Thy body lay.

Thine be the glory,
Risen, conquering Son;
Endless is the victory
Thou o'er death hast won!

Lo, Jesus meets us,
Risen from the tomb!
Lovingly He greets us,
Scatters fear and gloom.
Let the church with gladness
Hymns of triumph sing,
For her Lord now liveth,
Death hath lost its sting.

No more we doubt Thee,
Glorious Prince of life;
Life is naught without Thee:
Aid us in our strife;
Make us more than conquerors,
Through Thy deathless love;
Lead us in Thy triumph
To Thy home above.

552

THINE, O LORD, IS THE GREATNESS,
And the power and the glory.
Thine, O Lord, is the victory,
And majesty, and majesty.

All that is in heaven and earth is Thine,
Thou art exalted as head over all!

In Thy hand is power and might to make
    great,
In Thy hand is power to give strength to all!

Now is come salvation and power and might,
For the kingdom of our God has been given
  to His Christ!

553 Les Garrett.
Copyright © 1967 Scripture in Song,
a division of Integrity Music/
Adm. by Kingsway's Thankyou Music.

THIS IS THE DAY, this is the day
That the Lord has made, that the Lord has
  made;
We shall rejoice, we shall rejoice
And be glad in it, and be glad in it.
This is the day that the Lord has made,
We shall rejoice and be glad in it;
This is the day, this is the day
That the Lord has made.

554 Pauline Michael Mills.
Copyright © 1963, 1975 Fred Bock Music/
Kingsway's Thankyou Music.

THOU ART WORTHY, Thou art worthy,
Thou art worthy, O Lord.
To receive glory, glory and honour,
Glory and honour and power.
For Thou hast created, hast all things created,
Thou hast created all things;
And for Thy pleasure they are created,
Thou art worthy, O Lord.

555 Emily E. Steele Elliott.

THOU DIDST LEAVE THY THRONE and Thy
  kingly crown,
When Thou camest to earth for me;
But in Bethlehem's home there was found no
  room
For Thy holy nativity:
O come to my heart, Lord Jesus!
There is room in my heart for Thee.

Heaven's arches rang when the angels sang,
Proclaiming Thy royal degree;
But of lowly birth cam'st Thou, Lord, on earth,
And in great humility,
O come to my heart, Lord Jesus!
There is room in my heart for Thee.

The foxes found rest, and the birds had their
  nest,
In the shade of the cedar tree;
But Thy couch was the sod, O Thou Son of
  God,
In the deserts of Galilee.
O come to my heart, Lord Jesus!
There is room in my heart for Thee.

Thou camest, O Lord, with the living word
That should set Thy children free;
But with mocking scorn, and with crown of
  thorn,
They bore Thee to Calvary.
O come to my heart, Lord Jesus!
Thy cross is my only plea.

When heaven's arches shall ring, and her
  choirs shall sing,
At Thy coming to victory,
Let Thy voice call me home, saying, 'Yet there
  is room,
There is room at My side for thee.'
And my heart shall rejoice, Lord Jesus,
When Thou comest and callest for me.

556 Donn Thomas & Charles Williams.
Copyright © 1980 Spoone Music/
Word Music/Adm. by CopyCare.

THOU, O LORD, ART A SHIELD ABOUT ME,
You're my glory,
You're the lifter of my head.
Thou, O Lord, art a shield about me,
You're my glory,
You're the lifter of my head.

Hallelujah,
Hallelujah.
Hallelujah,
You're the lifter of my head.

557 John Marriott.

THOU, WHOSE ALMIGHTY WORD
Chaos and darkness heard,
And took their flight;
Hear us, we humbly pray,
And where the gospel-day
Sheds not its glorious ray,
Let there be light!

Thou who didst come to bring,
On Thy redeeming wing,
Healing and sight;
Health to the sick in mind,
Sight to the inly blind,
O now to all mankind
Let there be light!

Spirit of truth and love,
Life-giving, holy Dove,
Speed forth Thy flight;
Move on the waters' face,
Bearing the lamp of grace,
And in earth's darkest place
Let there be light!

Blessèd and holy Three,
Glorious Trinity,
Wisdom, love, might;
Boundless as ocean's tide
Rolling in fullest pride,
Through the world far and wide
Let there be light!

THROUGH OUR GOD *we shall do*
valiantly,
It is He who will tread down our enemies.
We'll sing and shout His victory,
Christ is King!
(Last time only)
Christ is King! Christ is King!

For God has won the victory
And set His people free;
His word has slain the enemy,
The earth shall stand and see that—

559 Fanny J. Crosby.

TO GOD BE THE GLORY! great things He
hath done!
So loved He the world that He gave us His
Son,
Who yielded His life an atonement for sin,
And opened the life-gate that all may go in.

Praise the Lord! Praise the Lord!
Let the earth hear His voice!
Praise the Lord! Praise the Lord!
Let the people rejoice!
O come to the Father through Jesus the
Son;
And give Him the glory, great things He
hath done!

O perfect redemption, the purchase of blood!
To every believer the promise of God;
The vilest offender who truly believes,
That moment from Jesus a pardon receives.

Great things He hath taught us, great things
He hath done,
And great our rejoicing through Jesus the
Son:
But purer and higher and greater will be
Our wonder, our worship, when Jesus we
see!

TO HIM WHO SITS ON THE THRONE and
unto the Lamb,
To Him who sits on the throne and unto the
Lamb
Be blessing and glory and honour and power
for ever,
Be blessing and glory and honour and power
for ever.

UNTO THEE, O LORD, do I lift up my soul,
Unto Thee, O Lord, do I lift up my soul.

O my God, I trust in Thee,
Let me not be ashamed,
Let not mine enemies triumph over me.

Yea, let none that wait on Thee be ashamed,
Yea, let none that wait on Thee be ashamed.

Show me Thy ways, Thy ways, O Lord,
Teach me Thy paths, Thy paths, O Lord.

Remember not the sins of my youth,
Remember not the sins of my youth.

The secret of the Lord is with them that fear
Him,
The secret of the Lord is with them that fear
Him.

Unto Thee, O Lord, do I lift up my soul,
Unto Thee, O Lord, do I lift up my soul.

UNTO YOU, O LORD,
Do I open up my heart.
Unto You, O Lord,
Do I lift my voice.
Unto You, O Lord,
Do I raise my hands,
Unto You, O Lord of hosts.

563
David J. Hadden.
Copyright © 1982 Restoration Music Ltd./
Adm. by Sovereign Music UK.

WE ARE A CHOSEN PEOPLE, *a royal*
priesthood,
A holy nation, belonging to God.
We are a chosen people, a royal
priesthood,
A holy nation, belonging to God.

You have called us out of darkness
To declare Your praise.
We exalt You and enthrone You,
Glorify Your name.

You have placed us into Zion
In the new Jerusalem.
Thousand thousand are their voices,
Singing to the Lamb.

564
Danny Daniels.
Copyright © 1987 Mercy/Vineyard
Publishing/Adm. by CopyCare.

WE ARE ALL TOGETHER
To call upon Your name;
There is nothing we like better
Than to sing and give You praise.

> *Lord, we welcome You,*
> *We welcome You,*
> *We welcome You,*
> *Come fill this place.*

Bring healing and salvation,
Let Your kingdom come
Right here just like in heaven,
Lord, may Your will be done.

Father, come fill this place,
We welcome You;
Jesus, we seek Your face,
'Cause all we want to do
Is give our love to You.

565
Trevor King.
Copyright © 1986 Trevor King/
Kingsway's Thankyou Music.

WE ARE A PEOPLE OF POWER,
We are a people of praise;
We are a people of promise,
Jesus has risen, He's conquered the grave!
Risen, yes, born again,
We walk in the power of His name;
Power to be the sons of God,
The sons of God! The sons of God!
We are the sons, sons of God!

566
Ian Traynar.
Copyright © 1977 Kingsway's
Thankyou Music.

WE ARE BEING BUILT INTO A TEMPLE,
Fit for God's own dwelling place;
Into the house of God which is the church,
The pillar and the ground of truth,
As precious stones that Jesus owns,
Fashioned by His wondrous grace.
And as we love and trust each other
So the building grows and grows.

567
Graham Kendrick.
Copyright © 1985 Kingsway's
Thankyou Music.

WE ARE HERE TO PRAISE YOU,
Lift our hearts and sing.
We are here to give You
The best that we can bring.
And it is our love
Rising from our hearts,
Everything within us cries:
'Abba Father.'
Help us now to give You
Pleasure and delight,
Heart and mind and will that say:
'I love You Lord.'

568
Ian Smale.
Copyright © 1987 Kingsway's
Thankyou Music.

WE ARE IN GOD'S ARMY,
We are in the army of the Lord, yeah,
yeah, yeah.
We are in God's army,
Glorie, Glorie, Glorie,
The Glorie Company.

The enemy's attacking, convinced he's
gaining ground,
But the only voice that he can hear is the one
he shouts around;
But we're not fooled by his lies, we know that
he is wrong—
We may be weak as soldiers, but as an army
we are strong.

The enemy's regrouping, as he tries another
plan,
He can't pick off an army but he can pick out
a man;
So we'll stay close together, and sing this
battle-song—
We may be weak as soldiers, but as an army
we are strong.

The enemy's realising that his future's looking
  poor,
Though he loves single combat, he's already
  lost the war;
United, not divided, together we belong—
We may be weak as soldiers, but as an army
  we are strong.

569 Geron Davis.
Copyright © 1983 Songchannel Music Co.
Meadowgreen Music /EMI Christian Music
Publishing/Adm. by CopyCare.

WE ARE STANDING on holy ground,
And I know that there are angels all around.
Let us praise Jesus now.
We are standing in His presence on holy ground.

570 John Pantry.
Copyright © 1990 Kingsway's
Thankyou Music.

WE ARE THE HANDS OF GOD,
Our task to do His will,
To lay our hands upon this world,
And by His Spirit see it healed.

> *We are the Church invincible,*
> *The flesh and blood of Christ.*
> *We are the Gospel visible,*
> *Our lives the Saviour's light to the world.*

We are the word of God,
And by the things we say
This world will judge the Prince of life
And be drawn in or turn away.

We are the feet of God,
Who walk the narrow way,
And every step we take is watched
By those for whom we fast and pray.

Though persecution comes,
And governments oppose,
Beneath the crushing weight of law
The church of Jesus grows and grows.

571 David Fellingham.
Copyright © 1986 Kingsway's
Thankyou Music.

WE ARE YOUR PEOPLE who are called by
  Your name.
We call upon You now to declare Your fame.
In this nation of darkness You've called us to
  be light.
As we seek Your face, Lord, stir up Your might.

Build Your church and heal this land,
Let Your kingdom come.
Build Your church and heal this land,
Let Your will be done.

572 Graham Kendrick.
Copyright © 1986 Kingsway's
Thankyou Music.

WE BELIEVE in God the Father,
Maker of the universe,
And in Christ His Son our Saviour,
Come to us by virgin birth.
We believe He died to save us,
Bore our sins, was crucified.
Then from death He rose victorious,
Ascended to the Father's side.

> *Jesus, Lord of all, Lord of all,*
> *Jesus, Lord of all, Lord of all,*
> *Jesus, Lord of all, Lord of all,*
> *Jesus, Lord of all, Lord of all.*
> *Name above all names,*
> *Name above all names.*
>   (Last time only)
> *Name above all names.*

We believe He sends His Spirit,
On His church with gifts of power.
God His word of truth affirming,
Sends us to the nations now.
He will come again in glory,
Judge the living and the dead.
Every knee shall bow before Him,
Then must every tongue confess.

573 Copyright © Central Board of Finance.

WE BREAK THIS BREAD to share in the body
  of Christ: *(Men)*
We break this bread to share in the body of
  Christ. *(Women)*

> *Though we are many, we are one body,*
> *Because we all share, we all share in one*
> *bread.*
>   (Repeat)

We drink this cup to share in the body of
  Christ: *(Men)*
We drink this cup to share in the body of
  Christ. *(Women)*

574

WE BRING THE SACRIFICE OF PRAISE
Into the house of the Lord,
We bring the sacrifice of praise
Into the house of the Lord.
We bring the sacrifice of praise
Into the house of the Lord,
We bring the sacrifice of praise
Into the house of the Lord.
And we offer up to You
The sacrifices of thanksgiving,
And we offer up to You
The sacrifices of joy.

575

(Men and women in canon)
WE DECLARE THAT THE KINGDOM OF GOD IS HERE,
*We declare that the kingdom of God is
here,*
Among you, among you.

(Last time)
*We declare that the kingdom of God is
here (Men)*
*We declare that the kingdom of God is
here (Women)*
We declare that the (Men)
Kingdom of God is here. (All)

The blind see, the deaf hear,
The lame men are walking;
Sicknesses flee at His voice.
The dead live again,
And the poor hear the good news:
Jesus is King, so rejoice!

576

WE DECLARE THERE'S ONLY ONE LORD,
And the earth belongs to Him,
We proclaim the day of salvation,
It's His kingdom and He's the King.

There is none like our mighty King,
He gave His life to free us.
There is none more worthy of
Our lives and our allegiance.

577

WE DECLARE YOUR MAJESTY,
We proclaim that Your name is exalted;
For You reign magnificently,
Rule victoriously,
And Your power is shown throughout the
earth.
And we exclaim our God is mighty,
Lift up Your name, for You are holy.
Sing it again, all honour and glory,
In adoration we bow before Your throne.

578

WE EXTOL YOU, our God and King.
We bless Your name
For ever and for ever,
For You open up Your hand
And shower us with goodness.
Your mercy and Your grace
Are freely lavished on us.

So we sing Your praise, (Jesus is Lord)
We extol Your name, (Jesus is Lord)
*Tell the glory of Your kingdom and Your
mighty power;*
Clothed in majesty, (Jesus is Lord)
Reigning sovereignly, (Jesus is Lord)
Your greatness is unsearchable, O God.

579

WE HAVE COME INTO THIS PLACE
And gathered in His name to worship Him,
We have come into this place
And gathered in His name to worship Him,
We have come into this place
And gathered in His name
To worship Christ the Lord,
Worship Him, Christ the Lord.

So forget about yourself
And concentrate on Him and worship Him,
So forget about yourself
And concentrate on Him and worship Him,
So forget about yourself
And concentrate on Him
And worship Christ the Lord,
Worship Him, Christ the Lord.

He is all my righteousness,
I stand complete in Him and worship Him,
He is all my righteousness,
I stand complete in Him and worship Him,
He is all my righteousness,
I stand complete in Him
And worship Christ the Lord,
Worship Him, Christ the Lord.

Let us lift up holy hands
And magnify His name and worship Him,
Let us lift up holy hands
And magnify His name and worship Him,
Let us lift up holy hands
And magnify His name
And worship Christ the Lord,
Worship Him, Christ the Lord.

580 Robert Newey.
Copyright © 1989 Kingsway's
Thankyou Music.

WE HAVE COME TO MOUNT ZION,
To the city of the living God,
To Jesus our Redeemer,
And the sprinkling of His blood.
We're part of a kingdom that cannot be shaken,
We've got a foundation that cannot be moved;
So let us praise Him,
Hallelujah,
Let us praise the living God.

Now we draw near to Him by faith,
Come through the veil,
For Jesus brings us by His new and living
    way into His holy place.
So let us come with boldness to the very
    throne of God the Father,
Enter in with confidence to meet Him face to
    face.

581 David J. Hadden.
Copyright © 1983 Restoration Music Ltd./
Adm. by Sovereign Music UK.

WE KNOW THAT ALL THINGS work together
    for our good
For good to those who love the Lord;
For God has called us to be just like His Son,
To live and walk according to His word.

We are more than conquerors,
We are more than conquerors,
Through Christ, through Christ.

I am persuaded that neither death nor life,
Nor angels, principalities, nor powers,
Nor things that are now, nor things that are to
    come,
Can separate us from the love of Christ.

If God is for us, who against us can prevail?
No one can bring a charge against His
    chosen ones;
And there will be no separation from our
    Lord,
He has justified us through His precious
    blood.

582 Diane Fung.
Copyright © 1979 Word's Spirit of Praise
Music/Adm. by CopyCare.

WE'LL SING A NEW SONG of glorious
    triumph,
For we see the government of God in our
    lives.
We'll sing a new song of glorious triumph,
For we see the government of God in our
    lives.

He is crowned, God of the whole world
    crowned,
King of creation crowned,
Ruling the nations now.
Yes, He is crowned, God of the whole world
    crowned,
King of creation crowned,
Ruling the nations now.

583 Graham Kendrick.
Copyright © 1989 Make Way Music.

WE'LL WALK THE LAND
With hearts on fire,
And every step
Will be a prayer.
Hope is rising,
New day dawning,
Sound of singing
Fills the air.

Two thousand years,
And still the flame
Is burning bright
Across the land.
Hearts are waiting,
Longing, aching,
For awakening
Once again.

Let the flame burn brighter
In the heart of the darkness,
Turning night to glorious day.
Let the song grow louder
As our love grows stronger,
Let it shine, let it shine.

We'll walk for truth,
Speak out for love;
In Jesus' name
We shall be strong,
To lift the fallen,
To save the children,
To fill the nation
With Your song.

584 Ramon Pink.
Copyright © 1983 Scripture in Song,
a division of Integrity Music/Adm.
by Kingsway's Thankyou Music.

WE PLACE YOU ON THE HIGHEST PLACE,
For You are the great High Priest,
We place You high above all else;
And we come to You and worship at Your
    feet.

585 Matthias Claudius.
Tr. Jane M. Campbell.

WE PLOUGH THE FIELDS and scatter
The good seed on the land,
But it is fed and watered
By God's almighty hand;
He sends the snow in winter,
The warmth to swell the grain,
The breezes and the sunshine,
And soft refreshing rain.

    All good gifts around us
    Are sent from heaven above;
    Then thank the Lord, O thank the Lord,
    For all His love.

He only is the Maker
Of all things near and far;
He paints the wayside flower,
He lights the evening star;
The winds and waves obey Him,
By Him the birds are fed;
Much more to us, His children,
He gives our daily bread.

We thank Thee, then, O Father,
For all things bright and good;
The seedtime and the harvest,
Our life, our health, our food.
No gifts have we to offer
For all Thy love imparts,
But that which Thou desirest,
Our humble, thankful hearts.

586 Ed Baggett.
Copyright © 1974, 1975 Celebration/
Kingsway's Thankyou Music.

WE REALLY WANT TO THANK YOU, LORD,
We really want to bless Your name,
Hallelujah! Jesus is our King!
We really want to thank You, Lord,
We really want to bless Your name,
Hallelujah! Jesus is our King!

We thank You, Lord, for Your gift to us,
Your life so rich beyond compare,
The gift of Your body here on earth
Of which we sing and share.

We thank You, Lord, for our life together,
To live and move in the love of Christ,
Tenderness which sets us free
To serve You with our lives.

587 Edith G. Cherry.

WE REST ON THEE, OUR SHIELD AND OUR DEFENDER!
We go not forth alone against the foe;
Strong in Thy strength, safe in Thy keeping
    tender,
We rest on Thee and in Thy name we go.
Strong in Thy strength, safe in Thy keeping
    tender,
We rest on Thee, and in Thy name we go.

Yes, in Thy name, O Captain of salvation!
In Thy dear name, all other names above,
Jesus our Righteousness, our sure Foundation,
Our Prince of glory and our King of love.
Jesus our Righteousness, our sure Foundation,
Our Prince of glory and our King of love.

We go in faith, our own great weakness
    feeling,
And needing more each day Thy grace to
    know:
Yet from our hearts a song of triumph pealing;
We rest on Thee, and in Thy name we go.
Yet from our hearts a song of triumph pealing;
We rest on Thee, and in Thy name we go.

We rest on Thee, our Shield and our Defender!
Thine is the battle, Thine shall be the praise;
When passing through the gates of pearly
    splendour,
Victors, we rest with Thee, through endless
    days.
When passing through the gates of pearly
    splendour,
Victors, we rest with Thee, through endless
    days.

588 Joan Parsons.
Copyright © 1978 Kingsway's
Thankyou Music.

WE SHALL BE AS ONE,
We shall be as one,
He the Father of us all,
We His chosen sons;
And by His command
Take each other's hand,
Live our lives in unity,
We shall be as one.

We shall be as one,
We shall be as one;
And by this shall all men know
Of the work He has done.
Love will take us on
Through His precious Son;
Love of Him who first loved us,
We shall be as one.

589 Graham Kendrick.
Copyright © 1988 Make Way Music.

WE SHALL STAND
With our feet on the Rock.
Whatever men may say,
We'll lift Your name up high.
And we shall walk
Through the darkest night.
Setting our faces like flint;
We'll walk into the light.

Lord, You have chosen me
For fruitfulness,
To be transformed into
Your likeness.
I'm gonna fight on through
Till I see You face to face.

Lord, as Your witnesses
You've appointed us.
And with Your Holy Spirit
Anointed us.
And so I'll fight on through,
Till I see You face to face.

590 Twila Paris.
Copyright © 1982 Singspiration Music/John T.
Benson Publishing Co./Adm. by CopyCare.

WE WILL GLORIFY the King of kings,
We will glorify the Lamb;
We will glorify the Lord of lords,
Who is the great 'I Am'.

Lord Jehovah reigns in majesty,
We will bow before His throne;
We will worship Him in righteousness,
We worship Him alone.

He is Lord of heaven, Lord of earth,
He is Lord of all who live;
He is Lord above the universe,
All praise to Him we give.

Hallelujah to the King of kings,
Hallelujah to the Lamb;
Hallelujah to the Lord of lords,
Who is the great 'I Am'.

591 Phil Lawson Johnston.
Copyright © 1987 Kingsway's
Thankyou Music.

WE WILL HONOUR YOU, *we will honour*
You,
We will exalt the Holy One of Israel.
We will honour You, yes, we will honour
You,
We will enthrone You in our praise.

You are the Alpha and Omega;
You are the beginning and the end.
There is no other we can turn to,
No other rock on which we can depend.

You will not share Your praise with idols;
All glory belongs to You alone.
Who in the skies can be compared with
The Lord Almighty Father God and King?

All of the earth will bow before You;
They will be left no place to hide.
No longer Satan's rule of darkness,
But the name of Jesus ever glorified.

592 Ge Baas.
Copyright © 1983 Kingsway's
Thankyou Music.

WE WORSHIP AND ADORE YOU,
Christ our King. (Christ our King.)
We worship and adore You,
Christ our King. (Christ our King.)
And we follow You together,
We follow You together,
And we follow You together,
Christ our King. (Christ our King.)

593 Joseph M. Scriven.

WHAT A FRIEND WE HAVE IN JESUS,
All our sins and griefs to bear!
What a privilege to carry
Everything to God in prayer!
O what peace we often forfeit!
O what needless pain we bear!
All because we do not carry
Everything to God in prayer.

Have we trials and temptations?
Is there trouble anywhere?
We should never be discouraged;
Take it to the Lord in prayer.
Can we find a friend so faithful
Who will all our sorrows share?
Jesus knows our every weakness;
Take it to the Lord in prayer.

Are we weak and heavy-laden,
Cumbered with a load of care?
Precious Saviour, still our refuge,
Take it to the Lord in prayer.
Do thy friends despise, forsake thee?
Take it to the Lord in prayer;
In His arms He'll take and shield thee,
Thou wilt find a solace there.

594 Keri Jones & David Matthews.
Copyright © 1978 Word's Spirit of Praise
Music/Adm. by CopyCare.

WHEN I FEEL THE TOUCH
Of Your hand upon my life,
It causes me to sing a song
That I love You, Lord.
So from deep within
My spirit singeth unto Thee,
You are my King, You are my God,
And I love You, Lord.

595 Wayne & Cathy Perrin.
Copyright © 1980 Integrity's Hosanna! Music.
Adm. Kingsway's Thankyou Music.

WHEN I LOOK INTO YOUR HOLINESS,
When I gaze into Your loveliness,
When all things that surround
Become shadows in the light of You;
When I've found the joy of reaching Your heart,
When my will becomes enthralled in Your love,
When all things that surround
Become shadows in the light of You:

I worship You, I worship You,
The reason I live is to worship You.
I worship You, I worship You,
The reason I live is to worship You.

596 Isaac Watts.

WHEN I SURVEY THE WONDROUS CROSS
On which the Prince of glory died,
My richest gain I count but loss,
And pour contempt on all my pride.

Forbid it, Lord, that I should boast,
Save in the death of Christ my God:
All the vain things that charm me most,
I sacrifice them to His blood.

See from His head, His hands, His feet,
Sorrow and love flow mingled down:
Did e'er such love and sorrow meet,
Or thorns compose so rich a crown?

Were the whole realm of Nature mine,
That were an offering far too small;
Love so amazing, so divine,
Demands my soul, my life, my all!

597 Tr. Edward Caswall.

WHEN MORNING GILDS THE SKIES
My heart awaking cries:
'May Jesus Christ be praised!'
Alike at work and prayer
To Jesus I repair:
'May Jesus Christ be praised!'

Does sadness fill my mind?
A solace here I find:
'May Jesus Christ be praised!'
When evil thoughts molest,
With this I shield my breast:
'May Jesus Christ be praised!'

To God, the Word, on high
The hosts of angels cry:
'May Jesus Christ be praised!'
Let mortals, too, upraise
Their voice in hymns of praise:
'May Jesus Christ be praised!'

Let earth's wide circle round
In joyful notes resound:
'May Jesus Christ be praised!'
Let air, and sea, and sky,
From depth to height, reply:
'May Jesus Christ be praised!'

Be this while life is mine
My canticle divine:
'May Jesus Christ be praised!'
Be this the eternal song,
Through all the ages long:
'May Jesus Christ be praised!'

598 Author unknown.

WHEN THE SPIRIT OF THE LORD is within my heart
I will sing as David sang.
When the Spirit of the Lord is within my heart
I will sing as David sang.
I will sing, I will sing,
I will sing as David sang.
I will sing, I will sing,
I will sing as David sang.

When the Spirit of the Lord is within my heart
I will clap ... dance ... praise ... *(etc.)*

599
John Henry Sammis.

WHEN WE WALK WITH THE LORD
In the light of His word,
What a glory He sheds on our way!
While we do His good will,
He abides with us still,
And with all who will trust and obey!

Trust and obey!
For there's no other way
To be happy in Jesus,
But to trust and obey.

Not a shadow can rise,
Not a cloud in the skies,
But His smile quickly drives it away;
Not a doubt nor a fear,
Not a sigh nor a tear,
Can abide while we trust and obey!

Not a burden we bear,
Not a sorrow we share,
But our toil He doth richly repay:
Not a grief nor a loss,
Not a frown nor a cross,
But is blessed if we trust and obey!

But we never can prove
The delights of His love
Until all on the altar we lay;
For the favour He shows,
And the joy He bestows,
Are for those who will trust and obey.

Then in fellowship sweet
We will sit at His feet,
Or we'll walk by His side in the way;
What He says we will do,
Where He sends we will go;
Never fear, only trust and obey!

600
Author unknown.

WHERE YOU GO I WILL GO,
Where you lodge I will lodge,
Do not ask me to turn away,
For I will follow you.
We'll serve the Lord together
And praise Him day to day,
For He brought us together
To love Him and serve Him always.

601
Graham Kendrick.
Copyright © 1986 Kingsway's
Thankyou Music.

WHETHER YOU'RE ONE or whether you're two
Or three or four or five,
Six or seven or eight or nine it's good to be alive.
It really doesn't matter how old you are,
Jesus loves you whoever you are.

La, la, la, la, la, la, la, la, la,
Jesus loves us all.
(Repeat)

Whether you're big or whether you're small
Or somewhere in between,
First in the class or middle or last,
We're all the same to Him.
It really doesn't matter how clever you are,
Jesus loves you whoever you are.

602
Nahum Tate.

WHILE SHEPHERDS WATCHED their flocks by night,
All seated on the ground,
The angel of the Lord came down
And glory shone around.

'Fear not' said he, for mighty dread
Had seized their troubled mind;
'Glad tidings of great joy I bring
To you and all mankind.

'To you in David's town this day
Is born of David's line
A Saviour, who is Christ the Lord,
And this shall be the sign.

'The heavenly babe you there shall find
To human view displayed,
All meanly wrapped in swaddling bands,
And in a manger laid.'

Thus spake the seraph; and forthwith
Appeared a shining throng
Of angels, praising God, who thus
Addressed their joyful song:

'All glory be to God on high
And on the earth be peace;
Goodwill henceforth from heaven to men
Begin and never cease.'

603 Dave Bilbrough.
Copyright © 1989 Kingsway's
Thankyou Music.

WHO CAN EVER SAY THEY UNDERSTAND
All the wonders of His master plan?
Christ came down and gave Himself to
    man
Forever more.

He was Lord before all time began,
Yet made Himself the sacrificial lamb,
Perfect love now reconciled to man
Forever more.

> *Forever more we'll sing the story*
> *Of love come down.*
> *Forever more the King of glory*
> *We will crown.*

He is coming back to earth again,
Every knee shall bow before His name,
'Christ is Lord', let thankful hearts proclaim
Forever more.

604 Graham Kendrick.
Copyright © 1988 Make Way Music.

WHO CAN SOUND THE DEPTHS OF SORROW
In the Father heart of God,
For the children we've rejected,
For the lives so deeply scarred?
And each light that we've extinguished
Has brought darkness to our land:
Upon our nation, upon our nation,
Have mercy, Lord.

We have scorned the truth You gave us,
We have bowed to other lords.
We have sacrificed the children
On the altars of our gods.
O let truth again shine on us,
Let Your holy fear descend:
Upon our nation, upon our nation,
Have mercy, Lord.

(Men only)
Who can stand before Your anger?
Who can face Your piercing eyes?
For You love the weak and helpless,
And You hear the victims' cries.
(All)
Yes, You are a God of justice,
And Your judgement surely comes:
Upon our nation, upon our nation,
Have mercy, Lord.

(Women only)
Who will stand against the violence?
Who will comfort those who mourn?
In an age of cruel rejection,
Who will build for love a home?
(All)
Come and shake us into action,
Come and melt our hearts of stone:
Upon Your people, upon Your people,
Have mercy, Lord.

Who can sound the depths of mercy
In the Father heart of God?
For there is a Man of sorrows
Who for sinners shed His blood.
He can heal the wounds of nations,
He can wash the guilty clean:
Because of Jesus, because of Jesus,
Have mercy, Lord.

605 Benjamin R. Hanby, alt.

WHO IS HE IN YONDER STALL,
At whose feet the shepherds fall?

> *'Tis the Lord!*
> *O wondrous story!*
> *'Tis the Lord, the King of glory!*
> *At His feet we humbly fall.*
> *Crown Him! Crown Him, Lord of all!*

Who is He to whom they bring
All the sick and sorrowing?

Who is He that stands and weeps
At the grave where Lazarus sleeps?

Who is He on yonder tree
Dies in pain and agony?

Who is He who from the grave
Comes to rescue, help, and save?

Who is He who from His throne
Sends the Spirit to His own?

Who is He who comes again,
Judge of angels and of men?

606 Judy Horner-Montemayor.
Copyright © 1975 Integrity's Hosanna! Music.
Adm. Kingsway's Thankyou Music.

WHO IS LIKE UNTO THEE,
O Lord, amongst gods?
Who is like unto Thee, glorious in holiness,
Fearful in praises, doing wonders?
Who is like unto Thee?

607 Frances R. Havergal.

WHO IS ON THE LORD'S SIDE?
Who will serve the King?
Who will be His helpers
Other lives to bring?
Who will leave the world's side?
Who will face the foe?
Who is on the Lord's side?
Who for Him will go?
By Thy call of mercy,
By Thy grace divine,
We are on the Lord's side;
Saviour, we are Thine.

Jesus, Thou hast bought us
Not with gold or gem,
But with Thine own life-blood,
For Thy diadem.
With Thy blessing filling
Each who comes to Thee
Thou hast made us willing,
Thou hast made us free.
By Thy grand redemption,
By Thy grace divine,
We are on the Lord's side;
Saviour, we are Thine.

Fierce may be the conflict,
Strong may be the foe,
But the King's own army
None can overthrow;
Round His standard ranging
Victory is secure;
For His truth unchanging
Makes the triumph sure.
Joyfully enlisting,
By Thy grace divine,
We are on the Lord's side;
Saviour, we are Thine.

Chosen to be soldiers
In an alien land,
Chosen, called, and faithful,
For our Captain's band;
In the service royal
Let us not grow cold,
Let us be right loyal,
Noble, true, and bold.
Master, Thou wilt keep us,
By Thy grace divine,
Always on the Lord's side,
Saviour, always Thine.

608 Phil Rogers.
Copyright © 1984 Kingsway's
Thankyou Music.

WHO IS THIS that grows like the dawn,
As bright as the sun, as fair as the moon?
Who is this that grows like the dawn,
As awesome as an army, as an army with
banners?

It is the church in the eyes of the Lord,
The bride of Christ preparing for her King.

Washed in His blood and clothed in
righteousness,
Anointed with the Spirit and waiting for her
Lord.
Who is this that grows like the dawn,
As awesome as an army, as an army with
banners?

609 Jane & Betsy Clowe.
Copyright © 1974, 1975 Celebration/
Kingsway's Thankyou Music.

WIND, WIND, BLOW ON ME,
Wind, wind, set me free,
Wind, wind, my Father sent
The blessèd Holy Spirit.

Jesus told us all about You,
How we could not live without You,
With His blood the power bought,
To help us live the life He taught.

When we're weary, You console us;
When we're lonely You enfold us;
When in danger You uphold us,
Blessèd Holy Spirit.

When unto the church You came
It was not in Your own but Jesus' name.
Jesus Christ is still the same,
He sends the Holy Spirit.

Set us free to love our brothers;
Set us free to live for others,
That the world the Son might see,
And Jesus' name exalted be.

610 Paul Field.
Copyright © 1987 Kingsway's
Thankyou Music.

WITH ALL MY HEART I thank You, Lord.
With all my heart I thank You, Lord,
For this bread and wine we break,
For this sacrament we take,
For the forgiveness that You make,
I thank You, Lord.

With all my soul I thank You, Lord.
With all my soul I thank You, Lord,
For this victory that You've won,
For this taste of things to come,
For this love that makes us one,
I thank You, Lord.

With all my voice I thank You, Lord.
With all my voice I thank You, Lord,
For the sacrifice of pain,
For the Spirit and the flame,
For the power of Your name,
I thank You, Lord.

611 Graham Kendrick.
Copyright © 1981 Kingsway's
Thankyou Music.

WITH MY WHOLE HEART I will praise You,
Holding nothing back, Hallelujah!
You have made me glad and now
I come with open arms to thank You,
With my heart embrace, Hallelujah!
I can see Your face is smiling.
With my whole life I will serve You,
Captured by Your love, Hallelujah!
O amazing love, O amazing love!

Lord, Your heart is overflowing
With a love divine, Hallelujah!
And this love is mine for ever.
Now Your joy has set You laughing
As You join the song, Hallelujah!
Heaven sings along, I hear the
Voices swell to great crescendos,
Praising Your great love, Hallelujah!
O amazing love, O amazing love!

Come, O Bridegroom, clothed in splendour,
My Belovèd One, Hallelujah!
How I long to run and meet You.
You're the fairest of ten thousand,
You're my life and breath, Hallelujah!
Love as strong as death has won me.
All the rivers, all the oceans
Cannot quench this love, Hallelujah!
O amazing love, O amazing love!

612 David Fellingham.
Copyright © 1990 Kingsway's
Thankyou Music.

WONDERFUL LOVE coming to me,
Wonderful grace, freedom and mercy;
Bought with a price, death on a cross,
Wonderful love, Jesus, You've given to me.

You are Christ, Son of God,
Suffering Lamb, pouring out Your life;
You've conquered death,
And You're reigning supreme in my life.

613 John Watson.
Copyright © 1986 Ampelos Music/
Adm. by CopyCare.

WORSHIP THE LORD! In His presence we
stand;
He cares for you and He understands.
Come Holy Spirit, reaching us now;
Grace, joy and peace, love abound.

Holy, holy, holy is the Lord.

(Additional choruses)
Worthy...
Faithful...
Mighty...

614 Dave Richards.
Copyright © 1979 Kingsway's
Thankyou Music.

WORTHY ART THOU, O Lord our God,
Of honour and power,
For You are reigning now on high, hallelujah!
Jesus is Lord of all the earth,
Hallelujah, hallelujah, hallelujah!

615 David J. Hadden.
Copyright © 1983 Restoration Music Ltd./
Adm. by Sovereign Music UK.

**WORTHY IS THE LAMB SEATED ON THE
THRONE,**
Worthy is the Lamb who was slain,
To receive power and riches
And wisdom and strength,
Honour and glory, glory and praise,
For ever and ever more.

616 Andy Park.
Copyright © 1990 Mercy/Vineyard
Publishing/Adm. by CopyCare.

WORTHY IS THE LAMB WHO WAS SLAIN.
Worthy is the Lamb who was slain,
Who was slain.
Worthy is the Lamb who was slain,
Who was slain.

To receive power and wealth,
To receive wisdom and strength.
To receive honour and glory.
To receive glory and praise.

Now to Him who sits on the throne
And to the Lamb who was slain,
Now be praise and honour and glory,
And power forever,
And power forever.

Worthy of power and wealth,
Worthy of wisdom and strength.
Worthy of honour and glory,
Worthy of glory and praise.

(Final chorus)
Unto the Lamb be power and wealth,
Unto the Lamb be wisdom and strength.
Unto the Lamb be honour and glory,
Unto the Lamb be glory and praise.

617 Mark Kinzer.
Copyright © 1976 The Word of God Music/
Adm. by CopyCare.

WORTHY, O WORTHY ARE YOU, LORD,
Worthy to be thanked and praised
And worshipped and adored.
Worthy, O worthy are You, Lord,
Worthy to be thanked and praised
And worshipped and adored.

Singing, Hallelujah, Lamb upon the throne,
We worship and adore You, make Your glory
  known.
Hallelujah, glory to the King:
You're more than a conqueror,
You're Lord of everything.

618 Ian White.
Copyright © 1986 Little Misty Music/
Kingsway's Thankyou Music.

WORTHY, THE LORD IS WORTHY,
And no one understands the greatness of His
  name.
Gracious, so kind and gracious,
And slow to anger, and rich, so rich in love.

  My mouth will speak in praise of my Lord,
  Let every creature praise His holy name.
  For ever, and ever more.
  For ever, and ever more.
  For ever, and ever more.
  For ever, and ever more.

Faithful, the Lord is faithful
To all His promises, and loves all He has made.
Righteous, in all ways righteous,
And He is near to all who call on Him in truth.

619 Richard Baxter.
John H. Gurney & Richard R. Chope altd.

YE HOLY ANGELS BRIGHT,
Who wait at God's right hand,
Or through the realms of light
Fly at your Lord's command,
Assist our song,
Or else the theme too high
Doth seem for mortal tongue.

Ye blessèd souls at rest,
Who see your Saviour's face,
Whose glory, e'en the least
Is far above our grace,
God's praises sound,
As in His sight
With sweet delight
Ye do abound.

Ye saints who toil below,
Adore your heavenly King,
And onward as ye go,
Some joyful anthem sing;
Take what He gives,
And praise Him still
Through good and ill,
Who ever lives.

My soul, bear thou thy part,
Triumph in God above,
And with a well-tuned heart
Sing thou the songs of love.
Let all thy days
Till life shall end,
Whate'er He send,
Be filled with praise.

620 Charles Wesley.

YE SERVANTS OF GOD,
Your Master proclaim,
And publish abroad
His wonderful name;
The name all-victorious
Of Jesus extol;
His kingdom is glorious
And rules over all.

God ruleth on high,
Almighty to save;
And still He is nigh,
His presence we have;
The great congregation
His triumph shall sing,
Ascribing salvation
To Jesus our King.

Salvation to God,
Who sits on the throne!
Let all cry aloud,
And honour the Son;
The praises of Jesus
The angels proclaim,
Fall down on their faces,
And worship the Lamb.

Then let us adore,
And give Him His right,
All glory and power,
All wisdom and might,
All honour and blessing,
With angels above,
And thanks never ceasing,
And infinite love.

621 Mark Altrogge.
Copyright © 1987 People of Destiny
International/Word Music/Adm. by CopyCare.

YOU ARE BEAUTIFUL beyond description,
Too marvellous for words,
Too wonderful for comprehension,
Like nothing ever seen or heard.
Who can grasp Your infinite wisdom?
Who can fathom the depth of Your love?
You are beautiful beyond description,
Majesty, enthroned above.

And I stand, I stand in awe of You.
I stand, I stand in awe of You.
Holy God, to whom all praise is due,
I stand in awe of You.

622 Mark Altrogge.
Copyright © 1989 People of Destiny
International/Word Music/Adm. by CopyCare.

YOU ARE COMPASSIONATE and gracious,
Patient and abounding in love;
As far as the east is from the west
You took the sins we were guilty of.
And You deal tenderly with us,
And You deal tenderly with us.

And higher than the heavens,
So great is Your love;
Yes, higher than the heavens
Is Your love for us.

623 John Sellers.
Copyright © 1984 Integrity's Hosanna! Music.
Adm. Kingsway's Thankyou Music.

YOU ARE CROWNED WITH MANY CROWNS,
And rule all things in righteousness.
You are crowned with many crowns,
Upholding all things by Your word.
You rule in power and reign in glory!
You are Lord of heaven and earth!
You are Lord of all.
You are Lord of all.

624 Patty Kennedy.
Copyright © 1985 Mercy/Vineyard Publishing/
Adm. by CopCare.

YOU ARE HERE and I behold Your beauty,
Your glory fills this place.
Calm my heart to hear You,
Cause my eyes to see You.
Your presence here is the answer
To the longing of my heart.

I lift my voice to worship and exalt You,
For You alone are worthy.
A captive now set free,
Your kingdom's come to me.
Glory in the highest,
My heart cries unto You.

625 Michael Ledner.
Copyright © 1981 Maranatha! Music/
Adm. by CopyCare.

YOU ARE MY HIDING PLACE,
You always fill my heart with songs of
    deliverance,
Whenever I am afraid
I will trust in You.
I will trust in You;
Let the weak say 'I am strong
In the strength of my God.'

626 Andy Park.
Copyright © 1988 Mercy/Vineyard
Publishing/Adm. by CopyCare.

YOU ARE THE HOLY ONE,
The Lord Most High.
You reign in majesty,
You reign on high.

You are the Worthy One
Lamb that was slain.
You bought us with Your blood,
And with You we'll reign.

We exalt Your name,
High and mighty One of Israel,
We exalt Your name.
Lead us on to war,
In the power of Your name.
We exalt Your name,
The Name above all names,
Our victorious King,
We exalt Your name.

You are the King of kings,
The Lord of lords;
All men will bow to You,
Before Your throne.

627

YOU ARE THE KING OF GLORY,
You are the Prince of Peace;
You are the Lord of heaven and earth,
You're the Sun of righteousness.
Angels bow down before You,
Worship and adore, for
You have the words of eternal life,
You are Jesus Christ the Lord.

Hosanna to the Son of David!
Hosanna to the King of kings!
Glory in the highest heaven,
For Jesus the Messiah reigns.

628

YOU ARE THE MIGHTY KING,
The living Word;
Master of everything,
You are the Lord.

And I praise Your name,
And I praise Your name.

You are Almighty God,
Saviour and Lord;
Wonderful Counsellor,
You are the Lord.

And I praise Your name,
And I praise Your name.

You are the Prince of Peace,
Emmanuel;
Everlasting Father,
You are the Lord.

And I love Your name,
And I love Your name.

You are the Mighty King,
The living Word;
Master of everything,
You are the Lord.

629

YOU ARE THE VINE,
We are the branches,
Keep us abiding in You.
You are the Vine,
We are the branches,
Keep us abiding in You.

Then we'll grow in Your love,
Then we'll go in Your name,
That the world will surely know
That You have power to heal and to save.

630

YOU ARE WORTHY,
Lord, You're worthy,
So I lift my heart, I lift my voice and cry
  'Holy'.
You have saved me, and I love You,
Jesus ever more I live to praise Your name.

631

YOU DID NOT WAIT FOR ME to draw near to
  You,
But You clothed Yourself in frail humanity.
You did not wait for me to cry out to You,
But You let me hear Your voice calling me.

And I'm forever grateful to You,
I'm forever grateful for the cross;
I'm forever grateful to You,
That You came to seek and save the lost.

632

YOU HAVE BEEN GIVEN the Name above all
  names,
And we worship You, yes we worship You.
You have been given the Name above all
  names,
And we worship You,
Yes we worship You.

We are Your people, made for Your glory,
And we worship You, yes we worship You.
We are Your people, made for Your glory,
And we worship You,
And we worship You.

You have redeemed us from every nation,
And we worship You, yes we worship You.
You have redeemed us from every nation,
And we worship You,
And we worship You.

633 Noel Richards.
Copyright © 1985 Kingsway's
Thankyou Music.

YOU LAID ASIDE YOUR MAJESTY,
Gave up everything for me,
Suffered at the hands of those You had
     created.
You took all my guilt and shame,
When You died and rose again;
Now today You reign,
In heaven and earth exalted.

I really want to worship You, my Lord,
You have won my heart
And I am Yours for ever and ever;
I will love You.
You are the only one who died for me,
Gave Your life to set me free,
So I lift my voice to You in adoration.

634 Patricia Morgan & Sue Rinaldi.
Copyright © 1990 Kingsway's
Thankyou Music.

YOU MAKE MY HEART FEEL GLAD.
You make my heart feel glad.
Jesus, You bring me joy;
You make my heart feel glad.

Lord, Your love brings healing and a peace
     into my heart,
I want to give myself in praise to You.
Though I've been through heartache
You have understood my tears,
O Lord, I will give thanks to You.

When I look around me, and I see the life You
     made,
All creation shouts aloud in praise;
I realise Your greatness, how majestic is Your
     name,
O Lord, I love You more each day.

635 Mark Veary & Paul Oakley.
Copyright © 1986 Kingsway's
Thankyou Music.

YOU, O LORD, rich in mercy,
Because of Your great love.
You, O Lord, so loved us,
Even when we were dead in our sins.

(Men)
You made us alive together with Christ,
And raised us up together with Him,
And seated us with Him in heavenly places,
And raised us up together with Him,
And seated us with Him in heavenly places in
     Christ.

(Women)
You made us alive together with Christ,
And raised us up,
And seated us,
And raised us up,
And seated us in Christ.

636 John W. Elliot.
Copyright © 1987 BMG Songs Inc/
Adm. by CopyCare.

YOU PURCHASED MEN with precious blood,
From every nation, tribe and tongue;
Brought from slavery, freed from prison
     chains;
Brought through death so they might rise
     again,
Born to serve and to reign:

> *Worthy is the Lamb that was slain, to*
>   *receive*
> *Highest honour, and glory, and power,*
>   *and praise!*
> *Worthy is the Lamb that was slain, to*
>   *receive*
> *Highest honour, and glory, and praise!*

Holy, holy to our God,
Who was, and is, and is to come;
Let us join the throng who see His face,
Bowing down to Him both night and day,
Lost in wonder and praise.

637 Wes Sutton.
Copyright © 1988 Sovereign Lifestyle Music.

YOUR MERCY FLOWS upon us like a river.
Your mercy stands unshakeable and true.
Most holy God, of all good things the Giver,
We turn and lift our fervent prayer to You.

> *Hear our cry,* (echo)
> *O Lord,* (echo)
> *Be merciful* (echo)
> *Once more;* (echo)
> *Let Your love* (echo)
> *Your anger stem,* (echo)
> *Remember mercy, O Lord, again.*

Your church once great, though standing
     clothed in sorrow,
Is even still the bride that You adore;
Revive Your church, that we again may honour
Our God and King, our Master and our Lord.

As we have slept, this nation has been taken
By every sin ever known to man;
So at its gates, though burnt by fire and broken,
In Jesus' name we come to take our stand.

638 Andy Park.
Copyright © 1987 Mercy/Vineyard
Publishing/Adm. by CopyCare.

YOUR WORKS, LORD, (Your works Lord)
Are awesome, (are awesome)
Your power (Your power)
Is great.
(Repeat)

> *Great are Your works Lord,*
> *Great are Your deeds,*
> *Awesome in power,*
> *So awesome to me.*

You will reign (You will reign)
For ever, (for ever)
In power (in power)
You will reign.
(Repeat)

Because of (because of)
Your greatness, (Your greatness)
All the earth (all the earth)
Will sing.
(Repeat)

639 Mark Altrogge.
Copyright © 1987 Integrity's Hosanna! Music/
People of Destiny Int./Adm. by Kingsway's
Thankyou Music.

YOU SAT DOWN at the right hand of the
  Father in majesty.
You sat down at the right hand of the Father
  in majesty.
You are crowned Lord of all,
You are faithful and righteous and true;
You're my Master, You're my Owner,
And I love serving You.

640 Steffi Geiser Rubin & Stuart Dauermann.
Copyright © 1975 Lillenas Publishing Co./
Adm. by CopyCare.

YOU SHALL GO OUT WITH JOY
And be led forth with peace,
And the mountains and the hills
Shall break forth before you.
There'll be shouts of joy,
And the trees of the field
Shall clap, shall clap their hands.
And the trees of the field shall clap their
  hands,
And the trees of the field shall clap their
  hands,
And the trees of the field shall clap their
  hands,
And you'll go out with joy.

641 Bob Baker.
Copyright © 1994 Mercy/Vineyard
Publishing/Adm. by CopyCare.

ABRAHAM'S SON, Chosen One,
Zion's cornerstone;
Passover Lamb, Son of Man,
Seated upon Your throne.

> *Hail to the King,*
> *Hail to the King,*
> *Hail to the King of kings.*
> (Repeat)

O promised Seed, beneath Your feet
Sin and death shall fall.
Now through us tread the serpent's head
Till You are all in all.

The world's yet to see Your glory,
But You'll be revealed in power,
And You will reign with the Bride ordained
For Your consummating hour.

642 Paul Oakley.
Copyright © 1997 Kingsway's
Thankyou Music.

> **ALL AROUND THE WORLD** *there's a new*
> *day dawning,*
> *There's a sound coming round,*
> *There's a new song rising up,*
> *Ah, it's a new day!*
> *Everywhere you go you can hear this*
> *story,*
> *There's a power coming down,*
> *There's a glimpse of glory now,*
> *Ah, it's a new day!*

There's a sound of praise,
There's a sound of war;
Lift the banner high, let the Lion roar.
Can you hear the sound in the tops of the
  trees?
Heaven's armies come! Crush the enemy!

Let the lame run, let the blind see!
Let Your power come, set the captives free!
Let the lost return to the Lover of our souls,
Let the prodigal find the way back home.

Lift your hands before the King,
The sovereign Ruler of the earth;
Let the nations come to Him,
Let the cry of hearts be heard:

Revive us! Revive us! Revive us again!
(Repeat)

643

ALL CONSUMING FIRE,
You're my heart's desire,
And I love You dearly, dearly Lord.
You're my meditation,
And my consolation,
And I love You dearly, dearly Lord.

Glory to the Lamb,
I exalt the great I AM;
Reigning on Your glorious throne,
You are my eternal home.

644

ALL CREATION BOWS at the name of Jesus,
Every star is in His hands.
Yet the glorious mystery of ages,
He delights in fragile man.

There is mercy in the name of Jesus,
Mercy to forgive our sin.
The mighty King of heaven became the
    humble servant,
To bring His children back to Him.
And this is why I will sing:

> Hallelujah, Christ is risen,
> Hallelujah, we are saved.
> He has purchased our salvation,
> Hallelujah, praise His name.

There is shelter in the name of Jesus,
He accepts the refugee;
And His mighty strength will never fail us,
His arm is always close to me.
And all my life I will sing:

645

ALL CREATURES OF OUR GOD AND KING,
Lift up your voice and with us sing:
Hallelujah, hallelujah!
Thou burning sun with golden beam,
Thou silver moon with softer gleam:

> O praise Him, O praise Him,
> Hallelujah, hallelujah, hallelujah!

Thou rushing wind that art so strong,
Ye clouds that sail in heaven along,
O praise Him, hallelujah!
Thou rising morn, in praise rejoice,
Ye lights of evening, find a voice:

Thou flowing water, pure and clear,
Make music for thy Lord to hear,
Hallelujah, hallelujah!
Thou fire so masterful and bright,
That givest man both warmth and light:

And all ye men of tender heart,
Forgiving others, take your part,
O sing ye, hallelujah!
Ye who long pain and sorrow bear,
Praise God and on Him cast your care:

Let all things their Creator bless,
And worship Him in humbleness,
O praise Him, hallelujah!
Praise, praise the Father, praise the Son,
And praise the Spirit, Three-in-One:

646

ALL I ONCE HELD DEAR, built my life upon,
All this world reveres, and wars to own,
All I once thought gain I have counted loss;
Spent and worthless now, compared to
    this.

> Knowing You, Jesus,
> Knowing You, there is no greater thing.
> You're my all, You're the best,
> You're my joy, my righteousness,
> And I love You, Lord.

Now my heart's desire is to know You
    more,
To be found in You and known as Yours.
To possess by faith what I could not earn,
All-surpassing gift of righteousness.

Oh, to know the power of Your risen life,
And to know You in Your sufferings.
To become like You in Your death, my Lord,
So with You to live and never die.

647

> **ALL THAT I AM** I lay before You;
> All I possess, Lord, I confess
> Is nothing without You.
> Saviour and King, I now enthrone You;
> Take my life, my living sacrifice to You.

Lord, be the strength within my weakness;
Be the supply in every need,
That I may prove Your promises to me,
Faithful and true in word and deed.

Into Your hands I place the future;
The past is nailed to Calvary,
That I may live in resurrection power,
No longer I but Christ in me.

648 David Fellingham.
Copyright © 1992 Kingsway's
Thankyou Music.

ALL THE ENDS OF THE EARTH will
    remember,
And turn to the Lord of glory;
All the families of the nations will bow down
    to the Lord,
As His righteous acts of power are displayed.

    And we will awaken the nations,
    To bring their worship to Jesus.
    And righteousness and praise shall spring
        forth
    In all the earth.
    And we will awaken the nations,
    To bring their worship to Jesus,
    And the kingdom shall be revealed in
        power,
    With signs, wonders and miracles,
    And righteousness and praise shall spring
        forth
    In all the earth.

Who will not fear the Lord of glory,
Or bring honour to His holy name?
For God has spoken with integrity and truth,
A word which cannot be revoked.

649 Jan Harrington.
Copyright © 1975 Celebration/Kingsway's
Thankyou Music.

ALL THE RICHES OF HIS GRACE,
All the fulness of His blessings,
All the sweetness of His love
He gives to you,
He gives to me.

    Oh, the blood of Jesus,
    Oh, the blood of Jesus,
    Oh, the blood of Jesus,
    It washes white as snow.

    Oh, the word of Jesus,
    Oh, the word of Jesus,
    Oh, the word of Jesus,
    It cleanses white as snow.

    Oh, the love of Jesus,
    Oh, the love of Jesus,
    Oh, the love of Jesus,
    It makes His Body whole.

650 John Gibson.
Copyright © 1996 Kingsway's
Thankyou Music.

(Leader) **ALL YOU PEOPLE,**
(All) *Sing unto the Lord.*
(Leader) *All you nations,*
(All) *Sing unto the Lord.*
Come with dancing,
Come and raise Your voice to the King,
Come and sing unto the Lord.

From the sun's rising
To the sun's setting,
In every place, every land,
He will be glorified;
Offerings of worship from every nation,
Let every tribe, every tongue,
Join in one song of praise.

(Leader) People of Africa,...
(All) Sing unto the Lord. *(After each line)*
Europe and Asia,...
All of Australasia,...
And all across America,...
The rich and poor will ...
The weak and strong can ...
Every generation, ...
Every tribe and nation, ...

651 Nathan Fellingham & Adrian Watts.
Copyright © 1997 Kingsway's
Thankyou Music.

ALMIGHTY GOD, I have heard of Your fame;
I stand in awe of Your wondrous deeds.
The heavens declare Your glorious name;
I worship You above all my needs.

The skies display the work of Your hands,
I will praise You for the rest of my days.
Who can You ask to approve Your plans?
For You are sovereign in all of Your ways.

    I will only worship You,
    There is nothing I want more
    Than to be with You,
    More and more I love You, Lord.
    The only One I bow before,
    I worship You with all that You've put in me;
    This is what You made me for.

652 Darlene Zschech.
Copyright © 1996 Darlene Zschech/Hillsongs
Australia/Kingsway's Thankyou Music.

ALMIGHTY GOD, MY REDEEMER,
My hiding place, my safe refuge;
No other name like Jesus,
No power can stand against You.

My feet are planted on this rock,
And I will not be shaken;
My hope it comes from You alone,
My Lord and my salvation.

Your praise is always on my lips,
Your word is living in my heart,
And I will praise You with a new song:
My soul will bless You, Lord.
You fill my life with greater joy;
Yes, I delight myself in You,
And I will praise You with a new song:
My soul will bless You, Lord.

When I am weak, You make me strong;
When I'm poor, I know I'm rich,
For in the power of Your name
All things are possible. (x4)

653 Carol Owen.
Copyright © 1993 Kingsway's
Thankyou Music.

AMONG THE GODS there is none like You,
O Lord, O Lord.
There are no deeds to compare with Yours, O
   Lord.
All the nations You have made will come;
They'll worship before You, O Lord,
O Lord.

For You are great and do marvellous
   deeds.
Yes, You are great and do marvellous
   deeds.
You alone are God, You alone are God.

You are so good and forgiving,
O Lord, O Lord.
You're rich in love to all who call to You.
All the nations You have made will come;
They'll glorify Your name, O Lord,
O Lord.

Teach me Your ways, O Lord,
And I'll walk in Your truth.
Give me an undivided heart,
That I may fear Your name.

654 Mark Altrogge.
Copyright © 1992 People of Destiny
International/Word Music/Adm. by CopyCare.

AND FROM YOUR FULNESS *we have all*
   received
Grace upon grace,
Kindness on kindness.
And from Your fulness we have all received
Grace upon grace,
Like wave upon wave
From the ocean of Your love.

Lord, You stand willing
And ready to bless,
You bid us bring You
Great requests;
Though many are saying
'Who will show us good?'
Day after day we see Your mercies.

Lord, You're the Author
Of every good gift;
You give us all
We need to live.
Lord, You became poor
To make us rich,
You crown our lives with Your compassion.

655 Graham Kendrick.
Copyright © 1991 Make Way Music.

AND HE SHALL REIGN *forever,*
His throne and crown shall ever endure.
And He shall reign forever,
And we shall reign with Him.

What a vision filled my eyes,
One like a Son of man,
Coming with the clouds of heaven
He approached an awesome throne.

He was given sovereign power,
Glory and authority.
Every nation, tribe and tongue
Worshipped Him on bended knee.

On the throne forever,
See the Lamb who once was slain.
Wounds of sacrificial love
Forever shall remain.

656 Donn Thomas.
Copyright © 1992 John T. Benson Publishing
Co/Adm. by CopyCare.

ANOINTING, FALL ON ME,
Anointing, fall on me;
Let the power of the Holy Ghost
Fall on me,
Anointing, fall on me.

Touch my hands, my mouth and my heart;
Fill my life, Lord, every part.
Let the power of the Holy Ghost
Fall on me,
Anointing, fall on me.

657 Noel & Tricia Richards.
Copyright © 1996 Kingsway's
Thankyou Music.

ARE WE THE PEOPLE

Who will see God's kingdom come,
When He is known in every nation?
One thing is certain,
We are closer than before;
Keep moving on, last generation.

These are the days for harvest,
To gather in the lost;
Let those who live in darkness
Hear the message of the cross.

We'll go where God is sending,
We'll do what He commands;
These years that He has waited
Could be coming to an end.

658 Richard Lewis.
Copyright © 1997 Kingsway's
Thankyou Music.

AS THE DEER PANTS for the water,
So my soul, it thirsts for You,
For You, O God,
For You, O God.
(Repeat)

When can I come before You
And see Your face?
My heart and my flesh cry out
For the living God,
For the living God.

Deep calls to deep
At the thunder of Your waterfalls.
Your heart of love is calling out to me.
By this I know that I am Yours
And You are mine.
Your waves of love are breaking over me.
Your waves of love are breaking over me.
Your waves of love are breaking over me.

659 Timothy Dudley-Smith.
Copyright © Timothy Dudley-Smith.

AS WATER TO THE THIRSTY,

As beauty to the eyes,
As strength that follows weakness,
As truth instead of lies;
As songtime and springtime
And summertime to be,
So is my Lord,
My living Lord,
So is my Lord to me.

Like calm in place of clamour,
Like peace that follows pain,
Like meeting after parting,
Like sunshine after rain;
Like moonlight and starlight
And sunlight on the sea,
So is my Lord,
My living Lord,
So is my Lord to me.

As sleep that follows fever,
As gold instead of grey,
As freedom after bondage,
As sunrise to the day;
As home to the traveller
And all he longs to see,
So is my Lord,
My living Lord,
So is my Lord to me.

660 David Baroni.
Copyright © 1992 Pleasant Hill Music/John T.
Benson Publishing Co/Adm. by CopyCare.

AS WE BEHOLD YOU, as we behold You,
We are changing into Your image.
As we behold You, as we behold You,
We are changing from glory to glory.

As we behold You in all of Your glory,
Lord, by Your Spirit we are changing
Into Your image from glory to glory,
As we behold You, living God.

661 Lex Loizides.
Copyright © 1996 Kingsway's
Thankyou Music.

AS WE SEE THE WORLD in tatters,
As we watch their dreams break down,
We can hear their quiet anguish:
'Come and help us!'
Brought to life by God's own Spirit,
Joined together in His Son,
Now the church with strength arises
Like an army.

Every place, every place
Where our feet shall tread,
Every tribe, every race
God has given us.

In the midst of boastful darkness
Shines a Light that cannot fail,
And the blind behold His glory,
Jesus! Jesus!
Not content with restoration
Of the remnant in the land,
He has filled us with His power
For the nations.

662
Derek Bond.
Copyright © 1992 Sovereign Music UK.

AT THE FOOT OF THE CROSS,
I can hardly take it in,
That the King of all creation
Was dying for my sin.
And the pain and agony,
And the thorns that pierced Your head,
And the hardness of my sinful heart
That left You there for dead.

And O what mercy I have found
At the cross of Calvary;
I will never know Your loneliness,
All on account of me.
And I will bow my knee before Your throne,
'cause Your love has set me free;
And I will give my life to You, dear Lord,
And praise Your majesty,
And praise Your majesty,
And praise Your majesty.

663
Gill Broomhall.
Copyright © 1992 Kingsway's
Thankyou Music & Sovereign Music UK.

BABY JESUS IN THE MANGER,
To the world He's still a stranger.
Wise men bring their gifts
Of gold and myrrh,
Baby Jesus in the manger.

Noel, Noel, Noel,
Hail the Immanuel.

Gentle Jesus, meek and lowly,
Full of love so pure and holy.
He will teach and pray,
Show mankind the way,
Gentle Jesus, meek and lowly.

Loving Jesus, mocked and beaten,
He the sin of man has taken.
He has paid the price,
He has given His life,
Loving Jesus, mocked and beaten.

Mighty Jesus, He is risen,
He has broken out of prison.
He has conquered sin,
Brought new life to men,
Mighty Jesus, He is risen.

664
Graham Kendrick.
Copyright © 1993 Make Way Music.

BEAUTY FOR BROKENNESS,
Hope for despair,
Lord, in Your suffering world
This is our prayer:
Bread for the children,
Justice, joy, peace;
Sunrise to sunset,
Your kingdom increase!

Shelter for fragile lives,
Cures for their ills,
Work for the craftsman,
Trade for their skills;
Land for the dispossessed,
Rights for the weak,
Voices to plead the cause
Of those who can't speak.

God of the poor,
Friend of the weak,
Give us compassion we pray:
Melt our cold hearts,
Let tears fall like rain;
Come, change our love
From a spark to a flame.

Refuge from cruel wars,
Havens from fear,
Cities for sanctuary,
Freedoms to share;
Peace to the killing-fields,
Scorched earth to green,
Christ for the bitterness,
His cross for the pain.

Rest for the ravaged earth,
Oceans and streams
Plundered and poisoned—
Our future, our dreams.
Lord, end our madness,
Carelessness, greed;
Make us content with
The things that we need.

Lighten our darkness,
Breathe on this flame
Until Your justice
Burns brightly again;
Until the nations
Learn of Your ways,
Seek Your salvation
And bring You their praise.

665
Dave Bilbrough.
Copyright © 1991 Kingsway's
Thankyou Music.

BE FREE *in the love of God,*
Let His Spirit flow within you.
Be free in the love of God,
Let it fill your soul.
Be free in the love of God,
Celebrate His name with dancing.
Be free in the love of God,
He has made us whole.

For His purpose He has called us,
In His hands He will uphold us.
He will keep us and sustain us
In the Father's love.

God is gracious, He will lead us
Through His power at work within us.
Spirit, guide us, and unite us
In the Father's love.

666
Billy Funk.
Copyright © 1991 Integrity's Praise!
Music/Adm. by Kingsway's Thankyou Music.

BE GLORIFIED, be glorified.
Be glorified, be glorified.
Be glorified in the heavens,
Be glorified in the earth;
Be glorified in the temple,
Jesus, Jesus,
Be Thou glorified.
Jesus, Jesus,
Be Thou glorified.

Worship the Lord, worship the Lord.
Worship the Lord, worship the Lord.
Worship the Lord in the heavens,
Worship the Lord in the earth;
Worship the Lord in the temple,
Jesus, Jesus,
Be Thou glorified.
Jesus, Jesus,
Be Thou glorified.

667
Gerald Coates & Noel Richards.
Copyright © 1991 Kingsway's
Thankyou Music.

BEHOLD THE LORD upon His throne;
His face is shining like the sun.
With eyes blazing fire, and feet glowing
  bronze,
His voice like mighty water roars.
Holy, holy, Lord God Almighty.
Holy, holy, we stand in awe of You.

The First, the Last, the living One
Laid down His life for all the world;
Behold He now lives forever more,
And holds the keys of death and hell.
Holy, holy, Lord God Almighty;
Holy, holy, we bow before Your throne.

So let our praises ever ring
To Jesus Christ, our glorious King.
All heaven and earth resound as we cry:
'Worthy is the Son of God!'
Holy, holy, Lord God Almighty;
Holy, holy, we fall down at Your feet.

668 Charles Wesley.

BEHOLD THE SERVANT OF THE LORD:
I wait Thy guiding eye to feel,
To hear and keep Thy every word,
To prove and do Thy perfect will;
Joyful from my own works to cease,
Glad to fulfil all righteousness.

Me if Thy grace vouchsafe to use,
Meanest of all Thy creatures, me.
The deed, the time, the manner choose:
Let all my fruit be found of Thee.
Let all my works in Thee be wrought,
By Thee to full perfection brought.

My every weak though good design
O'errule or change, as seems Thee meet:
Jesus, let all my work be Thine –
Thy work, O Lord, is all complete,
And pleasing in Thy Father's sight;
Thou only hast done all things right.

Here then to Thee Thine own I leave;
Mould as Thou wilt Thy passive clay;
But let me all Thy stamp receive,
But let me all Thy words obey,
Serve with a single heart and eye,
And in Thy glory live and die.

669 James Montgomery.

BE KNOWN TO US IN BREAKING BREAD,
But do not then depart;
Saviour, abide with us, and spread
Thy table in our heart.

There sup with us in love divine;
Thy body and Thy blood,
That living bread, that heavenly wine,
Be our immortal food.

We would not live by bread alone,
But by Thy word of grace,
In strength of which we travel on
To our abiding place.

670
Jim Bailey.
Copyright © 1996 Kingsway's
Thankyou Music.

BELLS THEY ARE RINGING,
Children are singing,
And we are exalting the Name over all.
Flags they are dancing,
The church is advancing,
As we are romancing the Name over all.

Jesus' kingdom can't be shaken,
Jesus' promise can't be broken,
Jesus, Lord of all creation,
Name over all.
Jesus, Truth of liberation,
Jesus, Light of our salvation,
Jesus, only way to heaven,
The Name over all.

671
Lex Loizides.
Copyright © 1995 Kingsway's
Thankyou Music.

BE STILL AND KNOW that I am God:
I will be glorified and praised in all the earth.
For My great name I will be found,
And I can never be resisted,
Never be undone;
I'm never lacking power
To glorify My Son.
The gates of hell are falling
And the church is coming forth,
My name will be exalted in the earth.

Be still and know that I am God;
I have poured out My Holy Spirit like a flood.
The land that cries for holy rain
Shall be inheriting her promises
And dancing like a child;
A holy monsoon deluge
Shall bless the barren heights,
And those who sat in silence
Shall speak up and shall be heard:
My name will be exalted in the earth.

Be still and know that I am God;
My Son has asked me for
The nations of the world.
His sprinkled blood has made a way
For all the multitudes of India and
    Africa to come;
The Middle East will find its peace
Through Jesus Christ My Son.
From London down to Cape Town,
From L.A. to Beijing,
My Son shall reign the undisputed King!

672
John L. Bell & Graham Maule.
Copyright © 1989 WGRG, Iona Community.

BE STILL AND KNOW THAT I AM GOD.
Be still and know that I am God.

673
Clinton Utterbach.
Copyright © 1988
Polygram Music Publishing Ltd.

BLESSÈD BE THE NAME OF THE LORD,
Blessed be the name of the Lord,
Blessed be the name of the Lord Most High!
(Repeat)

> *The Name of the Lord is a strong tower,*
> *The righteous run into it,*
> *And they are saved.*
> (Repeat)

Glory to the name of the Lord...

Holy is the name of the Lord...

674
Joey Holder.
Copyright © 1987 Far Lane Publishing/
Kingsway's Thankyou Music.

BLESSÈD JESUS, come to me,
Soothe my soul with songs of peace.
As I look to You alone,
Fill me with Your love.

> *Glorious, marvellous*
> *Grace that rescued me;*
> *Holy, worthy*
> *Is the Lamb who died for me.*

Mountains high and valleys low,
You will never let me go;
By Your fountain let me drink,
Fill my thirsty soul.

675
Gary Sadler & Jamie Harvill.
Copyright © 1992 Integrity's Praise! Music/
Adm. by Kingsway's Thankyou Music.

BLESSING AND HONOUR, glory and power
Be unto the Ancient of Days;
From every nation, all of creation
Bow before the Ancient of Days.

> *Every tongue in heaven and earth*
> *Shall declare Your glory,*
> *Every knee shall bow at Your throne*
> *In worship;*
> *You will be exalted, O God,*
> *And Your kingdom shall not pass away,*
> *O Ancient of Days.*

Your kingdom shall reign over all the earth:
Sing unto the Ancient of Days.
For none shall compare to Your matchless
    worth:
Sing unto the Ancient of Days.

676 Jacques Berthier/Taizé.
Copyright © Ateliers et Presses de Taize.

BLESS THE LORD, MY SOUL,
And bless His holy name.
Bless the Lord, my soul,
He rescues me from death.

It is He who forgives all your guilt,
Who heals every one of your ills,
Who redeems your life from the grave,
Who crowns you with love and compassion.

The Lord is compassion and love,
Slow to anger and rich in mercy.
He does not treat us according to our sins,
Nor repay us according to our faults.

As a father has compassion on his children,
The Lord has pity on those who fear Him;
For He knows of what we are made,
He remembers that we are dust.

677 Tina Pownall.
Copyright © 1987 Sovereign Music UK.

BREATHE ON ME, Spirit of Jesus.
Breathe on me, Holy Spirit of God.

Fill me again, Spirit of Jesus.
Fill me again, Holy Spirit of God.

Change my heart, Spirit of Jesus.
Change my heart, Holy Spirit of God.

Bring peace to the world, Spirit of Jesus.
Bring peace to the world, Holy Spirit of God.

678 Edwin Hatch, adpt. David Fellingham.
Copyright © 1995 Kingsway's Thankyou Music.

BREATHE ON ME, BREATH OF GOD,
And fill my life anew;
That I may love as You love,
And do the works that You do.
Holy Spirit, breathe on me.

Breathe on me, breath of God,
Until my heart is pure;
Until my will is one with Yours
Let holiness and love endure.
Holy Spirit, breathe on me.

And let every part of me
Glow with fire divine;
With passion in my life,
Jesus, let Your glory shine.
(Repeat)

679 Kent & Carla Henry.
Copyright © 1989 Kent Henry Ministries/
Kingsway's Thankyou Music.

BURN IT DEEP within my soul,
New strength and fire, O Lord.
Burn it deep within my soul,
New zeal and fire, O Lord.
Burn it deep within my soul,
New strength and fire,
It makes me whole.
Burn it deep,
Deep within my soul.

And You came
With the Holy Spirit's desire.
You came
With a zeal for Your Father's house.
Consume me, Lord,
With Your purifying fire,
And strengthen me
By Your mighty hand.

680 David Fellingham.
Copyright © 1997 Kingsway's
Thankyou Music.

BY YOUR BLOOD I can enter the holiest
    place,
To the throne of my Father and King.
There I find Your acceptance, mercy and
    grace,
And my life is renewed again.

Far away from the stress and the turmoil of
    life,
I now come to seek Your face.
In the house of the Lord where Your presence
    is found,
I now come to worship You.

I see the King upon the throne,
Jesus, full of majesty.
I will fall down at Your feet,
I will worship You alone.

In the light of Your presence I find deepest joy,
There is no other place I would be.
To behold Your beauty is all my desire,
You're the one my heart longs for,
You're the one my heart longs for.

681
Noel & Tricia Richards.
Copyright © 1992 Kingsway's
Thankyou Music.

CALLED TO A BATTLE, heavenly war;
Though we may struggle, victory is sure.
Death will not triumph, though we may die;
Jesus has promised our eternal life.

By the blood of the Lamb we shall
overcome,
See the accuser thrown down.
By the word of the Lord we shall
overcome,
Raise a victory cry,
Like thunder in the skies,
Thunder in the skies.

Standing together, moving as one;
We are God's army, called to overcome.
We are commissioned, Jesus says go;
In every nation, let His love be known.

682
Matt Redman.
Copyright © 1996 Kingsway's
Thankyou Music.

CAN A NATION BE CHANGED?
Can a nation be saved?
Can a nation be turned back to You?
(Repeat)

We're on our knees,
We're on our knees again.
We're on our knees,
We're on our knees again.

Let this nation be changed,
Let this nation be saved,
Let this nation be turned back to You.
(Repeat)

683
Matt Redman.
Copyright © 1995 Kingsway's
Thankyou Music.

CAN I ASCEND the hill of the Lord?
Can I stand in that holy place?
There to approach the glory of my God;
Come towards to seek Your face.
Purify my heart,
And purify my hands,
For I know it is on holy ground I'll stand.

I'm coming up the mountain, Lord;
I'm seeking You and You alone.
I know that I will be transformed,
My heart unveiled before You.
I'm longing for Your presence, Lord;
Envelop me within the cloud.
I'm coming up the mountain, Lord,
My heart unveiled before You,
I will come.

I'm coming to worship,
I'm coming to bow down,
I'm coming to meet with You.
(Repeat)

684
Chris Bowater.
Copyright © 1996 Sovereign Lifestyle Music.

CATCH THE FIRE,
Swim through the waters,
Fly on the wings of the Spirit.
(Repeat)

Hear the sound that fills heaven,
Hear the beat of my heart.
(Repeat)

As a Lover, gazing on His bride;
As a Father looking for His child;
As the Shepherd,
Searching for the one that's lost;
As the Saviour, weeping for the world.

685
John L. Bell & Graham Maule.
Copyright © 1989 WGRG, Iona Community.

CHRIST'S IS THE WORLD in which we move,
Christ's are the folk we're summoned to love,
Christ's is the voice which calls us to care,
And Christ is the One who calls us here.

To the lost Christ shows His face;
To the unloved He gives His embrace:
To those who cry in pain or disgrace,
Christ makes with His friends
A touching place.

Feel for the people we most avoid,
Strange or bereaved or never employed;
Feel for the women, and feel for the men
Who fear that their living is all in vain.

Feel for the parents who've lost their child,
Feel for the women whom men have defiled,
Feel for the baby for whom there's no breast,
And feel for the weary who find no rest.

Feel for the lives by life confused,
Riddled with doubt, in loving abused;
Feel for the lonely heart, conscious of sin,
Which longs to be pure but fears to begin.

686
Ian White.
Copyright © 1987 Little Misty Music/
Kingsway's Thankyou Music.

CLAP YOUR HANDS, ALL YOU NATIONS,
Shout to God with cries of joy,
O how awesome is the Lord most high,
The King over all the earth!

He subdued nations under us,
The peoples under our feet,
And He chose our inheritance for us,
The pride of Jacob, whom He loved.

Now our God has ascended
In the midst of shouts of joy,
And the Lord is in among the trumpet sound,
Among the trumpet sound.

Sing praise to God,
Sing praises to the King,
Sing praises to the King.
(Repeat)

For our God is King of all the earth,
Sing Him a psalm of praise,
For He rules above the nations on His throne,
On His holy throne.

All the people are gathered
Of the God of Abraham.
For the kings of all the earth belong to God,
And He is lifted high!

687 Patricia Morgan.
Copyright © 1991 Kingsway's
Thankyou Music.

CLOSER TO YOU, Lord, and closer still,
Till I am wholly in Your will.
Closer to hear Your beating heart,
And understand what You impart.
O Breath of Life, come purify
This heart of mine and satisfy,
My deep desire is to worship You,
Lord of my life, come closer still.

688 Valerie Collison.
Copyright © 1972 High-Fye Music.

COME AND JOIN THE CELEBRATION,
It's a very special day;
Come and share our jubilation,
There's a new King born today!

See the shepherds
Hurry down to Bethlehem;
Gaze in wonder
At the Son of God who lay before them.

Wise men journey,
Led to worship by a star,
Kneel in homage,
Bringing precious gifts from lands afar, so

'God is with us,'
'round the world the message bring;
He is with us,
'Welcome!' all the bells on earth are pealing.

689 Loralee Thiessen.
Copyright © 1993 Mercy/Vineyard Publishing/
Adm. by CopyCare.

COME, HOLY SPIRIT,
Come, Holy Spirit,
Come to this place,
We will embrace Your presence.

Come, soften our hearts,
Come, soften our hearts,
That we may obey,
Teach us Your way, come lead us.

Come, Holy Spirit.
Come, Holy Spirit.

690 Billy Funk.
Copyright © 1992 Integrity's Praise! Music/
Adm. by Kingsway's Thankyou Music.

COME INTO THE HEAVENLIES
And sing the song the angels sing,
Worthy, worthy.
Come into the heavenlies,
And sing the song the angels sing,
Worthy, worthy.

Worthy is the Lamb.
Worthy is the Lamb.
Worthy is the Lamb.
Worthy is the Lamb.

Worthy of blessing and honour,
Worthy of glory and power,
Worthy is the Lamb.
(Repeat)

691 Kevin Prosch.
Copyright © 1993 7th Time Music/Kingsway's
Thankyou Music.

COME LET US RETURN unto the Lord.
(Men – Women echo)
Come let us return unto the Lord.
(Men – Women echo)

(Repeat)

For He has torn us,
But He will heal us.
For He has wounded us,
But He will bandage us.

And He will come,
He'll come to us
Like rain, spring rain.
He will come to us
Like rain, spring rain.

692
Graham Kendrick.
Copyright © 1992 Make Way Music.

COME, LET US WORSHIP JESUS,
King of nations, Lord of all.
Magnificent and glorious,
Just and merciful.

Jesus, King of the nations,
Jesus, Lord of all.
Jesus, King of the nations,
Lord of all.

Lavish our hearts' affection,
Deepest love and highest praise.
Voice, race and language blending,
All the world amazed.

Bring tributes from the nations,
Come in joyful cavalcades,
One thunderous acclamation,
One banner raised.

Come, Lord, and fill Your temple,
Glorify Your dwelling place,
Till nations see Your splendour
And seek Your face.

Fear God and give Him glory,
For His hour of judgement comes.
Creator, Lord Almighty,
Worship Him alone.

693
John Pantry.
Copyright © 1992 Kingsway's
Thankyou Music.

COME, MY SOUL, AND PRAISE THE LORD.
(Men – Women echo)
Sing to Christ, the living Word,
(Men – Women echo)
Who heals my broken heart,
(Men – Women echo)
And binds my wounds. *(Men – Women echo)*

Holy, holy is the Lord, *(Men – Women echo)*
Who may stand before His word?
(Men – Women echo)
He knows my life so well,
(Men – Women echo)
Yet loves me still. *(Men – Women echo)*

As His eye is on the sparrow,
So His thoughts are for my life.
Not a moment passes by
But He thinks of me,
And He hears me when I cry.
So come my soul…

694
Noel Richards & Doug Horley.
Copyright © 1996 Kingsway's
Thankyou Music.

COME OUT OF DARKNESS into the light;
Come out of darkness into the light.
Come out of darkness into the arms of
*   love,*
Into the arms of love.

To a world in darkness,
To a world in pain,
At this time You've called us,
Your love to proclaim;
Through Your willing people
To the nations say,
To the nations say:

Do not be discouraged,
See what God has done;
He is working through us,
This world shall be won.
There will be a harvest
When the nations hear.
What are they going to hear?

By the blood of Jesus sin is washed away;
All who call upon Him, He will surely save.
This will be the promise that the nations hear,
When we sing it loud and clear.

695
Richard Lewis.
Copyright © 1996 Kingsway's
Thankyou Music.

COME TO THE POWER,
The power of the living God;
His name is higher,
Higher than any other name.
Mighty Jehovah, awesome Deliverer;
His power is greater,
Greater than any principality.

A mighty fortress is our God,
He sits enthroned in the heavens,
The Lord of Hosts is He.
A mighty fortress is our God,
He sits enthroned in the heavens,
He reigns in majesty.
(Repeat)
In majesty.

696
Chris Bowater.
Copyright © 1994 Sovereign Lifestyle Music.

CONFIDENCE, WE HAVE CONFIDENCE
To come, to ask for mercy.
Confidence, we have confidence,
To come, to ask for mercy.

Merciful God, we cry: 'Don't pass us by.'
Merciful God, we pray: 'Don't turn away;'
In Your love remember mercy.
In Your love remember mercy.

697 Geoff Bullock.
Copyright © 1997 Watershed Productions/
Kingsway's Thankyou Music.

DAY BY DAY and hour by hour,
Your love for me from heaven flows;
Like streams of water in the desert,
Living waters flow.
You walk beside me, gently guiding,
Leading me through every storm.
Everlasting, never changing
Grace and love divine.

Mercy's healing grace, relieving
Every spot and every stain.
Forgiven freely, no more guilty,
Love has conquered shame.
The broken mended, night has ended,
Lost and lonely lost no more;
For I am carried in the arms of
Grace and love divine.

I am carried in the arms
Of grace and love divine;
I am held by hands of healing,
Washed by water pure;
Lifting up my heavy heart,
Held in grace scarred hands,
I am carried in the arms
Of grace and love divine.

Never worthy, never earning,
All my works now left behind.
Ever onwards, ever upwards,
You've called me on to rise
Above my darkness, all my failure,
Every fear and every pain.
Always carried, always covered by
Grace and love divine.

698 David Fellingham.
Copyright © 1995 Kingsway's
Thankyou Music.

DAY OF FAVOUR, day of grace;
This is the day of jubilee.
The Spirit of the sovereign Lord
Is falling now on me.
Let the oil from heaven flow
From the presence of the King.
Jesus, let Your power flow
As we worship, as we sing.
Set us free to make You known
To a world that's full of shame.
Jesus, let Your glory fall,
Give us power to speak Your name.

Day of favour, day of grace;
This is the day of jubilee.
The Spirit of the sovereign Lord
Is falling now on me.
Open wide the prison doors,
Where satan's held the key.
Bring deliverance to the bound,
And set the captives free.
Bring the good news to the poor,
And cause the blind to see.
The Spirit of the Lord
Is falling now on me.

699 David Fellingham.
Copyright © 1994 Kingsway's
Thankyou Music.

DAYS OF HEAVEN here on the earth;
Touched by power, touched by love.
By Your word, and by Your Spirit
You send Your blessing here on us.

Lord, send the rain,
Let Your Spirit come and glorify Jesus.
Lord, send the rain,
Let Your Spirit come like a pent up flood,
Driven by the breath of God.

We bring our worship, we see Your face;
We stand in wonder of Your grace.
Your kingdom presence, Your majesty;
Jesus, You're here now, hear our plea.

700 Martin Smith.
Copyright © 1994 Curious? Music UK/Adm.
by Kingsway's Thankyou Music.

DID YOU FEEL THE MOUNTAINS TREMBLE?
Did you hear the oceans roar,
When the people rose to sing of
Jesus Christ, the risen One?

Did you feel the people tremble?
Did you hear the singers roar,
When the lost began to sing of
Jesus Christ, the saving One?

And we can see that God, You're moving,
A mighty river through the nations.
And young and old will turn to Jesus.
Fling wide you heavenly gates,
Prepare the way of the risen Lord.

Open up the doors
And let the music play,
Let the streets resound with singing.
Songs that bring Your hope,
Songs that bring Your joy,
Dancers who dance upon injustice.

Do you feel the darkness tremble,
When all the saints join in one song,
And all the streams flow as one river,
To wash away our brokenness?

And we can see that God, You're moving,
A time of jubilee is coming,
When young and old will turn to Jesus.
Fling wide you heavenly gates,
Prepare the way of the risen Lord.

701 Ian Smale.
Copyright © 1987 Kingsway's
Thankyou Music.

DON'T BE LAZY,
Lazy, lazy, lazy,
But copy those who through faith and
    patience
Receive what God has promised.

702 Brian Doerksen.
Copyright © 1994 Mercy/Vineyard Publishing/
Adm. by CopyCare.

DON'T LET MY LOVE GROW COLD;
I'm calling out, 'light the fire again.'
Don't let my vision die;
I'm calling out, 'light the fire again.'

You know my heart, my deeds;
I'm calling out, 'light the fire again.'
I need Your discipline;
I'm calling out, 'light the fire again.'

I am here to buy gold,
Refined in the fire:
Naked and poor,
Wretched and blind, I come.
Clothe me in white,
So I won't be ashamed:
Lord, light the fire again!

703 Andy Park.
Copyright © 1994 Mercy/Vineyard Publishing/
Adm. by CopyCare.

DOWN THE MOUNTAIN THE RIVER FLOWS,
And it brings refreshing wherever it goes.
Through the valleys and over the fields,
The river is rushing and the river is here.

The river of God sets our feet a-dancing,
The river of God fills our hearts with
    cheer;
The river of God fills our mouths with
    laughter,
And we rejoice for the river is here.

The river God is teeming with life,
And all who touch it can be revived.
And those who linger on this river's shore
Will come back thirsting for more of the Lord.

Up to the mountain we love to go
To find the presence of the Lord.
Along the banks of the river we run,
We dance with laughter, giving praise to the
    Son.

704 Geoff & Judith Roberts.
Copyright © 1996 Kingsway's
Thankyou Music.

DRAW ME CLOSE TO THE CROSS,
To the place of Your love,
To the place where You poured out Your
    mercy;
Where the river of life
That flows from Your wounded side
Brings refreshing to those who draw near.
Draw me close to Your throne
Where Your majesty is shown,
Where the crown of my life I lay down.
Draw me close to Your side,
Where my heart is satisfied,
Draw me close to You, Lord,
Draw me close.

705 David Fellingham.
Copyright © 1992 Kingsway's
Thankyou Music.

ETERNAL COVENANT of God
Down through time has been declared;
Drawing the heart of man
Into redemption's plan,
Mercy and grace revealed,
By the blood and Spirit sealed.
All our sins have been forgiven,
Raised from death to heights of heaven.

And we're living to the praise of His glory,
Eternally secure in His love;
The eyes of our hearts have been opened
To receive the blessing of God.
(Repeat)

706 Dave Bilbrough.
Copyright © 1995 Kingsway's
Thankyou Music.

FAITHFUL AND TRUE
Are all Your ways;
Your love for me will never fade away.
Always the same,
You never change;
Your love for me will never fade away.

Even in my hour of deepest need,
You are always there to walk with me.
You know my words before I speak;
Lord, I know that You will never forsake me.

707 Chris Bowater.
Copyright © 1990 Sovereign Lifestyle Music.

FAITHFUL GOD, faithful God,
All sufficient One, I worship You.
Shalom my peace,
My strong Deliverer,
I lift You up, faithful God.

708 David Fellingham.
Copyright © 1997 Kingsway's
Thankyou Music.

FAR ABOVE ALL OTHER LOVES,
Far beyond all other joys,
Heaven's blessings poured on me,
By the Holy Spirit's power.

Love's compelling power
Draws my heart into Yours;
Jesus, how I love You,
You're my Friend and my Lord.
You have died and risen
So what else can I say?
How I love You, Lord,
Love You, Lord.

All ambition now has gone,
Pleasing You my only goal;
Motivated by Your grace,
Living for eternity.

Looking with the eye of faith
For the day of Your return;
In that day I want to stand
Unashamed before Your throne.

709 Graham Kendrick.
Copyright © 1996 Make Way Music.

FAR AND NEAR hear the call,
Worship Him, Lord of all;
Families of nations come,
Celebrate what God has done.

Deep and wide is the love
Heaven sent from above;
God's own Son for sinners died,
Rose again, He is alive.

Say it loud, say it strong,
Tell the world what God has done;
Say it loud, praise His name,
Let the earth rejoice
For the Lord reigns.

At His name let praise begin,
Oceans roar, nature sing.
For He comes to judge the earth
In righteousness and in His truth.

710 Dave Bilbrough.
Copyright © 1995 Kingsway's
Thankyou Music.

FATHER GOD, fill this place
With Your love, with Your grace.
As we call on Your name,
Visit us in power again.

Lord, we worship You.
Lord, we worship You.
(Repeat)

Spirit come with Your peace;
Heal our wounds, bring release.
Lord we long for Your touch,
Fill our hearts with Your love.

711 John Barnett.
Copyright © 1989 Mercy/Vineyard Publishing/
Adm. by CopyCare.

FATHER, I COME TO YOU, lifting up my
hands
In the name of Jesus, by Your grace I stand.
Just because You love me and I love Your
Son,
I know Your favour, unending love.

I receive Your favour, Your unending love,
Not because I've earned it, not for what I've
done;
Just because You love me and I love Your
Son,
I know Your favour, unending love.

Unending love,
Your unending love.

It's the presence of Your kingdom as Your
glory fills this place,
And I see how much You love me as I look
into Your face.
Nothing could be better, there's nothing I
would trade
For Your favour, unending love.

712 Jim Bailey.
Copyright © 1996 Kingsway's
Thankyou Music.

FATHER IN HEAVEN, holy is Your name.
Your kingdom come, Your will be done,
Let it be the same.
(Repeat)
On earth as it is in heaven,
On earth as it is in heaven.
(Repeat)

Give us today all our daily bread,
As we forgive our debtors,
So You forgive our debts.
(Repeat)
And lead us not into temptation;
Deliver us from evil.
(Repeat)

For Yours is the kingdom,
The power and the glory,
Forever and ever and ever, amen.
(Repeat)

713 Paul McWilliams & William Thompson.
Copyright © 1993 Kingsway's
Thankyou Music.

FATHER, LIKE RAIN FROM THE SKIES,
Send Your word into our lives.
We cry out: 'Show us Your way,
Come to us, Father, we pray.'

Come and satisfy,
Come and satisfy my soul.
Come and satisfy,
Come and satisfy my soul
And make me whole.

When will our hearts understand,
You have our lives in Your hand?
We cry out: 'Come to us, Lord,
Guide us we pray with Your word.'

714 David Ruis.
Copyright © 1993 Mercy/Vineyard Publishing/
Adm. by CopyCare.

FATHER OF CREATION,
Unfold Your sovereign plan.
Raise up a chosen generation
That will march through the land.
All of creation is longing
For Your unveiling of power.
Would You release Your anointing;
O God, let this be the hour.

Let Your glory fall in this room,
Let it go forth from here to the nations.
Let Your fragrance rest in this place,
As we gather to seek Your face.

Ruler of the nations,
The world has yet to see
The full release of Your promise,
The church in victory.
Turn to us, Lord, and touch us,
Make us strong in Your might.
Overcome our weakness,
That we could stand up and fight.

(Men) Let Your kingdom come.
(Women) Let Your kingdom come.
(Men) Let Your will be done.
(Women) Let Your will be done.
(Men) Let us see on earth
(Women) Let us see on earth
(All) The glory of Your Son.

715 Robert Critchley.
Copyright © 1996 Kingsway's
Thankyou Music.

FATHER, YOU HAVE GIVEN
Precious gifts from heaven,
Equipping us to serve You
As You move upon the earth.
You've prepared us for this hour,
And anointed us with power
For humble acts of righteousness,
We freely volunteer to do Your work.

Ambassadors of reconciliation,
Preaching the good news of Jesus Christ;
Praying for the increase of Your kingdom,
Piercing the darkness with Your light.

Not to us, but to You be all the praises,
Not to us ,but to the glory of Your grace.
We will lift up a standard to this world,
Not for us, but for the honour of Your
*   name.*
Oh, Father, not for us,
But for the honour of Your name.

For the honour of Your name.
Oh, Your name.
(Repeat)

Father, You have chosen
The weak and the broken,
These ones are the vessels
Through whom You command Your
    strength.
We offer up our lives as living sacrifices,
Fill us with Your Spirit now,
And send us out to bring the harvest in.

Ambassadors of reconciliation...

716

FILLED WITH COMPASSION for all creation,
Jesus came into a world that was lost.
There was but one way that He could save us,
Only through suffering death on a cross.

    God, You are waiting,
    Your heart is breaking
    For all the people who live on the earth.
    Stir us to action,
    Filled with Your passion
    For all the people who live on the earth.

Great is Your passion for all the people
Living and dying without knowing You.
Having no Saviour, they're lost forever,
If we don't speak out and lead them to You.

From every nation we shall be gathered,
Millions redeemed shall be Jesus' reward.
Then He will turn and say to His Father:
'Truly my suffering was worth it all.'

717

FILL YOUR HEARTS WITH JOY and
    gladness,
Sing and praise your God and mine!
Great the Lord in love and wisdom,
Might and majesty divine!
He who framed the starry heavens
Knows and names them as they shine.

Praise the Lord, His people, praise Him!
Wounded souls His comfort know;
Those who fear Him find His mercies,
Peace for pain and joy for woe;
Humble hearts are high exalted,
Human pride and power laid low.

Praise the Lord for times and seasons,
Cloud and sunshine, wind and rain;
Spring to melt the snows of winter
Till the waters flow again;
Grass upon the mountain pastures,
Golden valleys thick with grain.

Fill your hearts with joy and gladness,
Peace and plenty crown your days;
Love His laws, declare His judgements,
Walk in all His words and ways;
He the Lord and we His children –
Praise the Lord, all people, praise!

718

    FIRE, there's a fire,
    Sweet fire burning in my heart.
    (Repeat)

And I will run with all of the passion
You've put in me.
I will spread the seed of the gospel
    everywhere.

And I can feel the power of Your hand upon
    me.
Now I know I'll never be the same again.
For as long as You will give me breath,
My heart is so resolved,
Oh, to lay my life before You, Lord,
Let everything I do be to Your praise.

Let me feel Your tongues of fire resting upon
    me;
Let me hear the sound of
Your mighty rushing wind.
Let my life be like an offering of worship;
Let me be a living sacrifice of praise.

719

5000+ HUNGRY FOLK,
5000+ hungry folk,
5000+ hungry folk
Came 4 2 listen 2 Jesus.

The 6 x 2 said 0 0 0,
The 6 x 2 said 0 0 0,
The 6 x 2 said 0 0 0,
Where can I get some food from?

Just 1 had 1 2 3 4 5,
Just 1 had 1 2 3 4 5,
Just 1 had 1 2 3 4 5,
Loaves and 1 2 fishes.

When Jesus blessed the 5 + 2,
When Jesus blessed the 5 + 2,
When Jesus blessed the 5 + 2,
They were increased many x over.

5000 + 8 it up,
5000 + 8 it up,
5000 + 8 it up,
With 1 2 3 4 5 6 7 8 9 10 11 12 basketfuls left
    over.

720 Ian White.
Copyright © 1988 Little Misty Music/
Kingsway's Thankyou Music.

FOCUS MY EYES on You, O Lord,
Focus my eyes on You;
To worship in spirit and in truth,
Focus my eyes on You.

Turn round my life to You, O Lord,
Turn round my life to You;
To know from this night You've made me
    new,
Turn round my life to You.

Fill up my heart with praise, O Lord,
Fill up my heart with praise;
To speak of Your love in every place,
Fill up my heart with praise.

721 Graham Kendrick.
Copyright © 1994 Make Way Music.

FOR THE JOYS AND FOR THE SORROWS,
The best and worst of times,
For this moment, for tomorrow,
For all that lies behind;
Fears that crowd around me,
For the failure of my plans,
For the dreams of all I hope to be,
The truth of what I am:

> *For this I have Jesus,*
> *For this I have Jesus,*
> *For this I have Jesus,*
> *I have Jesus.*
> *(Repeat)*

For the tears that flow in secret,
In the broken times,
For the moments of elation,
Or the troubled mind;
For all the disappointments,
Or the sting of old regrets,
All my prayers and longings
That seem unanswered yet:

For the weakness of my body,
The burdens of each day,
For the nights of doubt and worry,
When sleep has fled away;
Needing reassurance,
And the will to start again,
A steely-eyed endurance,
The strength to fight and win:

722 Matt Redman.
Copyright © 1994 Kingsway's
Thankyou Music.

FRIEND OF SINNERS, Lord of truth,
I am falling in love with You.
Friend of sinners, Lord of truth,
I have fallen in love with You.

> *Jesus, I love Your name,*
> *The name by which we're saved.*
> *Jesus, I love Your name,*
> *The name by which we're saved.*

Friend of sinners, Lord of truth,
I am giving my life to You.
Friend of sinners, Lord of truth,
I have given my life to You.

723 Wayne Drain.
Copyright © 1996 Kingsway's
Thankyou Music.

FROM EVERY TONGUE, tribe and nation,
Shouted out from all creation,
All the earth sings forth Your praise.
Even the trees clap their hands,
As the people of God take their stand,
Jesus Christ our banner we raise.

> *You're our God, our heart's desire,*
> *Breathe on our lives, release Your power.*
> *Deep in our hearts we already know*
> *That we'll be set free when we give up*
>   *control.*
> *Yeah, we'll be set free when we give up*
>   *control.*

In every circumstance or situation
We give thanks and adoration,
Jesus Christ is worthy of praise.
Whenever our minds give in to fear and
    doubting,
Feeling alone or left out,
We lift our hands and we start to sing.

724 Stuart Townend.
Copyright © 1995 Kingsway's
Thankyou Music.

La la la la la la. (x4)

FROM THE SLEEP OF AGES,
I am stirred by the kiss of love,
By the fragrant perfume
When His name is mentioned.
I have learned to wait for Him,
To receive His presence
With the sound of laughter,
And the joy of resting.
But listen, my Lover
Is coming from heaven's throne!

Over the mountains, leaping the hills,
He runs like a deer through the open plain;
Gazing through windows,
Peering through doors,
My Lover is calling and calling again:
'Rise up, my lovely, beautiful one,
The winter is past and the rains are gone;
Flowers appear all over the earth,
These are the promised days.'
This is the season of singing. (x4)

There is no preferring
In the Lover's loving;
We are all His treasure,
His desired inheritance.
He has come with blessings
From the Father's throne-room;
Gifts of power and healing,
For a needy people.
The wonder, the pleasure
Of knowing, of being known!

725 Chris Cartwright.
Copyright © 1991 Kingsway's
Thankyou Music.

FROM YOUR THRONE, O LORD,
Let Your fire fall upon us;
Let us feel the touch of the Spirit in our hearts,
To equip us and empower us,
Send us out to heal the land,
In Your name to shine the light of Christ.

From the Father's heart
Send us waves of Your compassion;
Move us, Lord, to pray for
Your will to come on earth.
Interceding for a nation
That is dying, lost and blind,
Let us see them with the eyes of Christ.

Lord, we lift one voice
In a song of joy and triumph;
Let Your word rise up from our lips, that in
  our lives
We will let the world know Jesus
Is the Victor and the King,
Let our anthem ring throughout the land.

726 Jim Bailey.
Copyright © 1997 Kingsway's
Thankyou Music.

GIVE ME A HEART OF COMPASSION,
Give me a hope for the lost.
Give me a passion for those
Who are broken and down.
Lord, I am ready and willing
To serve the weak and the young;
Help me to put into action
The words of this song.

And enable Your servants,
Enable Your servants
To preach good news,
To preach good news.
(Repeat)

I'll sing the songs of salvation,
Boldly I'll speak out Your word.
I'll let them know by my life,
I will show You are Lord.
I'll tell them all about Jesus,
I'll tell them all about You;
I'm not ashamed of the gospel
Or what it can do.

We're moving forward together,
As one voice boldly proclaim
The old and the young will be strong,
And we'll lift up Your name
On to the streets to the people,
Every man, woman and child,
And as we go You are with us,
You've given Your power.

You've enabled Your servants...

727 Dave Bilbrough.
Copyright © 1994 Kingsway's
Thankyou Music.

GIVE ME, LORD, A DREAM FROM HEAVEN,
Let me see the things You see;
Give me purpose and direction,
Holy Spirit, move on me.
I would set my face to serve You,
To do the things You'd have me do;
Stir within my heart a vision,
Lord, I will follow You.

By Your Spirit and Your word,
We would hasten Your return.
(Repeat)

Give to me a holy passion,
With every breath I will proclaim
The message of Your kingdom,
The glory of Your name.
Lead me into action,
Let me do the things You say;
Send me to the nations,
When You speak I will obey.

I believe that faith is rising,
I can see a tidal wave
Of Your Spirit that is moving
To end this final age.
There'll be shouts of acclamation
When You come back for Your Bride;
History's consummation
Is here before our eyes.

728 Author unknown.

GIVE ME OIL IN MY LAMP, keep me burning.
Give me oil in my lamp, I pray.
Give me oil in my lamp, keep my burning,
Keep me burning till the break of day.

Sing hosanna, sing hosanna,
Sing hosanna to the King of kings.
Sing hosanna, sing hosanna,
Sing hosanna to the King.

Give me joy in my heart, keep me praising…

Give me peace in my heart, keep me
   resting…

Give me love in my heart, keep me serving…

729 Dave Bilbrough.
Copyright © 1994 Kingsway's
Thankyou Music.

GIVE YOUR THANKS TO THE RISEN SON.
(Leader – all echo)
To the holy and anointed one. *(echo)*
Who fills our hearts with a joyful song. *(echo)*
Jesus. *(echo)*

Turn to Him, don't be afraid,
Give Him honour, give Him praise.
Lift Him up to the highest place.
Jesus.

Worship Him, crown Him King,
And give Him all your heart.
(Repeat)

730 Graham Kendrick & Steve Thompson.
Copyright © 1993 Make Way Music.

GOD IS GREAT, amazing!
Come, let His praises ring.
God is great, astounding!
The whole creation sings.

His clothing is splendour and majesty bright,
For He wraps Himself in a garment of light.
He spreads out the heavens – His palace of
   stars,
And rides on the wings of the wind.

What marvellous wisdom the Maker displays,
The sea vast and spacious, the dolphins and
   whales,
The earth full of creatures, the great and the
   small,
He watches and cares for them all.

The rain forest canopies darken the skies,
Cathedrals of mist that resound with the
   choirs,
Of creatures discordant, outrageous, ablaze
In colourful pageants of praise.

Above His creation the Father presides:
The pulse of the planets, the rhythm of tides,
The moon makes the seasons, the day
   follows night,
Yet He knows every beat of my heart.

Let cannons of thunder salute their acclaim,
The sunsets fly glorious banners of flame,
The angels shout 'holy' again and again
As they soar in the arch of the heavens.

731 Jim Bailey.
Copyright © 1997 Kingsway's
Thankyou Music.

GOD IS RAISING UP AN ARMY
Made of those who are still young.
God is lifting up their voices,
Through the weak He'll shame the strong.
It's been prophesied they will prophesy,
God's salvation they will show;
For the promise is to the children,
To our daughters and our sons.

Children of the cross,
A shining example,
Children of the cross
Are singing His praise.
Children of the cross
Are silencing the enemy,
Children of the cross
Are saying the Lord saves.

732 Author unknown.
Copyright Control.

GOD IS SO GOOD,
God is so good,
God is so good,
He's so good to me.

He took my sin,
He took my sin,
He took my sin,
He's so good to me.

Now I am free,
Now I am free,
Now I am free,
He's so good to me.

God is so good,
He took my sin,
Now I am free,
He's so good to me.

733

(And) **GOD IS SO GOOD.**
(And) God is so good.

He rides upon the wings of the wind,
He is exalted by His name Jah.
He walks in the midst of the stones of fire,
To be His sons is our desire.
For the natural things speak of the invisible.
Look around and see,
Who could deny the wonders of His love?

You reign on high in majesty,
And the widow's heart causes to sing.
You hear the cry of the fatherless,
And the depths of Your love who can
   comprehend?
For the natural things speak of the invisible.
Look around and see,
Who could deny the wonders of His love?

734

GOD OF HEAVEN, with the heart of a lover;
Conquering King, with compassion in His
   voice.
Sovereign Lord, with the care of a mother;
To You we bring our lives, knowing You will
   take us in.

Jesus Christ, You're the Alpha and Omega:
King of kings, who laid aside His crown.
Man of woes, but a Friend to the friendless:
To You we bring our fears, knowing You will
   set us free.

So let's be pure and holy, set apart for
   Jesus;
A covenant people, who reflect the heart
   of God.
With outstretched hands of mercy to the
   broken-hearted,
A covenant people who reveal the love of
   God.

735

GOD, OUR GOD, BLESSES US,
God blesses us,
That all the ends of the earth may fear Him.
(Repeat)

Let all the peoples praise Thee, O God,
Let all the peoples praise Him.

736

GOD SENT HIS SON, they called Him Jesus;
He came to love, heal, and forgive;
He lived and died to buy my pardon,
An empty grave is there to prove my Saviour
   lives.

Because He lives I can face tomorrow;
Because He lives all fear is gone;
Because I know He holds the future,
And life is worth the living
Just because He lives.

How sweet to hold a new-born baby,
And feel the pride and joy he gives;
But greater still the calm assurance,
This child can face uncertain days because
   He lives.

And then one day I'll cross the river;
I'll fight life's final war with pain;
And then as death gives way to victory,
I'll see the lights of glory and I'll know He
   lives.

737

GOD, YOU ARE AN AWESOME GOD,
And Your dominion reaches to the heavens,
And all nations sing Your praise;
As Your people, we declare Your holiness.

Holy, holy, holy is the Lord.
Holy, holy, holy is the Lord.

738

GO FORTH AND TELL! O Church of God,
   awake!
God's saving news to all the nations take:
Proclaim Christ Jesus, Saviour, Lord and
   King,
That all the world His worthy praise may sing.

Go forth and tell! God's love embraces all;
He will in grace respond to all who call:
How shall they call if they have never heard
The gracious invitation of His word?

Go forth and tell where still the darkness lies,
In wealth or want, the sinner surely dies;
Give us, O Lord, concern of heart and mind,
A love like Yours, compassionate and kind.

Go forth and tell! The doors are open wide:
Share God's good gifts – let no one be
  denied;
Live out your life as Christ your Lord shall
  choose,
Your ransomed powers for His sole glory use.

Go forth and tell! O church of God, arise!
Go in the strength which Christ your Lord
  supplies;
God till all nations His great name adore
And serve Him, Lord and King forever more.

739 Graham Kendrick.
Copyright © 1988 Make Way Music.

**GOOD NEWS, GOOD NEWS TO YOU WE
  BRING,**
Alleluia!
News of great joy that angels sing,
Alleluia!

> *Tender mercy He has shown us,*
> *Joy to all the world;*
> *For us God sends His only Son,*
> *Alleluia!*

Let earth's dark shadows fly away,
Alleluia!
In Christ has dawned an endless day,
Alleluia!

Now God with us on earth resides,
Alleluia!
And heaven's door is open wide,
Alleluia!

740 Bryn Haworth.
Copyright © 1991 Kingsway's
Thankyou Music.

GO TO ALL NATIONS, making disciples,
Baptising them in My name.
Go to all nations, making disciples,
Baptising them in My name.

> *I am coming soon.*
> *I am coming soon.*
> *I'm waiting at the gates*
> *For the Father's call.*
> *I am coming soon.*
> *Yes, I am coming soon.*

Teach them to do all I told you to do,
Teach them to walk in My ways.
I have authority in heaven and earth,
I will be with you always.

741 Doug Horley.
Copyright © 1993 Kingsway's
Thankyou Music.

Oh, it's **GREAT, GREAT, BRILL, BRILL,**
Wicked, wicked, skill, skill,
To have a friend like Jesus.
Great, great, brill, brill,
Wicked, wicked, skill, skill,
To have a friend like Him.
(Repeat)

He's always there,
He always listens,
He always hears me when I talk to Him.
He loves me now
And will forever,
I'll choose Him every day, day, day.

742 Noel Richards & Gerald Coates.
Copyright © 1992 Kingsway's
Thankyou Music.

GREAT IS THE DARKNESS that covers the
  earth,
Oppression, injustice and pain.
Nations are slipping in hopeless despair,
Though many have come in Your name.
Watching while sanity dies,
Touched by the madness and lies.

> *Come, Lord Jesus, come, Lord Jesus,*
> *Pour out Your Spirit we pray.*
> *Come, Lord Jesus, come, Lord Jesus,*
> *Pour out Your Spirit on us today.*

May now Your church rise with power and
  love,
This glorious gospel proclaim.
In every nation salvation will come
To those who believe in Your name.
Help us bring light to this world
That we might speed Your return.

Great celebrations on that final day
When out of the heavens You come.
Darkness will vanish, all sorrow will end,
And rulers will bow at Your throne.
Our great commission complete,
Then face to face we shall meet.

743 David & Nathan Fellingham.
Copyright © 1994 Kingsway's
Thankyou Music.

GREAT IS THE LORD;
Sovereign King,
We give You praise.

You spoke Your word and You rescued me,
You poured out Your grace and You set me
    free.
Now You've filled my life with the Spirit's
    power,
And You've set my heart on fire.

And by the power of Jesus' name
You have raised me up from my sin and
    shame.
You've anointed me with the Spirit's power,
And You've set my heart on fire.

By grace I'm saved through faith in God,
Not by works alone but by Jesus' blood.
Now I'm filled with strength by the Spirit's
    power,
And You've set my heart on fire.

Great is the Lord.
(Repeat)

744 Kenoly.
Copyright © 1987 Integrity's Hosanna! Music/
Adm. by Kingsway's Thankyou Music.

HALLELUJAH! JESUS IS ALIVE,
Death has lost its victory
And the grave has been denied;
Jesus lives forever,
He's alive, He's alive!
(Last time)
Hallelujah! Jesus is alive!

He's the Alpha and Omega,
The First and Last is He;
The curse of sin is broken
And we have perfect liberty.
The Lamb of God has risen,
He's alive, He's alive!

745 Doug Horley.
Copyright © 1996 Kingsway's
Thankyou Music.

HANDS, HANDS, FINGERS, THUMBS,
We can lift to praise You.
Hands, hands, fingers, thumbs,
We can lift to praise.
Hands, hands, fingers, thumbs,
We can lift to praise You.
Jump front, jump back, yeah!
We were made to praise.

We've got some hands that we can raise.
We've got a voice to shout Your praise,
    Jesus!
Got some feet a-made to dance;
Let's use them now we've got the chance.
(Repeat)

We were made to praise You,
We were made to praise.
We were made to praise You,
We were made to praise.
(Repeat)

746 Mick Gisbey.
Copyright © 1985 Kingsway's
Thankyou Music.

HAVE YOU GOT AN APPETITE?
Do you eat what is right?
Are you feeding on the word of God?
Are you fat or are you thin?
Are you really full within?
Do you find your strength in Him or are you
    starving?

You and me all should be
Exercising regularly,
Standing strong all day long,
Giving God the glory.
Feeding on the living Bread,
Not eating crumbs but loaves instead;
Standing stronger, living longer,
Giving God the glory.

If it's milk or meat you need,
Why not have a slap-up feed,
And stop looking like a weed and start to
    grow?
Take the full of fitness food,
Taste and see that God is good,
Come on, feed on what you should and be
    healthy.

747 Stuart Garrard.
Copyright © 1995 Curious? Music UK/
Adm. Kingsway's Thankyou Music.

HAVE YOU HEARD THE GOOD NEWS?
Have you heard the good news?
We can live in hope
Because of what the Lord has done.
(Repeat)

There is a way
When there seems to be no way,
There is a light in the darkness:
There is a hope,
An everlasting hope,
There is a God who can help us.

A hope for justice
And a hope for peace,
A hope for those in desperation:
We have a future,
If only we believe
He works in every situation.

748
Matt Redman.
Copyright © 1995 Kingsway's
Thankyou Music.

HAVE YOU NOT SAID as we pass through
   water,
You will be with us?
And You have said as we walk through fire,
We will not be burned.
We are not afraid, for You are with us;
We will testify to the honour of Your name.
We are witnesses, You have shown us
You are the One who can save.

   Fill us up and send us out
   In the power of Your name.
   Fill us up and send us out
   In the power of Your name.

Bring them from the west, sons and
   daughters,
Call them for Your praise.
Gather from the east all Your children,
Coming home again.
Bring them from afar, all the nations,
From the north and south,
Drawing all the peoples in.
Corners of the earth, come to see there's
Only one Saviour and King.

749
Russell Fragar.
Copyright © 1996 Russell Fragar/Hillsongs
Australia/Kingsway's Thankyou Music.

**HEAR THESE PRAISES FROM A GRATEFUL
   HEART,**
Each time I think of You the praises start:
Love You so much, Jesus,
Love You so much.

Lord I love You, my soul sings,
In Your presence, carried on Your wings:
Love You so much, Jesus,
Love You so much.

   How my soul longs for You,
   Longs to worship You forever
   In Your power and majesty.
   Lift my hands, lift my heart,
   Lift my voice towards the heavens,
   For You are my sun and shield.

750
Kevin Prosch.
Copyright © 1991 Mercy/Vineyard Publishing/
Adm. by CopyCare.

**HE BROUGHT ME TO HIS BANQUETING
   TABLE,** *(Men-Women echo)*
He brought me to His banqueting table,
   (Men-Women echo)
And His banner over me is love. *(All)*

I am my Belovèd's and He is mine, *(Men-
   Women echo)*
I am my Belovèd's and He is mine, *(Men-
   Women echo)*
And His banner over me is love. *(All)*
Yes, His banner over me is love.

And we can feel the love of God in this place,
We believe Your goodness, we receive Your
   grace.
We delight ourselves at Your table, O God,
You do all things well, just look at our lives.

751
David Fellingham.
Copyright © 1992 Kingsway's
Thankyou Music.

HE HAS BEEN GIVEN a Name above all
   names,
In earth and heaven, let all creation claim
That Jesus Christ is King, and Lord of all.
He is the Victor over satan's reign,
His blood has triumphed over sin and shame,
Jesus Christ is King and Lord of all.

He is the likeness of Jehovah,
Through whom the world was made.
By His word the universe is sustained,
Every power is subject to His name.

The name of Jesus in victory will resound,
In every nation let the good news sound:
Jesus Christ is King, and Lord of all.

752
Steve & Vikki Cook.
Copyright © 1990 Integrity's Hosanna Music!/
People of Destiny Int./Adm. by Kingsway's
Thankyou Music.

**HE HAS CLOTHED US WITH HIS
   RIGHTEOUSNESS,**
Covered us with His great love.
He has showered us with mercy,
And we delight to know the glorious favour,
Wondrous favour of God.

   We rejoice in the grace of God
   Poured upon our lives.
   Loving kindness has come to us
   Because of Jesus Christ.
   We rejoice in the grace of God,
   Our hearts overflow.
   What a joy to know the grace of God!

He's brought us into His family,
Made us heirs with His own Son.
All good things He freely gives us,
And we cannot conceive what God's
   preparing
God's preparing for us.

753

HE HAS RISEN,
He has risen,
He has risen,
Jesus is alive.

When the life flowed from His body,
Seemed like Jesus' mission failed.
But His sacrifice accomplished,
Victory over sin and hell.

In the grave God did not leave Him,
For His body to decay;
Raised to life, the great awakening,
Satan's power He overcame.

If there were no resurrection,
We ourselves could not be raised;
But the Son of God is living,
So our hope is not in vain.

When the Lord rides out of heaven,
Mighty angels at His side,
They will sound the final trumpet,
From the grave we shall arise.

He has given life immortal,
We shall see Him face to face;
Through eternity we'll praise Him,
Christ, the Champion of our faith.

754

HE IS LOVELY, *He is holy,*
Gave supremely, that all men may see.
He is gentle, tender-hearted,
Risen Saviour, He is God.

Master, Maker, Life Creator,
Come and dwell in me,
That my heart may know
Your tender mercy.
Shine through me that all may see
Your love so full and free;
And I'll declare Your praise
Through endless ages.

755

HE IS THE LORD, and He reigns on high:
He is the Lord.
Spoke into the darkness, created the light:
He is the Lord.
Who is like unto Him, never ending in days?
He is the Lord.
And He comes in power when we call on His
  name:
He is the Lord.

Show Your power, O Lord our God.
Show Your power, O Lord our God,
Our God.

Your gospel, O Lord, is the hope for our nation:
You are the Lord.
It's the power of God for our salvation:
You are the Lord.
We ask not for riches, but look to the cross:
You are the Lord.
And for our inheritance give us the lost:
You are the Lord.

Send Your power . . .

756

HE MADE THE EARTH, He made the sky,
He made the moon and the stars,
Jupiter and Mars.
He made the sun for everyone,
Our God made them all.
Our God is powerful, powerful,
Our God is great.
Our God is powerful, powerful,
Our God is great.

He made the fish, He made the birds,
Elephants and worms,
Creeping things that squirm.
Mice so small, giraffes so tall;
Our God made them all.
Our God is wonderful, wonderful,
Our God is great.
Our God is wonderful, wonderful,
Our God is great.

He made the boys, he made the girls,
He made our mums and dads,
To teach us good from bad.
He cares for me, He cares for You;
Our God loves us all.
Our God is beautiful, beautiful,
Our God is great.
Our God is beautiful, beautiful,
Our God is great.

757 Dave Bilbrough.
Copyright © 1996 Kingsway's
Thankyou Music.

HE PICKED ME UP

And He dusted me down,
Put my feet back on solid ground.
He welcomed me home
And He caused me to sing,
I'm in love, I'm in love with the King.

For all my days I'll sing His praise,
I'm so grateful.
Yes, I will give my everything
To the One who sets me free.

Once I was lost, but now I'm found,
Yes, He saved me.
He called my name and my life was changed
By the power of His love.

758 Paul Oakley.
Copyright © 1997 Kingsway's
Thankyou Music.

HERE I AM, and I have come
To thank You, Lord, for all You've done;
Thank You, Lord.
You paid the price at Calvary,
You shed Your blood, You set me free;
Thank You, Lord.
No greater love was ever shown,
No better life ever was laid down.

And I will always love Your name;
And I will always sing Your praise.
(Repeat)

You took my sin, You took my shame,
You drank my cup, You bore my pain;
Thank You, Lord.
You broke the curse, You broke the chains,
In victory from death You rose again;
Thank You, Lord.
And not by works, but by Your grace
You clothe me now in Your righteousness.

You bid me come, You make me whole,
You give me peace, You restore my soul;
Thank You, Lord.
You fill me up, and when I'm full,
You give me more till I overflow;
Thank You, Lord.
You're making me to be like You,
To do the works of the Father, too.

759 Craig Musseau.
Copyright © 1994 Mercy/Vineyard Publishing/
Adm. by CopyCare.

HERE I AM ONCE AGAIN,

I pour out my heart for I know that You hear
Every cry; You are listening,
No matter what state my heart is in.

You are faithful to answer
With words that are true
And a hope that is real.
As I feel Your touch,
You bring a freedom to all that's within.

In the safety of this place
I'm longing to...

Pour out my heart, to say that I love You,
Pour out my heart, to say that I need You.
Pour out my heart, to say that I'm thankful,
Pour out my heart, to say that You're
wonderful.

760 Rick Ridings.
Copyright © 1990 Ariose Music/EMI Christian
Music Publishing/Adm. by CopyCare.

HE REIGNS, *He reigns, Jesus reigns,*
He reigns enthroned in majesty.
Shout your praise, His banners raise,
For Jesus reigns.
Shout hosanna, Jesus reigns.

Our highest praise we bring
To our great eternal King.
His glory fills the skies,
Now from earth let praise arise.

He spoiled the hosts of hell,
And like blazing stars, they fell.
He led them forth in chains—
Now our mighty Victor reigns!

761 Chris Bowater.
Copyright © 1996 Sovereign Lifestyle Music.

HERE IN THE PRESENCE of the

Great and awesome God.
Here in the presence of the Holy One,
The only One.
Knowing not how best to bring adoring love,
To bow, to weep, to fall, and yet
You whisper, 'Child, draw near:

And stand in the presence of the Lord,
Stand in the presence of the Lord,
Stand in the presence of the Holy One,
Stand in the presence of the Lord.'

Here in the presence of the
Great and awesome God,
Majestic in His power yet full of grace:
I seek His face.
The passion in His eyes
Searches deep inside:
Such shining love intensifies,
Yet melts away my fears.

And I stand...

HERE IS BREAD, here is wine,
Christ is with us – He is with us;
Break the bread, drink the wine –
Christ is with us here.

Here is grace, here is peace,
Christ is with us – He is with us;
Know His grace, find His peace –
Feast on Jesus here.

In this bread there is healing,
In this cup there's life forever;
In this moment, by the Spirit
Christ is with us here.

Here we are, joined in one,
Christ is with us – He is with us;
We'll proclaim, till He comes –
Jesus crucified.

HERE IS THE RISEN SON,
Riding out in glory,
Radiating light all around.
Here is the Holy Spirit,
Poured out for the nations,
Glorifying Jesus the Lamb.

We will stand as a people
Who are upright and holy,
We will worship the Lord of hosts.
We will watch, we will wait
On the walls of the city,
We will look and see what He will say to us.

Every knee shall bow before Him,
Every tongue confess
That He is King of kings, Lord of lords,
And Ruler of the earth.

HERE WE ARE, LORD,
More weak than strong;
Still believing, still pressing on.
Make us ready
With hearts that are brave.
We will silence the lies of this age.

For such a moment we have been born.
We're gonna rise up,
Take this world by storm.
Let evil tremble,
We come in His name.
Our God is with us,
We're dangerous people.

All God's heroes failed as we do,
Sometimes doubting all that is true.
Yet He calls us great people of faith,
Working through us as history is made.

HERE WE STAND IN TOTAL SURRENDER,
Lifting our voices, abandoned to Your cause.
Here we stand, praying in the glory
Of the one and only Jesus Christ, the Lord.

This time revival!
Lord, come and heal our land;
Bring to completion
The work that You've begun.
This time revival!
Stir up Your church again,
Pour out Your Spirit
On Your daughters and Your sons.

Here we stand in need of Your mercy;
Father, forgive us for the time that we have
    lost.
Once again make us an army
To conquer this nation with the message of
    the cross.

HIS LOVE is higher than the highest of
    mountains.
His love goes deeper that the deepest of
    seas.
His love, it stretches to the farthest horizon,
And His love, it reaches to me.

His love is stronger than the angels and
  demons.
His love, it keeps me in my life's darkest hour.
His love secures me on the pathway to
  heaven,
And His love is my strength and power.

His love is sweeter than the sweetest of
  honey.
His love is better than the choicest of wine.
His love, it satisfies the deepest of hunger,
And His love, in Jesus it's mine.

Your love is higher…

767

HOLD ME CLOSER TO YOU EACH DAY;
May my love for You never fade.
Keep my focus on all that's true;
May I never lose sight of You.

In my failure, in my success,
If in sadness or happiness,
Be the hope I am clinging to,
For my heart belongs to You.

You are only a breath away,
Watching over me every day;
In my heart I am filled with peace
When I hear You speak to me.

No one loves me the way You do,
No one cares for me like You do.
Feels like heaven has broken through;
God, You know how I love You.

768

HOLINESS IS YOUR LIFE IN ME,
Making me clean through Your blood.
Holiness is Your fire in me,
Purging my heart like a flood.
I know You are perfect in holiness.
Your life in me, setting me free,
Making me holy.

Only the blood of Jesus covers all of my sin.
Only the life of Jesus renews me from within.
Your blood is enough, Your mercy complete.
Your work of atonement, paid for my debts,
Making me holy.
Only the blood of Jesus.

769

HOLY CHILD, how still You lie!
Safe the manger, soft the hay;
Faint upon the eastern sky
Breaks the dawn of Christmas Day.

Holy Child, whose birthday brings
Shepherds from their field and fold,
Angel choirs and eastern kings,
Myrrh and frankincense and gold:

Holy Child, what gift of grace
From the Father freely willed!
In Your infant form we trace
All God's promises fulfilled.

Holy Child, whose human years
Span like ours delight and pain;
One in human joys and tears,
One in all but sin and stain:

Holy Child, so far from home,
All the lost to seek and save:
To what dreadful death You come,
To what dark and silent grave!

Holy Child, before whose name
Powers of darkness faint and fall;
Conquered death and sin and shame –
Jesus Christ is Lord of all!

Holy Child, how still You lie!
Safe the manger, soft the hay;
Clear upon the eastern sky
Breaks the dawn of Christmas Day.

770

HOLY GHOST,
You wonderful Holy Ghost,
A wind blowing strong,
Blowing from heaven.
(Repeat)

We have decided to go
All the way with our God.
Revival in the land, that's our goal;
As soldiers in His army
We'll fight with heart and soul.

> (Final chorus)
> *Blood and fire,*
> *We call upon blood and fire,*
> *A wind blowing strong,*
> *Blowing from heaven.*
> (Repeat)

771 Nathan Fellingham.
Copyright © 1995 Kingsway's
Thankyou Music.

HOLY, HOLY,
Holy is the Lord God Almighty.
(Repeat)
Who was and is and is to come,
Who was and is and is to come.

Lift up His name with the sound of singing,
Lift up His name in all the earth.
Lift up your voice and give Him glory,
For He is worthy to be praised.

772 Jimmy Owens.
Copyright © 1972 Bud John Songs/EMI
Christian Music Publishing/Adm. by CopyCare.

HOLY, HOLY, HOLY, HOLY,
Holy, holy, Lord God Almighty!
And we lift our hearts before You
As a token of our love:
Holy, holy, holy, holy.

Gracious Father, gracious Father,
We're so glad to be Your children, gracious
        Father;
And we lift our heads before You
As a token of our love,
Gracious Father, gracious Father.

Precious Jesus, precious Jesus,
We're so glad that You've redeemed us,
        precious Jesus;
And we lift our hands before You
As a token of our love,
Precious Jesus, precious Jesus,

Holy Spirit, Holy Spirit,
Come and fill our hearts anew, Holy Spirit.
And we lift our voice before You
As a token of our love,
Holy Spirit, Holy Spirit.

Hallelujah, hallelujah,
Hallelujah, hallelujah –
And we lift our hearts before You
As a token of our love,
Hallelujah, hallelujah.

773 Bryn Haworth.
Copyright © 1991 Kingsway's
Thankyou Music.

HOLY, HOLY, HOLY IS THE LORD.
Holy, holy, holy is the Lord.

        And He is precious in God's sight,
        So precious in His eyes.

Worthy, worthy, worthy is the Lamb.
Worthy, worthy, worthy is the Lamb.

Glory, I give glory to the Lamb of God.
Glory, I give glory to the Lamb of God.

774 Richard Lewis.
Copyright © 1997 Kingsway's
Thankyou Music.

HOLY, HOLY, LORD GOD ALMIGHTY,
Who was and who is
And is to come.
(Repeat)

All the angels cry 'holy,'
All the angels cry 'holy,'
All the angels cry 'holy is Your name.
Holy is Your name.
Holy is Your name.
Holy is Your name.
Holy is Your name.'

775 John Paculabo.
Copyright © 1993 Kingsway's
Thankyou Music.

HOLY IS YOUR NAME,
Yeshua, my Deliverer.
Worthy of all praise,
You everliving God.

Perfect are Your ways,
Jehovah, my Father.
Faithful is Your love,
You gave Yourself for me.

        In You I have security;
        In You I put my trust.
        In You I have confidence,
        You meet my every need.

776 Mick Gisbey.
Copyright © 1993 Kingsway's
Thankyou Music.

HOLY ONE, my life is in Your hand;
My song an offering of my heart,
Redeemed, washed clean,
By faith I stand secure.
In You, Jesus, I live.

        To You the glory, to You the power,
        To You the honour forever more.
        Your love brings healing,
        Your love's eternal,
        Your love's the answer,
        The hope of the world,
        The hope of the world.

777
Charlotte Exon.
Copyright © 1991 Kingsway's
Thankyou Music.

HOLY SPIRIT, MOVE WITHIN ME,
Holy Spirit, come upon me now.
Holy Spirit, lead me to
The secret place of prayer,
Manifest the glory of God.
Holy Spirit, You are welcome,
Holy Spirit, we desire You.
Holy Spirit, worship through us,
Let us see the glory of God.

778
Robert Newey.
Copyright © 1994 Kingsway's
Thankyou Music.

HOPE OF THE WORLD,
You stepped into our time,
And yet they spurned You and then turned
  away.
To a dying world You reached out,
But they didn't want to hear
The words You had to say.

  But may the light
  You came to bring now shine
  In a world that finally lost its way.
  Holy love, now come,
  Come flow though me,
  Be my theme until my dying day.

Mercy, love, truth,
You shared all these
And then to bring them life
Became a dying seed.
Now to all who will receive
A new way has been opened,
And Your children are the light they need.

  And may the light...

779
Graham Kendrick & Steve Thompson.
Copyright © 1991 Make Way Music.

HOW CAN I BE FREE FROM SIN?
Lead me to the cross of Jesus.
From the guilt, the power, the pain?
Lead me to the cross of Jesus.
There's no other way,
No price that I could pay;
Simply to the cross I cling.
This is all I need,
This is all I plead,
That His blood was shed for me.

How can I know peace within?
Lead me to the cross of Jesus.
Sing a song of joy again!
Lead me to the cross of Jesus.
Flowing from above,
All-forgiving love
From the Father's heart to me!
What a gift of grace –
His own righteousness
Clothing me in purity!

How can I live day by day?
Lead me to the cross of Jesus.
Following His narrow way?
Lead me to the cross of Jesus.

780
Stuart Townend.
Copyright © 1995 Kingsway's
Thankyou Music.

HOW DEEP THE FATHER'S LOVE FOR US,
How vast beyond all measure,
That He should give His only Son
To make a wretch His treasure.
How great the pain of searing loss –
The Father turns His face away,
As wounds which mar the Chosen One
Bring many sons to glory.

Behold the man upon a cross,
My sin upon His shoulders;
Ashamed, I hear my mocking voice
Call out among the scoffers.
It was my sin that held Him there
Until it was accomplished;
His dying breath has brought me life –
I know that it is finished.

I will not boast in anything,
No gifts, no power, no wisdom;
But I will boast in Jesus Christ,
His death and resurrection.
Why should I gain from His reward?
I cannot give an answer;
But this I know with all my heart –
His wounds have paid my ransom.

781
Matt Redman.
Copyright © 1995 Kingsway's
Thankyou Music.

HOW LOVELY IS YOUR DWELLING PLACE,
O Lord Almighty.
My soul longs and even faints for You.
For here my heart is satisfied,
Within Your presence.
I sing beneath the shadow of Your wings.

Better is one day in Your courts,
Better is one day in Your house,
Better is one day in Your courts
Than thousands elsewhere.
(Repeat)

One thing I ask and I would seek;
To see Your beauty,
To find You in the place Your glory dwells.

My heart and flesh cry out
For You, the living God;
Your Spirit's water for my soul.
I've tasted and I've seen,
Come once again to me;
I will draw near to You,
I will draw near to You.

782 John Newton.

HOW SWEET THE NAME OF JESUS SOUNDS
In a believer's ear;
It soothes his sorrows, heals his wounds,
And drives away his fear.
It makes the wounded spirit whole,
And calms the troubled breast;
'Tis manna to the hungry soul
And to the weary, rest,
And to the weary, rest.

Dear name, the Rock on which I build,
My shield, and hiding place;
My never failing treasury, filled
With boundless stores of grace.
Jesus, my Shepherd, Saviour, Friend,
My Prophet, Priest, and King;
My Lord, my Life, my Way, my End,
Accept the praise I bring,
Accept the praise I bring.

Weak is the effort of my heart,
And cold my warmest thought;
But when I see You as You are,
I'll praise You as I ought.
I would Your boundless love proclaim
With every fleeting breath;
So shall the music of Your name
Refresh my soul in death,
Refresh my soul in death.

783 Dave Bilbrough.
Copyright © 1994 Kingsway's
Thankyou Music.

HOW WONDERFUL, how glorious
Is the love of God,
Bringing healing, forgiveness,
Wonderful love.

Let celebration echo through this land;
We bring reconciliation,
We bring hope to every man:

We proclaim the kingdom
Of our God is here;
Come and join the heavenly anthem,
Ringing loud and ringing clear:

Listen to the music
As His praises fill the air;
With joy and with gladness
Tell the people everywhere:

784 Dave Bilbrough.
Copyright © 1997 Kingsway's
Thankyou Music.

HUMBLE YOURSELVES
Under God's mighty hand,
So that He will lift you up.
(Repeat)

Cast all anxiety
On Him,
Because He cares for You.

Open your hearts
To the Lord your God,
And know His love for you.
(Repeat)

Cast all anxiety
On Him,
Because He cares for You.

I bow down
Before You, my Lord.
(Repeat)

785 Jim Bailey.
Copyright © 1996 Kingsway's
Thankyou Music.

I AM THE APPLE OF GOD'S EYE,
His BANANA over me is love.
He ORANGES His angels to look after me,
As His blessings PLUM-met from above.

Never have to play the GOOSEBERRY,
Feel like a LEMON, no not me.
For wherever this MAN-GOES,
A RASPBERRY it never blows.

The GREAT FRUIT of God,
The GREAT FRUIT of God,
The GREAT FRUIT of God it overflows.
(Repeat)

I will praise Him on the TANGERINE,
Praise Him on the MANDARIN;
SATSUMA or later you will see
There is always a CLEMENTINE
    for praising Him.

786 David Gate.
Copyright © 1997 Kingsway's
Thankyou Music.

I AM YOURS
And You are mine,
Friend to me
For all of time.

And all I have now
I give to You.
And all I want now
Is to be pure, pure like You.

I'm not afraid
Of earthly things,
For I am safe
With You, my King.

787 Wayne Drain.
Copyright © 1996 Kingsway's
Thankyou Music.

I BELIEVE IN GOD THE FATHER,
I believe in Jesus the Son:
I believe in God the Holy Spirit,
I believe in the Three in One.

I believe He was born of a virgin,
Was crucified and buried in the ground.
Descended into hell and won the battle,
But the devil, death and hell
Couldn't hold Him down.

O Lord, we're drowning in confusion,
So many of us going separate ways;
Wanting to be God is our delusion,
But some of us are standing up,
Not ashamed to say, I believe, I believe!

I believe He ascended into heaven,
Where He sits at God's right hand;
And I believe our King will be returning
To judge the living and the dead,
From every tribe and land.

788 Dave Bilbrough.
Copyright © 1991 Kingsway's
Thankyou Music.

I BELIEVE THERE IS A GOD IN HEAVEN
Who paid the price for all my sin;
Shed His blood to open up the way
For me to walk with Him.

Gave His life upon a cross,
Took the punishment for us,
Offered up Himself in love,
Jesus, Jesus.

'It is finished' was His cry;
Not even death could now deny
The Son of God exalted high,
Jesus, Jesus,
Jesus.

789 David Fellingham.
Copyright © 1992 Kingsway's
Thankyou Music.

I BOW DOWN in humble adoration,
Speak Your name with love and devotion,
Jesus, the Lamb sacrificed for me.
I see Your face, Your tender hands
Scarred for me.
I fall at Your feet with songs of praises
    singing;
My joy is complete, You fulfil my longing.
Prophet of God, my Priest and my King,
I worship and adore.

Before the Father's throne You ever intercede;
You always hear my prayer, whatever I may
    plead.
You wipe away my tears, You give me
    victory;
By Your blood I am cleansed, I am free.

790 Martin Smith.
Copyright © 1994 Curious? Music UK/Adm.
by Kingsway's Thankyou Music.

(Oh) **I COULD SING UNENDING SONGS**
Of how You saved my soul.
Well, I could dance a thousand miles
Because of Your great love.

My heart is bursting, Lord,
To tell of all You've done,
Of how You changed my life
And wiped away the past.
I wanna shout it out,
From every rooftop sing,
For now I know that God is for me,
Not against me.

Everybody's singing now,
'Cause we're so happy!
Everybody's dancing now,
'Cause we're so happy!
If only we could see Your face,
And see You smiling over us,
And unseen angels celebrate,
For joy is in this place!

791
Craig Musseau.
Copyright © 1990 Mercy/Vineyard Publishing/
Adm. by CopyCare.

I CRY OUT
For your hand of mercy to heal me.
I am weak,
I need Your love to free me.
O Lord, my Rock,
My strength in weakness,
Come rescue me, O Lord.

You are my hope,
Your promise never fails me.
And my desire
Is to follow You forever.
For You are good,
For You are good,
For You are good to me.
For You are good,
For You are good,
For You are good to me.

792
Ian Smale.
Copyright © 1996 Kingsway's
Thankyou Music.

I DON'T WANT TO BE A PHARISEE
Or anyone like that.
It's stupid swallowing camels
Whilst straining out a gnat.
To keep the letter of the law,
They forgot the people it was for.
So I don't want to be a Pharisee,
I don't want to be a Pharisee,
I don't want to be a Pharisee
Or anyone like that.

793
Matt Redman.
Copyright © 1996 Kingsway's
Thankyou Music.

I DREAM of tongues of fire
Resting on Your people,
I dream of all the miracles to come.
I hope to see the coming
Healing of the nations,
I long to see the prodigals return.
So many hopes and longings in You;
When will all the dreams come true?

I'm a believer in Your kingdom,
I am a seeker of the new things,
I am a dreamer with some old dreams,
Let them now come.

I hope to see You come down,
Rend the mighty heavens,
And let Your glory cover all the earth;
To see Your sons and daughters
Come to know and love You,
And find a purer passion in the church.
These are the things my heart will pursue:
When will all the dreams come true?

May Your church now reach out,
Sowing truth and justice,
Learn to love the poor and help the weak.
When Your kingdom's coming
It will touch the broken,
Place the lonely in a family.
So many hopes and longings in You:
When will all the dreams come true?

794
Graham Kendrick.
Copyright © 1987 Make Way Music.

IF MY PEOPLE, who bear My name,
Will humble themselves and pray;
If they seek My presence
And turn their backs on their wicked ways:
Then I will hear from heaven,
I'll hear from heaven and will forgive;
I will forgive their sins
And will heal their land,
Yes, I will heal their land.

795
Tommy Walker.
Copyright © 1996 WeMobile Music/Doulos
Publishing/Adm. by CopyCare.

I HAVE A MAKER,
He formed my heart;
Before even time began
My life was in His hand.

I have a Father,
He calls me His own;
He'll never leave me,
No matter where I go.

He knows my name,
He knows my every thought;
He sees each tear that falls,
And hears me when I call.

796
Matt Redman.
Copyright © 1995 Kingsway's
Thankyou Music.

I HAVE COME TO LOVE YOU,
I have come to love You today.
(Repeat)

And today and forever more
I'll love Your name.
And today and forever more
I'll love Your name.

I have come to worship,
I have come to worship today.
(Repeat)

I have come to thank You,
I have come to thank You today.
(Repeat)

797 Stuart Townend.
Copyright © 1997 Kingsway's
Thankyou Music.

I HAVE HEARD that You are swift to bless the
seeker,
And I believe that You will hear the constant
cry;
So I will call until I know I've had an
answer,
I need Your power, Lord!
As Jacob wrestled, so I'll wrestle with Your
angel,
And though I'm weary, I will not be
overcome;
For You have given me a passion for Your
kingdom,
O let Your glory fall!

I won't let go,
I won't let go until You bless me.
I won't take no for an answer;
Jesus, I won't let go!

I have heard that You show mercy to a
nation,
And I believe that You give power to Your
church;
So now I'm asking You to open up the
heavens,
Pour out Your mercy, Lord!
For Your gospel to be lived among Your
people,
For Your miracle of healing on the streets;
For the government to fear the Lord
Almighty,
We need Your power, Lord!

I'm not ungrateful for the blessings You have
given,
But I can see the need around me;
I'm not ashamed to say I need all that You
have,
So Father, hear me knocking,
See me holding out my hands to You.

For a hunger that will overcome my
weakness,
For a love that will not seek its own reward;
For my life to make a difference in this nation,
I need Your power, Lord!

798 Kent Henry.
Copyright © 1993 Integrity's Hosanna! Music/
Adm. by Kingsway's Thankyou Music.

(And) **I HAVE LOVED YOU** *with an*
everlasting love,
And I have drawn you with My loving
kindness.
And I have loved you with an everlasting
love,
And I have drawn you with My loving
kindness.

Because God loved you and to keep His own,
He brought you out with a mighty hand,
He redeemed you from the devil's yoke.
Oh, the Lord, He is the God
And faithful is He.
He'll keep His word and His covenant,
Giving mercy and prosperity.

And casting all of Your cares on Him
For He cares for you,
There's a love dimension
In the kingdom of God,
It's sure to take you through.
God commanded His love toward us,
Christ died on a tree,
Then He rose again, the living God,
More than conquerors now are we.

799 Lynn DeShazo.
Copyright © 1992 Integrity's Hosanna! Music/
Adm. by Kingsway's Thankyou Music.

**I HAVE MADE YOU TOO SMALL IN MY
EYES;**
O Lord, forgive me.
And I have believed in a lie
That You were unable to heal me.
But now, O Lord, I see my wrong;
Heal my heart, and show Yourself strong.
And in my eyes and with my song,
O Lord, be magnified,
O Lord, be magnified.

Be magnified, O Lord;
You are highly exalted.
And there is nothing You can't do,
O Lord, my eyes are on You,
Be magnified,
O Lord, be magnified.

I have leaned on the wisdom of men;
O God, forgive me.
And I have responded to them
Instead of Your light and Your mercy.
But now, O Lord, I see my wrong;
Heal my heart and show Yourself strong.
And in my eyes and with my song,
O Lord, be magnified,
O Lord, be magnified.

800 Don Moen.
Copyright © 1989 Integrity's Hosanna! Music/
Adm. by Kingsway's Thankyou Music.

I JUST WANT TO BE WHERE YOU ARE,
Dwelling daily in Your presence.
I don't want to worship from afar,
Draw me near to where You are.
I just want to be where You are,
In Your dwelling place forever.
Take me to the place where You are,
I just want to be with You.

> *I want to be where You are,*
> *Dwelling in You presence,*
> *Feasting at Your table,*
> *Surrounded by Your glory.*
> *In Your presence,*
> *That's where I always want to be,*
> *I just want to be,*
> *I just want to be with You.*

O my God, You are my strength and my
    song,
And when I'm in Your presence,
Though I'm weak, You're always strong.

801 Nathan Fellingham.
Copyright © 1997 Kingsway's
Thankyou Music.

I KNOW A PLACE
Where blessings from heaven are poured,
Mercy and grace abounding.
Through Jesus' blood
We have now been set free
Into the Father's loving.

I know a place
Where there is no guilt or fear,
As I come into His presence.
I can now know
A peace which surpasses all,
Nothing shall separate us.

> *And I will trust in You alone,*
> *My refuge and strength.*
> *For all the trials that come my way,*
> *Your grace is sufficient for me.*

I know a place
Where a wonderful river flows,
That fills me with His glory;
Bringing us life,
We're stirred to adore Him,
A perfect joy everlasting.

802 Randy & Terry Butler.
Copyright © 1993 Mercy/Vineyard Publishing/
Adm. by CopyCare.

I KNOW A PLACE, A WONDERFUL PLACE,
Where accused and condemned
Find mercy and grace.
Where the wrongs we have done,
And the wrongs done to us
Were nailed there with Him (You)
There on the cross.

(Men)   At the cross,
(Women)   At the cross,
(All)   He (You) died for my sin.
(Men)   At the cross,
(Women)   At the cross,
(All)   He (You) gave us life again.

803 Matt Redman.
Copyright © 1996 Kingsway's
Thankyou Music.

**I KNOW YOU LOVE TO CROWN THE
    HUMBLE,**
Pouring out grace for the broken heart.
You bless the meek, You meet the lowly;
Lord, as I bow, lift me to You.

> *I keep on bowing down, bowing down,*
> *Keep on bowing down,*
> *What else can I do?*
> *Keep on bowing down, bowing down.*
> *What else can I do,*
> *To give it all to You?*

I'd like to be one such believer,
Keeping my knees firmly on the ground.
I'd like to tread humbly before You;
Lord, as I bow, lift me to You.

Do You smile when You see
A humble believer on their knees?
And my Lord, will You be pleased
To look upon me, to look upon me?

804

I LIFT MY EYES TO THE QUIET HILLS,
In the press of a busy day;
As green hills stand in a dusty land,
So God is my strength and stay.

I lift my eyes to the quiet hills,
To a calm that is mine to share;
Secure and still in the Father's will,
And kept by the Father's care.

I lift my eyes to the quiet hills,
With a prayer as I turn to sleep;
By day, by night,
Through the dark and light,
My Shepherd will guard His sheep.

I lift my eyes to the quiet hills,
And my heart to the Father's throne;
In all my ways to the end of days,
The Lord will preserve His own.

805

I LONG FOR YOU, O LORD.
I long to know You more;
I long to have Your heart placed in me every
day.
I long for, I long for You, O Lord.

I hunger to eat the bread
Only You can give.
I'm thirsting to drink Your water
That I might live,
To grow in You,
To know in You
My every desire is found.

806

I LOVE THE LORD for He has heard me,
He has heard my mercy plea.
From deep within my troubled heart,
I cried 'O Lord, save me!'
I love the Lord for His compassion
And His gracious, righteous ways.
He protects the simple-hearted ones,
And in my need,
The Lord saw me, and saved.

For as long, for as long as I live,
I will call, I will call on His name.
Be at rest once more, my soul,
For the Lord is good,
And He has been good to you.

I love the Lord for all the goodness
That I never can repay,
But I lift the cup of salvation,
And call upon His name.
I will fulfil my vows before the Lord,
In the presence of His saints;
O, make me now Your servant, Lord,
You have freed me from,
You have freed me from these chains.

807

I LOVE YOU, LORD, MY STRENGTH,
For You heard my cry.
You have been my help in trouble.
I've put my trust in You,
My refuge and my hope,
You're the Rock on which I stand.

You're my stronghold,
You're my stronghold,
You're the stronghold of my life.
You're my stronghold,
You're my stronghold,
You're the stronghold of my life.

I love You, Lord, my strength,
You reached down from on high,
And You rescued me from trouble.
You've taken hold of me,
And set me on a rock,
And now this is where I stand.

I love You, Lord, my strength,
There is no other rock,
And now I will not be shaken.
The sea may roar and crash,
The mountains quake and fall,
Ah, but on this Rock I stand.

808

I'M A FRIEND OF JESUS CHRIST, *(echo)*
He's God's Son and He's alive, *(echo)*
I will trust in Him it's true, *(echo)*
He's always there to see me through.*(echo)*

Sound off, *Jesus!*
Sound off, is *Lord!*
Sound off, *Jesus!*
Sound off, is *Lord!*

The gift of God is eternal life through Jesus
Christ,
(Repeat x3)
Through Jesus, Jesus Christ.

Jesus is the Boss of my life,
He's the only one can make it come right.
Jesus is the Boss of my life,
Jesus is the Boss.

(Rap)
I said, come on everybody and move your
    feet;
The rhythm is hot, it's a powerful beat.
The time is right to do some business,
Get on your feet and be a witness
To the Holy One,
The King of kings, God's only Son;
Jesus Christ, that's His name,
He died to take our sin and shame.

809 Ian Smale.
Copyright © 1982 Kingsway's
Thankyou Music.

I'M LOOKING UP TO JESUS,
His face is shining beauty.
I'm feeling so unworthy,
Yet His Spirit leads me on.
I'm looking up to Jesus,
His radiance surrounds me.
I feel so pure and clean,
A taste of heaven on earth.

(Last time)
I'm looking up to Jesus.

810 Kevin Prosch.
Copyright © 1992 7th Time Music/Kingsway's
Thankyou Music.

I'M STANDING HERE TO TESTIFY, *(Leader)*
O, the Lord is good. *(All)*
To sing of how He changed my heart.
    (Leader)
O, the Lord is good. *(All)*
I was bound by hate and pride, *(Leader)*
O, the Lord is good. *(All)*
Never knowing of His light. *(Leader)*
O, the Lord is good. *(All)*

I did not think I could have peace, *(Leader)*
O, the Lord is good. *(All)*
Trapped inside by fear and shame. *(Leader)*
O, the Lord is good. *(All)*
He wiped away all of my grief, *(Leader)*
O, the Lord is good. *(All)*
When I believed upon His name. *(Leader)*

> *Come to the light, come as you are;*
> *You can be the friend of God.*
> *Humble yourself, give Him your heart,*
> *He will meet you where you are.*

(Last chorus)
Come to the light, just as you are;
Fall on the Rock for the wasted years.
He will restore all that was lost,
Surrender now, His power is here.

Clap Your hands, O God.
Clap Your hands, O God.
(Repeat)

811 Chris Bowater.
Copyright © 1995 Sovereign Lifestyle Music.

I NEED YOU like dew in the desert,
Like refreshing summer rain,
Come and pour Your love again on me.
I'm finding that every time I come
And ask for something more,
You never fail to pour Your love on me.

And peace like a river flows,
Waves of mercy ever roll;
Take me deeper,
I want to know You more.
Pour Your love, pour Your love,
Pour Your love on me.

812 David Fellingham.
Copyright © 1994 Kingsway's
Thankyou Music.

IN EVERY CIRCUMSTANCE of life
You are with me, glorious Father.
And I have put my trust in You,
That I may know the glorious hope
To which I'm called.
And by the power that works in me,
You've raised me up and set me free;
And now in every circumstance
I'll prove Your love without a doubt,
Your joy shall be my strength,
Your joy shall be my strength.

813 Jacques Berthier/Taizé.
Copyright © 1995 Ateliers et Presses de Taizé.

IN GOD ALONE my soul can find rest and
    peace,
In God my peace and joy.
Only in God my soul can find its rest,
Find its rest and peace.

Mon âme se repose en paix sur Dieu seul:
De lui vient mon salut.
Oui, sur Dieu seul mon âme se repose,
Se repose en paix.

814
Geoff Bullock.
Copyright © 1997 Watershed Productions/
Kingsway's Thankyou Music.

IN MY LIFE PROCLAIM YOUR GLORY,
In my heart reveal Your majesty;
Then my soul shall speak the wonders of
Your grace,
And this heart of mine shall sing Your praise.
In my words proclaim Your mercy,
In my life reveal Your power;
Then my soul shall be a mirror of Your love,
And this heart of mine shall sing Your praise.

Lord of all mercy, God of all grace,
Lord of all righteousness;
Lord of the heavens, Lord of the earth
Enthroned in majesty.
Worthy of honour, worthy of praise,
All glory and majesty;
I give You the honour, I give You the praise,
And proclaim Your glorious power.

In my soul unveil Your love, Lord,
Deep within my heart renewing me.
Day by day your life transforming all I am,
As this heart of mine reflects Your praise.
Lord of all, enthroned in glory,
Grace and mercy, truth and righteousness,
Every knee shall bow before this Christ, our Lord,
As all creation sings Your praise.

815
John Pantry.
Copyright © 1990 Kingsway's
Thankyou Music.

IN MYSTERY REIGNING, King over all,
Hear angels proclaiming, Jesus is Lord.
To each generation Your love is the same;
Wonderful Saviour, we worship Your name.

A beauty that's timeless, who can compare?
All earth stands in silence, when You appear.
Your kingdom is boundless, Your love
without end;
Wonder of wonders, this King is my friend!

All power has been given into Your hands;
Through blood and by suffering You now
command.
And no opposition can stand in Your light;
Crowned King of heaven, we kneel at the sight.

816
Wayne Drain.
Copyright © 1996 Kingsway's
Thankyou Music.

IN MY WEAKNESS You are strong,
When I fall short You carry me along.
Into my darkness You shine Your light,
When I feel blinded, You restore my sight.

You are the Lord, You never change,
You still the storm when I call Your name.
You're all I want, You're always there,
No matter when, no matter where.
You're the Lord, You never change.
You're the Lord, You never change.

I'm inconsistent, but You are true;
I don't trust myself, but I depend on You.
Look through my selfishness, and see my
heart;
Bring out the precious from the worthless
parts.

I need courage, Lord, to make a change;
It's time my independence got rearranged.
I'm tired of chasing after my own ways;
So I'll serve You, Lord,
Serve You, Lord, serve You, Lord,
For the rest, rest of my days.

817
Jacques Berthier/Taizé.
Copyright © Ateliers et Presses de Taize.

IN THE LORD I'll be ever thankful,
In the Lord I will rejoice!
Look to God, do not be afraid;
Lift up your voices, the Lord is near,
Lift up your voices, the Lord is near.

El Senyor és la meva força,
El Senyor el meu cant.
Ell m'haestat la salvació
En ell confio, i no tinc por.
En ell confio, i no tinc por.

818
Author unknown.

IN THE NAME OF JESUS,
In the name of Jesus,
We have the victory.
In the name of Jesus,
In the name of Jesus,
Demons will have to flee.
Who can tell what God can do?
Who can tell of His love for you?
In the name of Jesus, Jesus,
We have the victory.

819
Sue Rinaldi & Steve Bassett.
Copyright © 1994 Kingsway's
Thankyou Music.

IN THESE DAYS OF DARKNESS,
Who will bear the light?
In all of this confusion,
Who will rage against the night?
And who will light a beacon
In the face of this dark, dark sky?

Where there is oppression,
Who will raise the flame?
For the sake of all the children,
Who will touch the fields of shame?
And who will light a beacon
In the face of this dark, dark sky,
With a hope that is eternal,
With a love that will never die?

Oh I, I will carry the fire.
Oh I, I will carry the fire.

Who will burn with passion,
Blazing from the heart,
To forge a new tomorrow?
We must tell the world
Of a hope that is eternal,
Of a love that will never die.
And we will light a beacon
In the face of this dark, dark sky.

Oh I, I will carry the fire.
Oh I, I will carry the fire.
I will not rest, I will not tire,
With all my strength I'll carry the fire.
I will not rest, I will not tire,
With all my strength I'll carry the fire.

820 David Fellingham.
Copyright © 1996 Kingsway's
Thankyou Music.

IN THESE DAYS OF REFRESHING,
In these days of visitation,
There is a reason why You've come.
We have tasted of Your fulness,
One blessing after another,
And that is the reason we say 'come'.

It's not just to make us laugh or cry,
To shake or fall, but to glorify
Jesus, Jesus, Jesus,
And that is the reason we say 'come'.

And let me know the power to speak
And witness for the gospel,
Let me know the power to pray for the sick
And see them healed.
Let me know the faith that can
Move the mighty mountain,
Let me know the love that joins me
To Your people.

And we say more, Lord,
More of Your power.
We say more, Lord,
More of Your power.
We say more, Lord,
More of Your power,
More of Your power in me.

821 Maggi Dawn.
Copyright © 1993 Kingsway's
Thankyou Music.

INTO THE DARKNESS of this world,
Into the shadows of the night;
Into this loveless place You came,
Lightened our burdens, eased our pain,
And made these hearts Your home.
Into the darkness once again –
Oh come, Lord Jesus, come.

Come with Your love
To make us whole,
Come with Your light
To lead us on,
Driving the darkness
Far from our souls:
O come, Lord Jesus, come.

Into the longing of our souls,
Into these heavy hearts of stone,
Shine on us now Your piercing light,
Order our lives and souls aright,
By grace and love unknown,
Until in You our hearts unite –
Oh come, Lord Jesus, come.

O Holy Child, Emmanuel,
Hope of the ages, God with us,
Visit again this broken place,
Till all the earth declares Your praise
And Your great mercies own.
Now let Your love be born in us,
O come, Lord Jesus, come.

(Last Chorus)
Come in Your glory,
Take Your place,
Jesus, the Name above all names,
We long to see You face to face,
O come, Lord Jesus, come.

822 Ian Smale.
Copyright © 1994 Kingsway's
Thankyou Music.

I ONCE WAS FRIGHTENED OF SPIDERS,
I once was frightened of the dark;
I once was frightened of many, many
    things,
Especially things that barked.
But now I'm asking Jesus
To help these fears to go,
'Cause I don't want them to be part of me,
No, no, no, no, no.

I once was frightened by thunder,
And frightened by lightning too;
I once was frightened by many, many things
That crashed and banged and blew.
But now I'm asking Jesus
To help these fears to go,
'Cause I don't want them to be part of me,
No, no, no, no, no.

823 Graham Kendrick.
Copyright © 1994 Make Way Music.

IS ANYONE THIRSTY, anyone?
Is anyone thirsty?
Is anyone thirsty, anyone?
Is anyone thirsty? Jesus said:
'Let them come to me and drink,
Let them come to me.'

O, let the living waters flow,
O, let the living waters flow,
Let the river of Your Spirit
Flow through me.
(Repeat)
Flow through me.

Let the living waters flow.
Let the living waters flow.
Let the living waters flow.
Let the living waters flow.

824 Chris Falson.
Copyright © 1993 Chris Falson Music/
Maranatha! Music/Adm. by CopyCare.

I SEE THE LORD
Seated on the throne, exalted:
And the train of His robe
Fills the temple with glory:
The whole earth is filled,
The whole earth is filled,
The whole earth is filled
With Your glory.

Holy, holy,
Holy, holy,
Yes, holy is the Lord.
Holy, holy,
Holy, holy,
Yes, holy is the Lord of lords.

825 Craig Musseau.
Copyright © 1991 Mercy/Vineyard Publishing/
Adm. by CopyCare.

I SING A SIMPLE SONG OF LOVE
To my Saviour, to my Jesus.
I'm grateful for the things You've done,
My loving Saviour, oh precious Jesus.
My heart is glad that You've called me Your own;
There's no place I'd rather be,

(Than) in Your arms of love,
In Your arms of love,
Holding me still,
Holding me near
In Your arms of love.

826 Terry MacAlmon.
Copyright © 1989 Integrity's Hosanna! Music/
Adm. by Kingsway's Thankyou Music.

I SING PRAISES TO YOUR NAME, O Lord,
Praises to Your name, O Lord,
For Your name is great and greatly to be
    praised.
I sing praises to Your name, O Lord,
Praises to Your name, O Lord,
For Your name is great and greatly to be
    praised.

I give glory to Your name...

827 Martin Smith.
Copyright © 1996 Curious? Music UK/Adm. by
Kingsway's Thankyou Music.

IS IT TRUE TODAY that when people pray,
Cloudless skies will break,
Kings and queens will shake?
Yes it's true, and I believe it,
I'm living for You.

Well it's true today that when people pray
We'll see dead men rise,
And the blind set free?
Yes it's true and I believe it,
I'm living for You.

I'm gonna be a history maker in this land.
I'm gonna be a speaker of truth
To all mankind.
I'm gonna stand,
I'm gonna run into Your arms,
Into Your arms again,
Into Your arms, into Your arms again.

Well it's true today that when people stand
With the fire of God and the truth in hand,
We'll see miracles, we'll see angels sing,
We'll see broken hearts making history?
Yes it's true, and I believe it,
I'm living for You.

828

I STAND AMAZED when I realise
Your love for me is beyond all measure.
Lord, I can't deny
Your love for me is great.

It's as high, high as the heavens above,
Such is the depth of Your love
Toward those who fear You.
O Lord, far as the east is from west,
You have removed my transgressions.
You make my life brand new:
Father, I love You.

Your love is higher,
High as the heavens.
Your love is deeper,
Deeper than the deepest ocean.
Your love is stronger,
Stronger than the powers of darkness.
Your love is sweeter,
Sweeter than wine.

829

I STAND AMAZED IN THE PRESENCE
Of Jesus the Nazarene,
And wonder how He could love me,
A sinner, condemned, unclean.

How marvellous! How wonderful!
And my song shall ever be:
How marvellous! How wonderful!
Is my Saviour's love for me!

For me it was in the garden He prayed,
'Not My will, but Thine':
He had no tears for His own griefs,
But sweat drops of blood for mine.

In pity angels beheld Him,
And came from the world of light
To comfort Him in the sorrows
He bore for my soul that night.

He took my sins and my sorrows,
He made them His very own;
He bore the burden of Calvary,
And suffered and died alone.

When with the ransomed in glory
His face I at last shall see,
'Twill be my joy through the ages
To sing of His love for me.

830

I, THE LORD OF SEA AND SKY,
I have heard My people cry;
All who dwell in dark and sin
My hand will save.
I, who made the stars of night,
I will make their darkness bright.
I will speak My word to them.
Whom shall I send?

Here I am, Lord.
Is it I, Lord?
I have heard You calling in the night.
I will go, Lord,
If You lead me;
I will hold Your people in my heart.

I, the Lord of snow and rain,
I have borne my people's pain;
I have wept for love of them –
They turn away.
I will break their hearts of stone,
Give them hearts for love alone;
I will speak My word to them.
Whom shall I send?

I, the Lord of wind and flame,
I will tend the poor and lame,
I will set a feast for them –
My hand will save.
Finest bread I will provide
Till their hearts are satisfied;
I will give My life to them.
Whom shall I send?

831

IT IS GOOD TO GIVE THANKS TO THE LORD,
To remember all He has done;
Then God will remember our praises
When He looks with love on His people.

O give thanks to the Lord,
For His love endures forever.
O give thanks to the Lord,
For the Lord alone is good.

Our sin is the sin of our fathers,
We have done wrong, we all have been evil;
Like those who once lived in bondage,
We paid no heed to all You had done.

Our fathers forsook Your love,
At the Red Sea they questioned their God;
They fell from their faith in the desert,
And put God to the test in the wilderness.

Time after time He would rescue them,
Yet in malice they dared to defy Him;
Despite this He came to their aid
When He heard their cries of distress.

Save us, O Lord, in Your love;
Bring us back from all that offends You.
Look not alone at our sins,
But remember your promise of mercy.

Blessed be the Lord God of Israel
Both now and through all eternity;
Let nations and people cry out
And sing Amen! Alleluia!

832 Terry Butler.
Copyright © 1991 Mercy/Vineyard Publishing/
Adm. by CopyCare.

IT IS THE CRY OF MY HEART *to follow*
You.
It is the cry of my heart to be close to
You.
It is the cry of my heart to follow
All of the days of my life.

Teach me Your holy ways, O Lord,
So I can walk in Your truth.
Teach me Your holy ways, O Lord,
And make me wholly devoted to You.

Open my eyes so I can see
The wonderful things that You do.
Open my heart up more and more
And make it wholly devoted to You.

833 Ian Smale.
Copyright © 1993 Kingsway's
Thankyou Music.

IT'S A WONDERFUL, WONDERFUL,
WONDERFUL FEELING,
It's a wonderful feeling to
Know you're saved.
It's a wonderful, wonderful,
Wonderful WONDERFUL!
Wonderful feeling to
Know you're saved.

My life is built on rock, not sand;
It's a wonderful feeling to know you're saved.
And none can steal me from God's hand;
It's a wonderful feeling to know you're saved.

I once was lost but now I'm found:
It's a wonderful feeling to know you're saved.
In Father's arms I'm safe and sound:
It's a wonderful feeling to know you're saved.

My old life's gone, I'm now brand new:
It's a wonderful feeling to know you're saved
Much less of me, much more of You:
It's a wonderful feeling to know you're saved

834 Dave Bilbrough.
Copyright © 1995 Kingsway's
Thankyou Music.

IT'S GETTING CLEARER, the light is dawning
I'm pressing on to a higher place.
The past behind me, I'm moving forward,
And I will follow after You.

You are my strength, You are my shield,
You are the Rock on which I want to build
my life,
O Lord, O Lord.
I won't compromise, I won't be denied,
I want to keep my eyes on the prize
Of knowing You, knowing You.

There is a passion that burns within me,
I long to see Your kingdom come.
To know Your presence, to seek no other;
I hunger, Lord, for more of You.

835 Matt Redman & Martin Smith.
Copyright © 1995 Kingsway's
Thankyou Music.

IT'S RISING UP from coast to coast,
From north to south, and east to west;
The cry of hearts that love Your name,
Which with one voice we will proclaim.

The former things have taken place,
Can this be the new day of praise?
A heavenly song that comes to birth,
And reaches out to all the earth.
Oh, let the cry to nations ring,
That all may come and all may sing:

'Holy is the Lord.' (Every heart sing:)
'Holy is the Lord.' (With one voice sing:)
'Holy is the Lord.' (Every heart sing:)
'Holy is the Lord.'

And we have heard the Lion's roar,
That speaks of heaven's love and power.
Is this the time, is this the call
That ushers in Your kingdom rule?
Oh, let the cry to nations ring,
That all may come and all may sing:

'Jesus is alive!' (Every heart sing:)...

836 Pete Cant.
Copyright © 1997 Kingsway's
Thankyou Music.

I'VE FALLEN IN LOVE (I've fallen in love)
Since the first time we met,
(Since the first time we met)
There at the cross where You paid for my sin,
You opened the way to my heart and came
 in,
Oh, I've fallen in love, (I've fallen in love)
Yes, I've fallen in love. (I've fallen in love)

I've fallen in love (I've fallen in love)
Since the first time we met,
(Since the first time we met)
When I finally looked unto You,
You broke my hardened heart in two,
Oh, I've fallen in love, (I've fallen in love)
Yes, I've fallen in love. (I've fallen in love.)

Jesus my Lord, only You have my heart,
Only You can know;
Words don't express what my heart tries to
 say,
That I have fallen in love.

I've fallen in love (I've fallen in love)
Since the first time we met,
(Since the first time we met)
When You stole my love of the world
And placed my heart's affection on You,
Oh, I've fallen in love, (I've fallen in love)
Yes, I've fallen in love. (I've fallen in love.)

837 Matt Redman.
Copyright © 1993 Kingsway's
Thankyou Music.

I'VE GOT A LOVE SONG IN MY HEART,
It is for You, Lord my God.
I've got a love song in my heart,
It is for You, Lord my God.

> *La la la la la la la,*
> *La la la la la la la,*
> *La la la la la la la.*
> (Repeat)

I've got a passion in my heart...

I've got rejoicing in my heart...

And there is dancing in my heart...

I've never known a love like this...

838 Ian White.
Copyright © 1987 Little Misty Music/Kingsway's
Thankyou Music.

I WAITED PATIENTLY for the Lord,
He turned and heard my cry.
He lifted me from the pit,
Out from the mud and mire.
He put my feet on a rock,
And gave me a firm place to stand.
He put a new song in my mouth,
A hymn of praise to God,
A hymn of praise to God.

> *Many will see, many will fear,*
> *And many will put their trust in the Lord.*
> *Many will see, many will fear,*
> *And many will put their trust in the Lord.*

Blessed is the man who trusts the Lord,
And turns from all the proud,
From all those who have turned aside,
To follow what is false.
Many are the wonders that You have done,
All the things You have planned;
Were I to count they still would be
Too many to declare,
Too many to declare.

839 Chris Falson.
Copyright © 1990 Chris Falson Music/
Maranatha! Music/Adm. by CopyCare.

I WALK BY FAITH,
Each step by faith,
To live by faith,
I put my trust in You.
(Repeat)

Every step I take is a step of faith;
No weapon formed against me shall prosper.
And every prayer I make is a prayer of faith;
And if my God is for me,
Then who can be against me?

840 Paul Oakley & Alan Rose.
Copyright © 1997 Kingsway's
Thankyou Music.

I WANT TO BE HOLY,
I want to be righteous,
I want to live my life the way You want me to.
I want to be blameless,
Not walking in darkness,
I want to be a living sacrifice to You.

I'm gonna run the race,
I'm gonna run to win,
Throw off everything that hinders me.
I'm gonna fix my eyes upon the King,
And leave my sin behind.

I want to be so much better,
I want to be more like You.
Keep taking me further and deeper,
I want to right the wrong,
I want to live this song,
Now I'm pressing on,
I'm gonna leave my sin behind.

Singing, 'goodbye rage, goodbye hate,
Goodbye anger, goodbye malice,
Goodbye bitterness and slander,
Goodbye fear of man!'
(Repeat)

841 Doug Horley & Noel Richards.
Copyright © 1995 Kingsway's
Thankyou Music.

**I WANT TO BE OUT OF MY DEPTH IN YOUR
LOVE,**
Feeling Your arms so strong around me.
Out of my depth in Your love,
Out of my depth in You.
(Repeat)

Learning to let You lead,
Putting all trust in You;
Deeper into Your arms,
Surrounded by You.
Things I have held so tight,
Made my security;
Give me the strength I need
To simply let go.

842 Evan Rogers.
Copyright © 1997 Kingsway's
Thankyou Music.

I WANT TO KNOW
The glorious inheritance
That You have given to me.
And I want to know
The hope that You have called me to,
O Lord, I want to know Your truth.

I want to know You better,
The Spirit without measure,
To know the fulness that's in You.
I want to know Your mystery,
The grace You've given freely,
I know my life is hidden in You.

I want to know
Your wisdom and Your revelation,
Drawing me to You.
I want to know
The power of Your mighty strength
Which raised
Jesus from the dead.

843 Paul Oakley.
Copyright © 1995 Kingsway's
Thankyou Music.

I WAS LOST without a trace,
All except for the eyes of heaven.
Now my Saviour's love has found me,
And His love has brought me home.

I can sleep in peace tonight,
I won't worry about tomorrow,
Now I know my Daddy loves me,
And His perfect love will conquer all.

I'm like a child in His eyes,
And He will meet my needs
With all the riches of heaven;
And He loves me much too much
To let me go,
He will keep me in His love.

Heaven and earth may pass away,
And mountains fall into the ocean;
But His word is everlasting,
And His love goes on and on.

844 Brian Doerksen.
Copyright © 1994 Mercy/Vineyard Publishing/
Adm. by CopyCare.

I WILL BE YOURS,
You will be mine
Together in eternity.
Our hearts of love
Will be entwined,
Together in eternity,
Forever in eternity.

No more tears of pain in our eyes;
No more fear or shame,
For we will be with You,
For we will be with You.

845 Martin J. Nystrom.
Copyright © 1984 Integrity's Hosanna! Music/
Adm. by Kingsway's Thankyou Music.

I WILL COME AND BOW DOWN
At Your feet, Lord Jesus.
In Your presence is fulness of joy.
There is nothing, there is no one
Who compares with You;
I take pleasure in worshipping You, Lord.

846 Steve Bassett & Sue Rinaldi.
Copyright © 1994 Kingsway's
Thankyou Music.

I WILL CRY MERCY,
I will cry mercy for this land, O God.
I will cry justice,
I will cry justice for this land, O God,
For this land, O God.
Let Your tears flow from my eyes;
Let Your passion melt my heart of stone.
Let Your beauty be seen in my life;
Let Your heartbeat be my own.
So I'll cry mercy for this nation,
Let us see healing for the people,
And I'll cry justice for this nation, O God.

847 Matt Redman.
Copyright © 1995 Kingsway's
Thankyou Music.

I WILL DANCE, I will sing,
To be mad for my King.
Nothing, Lord, is hindering
The passion in my soul.
(Repeat)

And I'll become
Even more undignified than this.
(Some would say it's foolishness but)
I'll become
Even more undignified than this.

Na, na, na, na, na, na! Hey!
Na, na, na, na, na, na! Hey!

848 Ian White.
Copyright © 1992 Little Misty Music/
Kingsway's Thankyou Music.

I WILL EXTOL THE LORD with all my
heart.
I will extol the Lord with all my heart,
For holy and awesome,
For holy and awesome,
For holy and awesome is His name.

Holy and awesome is His name.
Holy and awesome is His name.
And the fear of the Lord
Is the start of wisdom.
Holy and awesome is His name.

Holy and awesome is His name.
Holy and awesome is His name.
Those who follow His ways
Have a good understanding.
Holy and awesome is His name.

Holy and awesome is His name.
Holy and awesome is His name.
And to Him belong eternal praise.
Holy and awesome is His name.
Holy and awesome is His name.
Holy and awesome is His name.

849 Sue Rinaldi.
Copyright © 1997 Kingsway's
Thankyou Music.

I WILL FOLLOW YOU TO THE CROSS
And lay myself down, lay myself down.
I will follow You to the cross,
And lay myself down, lay myself down.

Rid me of these dirty clothes,
Cleanse me from all this pollution.
I choose to walk in purity,
Oh, purify me, purify me.

Kiss me with Your healing touch,
Take me to the heat of the fire;
Bathe me in Your liquid love,
Oh, saturate me, saturate me.

Humbly I stand, humbly I kneel,
Humbly I fall at Your throne.
With a craving for You
That no words can describe:
Saturate me, saturate me;
Saturate me, saturate me;
Purify me, purify me;
Purify me, purify me;
Purify me, purify me.

850 Mark Altrogge.
Copyright © 1988 Integrity's Praise! Music/
People of Destiny Music/Adm. by Kingsway's
Thankyou Music.

I WILL GIVE THANKS TO THE LORD with all
my heart,
I will sing glorious praises to Your name;
I will be glad and exalt in You, my Lord,
Yesterday, today, forever, You're the same.

O Most High,
You who are my stronghold,
When troubles come,
You're my hiding place;
O Most High,
Those who know You trust You,
You will not forsake the ones
Who seek Your face.

851

I WILL OFFER UP MY LIFE

I WILL OFFER UP MY LIFE
In spirit and truth,
Pouring out the oil of love
As my worship to You.
In surrender I must give my every part;
Lord, receive the sacrifice
Of a broken heart.

Jesus, what can I give, what can I bring
To so faithful a friend, to so loving a King?
Saviour, what can be said, what can be
*   sung*
As a praise of Your name
For the things You have done?
Oh, my words could not tell, not even in
*   part,*
Of the debt of love that is owed by this
*   thankful heart.*

You deserve my every breath
For You've paid the great cost;
Giving up Your life to death,
Even death on a cross.
You took all my shame away,
There defeated my sin,
Opened up the gates of heaven,
And have beckoned me in.

852

I WILL PRAISE YOU,

I WILL PRAISE YOU,
O Lord, with all of my heart.
I will praise You,
O Lord, with all of my heart.
Before the gods I will sing Your praise.
Before the gods I will praise Your name.

The Lord will fulfil His purpose for me.
The Lord will fulfil His purpose for me.
Do not forsake the work of Your hands,
Revive me, Lord.

You have exalted above all things
Your name and Your word.
You have exalted above all things
Your name and Your word.
I called to You, and You answered me.
When I called to You, You made me strong.

For Your love, O Lord, endures forever,
And Your faithfulness is to the clouds.
Do not forsake the work of Your hands,
Revive me, Lord.

853

I WILL PRAISE YOU WITH THE HARP

I WILL PRAISE YOU WITH THE HARP
For Your faithfulness, O my God.
I will sing my praise to You
With the lyre, with the lyre.

O Holy One of Israel,   (x3)
My lips will shout for joy,
My lips will shout for joy.

When I sing my praise to You,   (x3)
For I have been redeemed,
I have been redeemed!

I'll speak of all Your righteous acts,   (x3)
And tell them all day long,
And tell them all day long.

Those who want to harm me
Are put to shame and confused.
I will sing my praise to You
With the lyre, with the lyre.

I've been redeemed, I've been redeemed!
I've been redeemed, I've been redeemed!

854

I WILL REST IN CHRIST

I WILL REST IN CHRIST
Like the calm within the storm;
I can find security in Him who leads me on.
I will put my faith, my trust and every hope,
For the peace of God will touch my soul,
In Him I will be whole.

I am not dismayed, I am not cast down;
I will never be alone, I need never fear.
I can always hope, I can always love;
For the love of God has touched my heart,
In Him I am secure.

I will rest in Christ;
I will hope in Him.
I will find a place of comfort,
I can find a place of rest,
Held in love, loved in Him,
Safe, I am secure,
As I rest in Christ,
As I hope in Him.

I will trust in Christ
Like a rock in stormy seas;
I have found a shelter in His life and peace in
    me.
I have found the way,
The truth, this perfect life;
And the hope in me is found in Him,
The lover of my soul.

855

I WILL SING, I WILL SING a song unto the
Lord, *(3 times)*
Alleluia, glory to the Lord.

Allelu, alleluia, glory to the Lord,
Allelu, alleluia, glory to the Lord,
Allelu, alleluia, glory to the Lord,
Alleluia, glory to the Lord.

We will come, we will come as one before
the Lord, *(3 times)*
Alleluia, glory to the Lord.

If the Son, if the Son shall make you free,
(3 times)
You shall be free indeed.

They that sow in tears shall reap in joy,
(3 times)
Alleluia, glory to the Lord!

Every knee shall bow and every tongue
confess, *(3 times)*
That Jesus Christ is Lord.

In His name, in His name we have the
victory, *(3 times)*
Alleluia, glory to the Lord.

856

I WILL SING OF THE LAMB,
Of the price that was paid for me,
Purchased by God,
Giving all He could give!
Here now I stand
In the garments of righteousness;
Death has no hold, for in Jesus I live.

I will sing of His blood
That flows for my wretchedness,
Wounds that are bared,
That I may be healed;
Power and compassion,
The marks of His ministry:
May they be mine as I harvest His field.

Oh, I will sing of the Lamb.
Oh, I will sing of the Lamb.
My heart fills with wonder,
My mouth fills with praise!
Hallelujah, hallelujah.

Once I was blind,
Yet believed I saw everything,
Proud in my ways,
Yet a fool in my part;
Lost and alone
In the company of multitudes,
Life in my body, yet death in my heart.

Oh, I will sing of the Lamb.
Oh, I will sing of the Lamb.
Oh, why should the King
Save a sinner like me?
Hallelujah, hallelujah.

What shall I give
To the Man who gave everything,
Humbling Himself
Before all He had made?
Dare I withold
My own life from His sovereignty?
I shall give all for the sake of His name!

Oh, I will sing of the Lamb.
Oh, I will sing of the Lamb.
I'll sing of His love
For the rest of my days!
Hallelujah, hallelujah.

857

I WILL WAIT for Your peace to come to me.
I will wait for Your peace to come to me,
And I'll sing in the darkness,
And I'll wait without fear,
And I'll sing in the darkness,
And I'll wait without fear.

858

I WILL WAVE MY HANDS in praise and
adoration,
I will wave my hands in praise and adoration,
I will wave my hands in praise and adoration,
Praise and adoration to the living God.

For He's given me hands that just love clapping:
One, two, one, two, three,
And He's given me a voice
That just loves shouting:
'Hallelujah!'
He's given me feet that just love dancing:
One, two, one, two, three,
And He's put me in a being
That has no trouble seeing
That whatever I am feeling
He is worthy to be praised.

859 David Ruis.
Copyright © 1991 Shade Tree Music/
Maranatha! Music/Adm. by CopyCare.

I WILL WORSHIP (I will worship)
WITH ALL OF MY HEART. (with all of my
   heart)
I will praise You (I will praise You)
With all of my strength. (all my strength)
I will seek You (I will seek You)
All of my days. (all of my days)
I will follow (I will follow)
All of Your ways. (all Your ways)

   I will give You all my worship,
   I will give You all my praise.
   You alone I long to worship,
   You alone are worthy of my praise.

I will bow down, (I will bow down)
Hail You as King. (hail You as King)
I will serve You, (I will serve You)
Give You everything. (give You everything)
I will lift up (I will lift up)
My eyes to Your throne, (my eyes to Your throne)
I will trust You, (I will trust You)
I will trust You alone. (trust You alone)

860 Nathan Fellingham, Luke Fellingham
& Louise Hunt.
Copyright © 1997 Kingsway's
Thankyou Music.

I WORSHIP YOU, ALMIGHTY KING, the Holy
   One,
For You alone have filled me with new life.
My greatest Friend, You've redeemed my soul;
You've won my heart with Your great love.

I have tasted of Your goodness
And I've heard of Your fame,
So we enter into Your presence
To praise Your holy name.

   We lift our voice and sing,
   There's an extravagant praise
   That fills our hearts,
   For You are Lord and King
   And we bless Your name.
   We dance for joy and bring
   Our adoration to our faithful God,
   To You our everything,
   We bring extravagant praise.
   Sing hallelujah, sing hallelujah.
   Sing hallelujah, sing hallelujah.

You've called me, Lord, to live for You in
   holiness,
I've been made clean and chosen as Your son.
Through Jesus Christ You've made me whole,
My heart is filled with love for You.

861 Callie Gerbrandt.
Copyright © 1993 Mercy/Vineyard Publishing/
Adm. by CopyCare.

I WORSHIP YOU, O LORD,
In spirit and truth;
I bow my face before Your throne,
I praise You, Lord.

I glorify Your name,
I magnify Your name;
And I exalt You Lord over all,
I praise You, Lord.

862 Evan Rogers.
Copyright © 1996 Kingsway's
Thankyou Music.

I WOULD RATHER BE a doorkeeper in Your
   house,
Than have the many things this world could
   offer.
All that I have gained I now count as loss,
There's nothing that compares to knowing
   You.

   In Your presence is where I want to be,
   The place where You reveal Your grace
      and glory.
   Your presence brings me to my knees,
   I bow down and declare that You are holy.

I would rather have one day in Your courts, O
   Lord,
Than have a thousand days somewhere else.
You are my sun and shield,
No good thing will you withhold,
For blessed are the ones who trust in You.

863 Andy Thorpe.
Copyright © 1993 Kingsway's
Thankyou Music.

JESUS, (Jesus)
Jesus, (Jesus)
It's the Name above all names.
(Repeat)

And at the name of Jesus
Every knee shall bow,
And every tongue confess He is Lord.

864 Chris Bowater.
Copyright © 1982 Sovereign Lifestyle Music.

JESUS, AT YOUR NAME we bow the knee.
Jesus, at Your name we bow the knee.
Jesus at Your name we bow the knee,
And acknowledge You as Lord.

You are Christ,
You are the Lord;
Through Your Spirit in our lives
We know who You are.

865 Matt Redman.
Copyright © 1995 Kingsway's
Thankyou Music.

JESUS CHRIST, I think upon Your sacrifice,
You became nothing, poured out to death.
Many times I've wondered at Your gift of life,
And I'm in that place once again.
And I'm in that place once again.

And once again I look upon
The cross where You died,
I'm humbled by Your mercy
And I'm broken inside.
Once again I thank You,
Once again I pour out my life.

Now You are exalted to the highest place,
King of the heavens, where one day I'll bow.
But for now, I marvel at this saving grace,
And I'm full of praise once again.
I'm full of praise once again.

Thank You for the cross,
Thank You for the cross,
Thank You for the cross, my Friend.
(Repeat)

866 Steve Israel & Gerrit Gustafson.
Copyright © 1988 Integrity's Hosanna! Music/
Adm. by Kingsway's Thankyou Music.

JESUS CHRIST IS THE LORD OF ALL,
Lord of all the earth.
Jesus Christ is the Lord of all,
Lord of all the earth.
Jesus Christ is the Lord of all,
Lord of all the earth.
Jesus Christ is the Lord of all,
Lord of all the earth.

Only one God over the nations,
Only one Lord of all.
In no other name is there salvation,
Jesus is Lord of all.

Jesus Christ is Lord of all.
Jesus Christ is Lord of all.
Jesus Christ is Lord of all.
Jesus Christ is Lord of all.

867 Martin Lore.
Copyright © 1993 Kingsway's
Thankyou Music.

JESUS, FORGIVE ME.
Jesus, free me.
Jesus, touch me.
Jesus, fill me.

I lift my head, lift my heart,
Lift my soul to You.
I give my life, give myself,
Give it all to You.

Jesus, teach me.
Jesus, lead me.
Jesus, guide me.
Jesus, use me.

868 Don Harris & Martin J Nystrom.
Copyright © 1993 Integrity's Hosanna! Music/
Adm. by Kingsway's Thankyou Music.

JESUS, I AM THIRSTY,
Won't You come and fill me?
Earthly things have left me dry,
Only You can satisfy,
All I want is more of You.

All I want is more of You,
All I want is more of You;
Nothing I desire, Lord,
But more of You.
(Repeat)
More of You.

869 Judith Butler & Paul Hemingway.
Copyright © 1996 Kingdom Faith Ministries.

JESUS, I LOVE YOU,
I worship and adore You.
Jesus, I love You,
Lord, I glorify Your name.

You are mighty, O Lord,
The Ancient of Days.
Your love stands forever,
Unfailing Your ways.

You are reigning on high,
Exalted King.
Your throne is eternal,
You are Lord over all.

870
Phil Lawson Johnston.
Copyright © 1991 Kingsway's
Thankyou Music.

JESUS IS THE NAME WE HONOUR;
Jesus is the name we praise.
Majestic Name above all other names,
The highest heaven and earth proclaim
That Jesus is our God.

We will glorify,
We will lift Him high,
We will give Him honour and praise.
We will glorify,
We will lift Him high,
We will give Him honour and praise.

Jesus is the name we worship;
Jesus is the name we trust.
He is the King above all other kings,
Let all creation stand and sing
That Jesus is our God.

Jesus is the Father's splendour;
Jesus is the Father's joy.
He will return to reign in majesty,
And every eye at last shall see
That Jesus is our God.

871
Bryn Haworth.
Copyright © 1993 Kingsway's
Thankyou Music.

JESUS, JESUS,
Son of God, Son of man,
Friend of sinners, gift of God.
Jesus, Jesus,
Light of life, Lord of all,
Full of grace and truth.

You have come to us,
Your presence has filled this place.
We will draw near to You,
We come, Lord, to seek Your face.

Jesus, Jesus,
My heart aches, my soul waits,
For Your healing, Lord, I pray.
Jesus, Jesus,
Mighty God, holy Child,
Name above all names.

Jesus, Jesus,
Son of God, Son of Man,
My soul thirsts for You.

872
Alan Rose.
Copyright © 1997 Kingsway's
Thankyou Music.

JESUS, LAMB OF GOD,
I stand redeemed,
Washed in Your blood.
And in the holy place I'll bow
To worship and adore.

Jesus, conquering King,
You died for me,
You bore my sins.
Your love has brought me to my knees
To worship and adore,
To worship and adore.

How I love You,
How I love You,
How I love You,
How I love You,
How I love You.

873
Paul Oakley.
Copyright © 1995 Kingsway's
Thankyou Music.

JESUS, LOVER OF MY SOUL,
All consuming fire is in Your gaze.
Jesus, I want You to know
I will follow You all my days.
For no one else in history is like You,
And history itself belongs to You.
Alpha and Omega, You have loved me,
And I will share eternity with You.

It's all about You, Jesus,
And all this is for You,
For Your glory and Your fame.
It's not about me,
As if You should do things my way;
You alone are God,
And I surrender to Your ways.

874
J. Ezzy, D. Grul, S. McPherson.
Copyright © 1992 Ezzy, Grul, McPherson/
Hillsongs Australia/Kingsway's
Thankyou Music.

JESUS, LOVER OF MY SOUL,
Jesus, I will never let You go:
You've taken me from the miry clay,
You've set my feet upon the rock and now I
    know:

I love You, I need You,
Though my world will fall,
I'll never let You go;
My Saviour, my closest Friend,
I will worship You until the very end.

875 Jacques Berthier/Taizé.
Copyright © 1978 Ateliers et Presses de Taize.

JESUS, REMEMBER ME
When You come into Your kingdom.
Jesus, remember me
When You come into Your kingdom.

876 Graham Kendrick.
Copyright © 1992 Make Way Music.

JESUS, RESTORE TO US AGAIN
The gospel of Your holy name,
That comes with power, not words alone,
Owned, signed and sealed from heaven's
    throne.
Spirit and word in one agreed;
The promise to the power wed.

*The word is near, here in our mouths
And in our hearts, the word of faith;
Proclaim it on the Spirit's breath: Jesus!*

Your word, O Lord, eternal stands,
Fixed and unchanging in the heavens;
The Word made flesh, to earth come down
To heal our world with nail-pierced hands.
Among us here You lived and breathed,
You are the Message we received.

Spirit of truth, lead us, we pray
Into all truth as we obey,
And as God's will we gladly choose,
Your ancient powers again will prove
Christ's teaching truly comes from God,
He is indeed the living Word.

Upon the heights of this great land
With Moses and Elijah stand.
Reveal Your glory once again,
Show us Your face, declare Your name.
Prophets and law, in You complete
Where promises and power meet.

Grant us in this decisive hour
To know the Scriptures and the power;
The knowledge in experience proved,
The power that moves and works by love.
May word and works join hands as one,
The word go forth, the Spirit come.

877 Tanya Riches.
Copyright © 1995 Tanya Riches/Hillsongs
Australia/Kingsway's Thankyou Music.

JESUS, WHAT A BEAUTIFUL NAME.
Son of God, Son of Man,
Lamb that was slain.
Joy and peace, strength and hope,
Grace that blows all fear away.
Jesus, what a beautiful name.

Jesus, what a beautiful name.
Truth revealed, my future sealed,
Healed my pain.
Love and freedom, life and warmth,
Grace that blows all fear away.
Jesus, what a beautiful name.

Jesus, what a beautiful name.
Rescued my soul, my stronghold,
Lifts me from shame.
Forgiveness, security, power and love,
Grace that blows all fear away.
Jesus, what a beautiful name.

878 Chris Bowater.
Copyright © 1991 Sovereign Lifestyle Music.

JUST THE MENTION OF YOUR NAME
Causes me to fall before You,
Tears flow as I adore You,
At the mention of Your name,
Just the mention of Your name.

Just the mention of Your name
Reaffirms the love that holds me,
Speaks once more of love that knows me,
At the mention of Your name,
Just the mention of Your name.

*Jesus, Jesus,
Jesus, Jesus.
At the mention of Your name,
I worship.*

879 George Herbert.

LET ALL THE WORLD in every corner sing:
'My God and King!'
The heavens are not too high;
His praise may thither fly:
The earth is not too low;
His praises there may grow.
Let all the world in every corner sing:
'My God and King!'

Let all the world in every corner sing:
'My God and King!'
The Church with psalms must shout,
No door can keep them out:
But, above all, the heart
Must bear the longest part.
Let all the world in every corner sing:
'My God and King!'

880
Matt Redman.
Copyright © 1997 Kingsway's
Thankyou Music.

LET EVERYTHING THAT,
Everything that,
Everything that has breath
Praise the Lord.
(Repeat)

Praise You in the morning,
Praise You in the evening,
Praise You when I'm young
And when I'm old.
Praise You when I'm laughing,
Praise You when I'm grieving,
Praise You every season of the soul.

If we could see how much You're worth,
Your power, Your might, Your endless love,
Then surely we would never cease to
      praise :

Praise You in the heavens,
Joining with the angels,
Praising You forever and a day.
Praise You on the earth now,
Joining with creation,
Calling all the nations to Your praise.

If they could see how much You're worth,
Your power, Your might, Your endless love,
Then surely they would never cease to
      praise:

881
Debbye Graafsma.
Copyright © 1992 WordPsalm Ministries Inc./
Kingsway's Thankyou Music.

LET EVERY TRIBE AND EVERY TONGUE
Bring praise to the Lamb,
For He has triumphed over all,
He has triumphed.
With His blood He has redeemed us
Forever to reign with Him in glory, amen.

We sing glory, glory to the Lamb;
Son of God, the Great I AM.
Awesome in splendour, triumphant King,
We give You praise and dominion over all.

Worthy, worthy is the Lamb;
Holy, resurrected Lamb.
Jesus, King Jesus, pre-eminent God,
We give You praise,
We give You praise over all.

882
Dave Bilbrough.
Copyright © 1997 Kingsway's
Thankyou Music.

LET THE CHIMES OF FREEDOM RING
All across this earth;
Lift your voice in praise to Him
And sing of all His worth,
And sing of all His worth.

Open wide your prison doors
To greet the Lord of life;
Songs of triumph fill the air,
Christ Jesus is alive,
Christ Jesus is alive.

Let all the people hear the news
Of the One who comes to save:
He's the Lord of all the universe,
And forever He shall reign.

And forever more, yes forever more,
And forever more He will reign.
(Repeat)

In every corner of this earth,
To every tribe and tongue,
Make known that God so loved this
      world
That He gave His only Son,
He gave His only Son.

Spread the news and make it plain,
He breaks the power of sin;
Jesus died and He rose again,
His love will never end,
His love will never end.

He will return in majesty
To take His rightful place
As the King of all eternity,
The Name above all names,
The Name above all names.

883
Phil Wilthew.
Copyright © 1996 Kingsway's
Thankyou Music.

LET THE CHURCH ARISE,
And let the darkness fall.
Say to those chains,
'You are now set free!'
Sickness has died its death
Through the blood of Christ.
To all the oppressed
He now promises life.

Jesus, Lord of all,
Come to us in a time of drought;
Send Your showers,
Let us know the riches of Your mercy.
Jesus, Lord of all,
Come to us in a time of need;
Send revival,
Let our nation see Your awesome glory.

Awake, O church,
Sing with all Your might;
The Lord of all the earth
Is in Your midst.
He is mending lives,
He is winning hearts;
In these coming days
Let revival start.

Come, let us go to the house of God,
With His praises in our hearts;
For the Lord has done great things for us,
And His glory's coming again.
(Repeat)

884 Bryn Haworth.
Copyright © 1991 Kingsway's
Thankyou Music.

LET THE RIGHTEOUS SING,
Come let the righteous dance,
Rejoice before your God,
Be happy and joyful,
Give Him your praise.
We give You our praise.
Shout for joy to God
Who rides upon the clouds,
How awesome are His deeds,
So great is His power.
Give Him your praise.
We give You our praise.

He gives the desolate a home,
He leads the prisoners out with singing.
Father to the fatherless,
Defender of the widow
Is God in His holy place.

885 David Fellingham.
Copyright © 1992 Kingsway's
Thankyou Music.

LET US DRAW NEAR to God
In full assurance of faith,
Knowing that as we draw near to Him,
He will draw near to us.
In the holy place
We stand in confidence,
Knowing our lives are cleansed in the blood
  of the Lamb,
We will worship and adore.

886 Mark Altrogge.
Copyright © People of Destiny Int./Word Music/
Adm. by CopyCare.

LET US DRAW NEAR WITH CONFIDENCE,
We have a Great High Priest.
There's mercy enough for all our sins,
We have a Great High Priest.
He was made weak and He was tried,
We have a Great High Priest.
He's able to feel and sympathise,
We have a Great High Priest.

He's the Lamb of God,
Slain before the ages,
The only Son,
The Servant crowned as King.
The One who came
To crush the works of darkness,
And He will fill all things, all things.

Let us each come with conscience cleansed,
We have a Great High Priest.
It's by His shed blood we enter in,
We have a Great High Priest.
We trust in no merits of our own,
We have a Great High Priest.
But look to the power of the cross alone,
We have a Great High Priest.

887 Paul Oakley.
Copyright © 1994 Kingsway's
Thankyou Music.

LET US GO up to the house of God
With a shout of praise,
With a song of celebration.
We'll ascend the hill of the Lord,
We can stand in the holy place.

We can have clean hands and a pure heart;
His blood can cleanse us from all our
  unrighteousness.
He has made a way though the cross;
Jesus' blood was shed for us.
We can draw near to our God.

Now His body has been broken,
And the curtain torn in two.
We can enter by a new and living way
Before His throne.
Yes, we can fellowship with Him,
The King of glory, King of kings.

888
Noel & Tricia Richards.
Copyright © 1996 Kingsway's
Thankyou Music.

Oh . . .
Oh . . .
Oh . . .
LET YOUR LOVE COME DOWN.
(Repeat)

There is violence in the air.
Fear touches all our lives.
How much pain can people bear?
Are we reaping what we've sown,
Voices silent for too long?
We are calling,
Let Your love come down.

There is power in Your love,
Bringing laughter out of tears.
It can heal the wounded soul.
In the streets where anger reigns
Love will wash away the pain.
We are calling,
Heaven's love come down.

889
David & Nathan Fellingham.
Copyright © 1992 Kingsway's
Thankyou Music.

LET YOUR WORD run freely through this
    nation,
Strong Deliverer, break the grip of satan's
    power.
Let the cross of Jesus stand above the idols
    of this land,
Let anointed lives rise up and take their
    stand.

And we will glorify the Lamb,
Slain from eternity.
Jesus is Lord, we declare His name,
And stand in His victory,
And stand in His victory.

With prophetic words of power, expose the
    darkness;
With apostolic wisdom build the church.
With zeal for the lost let the story be told,
Let the shepherds feed the lambs within their
    folds.

Let the Holy Spirit's fire burn within us,
Cleansed from sin and pure within we stand
    upright.
Not yielding to wrong, we will live in
    holiness,
Bringing glory to the Saviour, we will shine.

890
Dave Bilbrough.
Copyright © 1994 Kingsway's
Thankyou Music.

LIFT HIM UP, *lift Him high,*
Let His praises fill the sky.
Oh, heaven's gates are open wide
To those who hear the call.
(Repeat)

Through every generation
This truth will always shine,
That Christ came down among us,
Now He is glorified.

The message of the kingdom
Stands unshakeable through time:
That man can be forgiven,
If you seek then you will find.

891
Graham Kendrick.
Copyright © 1988 Make Way Music.

LIKE A CANDLE FLAME,
Flickering small in our darkness.
Uncreated light
Shines through infant eyes.

God is with us, alleluia. (Men)
God is with us, alleluia. (Women)
Come to save us, alleluia. (Men)
Come to save us, (Women)
Alleluia! (All).

Stars and angels sing,
Yet the earth sleeps in shadows;
Can this tiny spark
Set a world on fire?

Yet His light shall shine
From our lives, Spirit blazing,
As we touch the flame
Of His holy fire.

892
Timothy Dudley-Smith.
Copyright © 1967 Timothy Dudley-Smith.

LORD, FOR THE YEARS Your love has kept
    and guided,
Urged and inspired us, cheered us on our way,
Sought us and saved us, pardoned and
    provided:
Lord of the years, we bring our thanks today.

Lord, for that word, the word of life which
    fires us,
Speaks to our hearts and sets our souls ablaze,
Teaches and trains, rebukes us and inspires us:
Lord of the word, receive Your people's praise.

Lord, for our land in this our generation,
Spirits oppressed by pleasure, wealth and
    care:
For young and old, for commonwealth and
    nation,
Lord of our land, be pleased to hear our
    prayer.

Lord, for our world where men disown and
    doubt You,
Loveless in strength, and comfortless in pain,
Hungry and helpless, lost indeed without
    You:
Lord of the world, we pray that Christ may
    reign.

Lord for ourselves; in living power remake
    us –
Self on the cross and Christ upon the throne,
Past put behind us, for the future take us:
Lord of our lives, to live for Christ alone.

893 Dave Bilbrough.
Copyright © 1995 Kingsway's
Thankyou Music.

LORD, HAVE MERCY,
Lord, have mercy:
Move in power on this land.
(Repeat)

Hear our prayer,
Hear our prayer,
O Lord, O Lord.
(Repeat)

894 Robert & Dawn Critchley.
Copyright © 1989 Kingsway's
Thankyou Music.

**LORD, I COME BEFORE YOUR THRONE OF
    GRACE;**
I find rest in Your presence
And fulness of joy.
In worship and wonder
I behold Your face,
Singing what a faithful God have I.

What a faithful God have I,
What a faithful God.
What a faithful God have I,
Faithful in every way.

Lord of mercy, You have heard my cry;
Through the storm You're the beacon,
My song in the night.
In the shelter of Your wings,
Hear my heart's reply,
Singing what a faithful God have I.

Lord all sovereign, granting peace from heaven,
Let me comfort those who suffer
With the comfort You have given.
I will tell of Your great love for as long as I live,
Singing what a faithful God have I.

895 Geoff Bullock.
Copyright © 1992 Word Music/Adm.
by CopyCare.

LORD, I COME TO YOU,
Let my heart be changed, renewed,
Flowing from the grace
That I found in You.
And Lord, I've come to know
The weaknesses I see in me
Will be stripped away
By the power of Your love.

Hold me close,
Let Your love surround me.
Bring me near, draw me to Your side.
And as I wait
I'll rise up like the eagle,
And I will soar with You,
Your Spirit leads me on
In the power of Your love.

Lord, unveil my eyes,
Let me see You face to face,
The knowledge of Your love
As You live in me.
Lord, renew my mind
As Your will unfolds in my life,
In living every day
By the power of Your love.

896 Brian Doerksen.
Copyright © 1992 Mercy/Vineyard Publishing/
Adm. by CopyCare.

LORD, I HAVE HEARD OF YOUR FAME,
I stand in awe of Your deeds. O Lord,
I have heard of Your fame,
I stand in awe of Your deeds, O Lord.

Renew them, renew them,
In our day, and in our time
Make them known.
(Repeat)
In wrath remember mercy.

897 Rick Founds.
Copyright © 1989 Maranatha! Music/Adm.
by CopyCare.

LORD, I LIFT YOUR NAME ON HIGH;
Lord, I love to sing Your praises.
I'm so glad You're in my life;
I'm so glad You came to save us.

You came from heaven to earth to show
   the way,
From the earth to the cross,
My debt to pay.
From the cross to the grave,
From the grave to the sky,
Lord, I lift Your name on high.

898 Stephen McPherson.
Copyright © 1996 Stephen McPherson/
Hillsongs Australia/Kingsway's Thankyou
Music.

LORD, I LONG TO SEE YOU GLORIFIED
In everything I do;
All my heartfelt dreams I put aside,
To see Your Spirit move with power in my
life.

Jesus, Lord of all eternity,
Your children rise in faith;
All the earth displays Your glory,
And each word You speak
Brings life to all who hear.

   Lord of all,
   All of creation sings Your praise
   In heaven and earth.
   Lord, we stand,
   Hearts open wide,
   Be exalted.

899 Rick Founds.
Copyright © 1989 Maranatha! Music/Adm.
by CopyCare.

LORD, LOOK UPON MY NEED,
I need You, I need You.
Lord, have mercy now on me,
Forgive me, O Lord, forgive me,
And I will be clean.

   O Lord, You are familiar with my ways,
   There is nothing hid from You.
   O Lord, You know the number of my
     days,
   I want to live my life for You.

900 Darlene Zschech.
Copyright © 1997 Darlene Zschech/Hillsongs
Australia/Kingsway's Thankyou Music.

LORD, MY HEART CRIES OUT,
'Glory to the King';
My greatest love in life,
I hand You everything:
'Glory, glory',
I hear the angels sing.

Open my ears,
Let me hear Your voice,
To know that sweet sound,
Oh, my soul rejoice:
'Glory, glory',
I hear the angels sing.

   You're the Father to the fatherless,
   The answer to my dreams.
   I see You crowned in righteousness,
   We cry, 'Glory to the King'.
   Comforter to the lonely,
   The lifter of my head.
   I see You veiled in majesty;
   We cry, 'Glory, glory',
   We cry, 'Glory to the King'.

901 Joe King.
Copyright © 1990 Kingsway's
Thankyou Music.

LORD OF ALL CREATION,
Let this generation
See a visitation of Your power;
Put to flight all the powers of darkness,
O come, Lord Jesus, come.

   Lord of all creation,
   Let this generation
   See a visitation of Your power.
   Lord of all creation,
   There's an expectation
   Rising in this nation every hour.

Father God, forgive us,
Send Your cleansing rivers,
Wash us now and give us holy power;
Fill this land with Your awesome presence,
O come, Lord Jesus, come.

902 Jan Struther.
Copyright © Oxford University Press

LORD OF ALL HOPEFULNESS,
Lord of all joy,
Whose trust, ever child-like,
No cares could destroy;
Be there at our waking,
And give us, we pray,
Your bliss in our hearts, Lord,
At the break of the day.

Lord of all eagerness, Lord of all faith,
Whose strong hands were skilled
At the plane and the lathe;
Be there at our labours,
And give us, we pray,
Your strength in our hearts, Lord,
At the noon of the day.

Lord of all kindliness, Lord of all grace,
Your hands swift to welcome,
Your arms to embrace;
Be there at our homing,
And give us, we pray,
Your love in our hearts, Lord,
At the eve of the day.

Lord of all gentleness, Lord of all calm,
Whose voice is contentment,
Whose presence is balm;
Be there at our sleeping,
And give us, we pray,
Your peace in our hearts, Lord,
At the end of the day.

903 Kevin Prosch.
Copyright © 1995 7th Time Music/Kingsway's
Thankyou Music.

LORD OF THE DANCE,
You're the dancing Lord.
(Repeat x4)
Everybody dance, yeah!

Well everybody dance, now,
Get in the Holy Ghost.
Everybody praise the One, love the One,
You want the One, yeah,
The One you want the most, now.
Can't nobody stop me now,
I'm gonna give it everything I've got.
I come to You, run to You,
Run to You, yeah,
Just like a child.

It's just this love I have inside,
Yeah, I want it.
I feel You pleasure in my heart,
Yeah, I need it.
I want Your love
More and more each day.
And when I dance before You, Lord,
I'm gonna dance with all my might.

904 Ray Goudie, Dave Bankhead & Steve Bassett.
Copyright © 1993 Integrity's Hosanna! Music/
Adm. by Kingsway's Thankyou Music.

LORD, POUR OUT YOUR SPIRIT
On all the peoples of the earth;
Let Your sons and daughters
Speak Your words of prophecy.
Send us dreams and visions,
Reveal the secrets of Your heart;
Lord, our faith is rising,
Let all heaven sound the coming of Your
day.

There's gonna be a great awakening,
There's gonna be a great revival in our land.
There's gonna be a great awakening,
And everyone who calls on Jesus,
They will be saved.

Lord, pour out Your Spirit
On all the nations of the world;
Let them see Your glory,
Let them fall in reverent awe.
Show Your mighty power,
Shake the heavens and the earth;
Lord, the world is waiting,
Let creation see the coming of Your day.

905 Dave Bilbrough.
Copyright © 1993 Kingsway's
Thankyou Music.

LORD, WE COME IN ADORATION,
Lay our lives before You now.
We are here to reach the nations,
To tell the world of Jesus' power.
We would seek Your awesome glory,
All the gifts that You endow;
Called to reach this generation,
And now is the appointed hour.

We will go in Your name;
Go and proclaim Your kingdom.
Go in Your name,
For we have been chosen to tell all
creation
That Jesus is King of all kings.

We believe that You have spoken
Through Your Son to all the earth;
Given us this great commission
To spread the news of all Your worth.
Set apart to serve You only,
Let our lives display Your love;
Hearts infused that tell the story
Of God come down from heaven above.

Grant to us a fresh anointing,
Holy Spirit, be our guide;
Satisfy our deepest longing—
Jesus Christ be glorified.
Every tribe and every people,
Hear the message that we bring;
Christ has triumphed over evil,
Bow the knee and worship Him.

906 David Fellingham.
Copyright © 1994 Kingsway's
Thankyou Music.

LORD, WE CRY TO YOU: God, break through!
Let Your presence come in revival.
Like the gentle dew, our lives renew;
Let Your presence come in revival.

(Men) *O God, break through!*
(Women) *Send Your Spirit, Lord.*
(Men) *O God, break through!*
(Women) *Send Your Spirit.*
(All) *Let the name of Jesus be
    proclaimed.*
(Repeat)
(All) *O God, break through.*

Lord, we cry to You: God break through!
Move upon Your church in revival.
Like a mighty wind and tongues of fire,
Let Your Spirit come in revival.

Lord, we cry to You: God, break through!
Sweep across this land in revival.
Like the mighty rain, flood this land again;
Let Your power come in revival.

907

LORD, WE LONG TO SEE YOUR GLORY,

Gaze upon Your lovely face.
Holy Spirit, come among us,
Lead us to that secret place.

> *Holy God,*
> *We long to see Your glory,*
> *To touch Your holy majesty, O Lord.*
> *Holy God,*
> *Let us stay in Your presence,*
> *And worship at Your feet forever more.*
> *Holy God.*
> *Holy God.*

908

LORD, WE LONG TO SEE YOUR GLORY,

Lord, we long to feel Your power.
In these times of refreshing,
We long to know You more.
To behold You in Your majesty,
Our hearts are filled with joy;
As we look towards the coming King,
We cry 'Lord, let Your glory fall.'

There'll be a day when we will reign with
  Him,
The Bride of Christ born for perfect unity with
  Him.
We shall see Him face to face,
But until that day we shall pray,
'Show us Your glory.'

Help us to sing like the angels sing.
Help us to praise in the courts of our King.
Help us to dance like David danced,
Stirred by the love of Your Son,
Stirred by the love of Your Son.

909

LORD, WE'VE COME TO WORSHIP YOU,

Lord, we've come to praise:
Lord, we've come to worship You
In oh, so many ways.
Some of us shout,
And some of us sing,
And some of us whisper the praise we bring;
But Lord, we all are gathering
To give to You our praise.

910

LORD, YOU ARE THE AUTHOR OF MY LIFE,

You have begun a work in me,
You have predestined me
To do Your perfect will.
And Lord, You are the Lord of all my days,
You are the Lord of all my nights,
You have chosen me
To carry forth Your word.

So Lord, finish in me what You've begun,
Guide me by Your mighty hand, Lord:
Let me trust in You.
And Lord, let me seek Your holy face,
May I always walk with You, Lord,
And let Your will be done.

911

LORD, YOU ARE WORTHY,

Lord, You are worthy,
Lord, You are worthy,
We give You praise.

Lord, You are worthy...

Lord, You are holy...

Lord, we adore You...

Lord, You are worthy...

912 Martin Smith.
Copyright © 1992 Kingsway's
Thankyou Music.

LORD, YOU HAVE MY HEART,

And I will search for Yours;
Jesus, take my life and lead me on.
Lord, You have my heart,
And I will search for Yours;
Let me be to You a sacrifice.

And I will praise you, Lord. *(Men)*
I will praise You, Lord. *(Women)*
And I will sing of love come down. *(Men)*
I will sing of love come down. *(Women)*
And as You show Your face, *(Men)*
Show Your face, *(Women)*
We'll see Your glory here. *(All)*

913 Wayne Drain.
Copyright © 1996 Kingsway's
Thankyou Music.

LOST IN THE SHUFFLE,

I was lost as a goose,
The devil had a rope out,
And it looked just like a noose.
But just before I went off of that deep end,
My Father threw me out a line,
Forgave me of my sin.

Now we're dancin', me and the Father,
He's throwing me up in the air.
We're dancin', me and the Father,
He's swinging me,
I like it up there with my Father,
I like it up there with my Father.

He took me to the water,
And He cleaned me real good,
Then He raised me up to be with Him,
I feel just like I should.
He filled me with His Spirit,
I drank the whole cup,
Now when He calls I hear it,
Hey, turn that volume up!

'Cause we're dancin'...

God's got a big family, more than anyone can
  count;
There's always room for one more,
No need to be left out.
So come on, come on, come on,

And you could be dancin', you and the
  Father,
He'll throw you up in the air.
You'll be dancin', you and the Father,
He'll swing you up,
You'll like it up there with the Father,
You'll like it up there with the Father.

914 Noel & Tricia Richards.
Copyright © 1996 Kingsway's
Thankyou Music.

LOVE SONGS FROM HEAVEN are filling the
  earth,

Bringing great hope to all nations.
Evil has prospered, but truth is alive;
In this dark world the light still shines.

Nothing has silenced this gospel of Christ;
It echoes down through the ages.
Blood of the martyrs has made Your church
  strong;
In this dark world the light still shines.

For You we live,
And for You we may die;
Through us may Jesus be seen.
For You alone we will offer our lives;
In this dark world our light will shine.

Let every nation be filled with Your song:
This is the cry of Your people.
We will not settle for anything less,
In this dark world our light must shine.

915 Graham Kendrick.
Copyright © 1985 Kingsway's
Thankyou Music.

MAGNIFICENT WARRIOR, arrayed for
  battle,

We see You ready to slay Your enemies.
O Mighty Captain of heaven's armies,
We bow before You, we worship You.

So take Your sword upon Your side
O Mighty One, clothe Yourself
With splendour and with majesty,
And in Your majesty ride forth.
Ride forth victoriously for truth.
Humility and righteousness.
Let Your strong right hand
Display Your awesome deeds.

Magnificent Warrior, we hear Your strong
  command
To join the ranks of light and march into the
  fight;
By faith to overthrow ten thousand
  Jerichos,
To make Your judgements known in all the
  earth.

916

MAKES YOU WANNA DANCE, *(echo)*
Makes you wanna sing, *(echo)*
Makes you wanna shout all about it,
Shout all about it,
Shout it that Jesus is King.
(Repeat)

Every nation, power and tongue
Will bow down to Your name;
Every eye will see,
Every ear will hear Your name proclaimed,
This is gonna be our cry
Until You come again:
'Jesus is the only name
By which man can be saved.'

> *All over the world people just like us*
> *Are calling Your name, living in Your love.*
> *All over the world people just like us*
> *Are following Jesus.*
> (Repeat)

> (Last time)
> *We're worshipping Jesus,*
> *We're following Jesus,*
> *We're worshipping Jesus,*
> *We're calling on Jesus.*

917

MAKE US A HOUSE OF PRAYER,
That we might meet You there,
On behalf of the nation,
To a dying generation,
Make us a house of prayer.

And Lord, teach us to pray
Unceasingly night and day.
Make our intercession
For You a mighty weapon.
O Lord, teach us to pray.

918

MAY GOD BE GRACIOUS TO US and bless us,
Make His face to shine upon us.
May Your ways be known over the earth
And Your salvation among all nations.

> *May the peoples praise You;*
> *O God, may all the peoples praise You.*
> *May the peoples praise You;*
> *O God, may all the peoples praise You.*

May the nations be glad and sing for joy,
For with justice You rule the people You
  guide.
May Your ways be known over all the earth,
And Your salvation among all nations.

Then the harvest will come to the land,
And God, our God, will bless us.
God will bless us, and all the ends
Of earth will fear Him.

919

MAY I SING A SONG OF LOVE
To the One who saved my soul?
May I bow my head today
In the presence of the King?

You have called and I will come,
Lift my hands up to Your throne;
Worship You on holy ground –
That's what I long to do.

> *Draw me near into Your heart.*
> *All I have is broken love,*
> *And a thirst that cries for more.*
> *Draw me near to You.*

920

MAY OUR WORSHIP BE AS FRAGRANCE,
May our worship be as incense poured forth,
May our worship be acceptable
As a living sacrifice,
As a living sacrifice.

We are willing to pay the price,
We are willing to lay down our lives
As an offering of obedience,
As a living sacrifice,
As a living sacrifice.

921

MEN OF FAITH, rise up and sing
Of the great and glorious King;
You are strong when you feel weak,
In your brokenness complete.

> *Shout to the north and the south,*
> *Sing to the east and the west:*
> *Jesus is Saviour to all,*
> *Lord of heaven and earth.*

(Last time)
Lord of heaven and earth,
Lord of heaven and earth,
Lord of heaven and earth.

Rise up women of the truth,
Stand and sing to broken hearts,
Who can know the healing power
Of our glorious King of love.

We've been through fire,
We've been through rain;
We've been refined
By the power of His name.
We've fallen deeper in love with You,
You've burned the truth on our lips.

Rise up church with broken wings;
Fill this place with songs again,
Of our God who reigns on high:
By His grace again we'll fly.

922 John Chisum & Gary Sadler.
Copyright © 1994 Integrity's Hosanna! Music/
Adm. by Kingsway's Thankyou Music.

MERCIFUL GOD AND FATHER,
Loving us like no other,
Hear our prayer, the cry of our hearts,
As we come to You.
We acknowledge our transgressions,
We confess to You our sins;
Show us mercy and compassion,
Touch our lives
With Your healing grace again.

Release us from the past,
As we seek Your face.
Wash us free at last,
We receive Your love,
We receive Your healing grace.
We receive Your love,
We receive Your healing grace.

923 Chris Bowater and Mark & Helen Johnson.
Copyright © 1991 Sovereign Lifestyle Music.

MIGHTY GOD,
Everlasting Father,
Wonderful Counsellor,
You're the Prince of Peace.
(Repeat)

You are Lord of heaven,
You are called Emmanuel;
God is now with us,
Ever present to deliver.
You are God eternal,
You are Lord of all the earth;
Love has come to us,
Bringing us new birth.

A light to those in darkness,
And a guide to paths of peace;
Love and mercy dawns,
Grace, forgiveness and salvation.
Light for revelation,
Glory to Your people;
Son of the Most High,
God's love gift to all.

924 Eugene Greco, Gerrit Gustafson, Don Moen
Copyright © 1989 Integrity's Hosanna! Music/
Adm. by Kingsway's Thankyou Music.

MIGHTY IS OUR GOD,
Mighty is our King;
Mighty is our Lord,
Ruler of everything.
Glory to our God,
Glory to our King;
Glory to our Lord,
Ruler of everything.

His name is higher,
Higher than any other name;
His power is greater,
For He has created everything.

925 A. P. Douglas.
Copyright © 1997 Kingsway's
Thankyou Music.

MIGHTY IS THE LORD and most worthy of
   praise,
Praise Him all you people.
Look upon Him, God alone who saves:
Praise the Lord of all.
Nations will rise and nations will fall,
Praise Him all you people.
But there is One who is Lord of all:
Praise the Lord of all.

   He is Wonderful, Counsellor,
   Glorious Prince of Peace.
   He is Lord and King of everything,
   His praises never cease.
   (Repeat)

Awesome and great, like the strongest tower,
Praise Him all you people.
He is the one with limitless power,
Praise the Lord of all.
Leaders may come and presidents fall,
Praise Him all you people.
But there is One who is Lord of all:
Praise the Lord of all.

926
Carol Owen.
Copyright © 1994 Kingsway's
Thankyou Music.

MIGHTY, MIGHTY LORD.
Precious is Your name.
Wonderful Your ways,
Worthy of all praise, Jehovah.

Mighty, mighty Lord.
Holy is Your name.
Glorious and true,
Great in all You do, Jehovah,
Jehovah.

Hallowed be Your name,
Lord God Almighty,
For Yours is the kingdom,
The power and the glory,
Forever more.

927
Brian Doerksen.
Copyright © 1994 Mercy/Vineyard Publishing/
Adm. by CopyCare.

MORE THAN OXYGEN, I need Your love;
More than life-giving food
The hungry dream of.
More than an eloquent word
Depends on the tongue;
More than a passionate song
Needs to be sung.

More than a word could ever say,
More than a song could ever convey;
I need You more than all of these things.
Father, I need You more.

More than magnet and steel
Are drawn to unite;
More that poets love words
To rhyme as they write.
More than comforting warmth
Of sun in spring;
More than the eagle loves wind
Under its wings.

More than a blazing fire
On a winter's night;
More than tall evergreens
Reach for the light.
More than the pounding waves
Long for the shore;
More than these gifts You give,
I love You more.

928
Steve & Vikki Cook.
Copyright © 1991 People of Destiny
International/Word Music/Adm. by CopyCare.

MOST HOLY JUDGE,
I stood before You guilty,
When you sent Jesus to the cross for my sin.
There Your love was revealed,
Your justice vindicated,
One sacrifice has paid the cost
For all who trust in Jesus.

Now I'm justified,
You declare me righteous,
Justified by the blood of the Lamb.
Justified freely by Your mercy,
By faith I stand and I'm justified.

I come to You,
And I can call you 'Father',
There is no fear
There is no shame before You.
For by Your gift of grace
Now I am one of Your children,
An heir with those who bear Your name,
And share the hope of glory.

929
Author unknown.

MUKTI DILAYE Yesu naam,
Shanti dilaye Yesu naam.
(Repeat)
(Peace comes to you in Jesus' name,
Salvation in no other name.)

Yesu daya ka behta sagar
Yesu daya ka behta sagar
Yesu hai data mahan
Yesu hai data mahan
(Jesus is the Ocean of Grace:
You are majestic, Lord.)

Charni main tooney janamliya Yesu
Charni main tooney janamliya Yesu
Sooley pay kiya vishram
Sooley pay kiya vishram
(Jesus, You were born in a manger (Made of
wood:)
You were crucified on the cross (Made of wood.))

Peace comes to you in Jesus' name,
Salvation in no other name.

Ham sab key papon ko mitane
Ham sab key papon ko mitane
Yesu hua hai balidan
Yesu hua hai balidan
(For the remission of our sins,
Jesus has been sacrificed on the cross.)

Krus par apna khoon bahaa kar
Krus par apna khoon bahaa kar
Sara chukaya daam
Sara chukaya daam
(By shedding Your blood on the cross,
You paid the full price for our sins.)

930

MY FIRST LOVE is a blazing fire,
I feel His powerful love in me.
For He has kindled a flame of passion,
And I will let it grow in me.
And in the night I will sing Your praise, my
    love.
And in the morning I'll seek Your face, my
    love.

> *And like a child I will dance in Your*
>   *presence,*
> *Oh, let the joy of heaven pour down on*
>   *me.*
> *I still remember the first day I met You,*
> *And I don't ever want to lose that fire,*
> *My first love.*

My first love is a rushing river,
A waterfall that will never cease;
And in the torrent of tears and laughter,
I feel a healing power released.
And I will draw from Your well of life, my
    love,
And in Your grace I'll be satisfied, my love.

Restore the years of the church's slumber,
Revive the fire that has grown so dim;
Renew the love of those first encounters,
That we may come alive again.
And we will rise like the dawn throughout the
    earth,
Until the trumpet announces Your return.

931

MY GOD SHALL SUPPLY ALL MY NEEDS,
My God shall supply all my needs,
My God shall supply all my needs
'Cause it says so in the Bible,
'Cause it says so (where?)
In the book that came from heaven,
'Cause it says so (where?)
Isaiah fifty-eight eleven.
My God shall supply all my needs
'Cause it says so in the Bible.

932

MY HEART,
I want to give You my heart,
In service to the Lord, the One who cares
To ask for my life.
Take me,
Mould my life and make me
Into a child who longs to stay by Your side
And learn of Your ways.

For when I sought You, Lord, You heard me,
You delivered me from fear;
And by Your grace and mercy
You have brought us both so near.
I want to kneel before Your feet, Lord,
And to gaze upon Your face;
For the God who asks for my life
Loves me completely and always.

933

MY HEART IS NOT RAISED UP TOO HIGH,
My eyes don't search beyond the sky.
I do not seek what can't be known,
Nor fret myself over mysteries.

But I have calmed and soothed my soul,
Like a child at rest in its mother's arms;
Like this child sleeping by my side,
My soul, in God, knows peace and calm.

All you who love and trust your God,
In this God shall you put your hope,
For there you'll find unfailing love,
From this time forth, and forever more.

934

MY JESUS, MY LIFELINE,
I need You more than I've ever known.
There's no one quite like You,
I'm crying out for Your loving.

> *Oh Jesus, oh Jesus,*
> *I've never known a love like this before.*
> *Oh Jesus, oh Jesus,*
> *Accept this love I give to You,*
> *It's all I can do.*

I'm searching, I'm longing,
Please meet me just as You want to.
I'll stand here to offer,
Offer up this song of love to You.

935

MY JESUS, MY SAVIOUR,
Lord, there is none like You.
All of my days I want to praise
The wonders of Your mighty love.
My comfort, my shelter,
Tower of refuge and strength,
Let every breath, all that I am,
Never cease to worship You.

Shout to the Lord all the earth, let us sing
Power and majesty, praise to the King.
Mountains bow down
And the seas will roar
At the sound of Your name.
I sing for joy at the work of Your hands.
Forever I'll love You, forever I'll stand.
Nothing compares to the
Promise I have in You.

936

MY LIFE IS IN YOU, LORD,
My strength is in You, Lord,
My hope is in You, Lord,
In You, it's in You.
(Repeat)

(Last time)
In You.

I will praise You with all of my life;
I will praise You with all of my strength.
With all of my life,
With all of my strength;
All of my hope is in You.

937

MY LIPS SHALL PRAISE YOU,
My great Redeemer;
My heart will worship
Almighty Saviour.

You take all my guilt away,
Turn the darkest night to brightest day,
You are the restorer of my soul.

Love that conquers every fear,
In the midst of trouble You draw near,
You are the restorer of my soul.

You're the source of happiness,
Bringing peace when I am in distress,
You are the restorer of my soul.

938

MY TRUST IS IN THE NAME OF THE LORD
Who made heaven and earth;
My trust is in the name of the Lord
Who made heaven and earth.

Sing hallelujah, hallelujah.
Hallelujah, hallelu, hallelujah.

My hope is in the name of the Lord ...

My joy is in the name of the Lord ...

939

NAME OF ALL MAJESTY,
Fathomless mystery,
King of the ages
By angels adored;
Power and authority,
Splendour and dignity,
Bow to His mastery –
Jesus is Lord!

Child of our destiny,
God from eternity,
Love of the Father
On sinners outpoured;
See now what God has done,
Sending His only Son,
Christ the belovèd One –
Jesus is Lord!

Saviour of Calvary,
Costliest victory,
Darkness defeated
And Eden restored;
Born as a man to die,
Nailed to a cross on high,
Cold in the grave to lie –
Jesus is Lord!

Source of all sovereignty,
Light, immortality,
Life everlasting
And heaven assured;
So with the ransomed, we
Praise Him eternally,
Christ in His majesty –
Jesus is Lord!

940 Sarah Flower Adams.

NEARER, MY GOD, TO THEE,
Nearer to Thee:
E'en though it be a cross
That raiseth me,
Still all my song would be,
Nearer, my God, to Thee,
Nearer to Thee, nearer to Thee.

Though, like the wanderer,
The sun gone down,
Darkness be over me,
My rest a stone,
Yet in my dreams I'd be
Nearer, my God, to Thee,
Nearer to Thee, nearer to Thee.

There let the way appear,
Steps up to heaven;
All that Thou sendest me,
In mercy given;
Angels to beckon me
Nearer, my God, to Thee,
Nearer to Thee, nearer to Thee.

Then, with my waking thoughts
Bright with Thy praise,
Out of my stony griefs
Bethel I'll raise;
So by my woes to be
Nearer, my God, to Thee,
Nearer to Thee, nearer to Thee.

Or, if on joyful wing
Cleaving the sky,
Sun, moon, and stars forgot,
Upwards I fly,
Still all my song shall be,
Nearer, my God, to Thee,
Nearer to Thee, nearer to Thee.

941 Chris Roe.

NEVER LET MY HEART GROW COLD.
Lord, help my to love You
With a love that never dies.
Set my heart ablaze with burning desire
To see Jesus glorified,
To see Jesus glorified.

942 David Fellingham.

NEW COVENANT PEOPLE rejoice,
Lift up your eyes and see your King.
Reigning in power on His heavenly throne,
Angels are joyfully singing:

To the Father, our Creator,
To our Judge and Lord.
And to Jesus, Mediator,
Who has cleansed us in His blood.

Let us through Jesus draw near to God,
Offering up our sacrifice,
Confessing that Jesus is Lord over all,
Joining with heavenly praises:

We give thanks to You with fear,
Holy God, consuming fire,
Confessing that Jesus is Lord over all,
We bring our love and devotion:

943 Mark Altrogge.

NO EYE HAS SEEN,
And no ear has heard,
And no mind has ever conceived
The glorious things
That You have prepared
For everyone who has believed;
You brought us near and You called us Your own,
And made us joint heirs with Your Son.

How high and how wide,
How deep and how long,
How sweet and how strong is Your love;
How lavish Your grace,
How faithful Your ways,
How great is Your love, O Lord.

Objects of mercy,
Who should have known wrath,
We're filled with unspeakable joy;
Riches of wisdom
Unsearchable wealth,
And the wonder of knowing Your voice.
You are our treasure and our great reward,
Our hope and our glorious King.

944 Paul & Rita Baloche & Ed Kerr.

NO EYE HAS SEEN, NO EAR HAS HEARD,
No mind has conceived what the Lord has
    prepared;
But by His Spirit, He has revealed
His plan to those who love Him.
(Repeat)

We've been held by His everlasting love,
Led with loving kindness by His hand;
We have hope for the future yet to come,
In time we'll understand the mystery of His plan.

945
Carol Owen.
Copyright © 1994 Kingsway's
Thankyou Music.

NO ONE IS LIKE YOU, O LORD;
You are great and Your name is mighty.
No one is like You, O Lord;
You are great and Your name is mighty.
Who should not revere You,
O King of the nations?
Who should not revere You,
For this is Your due?
Among all wise men
In all of their kingdoms,
There is none like You.

No one is like You, O Lord;
You're enthroned over all the nations.
No one is like You, O Lord;
You're enthroned over all the nations.
Who should not revere You,
O King of the nations?
Who should not revere You,
For this is Your due?
Among all the wise men
In all of their kingdoms,
There is none like You.

None like You, O Lord,
The King and the Creator.
None like You, O Lord,
Our Father and our Maker.
None like You, O Lord,
Your faithfulness surrounds You.
How majestic is Your name,
As Your people we proclaim:

946
Robert Gay.
Copyright © 1988 Integrity's Hosanna! Music/
Adm. by Kingsway's Thankyou Music.

NO OTHER NAME but the name of Jesus,
No other name but the name of the Lord;
No other name but the name of Jesus
Is worthy of glory, and worthy of honour,
And worthy of power and all praise.

His name is exalted far above the earth,
His name is high above the heavens;
His name is exalted far above the earth,
Give glory and honour and praise unto His
  name.

947
Noel & Tricia Richards.
Copyright © 1989 Kingsway's
Thankyou Music.

NOTHING SHALL SEPARATE US
From the love of God.
Nothing shall separate us
From the love of God.

God did not spare His only Son,
Gave Him to save us all.
Sin's price was met by Jesus' death
And heaven's mercy falls.

Up from the grave Jesus was raised
To sit at God's right hand;
Pleading our cause in heaven's courts,
Forgiven we can stand.

Now by God's grace we have embraced
A life set free from sin;
We shall deny all that destroys
Our union with Him.

948
Tom Dowell.
Copyright © 1984 Christian Fellowship of
Columbia.

NO WEAPON FORMED, or army or king,
Shall be able to stand
Against the Lord and His anointed.
(Repeat)

All principalities and powers
Shall crumble before the Lord;
And men's hearts shall be released,
And they shall come unto the Lord.

No weapon formed, or army or king,
Shall be able to stand
Against the Lord and His anointed.

949
Alfred Vine.

O BREATH OF GOD, BREATHE ON US NOW,
And move within us while we pray;
The Spring of our new life art Thou,
The very light of our new day.

O strangely art Thou with us, Lord,
Neither in height nor depth to seek:
In nearness shall Thy voice be heard;
Spirit to spirit Thou dost speak.

Christ is our Advocate on high;
Thou art our Advocate within.
O plead the truth, and make reply
To every argument of sin.

But ah, this faithless heart of mine,
The way I know, I know my Guide;
Forgive me, O my Friend divine,
That I so often turn aside.

Be with me when no other friend
The mystery of my heart can share;
And be Thou known, when fears transcend,
By Thy best name of Comforter.

950 Graham Kendrick.
Copyright © 1992 Make Way Music.

O FATHER OF THE FATHERLESS,

In whom all families are blessed,
I love the way You father me.
You gave me life, forgave the past,
Now in Your arms I'm safe at last,
I love the way You father me.

Father me, forever You'll father me,
And in Your embrace I'll be forever secure.
I love the way You father me.
I love the way You father me.

When bruised and broken I draw near
You hold me close and dry my tears,
I love the way You father me.
At last my fearful heart is still,
Surrendered to Your perfect will,
I love the way You father me.

If in my foolishness I stray,
Returning empty and ashamed,
I love the way You father me.
Exchanging for my wretchedness
Your radiant robes of righteousness,
I love the way You father me.

And when I look into Your eyes
From deep within my spirit cries,
I love the way You father me.
Before such love I stand amazed
And ever will through endless days,
I love the way You father me.

951 William Cowper.

O FOR A CLOSER WALK WITH GOD,

A calm and heavenly frame,
A light to shine upon the road
That leads me to the Lamb.

Where is the blessèdness I knew
When I first saw the Lord?
Where is that soul-refreshing view
Of Jesus and His word?

What peaceful hours I once enjoyed!
How sweet their memory still!
But they have left an aching void
The world can never fill.

Return, O holy Dove! return,
Sweet messenger of rest!
I hate the sins that made Thee mourn,
And drove Thee from my breast.

The dearest idol I have known,
Whate'er that idol be,
Help me tear if from Thy throne,
And worship only Thee.

So shall my walk be close with God,
Calm and serene my frame;
So purer light shall mark the road
That leads me to the Lamb.

952 John Paculabo.
Copyright © 1993 Kingsway's
Thankyou Music.

O GOD, BE MY STRENGTH

Through my doubt and my fear.
O God, be my comfort
When darkness is near.
O Lord of all hope,
You're my Saviour and Guide.
O Lord, have mercy on me.

O God of all mercy
And God of all grace,
Whose infinite gift
Was to die in my place,
Eternal Creator,
Redeemer and Friend,
O Lord, have mercy on me.

O God of all power,
Invisible King,
Restorer of man,
My life I bring,
O Lord of my heart,
Grant Your peace now I pray:
O Lord, have mercy on me.

953 Michael Perry.
Copyright © Mrs B Perry/Jubilate Hymns.

O GOD BEYOND ALL PRAISING,

We worship You today,
And sing the love amazing
That songs cannot repay;
For we can only wonder
At every gift you send,
At blessings without number
And mercies without end:
We lift our hearts before You
And wait upon Your word,
We honour and adore You,
Our great and mighty Lord.

Then hear, O gracious Saviour,
Accept the love we bring,
That we who know Your favour
May serve You as our King;
And whether our tomorrows
Be filled with good or ill,
We'll triumph through our sorrows
And rise to bless You still:
To marvel at Your beauty
And glory in Your ways,
And make a joyful duty
Our sacrifice of praise!

O GOD, MOST HIGH, Almighty King,
The Champion of heaven, Lord of everything;
You've fought, You've won, death's lost its
    sting,
And standing in Your victory we sing.

*You have broken the chains
That held our captive souls.
You have broken the chains
And used them on Your foes.
All Your enemies are bound,
They tremble at the sound of Your name;
Jesus, You have broken the chains.*

The power of hell has been undone,
Captivity held captive by the risen One,
And in the name of God's great Son,
We claim the mighty victory You've won.

O GOD OF BURNING, CLEANSING FLAME:
Send the fire!
Your blood-bought gift today we claim:
Send the fire today!
Look down and see this waiting host,
And send the promised Holy Ghost;
We need another Pentecost!
Send the fire today!
Send the fire today!

God of Elijah, hear our cry:
Send the fire!
And make us fit to live or die:
Send the fire today!
To burn up every trace of sin,
To bring the light and glory in,
The revolution now begin!
Send the fire today!
Send the fire today!

It's fire we want, for fire we plead:
Send the fire!
The fire will meet our every need:
Send the fire today!
For strength to always do what's right,
For grace to conquer in the fight,
For power to walk the world in white:
Send the fire today!
Send the fire today!

To make our weak hearts strong and brave:
Send the fire!
To live, a dying world to save:
Send the fire today!
Oh, see us on Your altar lay,
We give our lives to you today,
So crown the offering now we pray:
Send the fire today!
Send the fire today!
Send the fire today!

OH, LEAD ME
To the place where I can find You.
Oh, lead me
To the place where You'll be.

Lead me to the cross
Where we first met;
Draw me to my knees,
So we can talk.
Let me feel Your breath,
Let me know You're here with me.

OH, OUR LORD AND KING,
*Our praise to You we bring,
There is no other Rock but You.
Seated high above,
You are the One we love,
This is our song of praise to You.*

King forever!
You are the First and You're the Last.
You are sovereign;
All Your commands will always
Come to pass, to give You glory!

Who is like You?
Who else is worthy of pur praise?
We exalt You;
You reign in majesty and
Awesome splendour,
King forever!

Abba Father,
Your steadfast love will never fail.
You are faithful,
You are God and I will
Worship in Your
Courts for ever.

958 Geoff Bullock.
Copyright © 1997 Watershed Productions/
Kingsway's Thankyou Music.

OH, THE MERCY OF GOD, the glory of grace,
That You chose to redeem us, to forgive and
restore,
And You call us Your children, chosen in Him
To be holy and blameless to the glory of God.

To the praise of His glorious grace,
To the praise of His glory and power;
To Him be all glory, honour and praise
Forever and ever and ever, amen.

Oh, the richness of grace, the depths of His
love,
In Him is redemption, the forgiveness of sin.
You called us as righteous, predestined in
Him
For the praise of His glory, included in Christ.

Oh, the glory of God expressed in His Son,
His image and likeness revealed to us all;
The plea of the ages completed in Christ,
That we be presented perfected in Him.

959 Craig Musseau.
Copyright © 1992 Mercy/Vineyard Publishing/
Adm. by CopyCare.

O LORD, ARISE, release Your power,
Scatter Your foes this very hour.
May we hold on to Your holy commands.
You are the Lord of every man.

You hold our lives, You give us breath,
You freed us from the power of death.
You're our salvation, our only hope,
You are the Lord of every man.

Your voice, it is like thunder
Over the waters.
Your voice echoes throughout the earth,
We will bow to the sound,
We will bow to the sound
Of Your voice.

960 Chris DePré.
Copyright © Heart of David Music.

**O LORD, HOW I LOVE TO SING YOUR
PRAISES.**
O Lord, how I love to dance for You.
O Lord, You have captured my affection,
Forever I will sing of Your love,
Forever I will bring to You my life,
Forever I will worship You.

And when I think of what You've done,
It makes me shout for joy.
And when I think of what's to come,
Living forever in Your presence,
Face to face with my magnificent obsession,
Forever, forever I will be with You.

Oh, la, la, la …
Oh, la, la, la …
Oh, la, la, la …
Forever, forever I will be with You.

961 Andy Park.
Copyright © 1991 Andy Park/Kingsway's
Thankyou Music.

O LORD I WANT TO SING YOUR PRAISES,
I want to praise Your name every day.
O Lord I want to sing Your praises,
I want to praise Your name every day.

Alleluia, allelu.
Alleluia, allelu.
(Alleluia.)

God, You are my God, and I will seek You;
I am satisfied when I find Your love.
God, You are my God, and I will seek You;
I am satisfied when I find Your love.

And I will praise You as long as I live,
For Your love is better than life.
In Your name I will lift up my hands,
For Your love is better than life.

962 Michael W. Smith.
Copyright © 1981 Meadowgreen Music/EMI
Christian Music Publishing/Adm. by CopyCare.

O LORD OUR LORD,
How majestic is Your name in all the earth.
O Lord our Lord,
How majestic is Your name in all the earth.
O Lord, we praise Your name;
O Lord, we magnify Your name.
Prince of Peace,
Mighty God,
O Lord God Almighty.

963
Jon Soper, Mark Robinson & John Peters.
Copyright © 1994 Kingsway's
Thankyou Music.

**O LORD, YOU ARE MY ROCK AND MY
REDEEMER;**
My song, You are the Strength of my life.
*O Lord, You are the Shepherd of Your
people;*
You keep us always walking in Your light.

You brought me out of darkness,
You took away my shame;
You broke the chains that bound me,
I praise Your name!

You carry all my sorrows,
You carry all my pain;
You fill me with Your Spirit,
I praise Your name!

964
Ian Smale.
Copyright © 1985 Kingsway's
Thankyou Music.

O LORD, YOU'RE GREAT, You are fabulous,
We love You more than any words can sing,
sing, sing.
O Lord, You're great, You are so generous,
You lavish us with gifts when we don't
deserve a thing.

Allelu, alleluia, praise You, Lord.
Alleluia, praise You, Lord.
Alleluia, praise You, Lord.
(Repeat)

O Lord, You're great, You are so powerful,
You hold the mighty universe in Your hand,
hand, hand.
O Lord, You're great, You are so beautiful,
You've poured out Your love on this
undeserving land.

965
Maggi Dawn.
Copyright © 1992 Kingsway's
Thankyou Music.

ONLY ONE THING I ask of the Lord:
Only one thing do I desire:
That I may dwell, may dwell in God's house
All of the days of my life,
All of the days of my life.

Even when days of trouble may come,
I will be safe if God is my home,
For I will hide in the shelter of love
All of the days of my life,
All of the days of my life.

I'll gaze on His beauty,
And sing of His glory;
While I have life within me,
What more could I need?

(Descant)
I'll sing to His holy name,
Forever He is the same,
His faithfulness never change,
Let all of the earth proclaim,
All of the days of my life.

966
Ian White.
Copyright © 1997 Little Misty Music/Kingsway's
Thankyou Music.

OPEN THE DOORS OF PRAISE.
Open the doors of praise.
Open the doors of praise
And let the Lord come in.
(Repeat)

In the spirit world
There's a battle going on,
And it rages endlessly.
But in the name of the Lord,
We can stand on His word,
For in Him we have the victory.

For He lives in the praises of His people, *(echo)*
Here among us to empower us!

And the demons will flee,
As He said it would be,
And the skies will ring with shouts of praise.
And the Lord Jesus Christ
Will be lifted high,
The Holy One who truly saves!

For He lives . . .

967
Maldwyn Pope.
Copyright © 1989 Samsongs/Coronation Music
Publishing/Kingsway's Thankyou Music.

O RIGHTEOUS GOD who searches minds and
hearts,
Bring to an end the violence of my foes,
And make the righteous more secure,
O righteous God.

*Sing praise to the name of the Lord most
high.*
*Sing praise to the name of the Lord most
high.*
*Give thanks to the Lord who rescues me,
O righteous God.*

O Lord my God, I take refuge in You;
Save and deliver me from all my foes.
My shield is God the Lord most high,
O Lord my God.

968 Samuel Trevor Francis.

O THE DEEP, DEEP LOVE OF JESUS!
Vast, unmeasured, boundless, free;
Rolling as a mighty ocean
In its fulness over me.
Underneath me, all around me,
Is the current of Thy love;
Leading onward, leading homeward,
To my glorious rest above.

O the deep, deep love of Jesus!
Spread His praise from shore to shore,
How He loveth, ever loveth,
Changeth never, nevermore;
How He watches o'er His loved ones,
Died to call them all His own;
How for them He intercedeth,
Watches over them from the throne.

O the deep, deep love of Jesus!
Love of every love the best:
'Tis an ocean vast of blessing,
'Tis a haven sweet of rest.
O the deep, deep love of Jesus!
'Tis a heaven of heavens to me;
And it lifts me up to glory,
For it lifts me up to Thee.

969 Brian Doerksen & Michael Hansen.
Copyright © 1990 Mercy/Vineyard Publishing/
Adm. by CopyCare.

OUR FATHER IN HEAVEN,
Holy is Your name.
Forgive us our sins, Lord,
As we forgive.
Our Father in heaven,
Give us our bread.
Lead us not into temptation,
But deliver us from the evil one.

Your kingdom come, Your will be done.
Your kingdom come, Your will be done

On the earth as it is in heaven.
Let it be done on the earth.
Amen. Amen.

970 Keith Routledge.
Copyright © 1992 Kingsway's
Thankyou Music/Sovereign Music UK.

OUR FATHER IN HEAVEN,
Hallowed be Your name,
Your kingdom come,
Your will be done on earth as in heaven.
Give us today our daily bread,
And forgive us our sins
As we forgive those who sin against us,
And lead us not into temptation,
But deliver us from evil;

For the kingdom, the power,
And the glory are Yours,
Now and forever, Amen.

(Last time)
For the kingdom, the power
And the glory are Yours,
Now and forever,
Now and forever,
Now and forever, Amen.

971 Noel & Tricia Richards.
Copyright © 1992 Kingsway's
Thankyou Music.

OUR GOD IS AWESOME IN POWER,
Scatters His enemies;
Our God is mighty in bringing
The powerful to their knees.
He has put on His armour,
He is prepared for war;
Mercy and justice triumph
When the Lion of Judah roars.

The Lord is a warrior,
We will march with Him.
The Lord is a warrior,
Leading us to win.
(Repeat)

Waken the warrior spirit,
Army of God, arise;
Challenge the powers of darkness,
There must be no compromise.
We shall attack their strongholds,
Our hands are trained for war;
We shall advance the kingdom,
For the victory belongs to God.

972 Dave Bilbrough.
Copyright © 1996 Kingsway's
Thankyou Music.

OUR GOD IS GREAT.
(Repeat x 4)

He gave us the wind,
The sun and the snow,
The sand on the sea shore,
The flowers that grow.
Morning and evening,
Winter and spring;
Come join all creation and sing.

The gifts that He brings
Are new every day,
From glorious sunset
To soft falling rain.
The mist on the hills,
The light and the shade;
Come join all creation in praise.

For music and dancing,
The sounds that we hear;
For colours and words,
The life that we share, we say:

OUR PASSION IS FOR YOU, Lord Jesus;
Your grace has fuelled a fire
That burns within our hearts.
There's nowhere that compares
With Your presence;
We've tasted of Your Spirit,
So there's just one thing we ask:

More, more, more, more, more.
More, more, more, more, more.
Pour out, pour out,
Pour out Your Spirit, O Lord.
Pour out, pour out,
Pour out Your Spirit, O Lord

OVER THE HEAVENS ABOVE,
Under the earth below,
Deeper than any sea
Shines the presence of Your glory.
A river with many streams
Flows to the heart of the holy King;
Full of such wonder and mystery,
Living in power and in glory.

Great are You Lord, and mighty,
Your splendour is reigning in the earth.
Your glory is revealed
In the hearts of those who You've redeemed.
Great are You, Lord, and mighty,
Great are You, Lord, and mighty.

OVER THE MOUNTAINS AND THE SEA
Your river runs with love for me,
And I will open up my heart,
And let the Healer set me free.
I'm happy to be in the truth,
And I will daily lift my hands,
For I will always sing of
When Your love came down, yeah.

I could sing of Your love forever,
I could sing of Your love forever.
I could sing of Your love forever,
I could sing of Your love forever.

Oh, I feel like dancing,
It's foolishness I know;
But when the world has seen the light,
They will dance with joy
Like we're dancing now.

OVERWHELMED BY LOVE,
Deeper than oceans,
High as the heavens.
Ever living God
Your love has rescued me.

All my sin was laid
On Your dear Son,
Your precious One.
All my debt He paid,
Great is Your love for me.

No-one could ever earn Your love,
Your grace and mercy is free.
Lord, these words are true,
So is my love for You.

PEACE, PERFECT PEACE, in this dark world of
sin?
The blood of Jesus whispers peace within.

Peace, perfect peace, by thronging duties
pressed?
To do the will of Jesus, this is rest.

Peace, perfect peace, with sorrows surging
round?
In Jesus' presence nought but calm is found.

Peace, perfect peace, with loved ones far
away?
In Jesus' keeping we are safe, and they.

Peace, perfect peace, our future all unknown?
Jesus we know, and He is on the throne.

Peace, perfect peace, death shadowing us
and ours?
Jesus has vanquished death and all its
powers.

It is enough: earth's struggles soon shall
cease,
And Jesus calls us to heaven's perfect peace.

978

POWER FROM ON HIGH,
Power from on high,
Lord, we are waiting
For power from on high.
Power from on high,
Power from on high,
Lord, we are waiting
For power from on high.

May we taste Your heaven
Here on the earth,
May Your Spirit bring us new birth.

May we take Your heaven
To those on the earth,
May Your Spirit bring them new birth.

May the truth and power
Of life that You give
Very soon be ours to live.

979

PRAISE AND GLORY,
Wisdom and honour,
Power and strength and thanksgiving
Be to our God forever and ever,
Amen.
(Repeat)

980

PRAISE GOD FROM WHOM ALL
BLESSINGS FLOW,
Praise Him all creatures here below.
Praise Him above, you heavenly host,
Praise Father, Son and Holy Ghost.
(Repeat)

Give glory to the Father,
Give glory to the Son,
Give glory to the Spirit
While endless ages run.
'Worthy the Lamb'
All heaven cries,
'To be exalted thus:'
'Worthy the Lamb'
Our hearts reply,
'For He was slain for us.'

Praise God from whom all blessings flow,
Praise God from whom all blessings flow.
(x4)

981

PRAISE THE LORD,
ALL YOU SERVANTS OF THE LORD,
Who minister by night within His house.
Lift up your hands
Within the sanctuary,
And praise the Lord.

May the Lord,
The Maker of heaven and earth,
May this Lord bless you from Zion;
Lift up your hands
Within the sanctuary
And praise the Lord.

We praise You, Lord,
We praise You, Lord;
Hallelujah, we praise You, Lord.

982

PROMISE OF THE FATHER,
Given through the Son,
Of power for His children,
The Holy Spirit's come.
Young men will see visions,
Old men will dream dreams;
Sons and daughters prophesy.
Father, send Your Spirit and I'll...

Catch the fire,
As You let the power from heaven fall.
I'll catch the fire,
As Your glory falls on me.
I'll catch the fire
As I open up my life to You.
Your power will set me free.
Let Your power fall on me.

Jesus in His glory
Sends His Spirit now,
That we might be proclaimers
Of the gospel's power.
In worship and in witness
We declare God's love,
Speaking to a dying world,
Jesus has the power to save, I'll...

983

QUIET MY MIND, Lord,
Make me still before You;
Calm my restless heart, Lord,
Make me more like You.
(Repeat)

Raise up my hands that are hanging down;
Strengthen my feeble knees.
May Your love and joy abound,
And fill me with Your peace.

984 Luke & Nathan Fellingham.
Copyright © 1997 Kingsway's
Thankyou Music.

RELEASE YOUR POWER *among us, Lord,*
That all may see Your glory.
(Repeat)

Lord, I give my life to You,
And trust Your holy name;
Help me grow in holiness,
And follow You in all Your ways.
Send Your Holy Spirit,
That I may truly be
Cleansed within my heart
And free from all impurity.

O Lord, as we come trusting our way to You,
Make our righteousness shine like the dawn.

Teach me, Lord, to listen
To the calling of Your Spirit,
Helping me and guiding me
To live my life as Jesus did.
I long to know Your power
And see the sick get healed;
Come and move among us, Lord,
That truth will be revealed.

985 Stuart Garrard.
Copyright © 1994 Kingsway's
Thankyou Music.

RELEASE YOUR POWER, O GOD.
Release Your power, O God,
The visions and dreams in our hearts.
(Repeat)

> *Come, Holy God.*
> *Come, Holy God.*

Release Your fire, O God.
Release Your fire, O God,
A passion that burns in our hearts.
(Repeat).

986 Jim Bailey.
Copyright © 1994 Kingsway's
Thankyou Music.

REMEMBER YOUR CREATOR
In the days of your youth.
(Repeat 4 times)

See people old and grey,
Hear them say:
'Wish I had been that way
When I was young.
I wasn't like you, you see,
Missed the opportunity,
And now I am old
And wish I was told.'

While you are young and strong
You can sing this song,
You can serve the Lord
With all you have.
And you will have no regrets,
You have done what's best;
You have not forgot, to...

987 Helena Barrington.
Copyright © 1988 Integrity's Praise! Music/
Adm. by Kingsway's Thankyou Music.

RIGHTEOUSNESS, PEACE, JOY IN THE HOLY
GHOST;
Righteousness, peace and joy in the Holy
Ghost,
That's the kingdom of God.
(Repeat)

Don't you want to be a part of the kingdom,
Don't you want to be a part of the kingdom,
Don't you want to be a part of the kingdom?
Come on, everybody!
(Repeat)

There's love in the kingdom,
So much love in the kingdom;
There's love in the kingdom.
Come on, everybody!

There's peace in the kingdom...

There's joy in the kingdom...

I'm an heir of the kingdom...

988 Peter Arajs.
Copyright © 1989 Kingsway's
Thankyou Music.

RISE UP, *let Your kingdom arise in us;*
We lift our eyes to the skies, and rise up
To the brightness of His rising.
(Repeat)

All creation awaits
The revealing of the sons of God,
And all the angels of heaven
Are listening for the prayers of us:
Hearing the sound of a powerful flood,
Saints of our God who've been bought by His
blood.

The redemption of God
Has given us a kingdom view,
And His promise to us,
The hope of glory, Christ in you.
Darkness shall run from the strength of His
    hand,
Our testimony, the blood of the Lamb.

989 Paul Oakley.
Copyright © 1996 Kingsway's
Thankyou Music.

RIVER OF GOD, *flood over me,*
And lift my feet up off the ground.
Carry me out into Your sea,
And in Your presence I'll be found.

I've felt Your fire and I've felt Your rain;
And I've heard Your voice whisper my
    name.
I've been wading in Your river,
I've ridden on Your waves;
I've tasted of Your goodness,
Still I'm longing to be changed.

There's something inside me that just won't
    let go;
Why am I afraid of losing control?
Oh, I know Your love is for me,
And You'll never do me harm;
So melt away my fears,
And Holy Spirit come!

I've had enough of holding back,
I see Your goodness all around,
This time I'm opening up my heart,
So come and fill me now.

Please help me, Lord, to be more like You,
To do all the things You've called me to do.
Let me help bring in Your harvest,
Oh, I want it for Your Son;
So fill me with Your power,
Holy Spirit come!

Come like a mighty rushing wind,
A tidal wave or a monsoon rain,
Like a stream in the desert,
Or a warm summer breeze;
Gentle Dove of heaven,
Bring me to my knees!

I've had enough of holding back...

990 David Fellingham.
Copyright © 1994 Kingsway's
Thankyou Music.

RUACH, Ruach,
Holy wind of God, blow on me.
Touch the fading embers, breathe on me.
Fan into a flame all that You've placed in me.
Let the fire burn more powerfully.
Ruach, Ruach,
Holy wind of God,
Holy wind of God, breathe on me.

991 Timothy Dudley-Smith.
Copyright © 1970 Timothy Dudley-Smith.

SAFE IN THE SHADOW OF THE LORD,
Beneath His hand and power,
I trust in Him,
I trust in Him,
My fortress and my tower.

My hope is set on God alone,
Though Satan spreads his snare,
I trust in Him,
I trust in Him,
To keep me in His care.

From fears and phantoms of the night,
From foes about my way,
I trust in Him,
I trust in Him,
By darkness as by day.

His holy angels keep my feet
Secure from every stone;
I trust in Him,
I trust in Him,
And unafraid go on.

Strong in the everlasting Name,
And in my Father's care,
I trust in Him,
I trust in Him,
Who hears and answers prayer.

Safe in the shadow of the Lord,
Possessed by love divine,
I trust in Him,
I trust in Him,
And meet His love with mine.

992 Adrian Howard & Pat Turner.
Copyright © 1985 Restoration Music Ltd/
Adm. by Sovereign Music UK.

SALVATION BELONGS TO OUR GOD,
Who sits on the throne,
And to the Lamb.
Praise and glory, wisdom and thanks,
Honour and power and strength:

Be to our God forever and ever,
Be to our God forever and ever,
Be to our God forever and ever, amen.

And we, the redeemed shall be strong
In purpose and unity,
Declaring aloud,
Praise and glory, wisdom and thanks,
Honour and power and strength:

993 Stuart Townend.
Copyright © 1994 Kingsway's
Thankyou Music.

SAY THE WORD, I will be healed;
You are the great Physician,
You meet every need.
Say the word, I will be free;
Where chains have held me captive,
Come sing Your songs to me,
Say the word.

Say the word, I will be filled;
My hands reach out to heaven,
Where striving is stilled.
Say the word, I will be changed;
Where I am dry and thirsty,
Send cool, refreshing rain,
Say the word.

His tears have fallen like rain on my life;
Each drop a fresh revelation.
I will return to the place of the cross,
Where grace and mercy
Pour from heaven's throne.

Say the word, I will be poor,
That I might know the riches
That You have in store.
Say the word, I will be weak;
Your strength will be the power
That satisfies the meek.
Say the word.

The Lord will see the travail of His soul,
And He and I will be satisfied.
Complete the work You have started in me:
O, come Lord Jesus, shake my life again.

994 Paul Oakley.
Copyright © 1997 Kingsway's
Thankyou Music.

SEARCH ME, O GOD,
And know my heart;
Know all my thoughts and my ways.
Cleanse me, O God,
Give me a pure heart,
That I may see Your face.

For You are an all consuming fire!
For You are an all consuming fire!

Teach me, O God,
Show me Your ways,
And I will walk in Your truth.
Keep me, O God,
Keep me from falling,
That I may stand before You.

Fill me, O God,
And send me out,
And I will make You known.
Give me Your heart
And Your compassion,
And let Your mercy flow.

995 Geoff Twigg.
Copyright © 1994 Kingsway's
Thankyou Music.

SEND FORTH YOUR LIGHT
AND YOUR TRUTH,
Let them guide me,
Let them bring me to Your holy mountain,
To the place where You dwell.
(Repeat)
(Last time)
O Lord.

Then I will come to the altar of God,
My joy and my delight;
Then I will offer the whole of my life,
A living sacrifice.

Jesus, the Way and the Truth and the Life,
My Saviour and my Lord;
Knowing Your presence will be my delight,
Your glory my reward.

996 John Pantry.
Copyright © HarperCollins Religious/Adm.
by CopyCare.

SEND ME OUT FROM HERE, Lord,
To serve a world in need.
May I know no man by the coat he wears,
But the heart that Jesus sees.
And may the light of Your face
Shine upon me, Lord.
You have filled my heart with the greatest
joy,
And my cup is overflowing.

'Go now, and carry the news
To all creation, every race and tongue.
Take no purse with you,
Take nothing to eat
For He will supply your needs.'

'Go now, bearing the light,
Living for others,
Fearlessly walking into the night;
Take no thought for your lives,
Like lambs among wolves,
Full of the Spirit, ready to die.'

997
David Wellington.
Copyright © 1995 Kingsway's
Thankyou Music.

SEND US THE RAIN, LORD,
Rain of Your Spirit,
Rain on this dry barren land.
Send us the rain, Lord,
Rain to revive us;
Cleanse us and fill us again.
Here we are, of one accord,
Calling to You, singing:
Send Your Spirit,
Send Your Spirit,
Send the rain on us again.

Pour out Your wine, Lord,
Wine of Your Spirit,
Wine that would teach us to love.
Pour out Your wine, Lord,
Oh, how we need You
To quench the thirst of our hearts.
Here we are, of one accord,
Calling to You, singing:
Send Your Spirit,
Send Your Spirit,
Pour Your wine on us again.

Breathe now upon us,
Breath of Your Spirit,
Breath to bring life to these bones.
Breathe now upon us,
Life of abundance,
Holiness, wisdom, love, truth.
Here we are, of one accord,
Calling to You, singing:
Send Your Spirit,
Send Your Spirit,
Breathe Your life on us again.

Send down the fire,
Fire of Your Spirit,
Refiner's fire to fulfil.
Send down the fire,
Fire to consume us,
Reveal Your power once more.
Here we are, of one accord,
Calling to You, singing:
Send Your Spirit,
Send Your Spirit,
Send the fire on us again.

998
Dave Bilbrough.
Copyright © 1995 Kingsway's
Thankyou Music.

SEND YOUR RAIN down from the heavens;
Send Your rain to this earth.
Let there be a great outpouring;
Holy Spirit, come to us.

Send Your fire down from the heavens;
The fire of revival to Your church.
We can see the world is waiting;
Holy Spirit, come to us.

Fill this land with Your grace and mercy;
Cause our hearts to worship You.

999
Andy Park.
Copyright © 1989 Mercy/Vineyard Publishing/
Adm. by CopyCare.

SHOW ME, DEAR LORD, how You see me in
Your eyes,
So that I can realise Your great love for me.
Teach me, O Lord, that I am precious in Your
sight,
That as a father loves his child, so You love me.

*I am Yours because You have chosen me.
I'm Your child because You've called my
name,
And Your steadfast love will never change;
I will always be Your precious child.*

Show me, dear Lord, that I can never earn
Your love,
That a gift cannot be earned, only given.
Teach me, O Lord, that Your love will never
fade,
That I can never drive away Your great mercy.

1000
Matt Redman.
Copyright © 1996 Kingsway's
Thankyou Music.

SHOW ME THE WAY OF THE CROSS once
again,
Denying myself for the love that I've gained.
Everything's You now, everything's changed;
It's time You had my whole life,
You can have it all.

*Yes, I resolve to give it all;
Some things must die, some things must
live,
Not 'what can I gain', but 'what can I give'.
If much is required when much is
received,
Then You can have my whole life,
Jesus, have it all.*

I've given like a beggar but lived like the rich,
And crafted myself a more comfortable cross.
Yet what I am called to is deeper than this;
It's time You had my whole life,
You can have it all.

1001

SING A SONG OF CELEBRATION,
Lift up a shout of praise,
For the Bridegroom will come,
The glorious One.
And oh, we will look on His face;
We'll go to a much better place.

Dance with all your might,
Lift up your hands and clap for joy:
The time's drawing near
When He will appear.
And oh, we will stand by His side;
A strong, pure, spotless Bride.

*Oh, we will dance on the streets that are
golden,
The glorious Bride and the great Son of
Man,
From every tongue and tribe and nation
Will join in the song of the Lamb.*

(Men-Women echo)
Sing aloud for the time of rejoicing is near.
The risen King, our Groom is soon to appear.
The wedding feast to come is now near at
hand.
Lift up your voice, proclaim the coming
Lamb.

1002

SING TO GOD NEW SONGS of worship:
All His deeds are marvellous;
He has brought salvation to us
With His hand and holy arm:
He has shown to all the nations
Righteousness and saving power;
He recalled His truth and mercy
To His people Israel.

Sing to God new songs of worship:
Earth has seen His victory;
Let the lands of earth be joyful
Praising Him with thankfulness:
Sound upon the harp His praises,
Play to Him with melody;
Let the trumpets sound His triumph,
Show your joy to God the King!

Sing to God new songs of worship:
Let the sea now make a noise;
All on earth and in the waters
Sound your praises to the Lord:
Let the hills be joyful together,
Let the rivers clap their hands,
For with righteousness and justice
He will come to judge the earth.

1003

SING TO THE LORD with all of your heart;
Sing of the glory that's due to His name.
Sing to the Lord with all of your soul,
Join all of heaven and earth to proclaim:

*You are the Lord, the Saviour of all,
God of creation, we praise You.
We sing the songs that awaken the
dawn,
God of creation, we praise You.*

Sing to the Lord with all of your mind,
With understanding give thanks to the King.
Sing to the Lord with all of your strength,
Living our lives as a praise offering.

1004

SOFTEN MY HEART,
That I may know
The love You have for me,
More than words or well-worn phrases.

Soften my heart,
For love to grow,
The love I have for You,
That keeps my motives pure and
blameless.

Enter in,
Come and have free reign
As I walk with You today.
Risen Lamb,
Holy One,
Overshadow me today.

1005

SOMETIMES WHEN I FEEL YOUR LOVE
As I walk along the busy street,
I whisper Your name under my breath.
And sometimes when I feel Your touch
In the quiet place of my room,
I sing Your name in adoration.
And there are times when I feel like I'm
    bursting
With Your love so strong and so true;
And in my heart I feel such a yearning,
And I want all the world
To know You love them, too.

I love Your love,
Gonna shout it out aloud.
I love Your love,
Wanna tell the world about it.
I love Your love,
'Cause I've found it to be true,
And I live to love You, too.

1006

SON OF MAN and Man of heaven,
Full of grace and truth;
Sinner's friend yet without sin,
I want to be like You:
Perfect in holiness,
Full of faithfulness and love.

I want to be like Jesus,
I want to be like Jesus,
I want to be like You,
O Lord, our God.
(Repeat)

You began a work in me,
I know You'll see it through.
There's a new song in my heart,
And I want to sing to You.
You lifted me from mire,
From sin and from shame You set me free,
And I know Your tenderness,
I know Your power at work in me.

You're making me like Jesus ...

1007

SOON, AND VERY SOON,
We are going to see the King;
Soon, and very soon,
We are going to see the King;
Soon, and very soon,
We are going to see the King;
Alleluia, alleluia,
We're going to see the King!

No more crying there ...

No more dying there ...

Alleluia, alleluia,
Alleluia, alleluia.

Soon, and very soon ...

Alleluia ...

1008

SOUND THE TRUMPET, strike the drum,
See the King of glory come,
Join the praises rising from
The people of the Lord.
Let your voices now be heard,
Unrestrained and unreserved,
Prepare the way for His return,
You people of the Lord.

Sing Jesus is Lord;
Jesus is Lord.

Bow down to His authority,
For He has slain the enemy.
Of heaven and hell He holds the key.
Jesus is Lord;
Jesus is Lord.

1009

SPIRIT OF GOD, SHOW ME JESUS,
Remove the darkness,
Let truth shine through!
Spirit of God, show me Jesus,
Reveal the fulness of His love to me.

1010 Christopher Idle.
Copyright © Christopher Idle/Jubilate Hymns.

SPIRIT OF HOLINESS,
Wisdom and faithfulness,
Wind of the Lord,
Blowing strongly and free:
Strength of our serving
And joy of our worshipping;
Spirit of God,
Bring Your fulness to me!

You came to interpret
And teach us effectively
All that the Saviour
Has spoken and done;
To glorify Jesus is all Your activity;
Promise and Gift
Of the Father and Son:

You came with Your gifts
To supply all our poverty,
Pouring Your love
On the church in her need;
You came with Your fruit
For our growth to maturity,
Richly refreshing
The souls that You feed:

1011 Darlene Zschech.
Copyright © 1996 Darlene Zschech/Hillsongs
Australia/Kingsway's Thankyou Music.

STANDING IN YOUR PRESENCE,
Lord, my heart and life are changed;
Just to love You and to live to
See Your beauty and Your grace.

Heaven and earth cry out Your name,
Nations rise up and see Your face;
And Your kingdom is established
As I live to know You more.
Now I will never be the same;
Spirit of God, my life You've changed,
And I'll forever sing Your praise.
I live to know You, Lord.
I live to know You, Lord.

You've called me, I will follow;
Your will for me I'm sure.
Let Your heartbeat be my heart's cry,
Let me live to serve Your call.

1012 Dave Browning.
Copyright © 1986 Glory Alleluia Music/Tempo
Music Publications/Adm. by CopyCare.

TAKE ME PAST THE OUTER COURTS,
And through the holy place,
Past the brazen altar,
Lord, I want to see Your face.
Pass me by the crowds of people,
And the priests who sing their praise;
I hunger and thirst for Your righteousness,
But it's only found one place,

So take me into the Holy of holies,
Take me in by the blood of the Lamb;
So take me into the Holy of holies,
Take the coal, cleanse my lips, here I am.

1013 Graham Kendrick & Steve Thompson.
Copyright © 1993 Make Way Music.

TEACH ME TO DANCE *to the beat of Your*
heart,
Teach me to move in the power of Your
Spirit,
Teach me to walk in the light of Your
presence,
Teach me to dance to the beat of Your
heart.
Teach me to love with Your heart of
compassion,
Teach me to trust in the word of Your
promise,
Teach me to hope in the day of Your
coming,
Teach me to dance to the beat of Your
heart.

You wrote the rhythm of life,
Created heaven and earth;
In You is joy without measure.
So, like a child in Your sight,
I dance to see Your delight,
For I was made for Your pleasure,
Pleasure.

Let all my movements express
A heart that loves to say 'yes',
A will that leaps to obey You.
Let all my energy blaze
To see the joy in Your face;
Let my whole being praise You,
Praise You.

1014 Kevin Prosch.

TEACH US, O LORD, what it really means
To rend our hearts instead of outer things.
And teach us, O God, what we do not see
About our hearts and of Your ways.
And Father deal with our carnal desires,
To move in Your power, but not live the life,
And to love our neighbour with all that we
    have,
And keep our tongues from saying things we
    have not seen.

*O, break our hearts with the things that
    break Yours,*
If we sow in tears, we will reap in joy,
*That we might pass through Your refining
    fire,*
*Where brokenness awaits on the other
    side.*

Raise up an army like Joel saw,
Your church that is stronger than ever
    before.
They do not break ranks when they plunge
    through defences,
But the fear of the Lord will be their wisdom.
That they might weep as Jesus wept,
A fountain of tears for the wounded and lost;
Whoever heard of an army, O God,
That conquered the earth by weeping,
And mourning, and brokenness?

*But there will be a day when the nations
    will bow*
*And our Lord will be King over all the
    earth;*
And He will be the only One,
And also His name will be the only One.

1015 Martin Smith.

THANK YOU FOR SAVING ME;
What can I say?
You are my everything,
I will sing Your praise.
You shed Your blood for me;
What can I say?
You took my sin and shame,
A sinner called by name.

Great is the Lord.
Great is the Lord.
For we know Your truth has set us free;
You've set Your hope in me.

Mercy and grace are mine,
Forgiven is my sin;
Jesus, my only hope,
The Saviour of the world.
'Great is the Lord,' we cry;
God, let Your kingdom come.
Your word has let me see,
Thank You for saving me.

1016 Richard Lewis.

THE ANGELS AROUND YOUR THRONE,
They cry, 'Holy is the Lamb.'
The angels around Your throne,
They cry, 'Holy is the Lamb.'
So we sing holy, holy, holy,
Holy is the Lamb.
So we sing holy, holy, holy,
Holy is the Lamb.

The angels around Your throne,
They cry, 'Worthy is the Lamb.'
The angels around Your throne,
They cry, 'Worthy is the Lamb.'
So we sing worthy, worthy, worthy,
Worthy is the Lamb.
So we sing worthy, worthy, worthy,
Worthy is the Lamb.

1017 Matt Redman.

THE ANGELS, LORD, THEY SING
Around Your throne;
And we will join their song:
Praise You alone.
(Repeat)

Holy, holy, holy,
Lord our God,
Who was and is and is to come.
(Repeat)

The living creatures, Lord,
Speak endless praise;
And joining at Your throne,
We'll sing their sweet refrain.
(Repeat)

The elders, Lord, they fall
Before Your throne;
Our hearts we humbly bow
To You alone.
(Repeat)

1018 Doug Horley.
Copyright © 1994 Kingsway's
Thankyou Music.

THE BATTLE IS THE LORD'S,
The battle is the Lord's,
The battle is the Lord's
That is our victory cry.
(Repeat)

We refuse to bow to satan's schemes,
Set our wills for righteousness;
We declare we'll choose for truth
In every situation.
We could battle in the heavenlies,
Yet in our lives neglect to fight:
Saying no to self and no to sin
Is where our warfare must begin.

As we're taking ground in daily war,
Living lives of righteousness,
We will grow in strength to face
The bigger situations.
And the more of us that battle through,
The purer then this church will be;
Who will stop us then as we proclaim:
'Strongholds, you have had your day!'

1019 Matt Redman & Martin Smith.
Copyright © 1995 Kingsway's
Thankyou Music.

THE CROSS HAS SAID IT ALL,
The cross has said it all.
I can't deny what You have shown,
The cross speaks of a God of love;
There displayed for all to see,
Jesus Christ, our only hope,
A message of the Father's heart:
'Come, my children, come on home.'

As high as the heavens are above the
earth,
So high is the measure of Your great love;
As far as the east is from the west,
So far have You taken our sins from us.
(Repeat)

The cross has said it all,
The cross has said it all.
I never recognised Your touch
Until I met You at the cross;
We are fallen, dust to dust,
How could You do this for us?
Son of God shed precious blood:
Who can comprehend this love?

How high, how wide, how deep;
(Repeat x4)
How high!

1020 Martin Smith.
Copyright © 1993 Kingsway's
Thankyou Music.

THE CRUCIBLE FOR SILVER
And the furnace for gold,
But the Lord tests the heart of this child.
Standing in all purity,
God, our passion is for holiness,
Lead us to the secret place of praise.

Jesus, Holy One,
You are my heart's desire.
King of kings, my everything,
You've set this heart on fire.
(Repeat)

Father, take our offering, with our song we
humbly praise You.
You have brought Your holy fire to our lips.
Standing in Your beauty, Lord,
Your gift to us is holiness;
Lead us to the place where we can sing:

1021 Dave Bilbrough & Andy Piercy.
Copyright © 1995 Kingsway's
Thankyou Music/I Q Music.

THE DAY OF THE STREAMS *is over,*
The time of the river is here.
(Repeat x4)

I hear the sound of a mighty river,
Of rushing water running free
To every land, through every border,
Flowing now across this earth.

There is a time I know is coming,
When all God's people join as one;
They will become a great awakening,
Bringing life to all the world.

And the river is flowing,
Getting wider and wider,
Deeper and deeper
As it flows from the throne;
And the leaves on the trees
Are for the healing of the nations,
It's as clear as crystal,
It's the water of life.

1022 Geoff Bullock.
Copyright © 1997 Watershed
Productions/Kingsway's Thankyou Music.

THE EARTH RESOUNDS IN SONGS OF PRAISE;
Creation shouts Your glorious name,
And the skies speak forth Your majesty,
And the heavens declare Your glory.
Your kingdom rules from age to age;
Every tribe and tongue shall bring You praise,
And we come to bow before the throne
Of the Lord of the heavens and earth.

Jesus, King of kings,
Jesus, Lord of lords,
We proclaim Your kingdom come,
Jesus, Son of God.
Lord, enthroned on high
Above the heavens and the earth,
We proclaim Your kingdom come!

1023

THE GRACE OF GOD upon my life
Is not dependent upon me,
On what I have done
Or deserved,
But a gift of mercy from God
Which has been given unto me
Because of His love,
His love for me.

It is unending, unfailing,
Unlimited, unmerited,
The grace of God given unto me.
It is unending, unfailing,
Unlimited, unmerited,
The grace of God given unto me.

1024

THE HEAVENS THEY PREACH, they preach,
They preach the glorious splendour of God.
The stars in the sky seem so out of reach,
Yet they whisper His wonderful love.
Day after day in a sermon of nature
The works of His hands lift their voice:
'Wake up, you nations, and serve Your Creator,
There's mercy in Him, so rejoice!'

And I'll lift my heart and my hands to Him,
And I'll let my life shine with love
To God's wonderful Son.
He wears the crown, He's the King.
Come and behold Him now,
Come and delight in His excellent virtues;
Seek Him while He can be found,
For He is the help and the hope
For all the world.

The prophets, they preached, they preached,
They preached that one day a Saviour would
   come;
And suddenly men heard a heavenly speech,
The voice of God's only Son.
Day after day in the streets and the temple
He taught them and met their needs,
And now through His death and His great
   resurrection
His glorious purpose succeeds.

Your people will preach, we'll preach,
We'll preach the unfailing riches of Christ;
There's no one who's fallen too far from His
   reach,
Who can't come from death into life.
Day after day at the dawn of revival
The multitudes seek His face,
As we work to speed on His final arrival
And crown Him with glory and praise!

1025

THE KING OF LOVE is my delight,
His eyes are fire, His face is light,
The First and Last, the Living One,
His name is Jesus.
And from His mouth there comes a sound
That shakes the earth and splits the ground,
And yet this voice is life to me,
The voice of Jesus.

And I will sing my songs of love,
Calling out across the earth;
The King has come,
The King of love has come.
And troubled minds can know His peace,
Captive hearts can be released;
The King has come,
The King of love has come.

My Lover's breath is sweetest wine,
I am His prize, and He is mine;
How can a sinner know such joy?
Because of Jesus.
The wounds of love are in His hands,
The price is paid for sinful man;
Accepted child, forgiven son,
Because of Jesus.

And my desire is to have You near;
Lord, You know that You are welcome here.
Before such love, before such grace
I will let the walls come down.

1026

THE LIGHT OF CHRIST
Has come into the world;
The light of Christ
Has come into the world.

All men must be born again
To see the kingdom of God;
The water and the Spirit
Bring new life in God's love.

God gave up His only Son
Out of love for the world,
So that all men who believe in Him
Will live forever.

The light of God has come to us
So that we might have salvation;
From the darkness of our sins we walk
Into glory with Christ Jesus.

1027 Merrilyn Billing.
Copyright © 1989 Arise Ministries/
Kingsway's Thankyou Music.

THE LORD FILLS ME WITH HIS STRENGTH,
And protects me wherever I go.
The Lord fills me with His strength,
And protects me wherever I go.

Wherever I go, wherever I go,
The Lord protects me wherever I go.
Wherever I go, wherever I go,
The Lord protects me wherever I go.

1028 Paul Oakley.
Copyright © 1991 Kingsway's
Thankyou Music.

THE LORD HAS SPOKEN. (Men/Women echo)
His purpose stands. (Men/Women echo)
The Lord has spoken. (Men/Women echo)
His purpose stands. (Men/Women echo)

Does God speak and then not act?
Make a vow and not fulfil?
I will choose to serve the Lord
Wholeheartedly, wholeheartedly.

> (Ch 1.)
> *Oh, raise up a church*
> *With a different spirit,*
> *Like Caleb's spirit, believing Your word.*
> *Oh, raise up a church who will not sin,*
> *They press on in to possess the land.*

You began with just one man,
A covenant with Abraham,
Promising that through his seed
The nations would be blessed,
And now Your plan is manifest.

> (Repeat Ch1.)

> (Ch2.)
> *Oh, raise up a church who walk by faith,*
> *In the fear of God they overcome.*
> *Oh, raise up a church*
> *Whose God is with them,*
> *They walk in wisdom, they fear no harm.*

Deliver us from the fear of man,
And by Your grace we shall stand.
We'll call to mind Your mighty works
And Your acts of sovereign power;
We'll gather strength as we agree
The battle belongs to the Lord.

> (Repeat Ch1. & Ch2.)

> (Ch 3.)
> *Oh, raise up a church*
> *Who revere Your judgements,*
> *They lift up a banner of mercy and love.*
> *Oh, raise up a church*
> *Who'll not keep silent,*
> *They speak of the glory of Your dear Son.*

1029 Daniel C Stradwick.
Copyright © 1980 Scripture in Song, a
division of Integrity Music/Adm. by
Kingsway's Thankyou Music.

THE LORD REIGNS, *the Lord reigns,*
The Lord reigns,
Let the earth rejoice, let the earth rejoice,
Let the earth rejoice.
Let the people be glad
That our God reigns.

A fire goes before Him
And burns up all His enemies;
The hills melt like wax
At the presence of the Lord,
At the presence of the Lord.

The heavens declare His righteousness,
The peoples see His glory;
For You, O Lord, are exalted
Over all the earth,
Over all the earth.

1030 Stuart Townend.
Copyright © 1996 Kingsway's
Thankyou Music.

THE LORD'S MY SHEPHERD, I'll not want.
He makes me lie in pastures green.
He leads me by the still, still waters,
His goodness restores my soul.

> *And I will trust in You alone.*
> *And I will trust in You alone,*
> *For Your endless mercy follows me,*
> *Your goodness will lead me home.*

> (Descant)
> *I will trust, I will trust in You.*
> *I will trust, I will trust in You.*
> *Endless mercy follows me,*
> *Goodness will lead me home.*

He guides my ways in righteousness,
And He anoints my head with oil,
And my cup, it overflows with joy,
I feast on His pure delights.

And though I walk the darkest path,
I will not fear the evil one,
For You are with me, and Your rod and staff
Are the comfort I need to know.

1031

THE LOVE OF GOD, heaven's hope;
This perfect peace, this rest for my soul.
This love divine, portrayed in pain,
The cross stands alone,
Unfailing love.

This love of God, creation's cry;
Perfection portrayed, broken for me.
The Author of life has suffered our pain.
The cross stands alone,
Unfailing love.

> *The love of God was found in the nails;*
> *The love of God was seen in the scars.*
> *The light and the life was darkened by*
> *   death,*
> *My hope and salvation carried to life,*
> *Unfailing love.*

The love of God, written in blood;
This empty grave, the stone rolled away!
The mercy of God has triumphed in Christ.
The cross stands alone,
Unfailing love.

1032

THE NAME OF THE LORD is a strong tower;
The name of the Lord brings refuge and
   strength.
The name of the Lord gives hope to the
   hopeless;
The name of the Lord breathes life to the
   dead.

The name of the Lord give strength to the
   weary,
The name of the Lord brings freedom from
   fear;
The name of the Lord gives peace to the
   restless,
The name of the Lord will heal the oppressed.

O Lord, You never change,
Holy God, You remain the same,
For Your love, it never fades,
Your faithfulness surrounds me.

> *For You alone are God, and I bow before*
> *   You.*
> *You alone are God, I worship, adore You.*
> *You alone are God, none other before You,*
> *And I offer up my life again.*

The name of the Lord covers me with mercy,
The name of the Lord brings everlasting joy;
The name of the Lord will lift all my
   burdens,
The name of the Lord, it makes me
   complete.

I call, and You answer me,
For You know my every need.
In Your love I put my trust,
Your faithfulness surrounds me.

O taste and see
That the Lord is good.
How blessèd is the man
Who hides himself in Him.

1033

THERE IS A HOME that wanderers seek,
There is a strength that lifts the weak;
There is hope for those that know despair.
There is a cup that satisfies,
There is a Friend who dries my eyes;
There is peace for those with heavy hearts.

> *Tender mercy,*
> *The tender mercy of our God,*
> *From lips of sinners*
> *He has heard the faintest cry.*
> *Tender mercy,*
> *The tender mercy of our God,*
> *He has relented and His grace is my*
> *   delight.*

I have resolved to know Him more,
He whom the hosts of heaven adore,
Mighty King, whose reign will never end.
Yet as I gaze at the Holy One,
He beckons me to closer come,
Bares the scars that show to me my worth.

1034 Matt Redman.
Copyright © 1996 Kingsway's
Thankyou Music.

THERE IS A LOUDER SHOUT TO COME,
There is a sweeter song to hear;
All the nations with one voice,
All the people with one fear.
Bowing down before Your throne,
Every tribe and tongue will be;
All the nations with one voice,
All the people with one King.
And what a song we'll sing upon that day.

O what a song we'll sing and
O what a tune we'll bear;
You deserve an anthem of the highest
praise.
O what a joy will rise and
O what a sound we'll make;
You deserve an anthem of the highest
praise.

Now we see a part of this,
One day we shall see in full;
All the nations with one voice,
All the people with one love.
No one else will share Your praise,
Nothing else can take Your place;
All the nations with one voice,
All the people with one Lord.
And what a song we'll sing upon that day.

Even now upon the earth
There's a glimpse of all to come;
Many people with one voice,
Harmony of many tongues.
We will all confess Your name,
You will be our only praise;
All the nations with one voice,
All the people with one God.
And what a song we'll sing upon that day.

1035 Lenny LeBlanc.
Copyright © 1991 Integrity's Hosanna! Music/
Adm. by Kingsway's Thankyou Music.

THERE IS NONE LIKE YOU,
No one else can touch my heart like You do.
I could search for all eternity long and find
There is none like You.

Your mercy flows like a river wide,
And healing comes from Your hands.
Suffering children are safe in Your arms;
There is none like You.

1036 Noel & Tricia Richards.
Copyright © 1996 Kingsway's
Thankyou Music.

THERE IS NO ONE LIKE OUR GOD *in all*
the earth.
There is no one like our God in all the
earth.
No one like our God,
No one like our God.

Our God has made the heavens,
Our God has made the earth;
And everything that lives,
His word has brought to birth.

He numbers every star,
And calls each one by name;
He fills the skies with clouds,
Supplies the earth with rain.

Sing praises to our God,
Sing praises to His name;
His love will never end,
His word will never fail.

God is with us.
God is with us.
God is with us.

1037 David Ruis.
Copyright © 1996 Mercy/Vineyard Publishing/
Adm. by CopyCare.

THERE IS NO OTHER FRIEND,
There is no other friend like You, O Lord;
No other brother, no other sister like You.
There is no other love,
There is no other love like You, O Lord;
No other sweeter, no other fountain but You.

How long until I'm satisfied?
I must have more of You.
For I was born in Zion,
Awakened love is crying out for You.
Lord, it must be You!

If I am healed by just one touch of Your
garment, Lord,
Then how much more of Your love is for me
Than I'm tasting, Lord?
Draw me, take me, I will run
Over the mountains and down
Into the valley, I will run with You.

Ah, all my fountains are in You.
(Repeat)

1038 Robert Critchley.
Copyright © 1993 Kingsway's
Thankyou Music.

THERE IS ONE NAME under heaven
By which men can be saved,
Jesus alone.
Only one name under heaven,
Jesus, and Jesus alone.

One sacrifice,
One holy Lamb
Shed His own blood,
Paid for my sin;
And this righteous One,
God's only Son,
I sing my praises to Him,
I sing my praises to Him.

1039 Geoff Bullock.
Copyright © 1997 Watershed Productions/
Kingsway's Thankyou Music.

THERE'S A LIGHT THAT SHINES, a lamp that
    burns,
The hope, the peace of righteousness.
And You who hear the prayers of all,
You call us near to You.

There's a path that leads, a way that's true,
The life, the light, the perfect truth.
We come to You forgiven, free,
You call us near to You.

   And the light shines so we can see,
   And the truth came so we could know.
   And the light of God is the light of men,
   And His life gives life to all.

No other way, no other life,
No other truth, no other light.
The way ahead is found in Christ,
You call us near to You.

We will dance and sing, for freedom comes
To heal our hearts and dry our tears.
Forever more in glorious light
You call us near to You.

1040 Richard Lewis.
Copyright © 1997 Kingsway's
Thankyou Music.

THERE'S AN AWESOME SOUND
On the winds of heaven,
Mighty thunder clouds
In the skies above.
The immortal King,
Who will reign forever,
Is reaching out with His arms of love,
His arms of love,
His arms of love.

All creation sings
Of the Lamb of glory,
Who laid down His life
For all the world.
What amazing love,
That the King of heaven
Should be crucified,
Stretching out His arms,
His arms of love,
His arms of love.

   Send revival to this land,
   Fill this nation with Your love.
   (Repeat)

1041 Paul Oakley.
Copyright © 1995 Kingsway's
Thankyou Music.

**THERE'S A PLACE WHERE THE STREETS
    SHINE**
With the glory of the Lamb.
There's a way, we can go there,
We can live there beyond time.

   Because of You, because of You,
   Because of Your love,
   Because of Your blood.

No more pain, no more sadness,
No more suffering, no more tears.
No more sin, no more sickness,
No injustice, no more death.

   Because of You, because of You,
   Because of Your love,
   Because of Your blood.

   All our sins are washed away,
   And we can live forever,
   Now we have this hope,
   Because of You.
   Oh, we'll see You face to face,
   And we will dance together
   In the city of our God,
   Because of You.

There is joy everlasting,
There is gladness, there is peace.
There is wine ever flowing,
There's a wedding, there's a feast.

1042 Malcolm du Plessis.
Copyright © 1991 Maranatha! Music/
Adm. by CopyCare.

THERE'S A RIVER flowing from the throne,
Not a gentle stream but powerful flow.
It brings the city of our God such joy,
And springs up fountains in her midst.
On the banks the trees are full of life,
The fruit just grows and grows all the year
   round.
The leaves are green and never seem to die,
They're for the healing of this world.

There's a river, there's a river,
There's a river flowing from the throne.
There's a river, there's a river
And it flows through out the world.
There's a river, there's a river,
There's a river flowing from the throne.
There's a river, there's a river
And it's flooding over me.

You invited me to come for free,
Enjoy the feast You had prepared for me;
Draw with laughter from Your sparkling wells,
Bathe in Your river of delights.
First You led me to the edge of the stream,
Cautiously I put my ankles in;
The thrill was just too much to describe,
And I heard You call me deeper still!

1043 Taran Ash, James Mott & Matthew Pryce.
Copyright © 1997 Kingsway's
Thankyou Music.

THERE'S A RIVER OF JOY that flows from
   Your throne,
O river of joy flow through me.
There's a river of joy that flows from Your throne:
Come, Holy Spirit, with joy,
Come, Holy Spirit, with joy.

I will rise up on the wings of an eagle;
With joy I receive Your love.
I will praise You with a song everlasting.
Thank You, Lord, for Your love.
Thank You, Lord, for Your love.

1044 David Ruis.
Copyright © 1994 Mercy/Vineyard Publishing/
Adm. by CopyCare.

THERE'S A WIND A-BLOWING
All across the land;
Fragrant breeze of heaven
Blowing once again.
Don't know where it comes from,
Don't know where it goes,
But let it blow over me.
Oh, sweet wind,
Come and blow over me.

There's a rain a-pouring,
Showers from above;
Mercy drops are coming,
Mercy drops of love.
Turn your face to heaven,
Let the water pour,
Well, let it pour over me.
Oh, sweet rain,
Come and pour over me.

There's a fire burning,
Falling from the sky;
Awesome tongues of fire,
Consuming you and I.
Can you feel it burning,
Burn the sacrifice?
Well, let it burn over me.
Oh, sweet fire,
Come and burn over me.

1045 Eddie Espinosa
Copyright © 1990 Mercy/Vineyard Publishing/
Adm. by CopyCare.

THERE'S NO ONE LIKE YOU, my Lord,
No one could take Your place;
My heart beats to worship You,
I live just to seek Your face.
There's no one like You, my Lord,
No one could take Your place;
There's no one like You, my Lord,
No one like You.

You are my God,
You're everything to me;
There's no one like You, my Lord,
No one like You.
You are my God.
You're everything to me;
There's no one like You, my Lord,
No one like You.

There's no one like You, my Lord,
No one could take Your place;
I long for Your presence, Lord,
To serve You is my reward.
There's no one like You, my Lord,
No one could take Your place;
There's no one like You, my Lord,
No one like You.

1046 Ian Smale.
Copyright © 1994 Kingsway's
Thankyou Music.

THERE'S NOTHING I LIKE BETTER THAN TO PRAISE.

There's nothing I like better
Than to praise.
'Cause Lord, I love You,
And there's nothing I would rather do
Than whisper about it,
Talk all about it.
Shout all about it all my days.

1047 Robin Mark.
Copyright © 1997 Daybreak Music Ltd.

THESE ARE THE DAYS OF ELIJAH,

Declaring the word of the Lord:
And these are the days of Your servant
   Moses,
Righteousness being restored.
And though these are days of great trial,
Of famine and darkness and sword,
Still, we are a voice in the desert crying
'Prepare ye the way of the Lord.'

> *Behold He comes riding on the clouds,*
> *Shining like the sun at the trumpet call;*
> *Lift your voice, it's the year of jubilee,*
> *Out of Zion's hill salvation comes.*

These are the days of Ezekiel,
The dry bones becoming as flesh;
And these are the days of Your servant David,
Rebuilding the temple of praise.
These are the days of the harvest,
The fields are as white in the world,
And we are the labourers in the vineyard,
Declaring the word of the Lord.

1048 Mick Gisbey.
Copyright © 1985 Kingsway's
Thankyou Music.

THE SKY IS FILLED with the glory of God.

Triumphantly the angels sing:
'Rejoice, good news, a Saviour is born,
And life will never be the same.'

> *Emmanuel.*
> *Emmanuel.*
> *Emmanuel.*

Praise and adoration spring from our hearts,
We lift our voices unto You;
You are the One, God's only Son,
King of kings forever more!

1049 Andy Park.
Copyright © 1992 Mercy/Vineyard Publishing/
Adm. by CopyCare.

THE SPIRIT OF THE SOVEREIGN LORD is

upon you,
Because He has anointed you
To preach good news.
(Repeat)

He has sent you to the poor, *(Men)*
This is the year: *(Women)*
To bind up the brokenhearted, *(Men)*
This is the day: *(Women)*
To bring freedom to the captives, *(Men)*
This is the year: *(Women)*
And to release the ones in darkness. *(All)*

> *This is the year of the favour of the Lord.*
> *This is the day of the vengeance of our*
>   *God.*
> *This is the year of the favour of the Lord.*
> *This is the day of the vengeance of our*
>   *God.*

The Spirit of the Sovereign Lord is upon us,
Because He has anointed us
To preach good news.
(Repeat)

He will comfort all who mourn *(Men)*
This is the year: *(Women)*
He will provide for those who grieve; *(Men)*
This is the day: *(Women)*
He will pour out the oil of gladness, *(Men)*
This is the year: *(Women)*
Instead of mourning you will praise. *(All)*

1050 Author unknown.

THE VIRGIN MARY HAD A BABY BOY,

The Virgin Mary had a baby boy,
The Virgin Mary had a baby boy,
And they said that His name was Jesus.

> *He come from the glory,*
> *He come from the glorious kingdom.*
> *He come from the glory,*
> *He come from the glorious kingdom.*
> *Oh, yes! believer.*
> *Oh, yes! believer.*
> *He come from the glory,*
> *He come from the glorious kingdom.*

The angels sang when the baby was born,
The angels sang when the baby was born,
The angels sang when the baby was born,
And proclaiming Him the Saviour Jesus.

The wise men saw where the baby was born,
The wise men saw where the baby was born,
The wise men saw where the baby was born,
And they saw that His name was Jesus.

1051 Dave Bilbrough.
Copyright © 1996 Kingsway's
Thankyou Music.

THE WAVES ARE BREAKING, the tide is
   turning,
God's Spirit is coming to this earth;
The harvest is waiting,
And we have been called
To go to the nations of this world.

> *To the ends of the earth,*
> *To the ends of the earth,*
> *To the ends of the earth we will go;*
> *Bearing the message*
> *That our God can be known,*
> *To the ends of the earth we will go.*

The fire is falling, the wind is blowing,
The flame is spreading across our land;
Revival is coming, let the world hear,
Tell every woman, child and man.

The drums are beating,
The trumpet is sounding,
A warrior spirit He's put in our hearts;
In the name of the Father, Spirit and Son,
We'll take this word to everyone.

1052 Noel & Tricia Richards.
Copyright © 1994 Kingsway's
Thankyou Music.

THE WORLD IS LOOKING FOR A HERO;
We know the greatest One of all:
The mighty Ruler of the nations,
King of kings and Lord of lords;
Who took the nature of a servant,
And gave His life to save us all.

> *We will raise a shout,*
> *We will shout it out,*
> *He is the Champion of the world.*
> (Repeat)

The Lord Almighty is our hero,
He breaks the stranglehold of sin.
Through Jesus' love we fear no evil;
Powers of darkness flee from Him.
His light will shine in every nation,
A sword of justice He will bring.

1053 Kevin Prosch.
Copyright © 1995 7th Time Music/
Kingsway's Thankyou Music.

THEY THAT WAIT ON THE LORD
Will renew their strength,
Run and not get weary,
Walk and not faint.
(Repeat)

Do you not know?
Have you not heard?
My Father does not get weary.
He'll give passion to a willing heart:
Even the youths get tired and faint,
But strength will come for those who wait.

If you wait on the Lord
You'll renew your strength,
Run and not get weary,
Walk and not faint.
(Repeat)

I will wait, I will wait, I will wait on You;
I will run, I will run, I will run with You;
My love, my love, my love for You.

1054 Christopher Idle.
Copyright © Christopher Idle/Jubilate Hymns.

THIS EARTH BELONGS TO GOD,
The world, its wealth, and all its people;
He formed the waters wide
And fashioned every sea and shore.
Who may go up the hill of the Lord
And stand in the place of holiness?
Only the one whose heart is pure,
Whose hands and lips are clean.

Lift high your heads, you gates,
Rise up, you everlasting doors,
As here now the King of glory
Enters into full command.
Who is the King, this King of glory?
Where is the throne He comes to claim?
Christ is the King, the Lord of glory,
Fresh from His victory.

Lift high your heads, you gates,
And fling wide open the ancient doors,
For here the King of glory
Takes universal power.
Who is this king, this King of glory,
What is the power by which He reigns?
Christ is the King, His cross of glory,
And by love He rules.

All glory be to God
The Father, Son and Holy Spirit;
From ages past it was,
Is now, and ever more shall be.

1055 Kent Henry & David Ortinau.
Copyright © 1995 Kent Henry
Ministries/Kingsway's Thankyou Music.

THIS GOD IS OUR GOD,
God of power, God of might.
This God is our God,
God of wisdom and light.
(Repeat)

And we meditate on Your great love,
Your praises fill the earth.
The villages of Judah shout
That you will be, forever be
Our guide unto the end.

As we have heard, so we have seen
The safety of our God,
That we might tell all generations
You will be, forever be
Our guide unto the end.

1056 Mark Altrogge.
Copyright © 1992 People of Destiny
International/Word Music/Adm.
by CopyCare.

THIS I KNOW, *my God is for me,*
This I know.
This I know, my God is on my side;
My God is for me, this I know.

If God did not spare His only Son,
But delivered Him up for us all,
Will He not give us every good thing
When we come in His name and call?

Let us draw near the throne of grace
For mercy and help in our need;
For Jesus is ever praying for us,
He is living to intercede.

1057 Christopher Beatty.
Copyright © 1979 Birdwing Music/BMG
Songs/EMI Christian Music Publishing/Adm.
by CopyCare.

THIS IS HOLY GROUND,
We're standing on holy ground,
For the Lord is here
And where He is holy.
This is holy ground,
We're standing on holy ground,
For the Lord is here
And where He is holy.

These are holy hands,
He's given us holy hands,
He works through these hands
And so these hands are holy.
These are holy hands,
He's given us holy hands,
He works through these hands
And so these hands are holy.

1058 Graham Kendrick.
Copyright © 1985 Kingsway's
Thankyou Music.

THIS IS MY BELOVÈD SON
Who tasted death
That you, my child, might live.
See the blood He shed for you,
What suffering!
Say what more could He give?
Clothed in His perfection,
Bring praise, a fragrance sweet,
Garlanded with joy,
Come worship at His feet:

> *That the Lamb who was slain*
> *Might receive the reward,*
> *Might receive the reward of His*
> *suffering.*

Look, the world's great harvest fields
Are ready now,
And Christ commands us: 'Go!'
Countless souls are dying
So hopelessly,
His wondrous love unknown.
Lord, give us the nations
For the glory of the King.
Father, send more labourers,
The lost to gather in.

Come the day when we will stand
There face to face,
What joy will fill His eyes.
For at last His Bride appears,
So beautiful,
Her glory fills the skies.
Drawn from every nation,
People, tribe and tongue;
All creation sings,
The wedding has begun.

> *And the Lamb who was slain*
> *Shall receive the reward,*
> *Shall receive the reward of His*
> *suffering.*

1059

THIS IS MY PILGRIMAGE,
To climb into You.
This is my pilgrimage,
To be absorbed by You.

I'm so restless for more of You, O God.
I'm so restless, hear these words, O God.

Give me the eyes of a prophet,
Help me to see the unseen,
I long to hear the music of heaven,
As the angels play in my ears.
Sometimes I'm war torn and weary,
Sometimes I'm willing and strong,
But at this moment I'm standing before You
As Your restless pilgrim.

I'll fix my eyes on You,
I'll tread the path with You,
I'll be a warrior of love for You.

But I'm so restless . . .

1060

THIS IS THE MYSTERY,
That Christ has chosen you and me
To be the revelation of His glory;
A chosen, royal, holy people,
Set apart and loved,
A Bride preparing for her King.

Let the Bride say 'come',
Let the Bride say 'come',
Let the Bride of the Lamb
Say 'come, Lord Jesus!'
Let the Bride say 'come',
Let the Bride say 'come',
Let the Bride of the Lamb
Say 'come, Lord Jesus, come!'

She's crowned in splendour
And a royal diadem,
The King is enthralled by her beauty.
Adorned in righteousness,
Arrayed in glorious light,
The Bride in waiting for her King.

Now hear the Bridegroom call,
'Beloved, come aside;
The time of betrothal is at hand.
Lift up your eyes and see
The dawning of the day,
When as King, I'll return to claim My Bride.'

1061

THIS IS THE PLACE
Where dreams are found,
Where vision comes,
Called holy ground.

Holy ground,
I'm standing on holy ground,
For the Lord my God
Is here with me.

Your fire burns
But never dies;
I realise
This is holy ground.

The Great I AM,
Revealed to man;
Take off your shoes,
This is holy ground.

1062

THIS LOVE, this hope,
This peace of God, this righteousness,
This faith, this joy,
This life complete in me.

Now healed and whole,
And risen in His righteousness,
I live in Him,
He lives in me,
And filled with this hope in God,
Reflecting His glory.

Now is the time to worship You,
Now is the time to offer You
All of my thoughts, my dreams and plans;
I lay it down.
Now is the time to live for You,
Now is the time I'm found in You.
Now is the time Your kingdom comes.

1063

THOUGH I FEEL AFRAID
Of territory unknown,
I know that I can say
That I do not stand alone.
For Jesus, You have promised
Your presence in my heart;
I cannot see the ending,
But it's here that I must start.

And all I know is You have called me,
And that I will follow is all I can say.
I will go where You will send me,
And Your fire lights my way.

What lies across the waves
May cause my heart to fear;
Will I survive the day,
Must I leave what's known and dear?
A ship that's in the harbour
Is still and safe from harm,
But it was not built to be there,
It was made for wind and storm.

1064 James Wright.
Copyright © 1996 Kingsway's
Thankyou Music.

THROUGHOUT THE EARTH YOUR GLORY WILL COME,
A day of power, of salvation.
To thirsty hearts Your rivers will run,
Changing lives for the glory of God.
From Satan's hold this land will be free,
The deaf will hear, the blind will see;
To walk in truth, in victory,
To live for the glory of God.

*Lord, come and reign by the power of
Your Spirit,
Shower this land with Your rivers of
life,
That Jesus the Son would be glorified
Within the heart of Your Bride,
Lord, come and reign.*

Upon the earth may Your kingdom come,
Within our lives may Your will be done;
Under the reign of Jesus the Son
We will live for the glory of God.
The gates of heaven are open wide,
To bless this land, to turn back the tide,
To welcome in Your glorious Bride,
To live for the glory of God.

1065 Edward Hayes Plumptre.

THY HAND, O GOD HAS GUIDED
Thy flock, from age to age;
The wondrous tale is written,
Full clear on every page.
Our fathers owned Thy goodness,
And we their deeds record;
And both of this bear witness:
One Church, one Faith, one Lord.

Thy heralds brought glad tidings
To greatest as to least;
They bade them rise and hasten
To share the great King's feast.
And this was all their teaching
In every deed and word;
To all alike proclaiming:
One Church, one Faith, one Lord.

Through many a day of darkness,
Through many a scene of strife,
The faithful few fought bravely
To guard the nation's life.
Their gospel of redemption,
Sin pardoned, man restored,
Was all in this enfolded:
One Church, one Faith, one Lord.

Thy mercy will not fail us,
Nor leave Thy work undone;
With Thy right hand to help us,
The victory shall be won.
And then, by men and angels,
Thy name shall be adored,
And this shall be their anthem:
One Church, one Faith, one Lord.

1066 Amy Grant & Michael W. Smith.
Copyright © 1983 Bug & Bear Music/LCS
Music Group Inc./Meadowgreen Music/EMI
Christian Music Publishing/Adm. by
CopyCare.

THY WORD *is a lamp unto my feet
And a light unto my path.*
(Repeat)

When I feel afraid,
Think I've lost my way,
Still You're there right beside me.
And nothing will I fear
As long as You are near;
Please be near me to the end.

I will not forget
Your love for me, and yet
My heart forever is wandering.
Jesus, be my guide
And hold me to Your side,
And I will love You to the end.

1067 Noel Richards.
Copyright © 1991 Kingsway's
Thankyou Music.

TO BE IN YOUR PRESENCE,
To sit at Your feet,
Where Your love surrounds me,
And makes me complete.

This is my desire, O Lord,
This is my desire.
This is my desire, O Lord,
This is my desire.

To rest in Your presence,
Not rushing away;
To cherish each moment,
Here I would stay.

1068 Bryn Haworth.
Copyright © 1996 Kingsway's
Thankyou Music.

TO HIM WHO LOVES US,
And has freed us from our sins
By His blood,
And has made us to be a kingdom
And priests to serve His God.
(Repeat)
And Father.

(Men-Women echo each line)
To Him be glory
And power
Forever
And ever.
To Him be glory
And power
Forever,
Amen. (Together)

1069 Sue Rinaldi & Steve Bassett.
Copyright © 1988 Word's Spirit of Praise
Music/Adm. by CopyCare.

TO YOUR MAJESTY,
And Your beauty I surrender.
To Your holiness,
And Your love I surrender.
For You are an awesome God who is mighty,
You deserve my deepest praise;
With all of my heart,
With all of my life I surrender.

1070 Kirk & Deby Dearman.
Copyright © Ariose Music/EMI Christian
Music Publishing/Adm. by CopyCare.

VISIT US, O LORD, with Your awesome
   presence.
Dwell in our midst in Your glory and power,
In Your strength and in Your love.

This is our cry, O Lord,
Let Your presence fill this place,
Fill this place.
(Repeat)

1071 Mick Gisbey.
Copyright © 1995 Kingsway's
Thankyou Music.

WAITING FOR YOUR SPIRIT,
Thirsty for Your Spirit;
Touching us, Lord, as we pray,
Filling our lives with You again.
Fall on us, Lord,
As we call on You.

1072 Matt Redman.
Copyright © 1994 Kingsway's
Thankyou Music.

WAKE UP, MY SOUL,
Worship the Lord of truth and life.
Have strength, my heart,
Press on as one who seeks the prize.
I'll run for You, my God and King,
I'll run as one who runs to win.
I'm pressing on, not giving in.
I will run, I will run for You, my King.

And Spirit come, give life to us,
Come breathe the Father's love in us.
Won't You fill us once again?
And we will run and run with Him.
We'll run with strength,
With all our might,
We'll fix our eyes on Jesus Christ;
He has conquered death and sin,
And we will run and run and run
With Him.

1073 Nathan Fellingham.
Copyright © 1996 Kingsway's
Thankyou Music.

WAKE UP, WAKE UP O SLEEPER,
And rise from the dead.
(Repeat)

We are His people drawn by grace,
Chosen by His glorious name,
Called to give Him all our praise,
Set apart to worship Him.
We must be humble now and pray,
And turn from all our careless ways,
And in our hearts wait for the hour
For Christ to come in awesome power.

We are called to righteousness,
To be like God in holiness;
So let all slander now subside,
And flee from bitterness and rage.
And soon the night will fade away,
And in its place will come the day;
So we must clothe ourselves in light,
The armour that will help us fight.

Revere the name of the Lord,
And He will shine on you;
He will arise with healing
And set you free.

1074 Maggi Dawn.
Copyright © 1994 Kingsway's
Thankyou Music.

WASH ME CLEAN in that cool river;
Wash my soul in the pure water.
Wash me clean in that cool river;
Lord, make me new.

1075 Kevin Prosch.
Copyright © 1991 Mercy/Vineyard
Publishing/Adm. by CopyCare.

WE ARE HIS PEOPLE,
He gives us music to sing.
There is a sound now,
Like the sound of the Lord when His enemies
    flee.
But there is a cry in our hearts,
Like when deep calls unto the deep,
For Your breath of deliverance,
To breathe on the music we so desperately
    need.

But without Your power
All we have are these simple songs.
If You'd step down from heaven,
Then the gates of hell would surely fall.

> *Shout to the Lord, shout to the Lord,*
> *Shout to the Lord of Hosts.*
> *Shout to the Lord, shout to the Lord,*
> *Shout to the Lord of Hosts.*
> *And it breaks the heavy yoke, breaks the*
>   *heavy yoke*
> *When you shout, you shout to the Lord.*
> *It breaks the heavy yoke, breaks the heavy*
>   *yoke,*
> *When you shout, you shout to the Lord.*

1076 Tr. Anders Nyberg.
Copyright © 1990 Wild Goose Publications.

WE ARE MARCHING IN THE LIGHT OF GOD,
We are marching in the light of God.
(Repeat)

We are marching, marching,
We are marching, marching,
We are marching in the light of God.
(Repeat)

Siyahamb' ekukhanyen' kwenkhos',
Siyahamb' ekukhanyen' kwenkhos'.
(Repeat)

Siyahamba, hamba, siyahamba, hamba,
Siyahamb' ekukhanyen' kwenkhos'.
(Repeat)

We are living in the love of God...

We are moving in the power of God...

1077 Lex Loizides.
Copyright © 1997 Kingsway's
Thankyou Music.

**WE ARE MARCHING TO A DIFFERENT
    ANTHEM,**
We are dancing to a different song;
And our hearts have come alive with freedom,
Mercy has come, the God of mercy has come.
He is moving through the towns and cities,
He is binding up the broken ones;
And His healing hand is working wonders,
See how they come, He sets them free when
    they come.
And I sing:

> *I love the God of heaven,*
> *I love His precious Son;*
> *And in the Holy Spirit,*
> *He's making us strong,*
> *And giving us the victory.*
> *I love the God of heaven,*
> *I love His precious Son;*
> *And in the Holy Spirit,*
> *He's making us strong,*
> *And giving us a victory song.*

He is training up our hands for battle,
And equipping us to take the land;
For the promises to us are mighty,
We will be strong, and move together as
    one.
We are heading for our finest hour,
When our Saviour will be magnified,
And His glory will outshine all others:
Jesus is Lord, let Him be praised and
    adored.
And I sing:

1078 Bob Fitts.
Copyright, © 1992 Integrity's Hosanna! Music/
Adm. by Kingsway's Thankyou Music.

WE ARE SALT and we are the light;
We've come to break the powers of night,
And by the love of God proclaim His liberty.
We're ambassadors of grace,
In His name we take this place;
Lord, let Your will be done,
Let Your kingdom come,
Lord, let it rain, let it rain.

Let Your blessings pour
On the nations, Lord, let it rain.
Let Your blessings pour
On the nations, Lord, let it rain.
As we sing Your praises,
Break the curses, let it rain.
Hear Your people praying,
Send Your blessing, let it rain.
Oh, let it rain.

You have won the fight, O Lord;
By Your death our life's been restored,
And You have risen now
To vanquish all our foes.
Come, abolish every curse
O'er the nations of the earth;
In Your name we'll go,
To proclaim You rose to live and reign.
Lord, come and reign.

1079 Kevin Prosch.
Copyright © 1990 Mercy/Vineyard Publishing/
Adm. by CopyCare.

WE ARE THE ARMY OF GOD,
Sons of Abraham,
We are a chosen generation.
Under a covenant,
Washed by His precious blood,
Filled with the mighty Holy Ghost.

And I hear the sound of the coming rain,
As we sing the praise to the great I AM.
And the sick are healed,
And the dead shall rise,
And Your church is the army that was
   prophesied.

1080 Paul Oakley.
Copyright © 1996 Kingsway's
Thankyou Music.

WE ARE YOUR INHERITANCE,
We are Your reward.
(Repeat)
And You're our glory
And the lifter of our heads;
You're our glory
And the lifter of our heads.

Listen, can you hear it?
The Spirit and the Bride.
(Repeat)
Whisper 'Jesus!
Maranatha! Come!'
Whisper 'Jesus!
Maranatha! Come!'

O come, O come to us!
O come, O come to us!
Jesus, Jesus, Jesus!
O come, O come to us!

1081 Richard Lewis.
Copyright © 1994 Kingsway's
Thankyou Music.

WE ASK YOU, O LORD,
For the rain of Your Spirit.
We ask You, O Lord,
For the rain of Your Spirit.
For now is the time,
For now is the time
Of the latter rain,
Of the latter rain.

Send Your rain, cleanse us by Your word;
Let us be Your pure and radiant Bride.
Make us strong, prepare us for revival;
Let us see the nations turn their hearts,
Let us see the nations turn their hearts,
Let us see the nations turn their hearts
To You, to You.

Send Your rain, mercy from heaven.
Send Your rain, the grace of Your Son.
Send Your rain, Word of Your power,
Send Your rain, come fill everyone.
(Repeat)

1082 David & Nathan Fellingham.
Copyright © 1995 Kingsway's
Thankyou Music.

WE BEHOLD YOUR GLORY,
Fountain of life, the Lord Jesus Christ.
Lord of the universe,
You die in weakness;
Strong Deliverer,
How You were wounded.
Sustainer of life,
Disfigured and shamed,
This is the medicine
That saves and heals us.
A crown of thorns
Was placed on Your brow;
Though You were scourged,
Blow after blow,
By Your stripes we are healed.

We behold Your glory,
Fountain of life, the Lord Jesus Christ.
Though You were fettered,
We are delivered;
Though You were condemned,
We are absolved.
Though You were exposed
To mocking and shame,
We are established
And raised up in honour.
Though You were laid
In the dust of death,
Though You went down
To hell's darkest depths,
The kingdom of heaven is ours.

1083 Ian Smale.
Copyright © 1996 Kingsway's
Thankyou Music.

WE BELIEVE IN HEBREWS THIRTEEN, EIGHT,
Jesus Christ is never out of date.
If it's yesterday or today, or forever more,
Jesus stays the same and that is great.

1084 Viola Grafstrom.
Copyright © 1996 Kingsway's
Thankyou Music.

WE BOW DOWN and confess
You are Lord in this place.
We bow down and confess
You are Lord in this place.
You are all I need;
It's Your face I seek.
In the presence of Your light
We bow down, we bow down.

1085 Kevin Prosch.
Copyright © 1991 Mercy/Vineyard
Publishing/Adm. by CopyCare.

WE CONFESS THE SINS OF OUR NATION,
And, Lord, we are guilty
Of a prayerless life.
We've turned away our hearts from Your laws,
And have taken for granted Your unchanging
grace.
Turn away this curse from our country;
We say that we've robbed You,
And our storehouses are bare.
Open wide the floodgates of heaven,
Rebuke the devourer so we may not be
destroyed.

You said that if we'd humble ourselves
And begin to pray,
You would heal our barren land,
And cleanse us with Your rain.

Don't pass us by,
Let this be the generation, Lord,
That lifts up Your name to all the world.
Save us, O God,
Save a people for Yourself, O Lord,
Let the fear of the Lord be a standard.
Save us, O God,
Cleanse us from our unfaithfulness,
Let the place where we live
Be called a house of prayer.

1086 Mark Altrogge.
Copyright © 1992 Integrity's Hosanna! Music/
People of Destiny Int./Adm. by Kingsway's
Thankyou Music.

WE GIVE THANKS TO YOU, O Lord,
Almighty God,
The One who is, who was
And is to come.
You've taken up Your power
And begun to reign,
The nations bow before the Holy One.

Now Your salvation,
And Your power and Your kingdom
Have all come,
And You are Lord of all.
The accuser of the brothers
Has been hurled down forever,
Overcome by the blood,
Overcome by the blood,
Overcome by the blood of the Lamb.

1087 Chris Falson.
Copyright © 1990 Chris Falson Music/Adm.
by Kingsway's Thankyou Music.

WE HAVE A VISION for this nation;
We share a dream for this land.
We join with angels in celebration,
By faith we speak revival to this land.

Where every knee shall bow and worship You,
And every tongue confess that You are Lord;
Give us an open heaven, anoint our prayers
this day,
And move Your sovereign hand across this
nation.

1088 Stuart Garrard.
Copyright © 1992 Kingsway's
Thankyou Music.

WE HAVE CALLED ON YOU, LORD,
And You have heard us.
We have called on Your name,
And You have answered.
Mercy has triumphed over judgement.
Mercy has triumphed over judgement.

You have stretched out Your hand,
And You have touched us,
Sent us Your holy fire,
And You have purged us.
Light has triumphed over darkness.
Light has triumphed over darkness.

We love You, and sing to You,
God of our salvation.
You've rescued us and we declare
Your glory to the nations.
We give our lives, a living sacrifice,
Empty and ready to be filled
With Your power.

1089 Robert Newey.
Copyright © 1997 Kingsway's
Thankyou Music.

WE HAVE COME TO SEEK YOUR FACE,
Filled with wonder at Your grace,
Amazed at how You've come
And touched our lives.
But even as we've felt Your touch,
Desire for You has grown so much,
It only serves to make us realise
That the way ahead is in Your strength alone.
So we stand before You now and we cry,
'Lord, lead us on!'

'Cause after all You've brought us through,
We find we're even more dependent on You,
Not in power, not in might,
But through Your Spirit's guiding light.
We're driven by the things He says,
And glory in our weaknesses,
And knowing how we need You now, we
    come:
Here we stand before You.

And we will wait for You, wait for You;
Show us, Lord, what You would have us do.
We will wait for You, wait for You;
Show us, Lord, what You would have us do.

1090 Martin Smith.
Copyright © 1994 Curious? Music UK/Adm.
by Kingsway's Thankyou Music.

WE HAVE FLOODED THE ALTAR with our
tears;
We have wearied You, Lord, with our words.
Great God, our promises we've broken,
O Lord, forgive me.

You are breaking the pride in our hearts;
You have given us tears for the lost.
You crown the humble with salvation;
O Lord, humble me.

So lead me, oh lead me into Your arms;
I will be safe in the shadow of Your wing.
Lead me, oh lead me into Your arms;
I will be safe in Almighty.

You have paid back our sin with Your love;
Lover's arms You have offered us.
Faithful One, raise up a faithful people
Who find their treasure here.

1091 Paul Oakley.
Copyright © 1994 Kingsway's
Thankyou Music.

WE HAVE PRAYED THAT YOU WOULD HAVE
    MERCY;
We believe from heaven You've heard.
Heal our land, so dry and so thirsty;
We have strayed so far from You, Lord.
Your cloud appeared on the horizon,
Small as a man's hand.
But now You're near,
Filling our vision,
Pour out Your Spirit again.

I felt the touch of Your wind on my face:
I feel the first drops of rain.

Let it rain, let it rain.
I will not be the same.
Let it rain, rain on me.
Let it pour down on me,
Let it rain.

Let it rain, let it rain,
Let it rain, let it rain on me.
Let it rain, let it rain,
Let it rain.

1092 Stuart Townend.
Copyright © 1997 Kingsway's
Thankyou Music.

WE HAVE SUNG OUR SONGS OF VICTORY,
We have prayed to You for rain;
We have cried for Your compassion
To renew the land again.
Now we're standing in Your presence,
More hungry than before;
Now we're on Your steps of mercy,
And we're knocking at Your door.

How long before You drench the barren
    land?
How long before we see Your righteous
    hand?
How long before Your name is lifted high?
How long before the weeping turns to
    songs of joy?

Lord, we know Your heart is broken
By the evil that You see,
And You've stayed Your hand of judgement
For You plan to set men free.
But the land is still in darkness,
And we've fled from what is right;
We have failed the silent children
Who will never see the light.

But I know a day is coming
When the deaf will hear His voice,
When the blind will see their Saviour,
And the lame will leap for joy.
When the widow finds a Husband
Who will always love His bride,
And the orphan finds a Father
Who will never leave her side.

How long before Your glory lights the
  skies?
How long before Your radiance lifts our
  eyes?
How long before Your fragrance fills the air?
How long before the earth resounds with
  songs of joy?

1093 Noel Richards.
Copyright © 1991 Kingsway's
Thankyou Music.

WELCOME, KING OF KINGS!
How great is Your name.
You come in majesty
Forever to reign.

You rule the nations,
They shake at the sound of Your name.
To You is given all power,
And You shall reign.

Let all creation bow down
At the sound of Your name.
Let every tongue now confess,
The Lord God reigns.

1094 David Fellingham.
Copyright © 1997 Kingsway's
Thankyou Music.

WE LIFT UP OUR HEADS,
And we will sing our praise
To Him who sits on the throne.
We lift up our heads
To the King of kings,
Who reigns in heaven and earth.

Holy and mighty,
Awesome in power,
Full of compassion
And love.

Glorious in holiness,
Fearful in praises,
Working His wonders
In us.

1095 Martin Smith.
Copyright © 1995 Curious? Music UK/Adm.
by Kingsway's Thankyou Music.

WELL, I HEAR THEY'RE SINGING in the
  streets
That Jesus is alive,
And all creation shouts aloud
That Jesus is alive.
Now surely we can all be changed
'cause Jesus is alive;
And everybody here can know
That Jesus is alive.

And I will live for all my days
To raise a banner of truth and light,
To sing about my Saviour's love—
And the best thing that happened,
It was the day I met You.

I've found Jesus.
I've found Jesus.
I've found Jesus.
I've found Jesus.

Well, I feel like dancing in the streets
'Cause Jesus is alive,
To join with all who celebrate
That Jesus is alive.
The joy of God is in this town
'Cause Jesus is alive;
For everybody's seen the truth
That Jesus is alive.

And I will live for all my days…

Well, You lifted me from where I was,
Set my feet upon a rock,
Humbled that You even know about me.
Now I have chosen to believe,
Believing that You've chosen me;
I was lost but now I've found…

1096 Bob Baker.
Copyright © 1994 Mercy/Vineyard
Publishing/Adm. by CopyCare.

WELL, I THANK YOU, LORD,
That You are my Saviour;
You're my strength
And You're the Rock on which I stand.
You give me life,
And a grace that's greater,
When I humble myself
Beneath Your mighty hand.

You bring times of refreshing,
You bring times of refreshing,
You bring times of refreshing to my soul.
When I'm weary from the fight,
And trying to do what's right,
You bring times of refreshing to my soul.

For the day will come
When we'll all be gathered,
And the sun will rise with healing in its wings;
And all the years of pain
Won't seem to matter,
When our eyes behold
Our Teacher and our King.

1097 Chris Bowater.
Copyright © 1996 Sovereign Lifestyle Music.

WE'RE HERE FOR THE HARVEST,
Get ready to reap,
The call is for action,
It's not time to sleep.
We're here for the harvest,
The yield will be great;
The fields are now ripened,
So don't hesitate.

There's need for more labourers,
For many, not few,
The challenge set before us
Is who? And we cry:
Lord of the harvest,
In this day of Your power,
Hear the anthem of voices: 'send me!'

Send me, send me,
Lord of the harvest, send me!
Send me, send me,
Lord of the harvest, send me!

The Spirit is upon us,
To cause the blind to see;
The Spirit of the Sovereign Lord
To set the captive free.
The homeless and the needy
Can no longer be ignored,
And all oppressed will celebrate
The favour of the Lord.

There's need for more labourers…

1098 Carol Owen.
Copyright © 1994 Kingsway's
Thankyou Music.

**WE REJOICE IN THE GOODNESS OF OUR
GOD,**
We rejoice in the wonders of Your favour.
You've set the captives free,
You've caused the blind to see,
Hallelujah,
You give us liberty, hallelujah.

Always the same, You never change,
And Your mercies are new every day.
Compassionate and gracious,
Our faithful loving God,
Slow to anger, rich in love.

You give us hope, You give us joy,
You give us fulness of life to enjoy.
Our Shepherd and Provider,
Our God who's always there,
Never failing, always true.

1099 Matt Redman.
Copyright © 1997 Kingsway's
Thankyou Music.

WE'RE LOOKING TO YOUR PROMISE of old,
That if we pray and humble ourselves,
You will come and heal our land,
You will come,
You will come.

We're looking to the promise You made,
That if we turn and look to Your face,
You will come and heal our land,
You will come,
You will come to us.

Lord, send revival, start with me.
For I am one of unclean lips,
And my eyes have seen the King;
Your glory I have glimpsed.
Send revival, start with me.

1100 Ian White.
Copyright © 1997 Little Misty Music/
Kingsway's Thankyou Music.

WE'RE REACHING OUT TO YOU AGAIN.
We're in the upper room again.
We feel the Spirit's wave,
We're in pre-revival days.
We're kneeling on the floor again.
We're crying out for more again.
We're seeking for Your face
We're in pre-revival days.

You say where our treasure is,
There is our heart.
You say where our treasure is,
There is our heart.

We're looking at our lives again.
Your love has filled our eyes again.
We cherish Your embrace,
We're in pre-revival days.
We're praying for the lost again.
The hardened heart is soft again.
No one is turned away,
We're in pre-revival days.

We're talking in the streets again.
You're showing us what to speak again.
The demons scream with rage,
We're in pre-revival days.

But a single song
Can never change our ways,
So we cry to You, Lord,
You are mighty to save.

Jesus out in front again.
Jesus on our tongues again.
We're rising up in faith
To see revival days.
We're praying for our land again.
You've stayed Your patient hand again.
This nation needs Your grace
To see revival days.

1101 Richard Lewis & Chris Cartwright.
Copyright © 1994 Kingsway's
Thankyou Music.

WE'RE SO THANKFUL TO YOU,
We're so grateful for the things You've done,
That You died for us on the cross—
Such a painful death,
That You paid the price for us,
You paid the price for us.

And we say thank You, Lord.
We say thank You, Lord.
We say thank You for what You have
done.
And we say thank You, Lord.
We say thank You, Lord.
We say thank You
For the things You have done.

It's so wonderful that you rose,
Victorious over death and hell.
All authority is now Yours,
And the Comforter
You have sent in fulness to us,
You have come to us.

1102 Stuart Garrard.
Copyright © 1993 Kingsway's
Thankyou Music.

WE'RE STANDING HERE with open hearts,
Our voices joined in unity.
We know we don't lead perfect lives,
And we cry to You for mercy.
Father in heaven, we honour Your name,
That we might bring You glory and fame;
Pour out Your Spirit upon us we pray,
To heal and deliver and save.

This is our heart cry;
This is our heart cry.
(Repeat)

We stand before the throne of grace,
A people for Your possession;
We hunger and thirst, we seek Your face,
Come touch us with Your presence.
Father in heaven, holy and true,
Stretch out Your hand, let power break
   through;
Pour out Your Spirit upon us today,
To heal and deliver and save.

1103 Lex Loizides.
Copyright © 1996 Kingsway's
Thankyou Music.

WE STAND TOGETHER before our Saviour,
We stand together in the cause of our God.
We have a vision, we've been commissioned
To raise a banner in the name of our God.

Once, when we were dead in our sin,
Our hearts were turned away,
But then the light of Christ broke in
And made us live again.
And if You could heal our blindness,
You can save our nation too,
So we give ourselves this day to follow You.

We'll preach the gospel, we'll tell the people.
About a Saviour who has died on a cross.
With true compassion, without distraction,
While we have time we will deliver the lost.

Someday soon the King will come
With glory, power and might,
And all the hosts of heaven and hell
Will bow before the light.
And the nations will be gathered
For the righteous Judge will come,
And the blood-bought church
Will join the Risen One.

1104 Sue Rinaldi.
Copyright © 1996 Kingsway's
Thankyou Music.

WE WANNA CHANGE THIS WORLD,
We wanna change this world.
(Repeat)

So wave those flags of justice
Over the nations,
And hit those drums of peace
Among the peoples.
We hear the sound of history in the making,
Let God's love run around the earth
And bring freedom!

So hold each other's hands
Across the oceans,
And play those chords of peace
Among the peoples.
We hear the sound of reconciliation:
Let God's love dance around the earth
And bring freedom!

And we wanna change this world
As we live out holy lives.
And we wanna change this world
As You wash our motives clean.
(Repeat)
Oh, wash us clean!

1105 Doug Horley.
Copyright © 1993 Kingsway's
Thankyou Music.

WE WANT TO SEE JESUS LIFTED HIGH,

A banner that flies across this land,
That all men might see the truth and know
He is the way to heaven.
(Repeat)

> *We want to see, We want to see,*
> *We want to see Jesus lifted high.*
> *We want to see, we want to see,*
> *We want to see Jesus lifted high.*

Step by step we're moving forward,
Little by little taking ground,
Every prayer a powerful weapon,
Strongholds come tumbling down,
And down, and down, and down.

> *We're gonna see, we're gonna see,*
> *We're gonna see Jesus lifted high.*
> *We're gonna see, we're gonna see,*
> *We're gonna see Jesus lifted high.*

1106 Steve Cantellow & Matt Redman.
Copyright © 1996 Kingsway's
Thankyou Music.

WE WILL GIVE OURSELVES NO REST

Till Your kingdom comes on earth;
You've positioned watchmen on the walls.
Now our prayers will flow like tears,
For You've shared Your heart with us;
God of heaven, on our knees we fall.
Come down in power,
Reveal Your heart again;
Come hear our cries,
The tears that plead for rain.

We're knocking,
Knocking on the door of heaven,
We're crying,
Crying for this generation;
We're praying for Your name to be known
In all of the earth.
We're watching,
Watching on the walls to see You,
We're looking,
Looking for a time of breakthrough;
We're praying for Your word to bear fruit
In all of the earth, in all of the earth.

1107 Dave Bilbrough.
Copyright © 1991 Kingsway's
Thankyou Music.

WE WILL TEAR DOWN EVERY STRONGHOLD

Through the power of His word.
We will seek to bring His kingdom in,
Make a way for His return.

We will tell of His salvation,
For the church of Christ is called
To bring healing to the nations,
See His righteousness restored.

> *Satan is defeated,*
> *Christ has overcome,*
> *Seated at the Father's hand,*
> *Lord, on earth may Your will now be done.*

1108 Dennis Jernigan.
Copyright © 1989 Shepherd's Heart Music/
Sovereign Lifestyle Music.

WE WILL WORSHIP THE LAMB OF GLORY,

We will worship the King of kings;
We will worship the Lamb of Glory,
We will worship the King.

> *And with our hands lifted high*
> *We will worship and sing,*
> *And with our hands lifted high*
> *We come before You rejoicing.*
> *With our hands lifted high to the sky,*
> *When the world wonders why,*
> *We'll just tell them we're loving our King.*
> *Oh, we'll just tell them we're loving our*
> *King.*
> *Yes, we'll just tell them loving our King.*

Bless the name of the Lamb of Glory,
I bless the name of the King of kings;
Bless the name of the Lamb of Glory,
Bless the name of the King.

1109

WHAT A FRIEND I'VE FOUND,
Closer than a brother;
I have felt Your touch,
More intimate than lovers.

    Jesus, Jesus,
    Jesus, Friend forever.
    (Repeat)

What a hope I've found,
More faithful than a mother;
It would break my heart
To ever lose each other.

1110

WHATEVER I HAVE GAINED,
Whatever I have done,
I leave it all behind to follow You.
The things that I attained,
The goals I may have gained,
A prize or any glory of my own.

    For I am lost without Your love,
    All things are loss without Your love;
    For I am lost without Your love,
    All things are loss without Your love.

The wonder of Your love,
The wonder of Your grace;
To gain You and to know You as my Lord.
That I am found in You,
Your righteousness alone,
Is more than I could dream or ever ask.

1111

WHAT KIND OF LOVE IS THIS
That gave itself for me?
I am the guilty one,
Yet I go free.
What kind of love is this,
A love I've never known;
I didn't even know His name—
What kind of love is this?

What kind of man is this,
That died in agony?
He who had done no wrong
Was crucified for me.
What kind of man is this,
Who laid aside His throne
That I may know the love of God—
What kind of man is this?

By grace I have been saved;
It is the gift of God.
He destined me to be His son,
Such is His love.
No eye has ever seen,
No ear has ever heard,
Nor has the heart of man conceived
What kind of love is this.

1112

WHEN CAN I GO AND MEET WITH GOD?
My soul is weak, my body tired.
Can it be here, can it be now?
I need to find that place again.

When can I come and meet You, God?
I thirst inside for heaven's touch.
Let it be here, let it be now;
I need to find that place again...

    Where deep calls to deep
    In the roar of Your waterfalls,
    You're calling me
    With the force of Your love.
    Let Your waves sweep
    Over all the dry places, Lord;
    Usher me in to the depths of Your
      heart,
    Where deep calls to deep,
    Where deep calls to deep,
    Where deep calls to deep,
    Where deep calls to deep.

I want to know Your risen power.
I need to share Your sufferings;
And as I die to my own will,
Lord, raise me to that place again.

1113

WHEN THE MUSIC FADES, all is stripped
    away,
And I simply come;
Longing just to bring something that's of
    worth
That will bless Your heart.

I'll bring You more than a song,
For a song in itself
Is not what You have required.
You search much deeper within
Through the way things appear;
You're looking into my heart.

I'm coming back to the heart of worship,
And it's all about You,
All about You, Jesus.
I'm sorry, Lord, for the thing I've made it,
When it's all about You,
All about You, Jesus.

King of endless worth, no one could express
How much You deserve.
Though I'm weak and poor, all I have is Yours,
Every single breath.

1114
Noel Richards.
Copyright © 1996 Kingsway's
Thankyou Music.

WHEN WE'RE IN TROUBLE,
When there are cares;
When faith is shaken up,
When we despair,
We call on Jesus,
Give Him our thanks;
We let His peace and joy
Come to our hearts.

We're gonna keep on praying,
Keep on praying.
We're gonna keep on praying,
Keep on praying.

When there is sickness,
When there is pain,
There is a healing touch,
Each time we pray.
God always listens,
Cares for our needs;
Prayers of the righteous one
Have power indeed.

Prayers for the nation,
Prayers for the world.
Prayers for the government,
Prayers for the church.
Prayers for the seekers,
Prayers for the saints,
Praying that people will come to faith.

1115
Kevin Prosch.
Copyright © 1995 7th Time Music/
Kingsway's Thankyou Music.

WHEN YOU'VE BEEN BROKEN, broken to
pieces,
And your heart begins to faint,
'Cause you don't understand.
And when there is nothing
To rake from the ashes,
And you can't even walk
Onto the fields of praise.
But I bow down and kiss the Son.
Oh, I bow down and kiss the Son.

When the rock falls, falls upon you,
And you get ground to dust,
No music for your pain.
You open the windows,
The windows of heaven,
And then You opened me,
And You crushed me like a rose.
But I bow down and kiss the Son.
Oh, I bow down and kiss the Son.
Oh, I bow down and kiss the Son.

Let the praise of the Lord be in my mouth,
Let the praise of the Lord be in my mouth.

Though You slay me, I will trust You, Lord.
(Repeat x4)

1116
Tommy Walker.
Copyright © 1992 Integrity's Hosanna! Music/
Adm. by Kingsway's Thankyou Music.

WHERE THERE ONCE WAS ONLY HURT,
He gave His healing hand;
Where there once was only pain,
He brought comfort like a friend.
I feel the sweetness of His love
Piercing my darkness.
I see the bright and morning sun
As it ushers in His joyful gladness.

He's turned my mourning into dancing
again,
He's lifted my sorrow.
I can't stay silent, I must sing
For His joy has come.

His anger lasts for a moment in time;
But His favour is here
And will be on me for all my lifetime.

1117
Paul Oakley.
Copyright © 1995 Kingsway's
Thankyou Music.

WHO IS THERE LIKE YOU,
And who else would give their life for me,
Even suffering in my place?
And who could repay You?
All of creation looks to You,
And You provide for all You have made.

So I'm lifting up my hands,
Lifting up my voice,
Lifting up Your name,
And in Your grace I rest,
For Your love has come to me
And set me free.
And I'm trusting in Your word,
Trusting in Your cross,
Trusting in Your blood
And all Your faithfulness,
For Your power at work in me
Is changing me.

1118 Stuart Townend.
Copyright © 1995 Kingsway's
Thankyou Music.

WHO PAINTS THE SKIES into glorious day?
Only the splendour of Jesus.
Who breathes His life into fists of clay?
Only the splendour of Jesus.
Who shapes the valleys and brings the rain?
Only the splendour of Jesus.
Who makes the desert to live again?
Only the splendour of Jesus.

Teach every nation His marvellous ways;
Each generation shall sing His praise.

He is wonderful, He is glorious,
Clothed in righteousness,
Full of tenderness.
Come and worship Him,
He's the Prince of life,
He will cleanse our hearts
In His river of fire.

Who hears the cry of the barren one?
Only the mercy of Jesus.
Who breaks the curse of the heart of stone?
Only the mercy of Jesus.
Who storms the prison and sets men free,
Only the mercy of Jesus.
Purchasing souls for eternity?
Only the mercy of Jesus.

1119 Alex Muir.
Copyright © 1993 Kingsway's
Thankyou Music.

WHOSE LIPS WILL PLEAD
For the people of this land?
Who'll stand in the gap,
And who'll build up the wall,
Before the long day of God's patience is
    over,
Before the night comes
When His judgement will fall?

And whose eyes will weep
For the people of this land?
And whose hearts will break
For the hearts made of stone,
For those who are walking out into
    darkness,
Away from God's love,
Without Christ, so alone?

And whose ears can hear
What the Spirit is saying
To those who are willing
To watch and to pray?
Pray on till God's light
Fills the skies over this land,
The light of revival that brings a new day.

1120 Graham Maule & John L. Bell.
Copyright © 1987 WGRG,
Iona Community.

WILL YOU COME AND FOLLOW ME
If I but call your name?
Will you go where you don't know
And never be the same?
Will you let My love be shown,
Will you let My name be known,
Will you let My life be grown in you,
And you in Me?

Will you leave yourself behind
If I but call your name?
Will you care for cruel and kind
And never be the same?
Will you risk the hostile stare,
Should your life attract or scare?
Will you let Me answer prayer
In you and you in Me?

Will you let the blinded see
If I but call your name?
Will you set the prisoners free
And never be the same?
Will you kiss the leper clean,
And do such as this unseen,
And admit to what I mean
In you and you in Me?

Will you love the 'you' you hide
If I but call your name?
Will you quell the fear inside
And never be the same?
Will you use the faith you've found
To reshape the world around,
Through My sight and touch and
    sound
In you and you in Me?

Lord, Your summons echoes true
When You but call my name.
Let me turn and follow You
And never be the same.
In Your company I'll go
Where Your love and footsteps show;
Thus I'll move and live and grow
In You and You in me.

1121 Ruth Dryden.
Copyright © 1978 Genesis Music/
Kingsway's Thankyou Music.

WITHIN THE VEIL I now would come,
Into the holy place, to look upon Thy face.
I see such beauty there, no other can
    compare;
I worship Thee, my Lord, within the veil.

1122 Carol Owen.
Copyright © 1995 Kingsway's
Thankyou Music.

WORTHY IS THE LAMB,
Worthy is the Lamb,
Worthy is the Lamb who was slain.
(Repeat)

My Lord and Saviour,
My great Redeemer,
Your blood has purchased me for God.
My Lord and Saviour,
My great Redeemer,
You came to set the captives free.

Holy is the Lamb . . .

Jesus, You're the Lamb . . .

Glory to the Lamb . . .

1123 Carl Tuttle.
Copyright © 1992 Mercy/Vineyard Publishing/
Adm. by CopyCare.

YET THIS WILL I CALL TO MIND,
And therefore I will hope,
Because of the Lord's great love
I've been redeemed.
The Lord is gracious and kind
To all who call on His name,
Because of the Lord's great love
I've been redeemed.

Because of the Lord's great love,
Because of the Lord's great love,
Because of the Lord's great love
I've been redeemed.

I know of His steadfast love,
His mercy renewed each day,
Because of the Lord's great love
I've been redeemed.
Washed in the blood of the Lamb,
Guiltless for ever I stand,
Because of the Lord's great love
I've been redeemed.

1124 Ian White.
Copyright © 1997 Little Misty Music/
Kingsway's Thankyou Music.

YOU ARE MERCIFUL TO ME,
You are merciful to me,
You are merciful to me, my Lord.
(Repeat)

Every day my disobedience
Grieves Your loving heart;
But then redeeming love breaks through,
And causes me to worship You.

(Men – Women echo))
Redeemer,
Saviour,
Healer
And Friend.
Every day
Renew my ways,
Fill me with love
That never ends.

1125 Craig Musseau.
Copyright © 1989 Mercy/Vineyard Publishing/
Adm. by CopyCare.

YOU ARE MIGHTY,
You are holy,
You are awesome in Your power.
You have risen, You have conquered,
You have beaten the power of death.

Hallelujah, we will rejoice.
Hallelujah, we will rejoice.

1126 Brian Doerksen.
Copyright © 1991 Mercy/Vineyard Publishing/
Adm. by CopyCare.

YOU ARE MY KING, (You are my King)
And I love You.
You are my King, (You are my King)
And I worship You.

Kneeling before You now,
All of my life I gladly give to You.
Placing my hopes and dreams
In Your hands,
I give my heart to You.

I love You, love You, Jesus.
Yes, I love You, love You, Jesus,
My King.

1127 Noel & Tricia Richards.
Copyright © 1995 Kingsway's
Thankyou Music.

YOU ARE MY PASSION,
Love of my life,
Friend and companion, my Lover.
All of my being
Longs for Your touch;
With all my heart I love You.

Now You will draw me close to You,
Gather me in Your arms;
Let me hear the beating of Your heart,
O my Jesus,
O my Jesus.

1128 Wynne Goss.
Copyright © 1992 Kingsway's
Thankyou Music.

YOU ARE RIGHTEOUS in all Your ways,
You are good, You are good.
You are truthful in all You say,
You are good, You are good.

And I bow my knee before You,
In honour of Your name,
For You alone are worthy,
Worthy of my praise,
Worthy of my praise.

You are holy, faithful and true,
You are good, You are good.
You are gracious in all You do,
You are good, You are good.

1129 Tommy Walker.
Copyright © 1991 WeMobile Music/Doulos
Publishing/Adm. by CopyCare.

YOU ARE THE GREAT I AM,
Forever You will be.
Let every angel sing
Of Your perfect authority.
Every knee will bow
And every tongue confess;
You are the great I AM,
The First and Last

Mighty, (Mighty)
Eternal, (Eternal)
Immortal, (Immortal)
Awesome One. (Awesome One)
Mysterious, (Mysterious)
The Wonderful, (the Wonderful)
The Holy One, (the Holy One)
The Beginning and the End.

1130 Steve & Vikki Cook.
Copyright © 1994 People of Destiny
International/Word Music/Adm. by CopyCare.

**YOU ARE THE PERFECT AND RIGHTEOUS
GOD**
Whose presence bears no sin;
You bid me come to Your holy place:
How can I enter in
When Your presence bears no sin?
Through Him who poured out His life for me,
The atoning Lamb of God,
Through Him and His work alone I boldly come.

I come by the blood, I come by the cross,
Where Your mercy flows
From hands pierced for me.
For I dare not stand on my righteousness,
My every hope rests on what Christ has
done,
And I come by the blood.

You are the high and exalted King,
The One the angels fear;
So far above me in every way,
Lord, how can I draw near
To the One the angels fear?
Through Him who laid down His life for me
And ascended to Your side,
Through Him, through Jesus alone I boldly
come.

1131 Per Soetorp.
Copyright © 1992 His Music/
Kingsway's Thankyou Music.

YOU ARE WONDERFUL,
Counsellor, Mighty God.
You are Prince of Peace,
Our Father forever more.
You're the Alpha and Omega,
Lord of all lords.
You are Wonderful,
Counsellor, Mighty God.

1132 John Pantry.
Copyright © 1990 Kingsway's
Thankyou Music.

YOU ARE WORTHY TO RECEIVE
All the honour and praise.
Lamb of God, Prince of Peace,
We lift high Your name.

For Yours is the greatness,
The power and the glory;
Lord of the nations,
Have mercy on us.
Though heaven be shaken,
And earth's kingdoms fall,
We will still worship You.

In the footsteps of our King,
We walk unafraid;
Though the battle may rage,
Our praises will ring.

1133 Terry Butler.
Copyright © 1992 Mercy/Vineyard Publishing/
Adm. by CopyCare.

YOU BLESS MY LIFE, and heal me inside,
Over and over again.
You touched my heart and brought peace of
mind,
Over and over again.

All I can say is I love You.
All I can say is I need You.
All I can say is I thank You, Lord,
For all that You've done in my life.

You've been so kind and patient with me,
Over and over again.
When I have strayed You showed me the
way,
Over and over again.

1134 Robert Newey.
Copyright © 1990 Kingsway's
Thankyou Music.

YOU CAME to heal the brokenhearted;
You came to make the blind eyes see.
Your light is burning now within us,
As Your word of truth sets us free.

And we will fill the earth with the love of
God
That's been shed abroad in our hearts,
Share with every nation and every land
The grace that He imparts.
And we will sing a new song of joy and
peace,
A resounding trumpet call,
Causing hearts to rise, opening eyes to
see
That Jesus, Jesus is Lord of all.

You come in all Your mighty power,
You come to bring the latter rain;
We know You've filled us with Your Spirit
And a love we cannot contain.

You'll come in glory and splendour,
You'll come to reign upon the earth;
We know we'll live with You forever
And declare Your mighty worth.

1135 Mark Altrogge.
Copyright © 1991 People of Destiny
International/Word Music/Adm. by CopyCare.

YOU HAVE BECOME FOR US WISDOM;
You have become for us righteousness.
You have become our salvation;
You have become all our holiness.

All that we need is found in You;
Oh, all that we need is in You.
All that we need is found in You;
You are our all in all.
You have become our all in all.

You have become our provision;
In union with You we have victory.
In You we have died and have risen;
You are our great hope of glory.

1136 Andy Park.
Copyright © 1991 Mercy/Vineyard Publishing/
Adm. by CopyCare.

YOU HAVE CALLED US CHOSEN,
A royal priesthood,
A holy nation,
We belong to You.
(Repeat)

Take our lives as a sacrifice;
Shine in us Your holy light.
Purify our hearts' desire;
Be to us a consuming fire.

You have shown us mercy,
You have redeemed us;
Our hearts cry 'Father,
We belong to You.'
(Repeat)

1137 Alun Leppitt.
Copyright © 1994 Kingsway's
Thankyou Music.

YOU HAVE LIFTED UP THE HUMBLE,
Filled the hungry with good things;
Shown Your mercy to the fearful,
You have healing in Your wings.
The rich will leave with nothing,
But the poor will have it all,
And the pure in heart will see their holy God.

You will light the road from darkness,
As You lead us to Your throne;
You give strength to the weary,
And shelter from the storm.
You pour out living waters
So we will never thirst,
And You wipe away the tears from our eyes.

Holy is Your name,
Holy is Your name;
Perfect grace and rich in love,
Your mercy never ends.
Holy is Your name,
Holy is Your name;
Precious Lamb of sacrifice,
Forever You will reign.

You bring justice to the nations,
Salvation's at Your hand;
With your blood You made the purchase
From every tribe and land,
To be priests within Your kingdom,
Your Spirit's on us all
To show the love and favour of the Lord.

1138 Tom Davis & Kevin Prosch.
Copyright © 1991 Mercy/Vineyard Publishing/
Adm. by CopyCare.

YOU HAVE TAKEN THE PRECIOUS
From the worthless and given us
Beauty for ashes, love for hate.
You have chosen the weak things
Of the world to shame that which is strong,
And the foolish things to shame the wise.

You are help to the helpless,
Strength to the stranger,
And a father to the child that's left alone.
And the thirsty You've invited
To come to the waters,
And those who have no money, come and
buy.

So come, so come.
So come, so come.

Behold the days are coming
For the Lord has promised,
That the ploughman will overtake the
reaper.
And our hearts will be the threshing floor,
And the move of God we've cried out for
Will come, it will surely come.

For You will shake the heavens,
And fill Your house with glory,
And turn the shame of the outcast into
praise.
And all creation groans and waits
For the Spirit and the Bride to say
The word that Your heart has longed to
hear.

1139 Darlene Zschech & Russell Fragar.
Copyright © 1996 Darlene Zschech & Russell
Fragar/Hillsongs Australia/Kingsway's
Thankyou Music.

YOU MAKE YOUR FACE TO SHINE ON ME,
And that my soul knows very well;
You lift me up, I'm cleansed and free,
And that my soul knows very well.

When mountains fall I'll stand
By the power of Your hand,
And in Your heart of hearts I'll dwell,
And that my soul knows very well.
(Repeat)

Joy and strength each day I'll find,
And that my soul knows very well;
Forgiveness, hope I know is mine,
And that my soul knows very well.

1140 Ian Smale.
Copyright © 1994 Kingsway's
Thankyou Music.

**YOU NEVER PUT A LIGHT UNDER A DIRTY
OLD BUCKET.**
You never put a light under a dirty old
bucket.
You never put a light under a dirty old
bucket
If you want light to shine around, round,
round.

Shine, shine around, round round.
Shine, shine around, round, round.
Shine a light that everyone can see.
Lord, help me let my little light shine,
Not just Sundays, all the time,
So friends give praise to You
When they see me.

1141 Carol Mundy.
Copyright © 1993 Kingsway's
Thankyou Music.

YOU'RE AMAZING,
An amazing mighty God,
Full of compassion and true.
You're a loving heavenly Father
To whom all praise is due.
You're so amazing,
Father, I love You.

1142

YOU RESCUED ME, and picked me up,
A living hope of grace revealed,
A life transformed in righteousness,
O Lord You have rescued me.
 Forgiving me, You healed my heart,
And set me free from sin and death.
You brought me life, You made me whole,
O Lord, You have rescued me.

And You loved me before I knew You,
And You knew me for all time.
I've been created in Your image,
O Lord.
And You bought me, and You sought me,
Your blood poured out for me;
A new creation in Your image,
O Lord.
You rescued me, You rescued me.

1143

YOU'RE THE LION OF JUDAH,
The Lamb that was slain,
You ascended to heaven
And ever more will reign;
At the end of the age
When the earth You reclaim,
You will gather the nations before You.
And the eyes of all men will be
Fixed on the Lamb who was crucified,
For with wisdom and mercy and justice
You'll reign at Your Father's side.

And the angels will cry:
'Hail the Lamb
Who was slain for the world,
Rule in power.'
And the earth will reply:
'You shall reign
As the King of all kings
And the Lord of all lords.'

There's a shield in our hand
And a sword at our side,
There's a fire in our spirit
That cannot be denied;
As the Father has told us,
For these You have died,
For the nations that gather before You.
And the ears of all men need to hear
Of the Lamb who was crucified,
Who descended to hell yet was raised up
To reign at the Father's side.

1144

YOUR EYE IS ON THE SPARROW,
And Your hand, it comforts me.
From the ends of the earth
To the depths of my heart,
Let Your mercy and strength be seen.
You call me to Your purpose,
As angels understand.
For Your glory may You draw all men,
As Your love and grace demands.

And I will run to You,
To Your words of truth;
Not by might, not by power
But by the Spirit of God.
Yes, I will run the race,
Till I see Your face.
Oh, let me live in the glory of Your grace.

1145

YOUR LOVE LOOKS AFTER ME,
It never fails.
Your word takes care of me,
And keeps my mind on You.
(Repeat)

You are majestic
Through all the earth;
I am Your servant
For the rest of my days.

You are magnificent,
The God of glory;
I'm going to worship You
For the rest of my days,
For the rest of my days,
For the rest of my days.

1146

YOUR LOVE, O LORD,
It reaches to the heavens;
Your faithfulness,
It reaches to the skies.
Your righteousness is like
The mighty mountains;
How priceless is Your faithful love.

I will exalt You, O Lord,
I will exalt You, O Lord.
Praise Your holy name,
That my heart may sing to You;
I will exalt You, O Lord.

Your name, O Lord,
It is a mighty tower;
Your glory
It covers all the earth.
In Your hands alone
Are strength and power,
All praise to be Your glorious name.

1147 David Wellington.
Copyright © 1994 Kingsway's
Thankyou Music.

YOUR NAME IS PEACE
Saviour so holy;
King of righteousness
Merciful and mighty.
God with us,
Revealed to us,
Awesome and eternal God,
Your name is peace.
Wonderful Counsellor,
Everlasting Father,
Lord, Your name is peace,
Your name is peace.

1148 Paul Oakley.
Copyright © 1997 Kingsway's
Thankyou Music.

YOUR VOICE IS LIKE THUNDER,
Your eyes like fire;
Your throne is forever,
In unapproachable light.
Your grace is so tender,
Your love like wine;
To You I surrender,
I lay down my life.

And all I want to do . . .

*Is to build a house of gold,
Purest silver and costly stones;
Let it stand when the fire comes,
When the day brings Your light.
Be my wisdom and be my strength,
Fill me up with Your faithfulness;
Keep me loving until the end.
Let the fire in Your eyes
See a living sacrifice,
Pleasing in Your sight.*

Let me build a house of gold . . .

1149 Dougie Brown.
Copyright © 1991 Sovereign Lifestyle Music.

YOUR WILL, NOT MINE, that is what I desire
    to see,
Walking in righteousness, and holy liberty.
Your life, not mine, that is what I desire to
    live,
Forgiving others, as always You forgive.

*I bow before Your majesty,
I fall before Your throne;
I cannot understand Your love,
But I claim it as my own.
I rise and stand before You
As a living sacrifice;
I seek to do Your will, O God,
For the rest of my life.*

Your voice, not mine, that is what I desire to
    hear;
Speak in the stillness and whisper in my ear.
Your mind, not mine, that is what I desire to
    have;
To prophesy Your word, release the captive
    heart.

Your race, not mine, that is what I desire to
    run;
To finish off the work that others have begun.
Your work, not mine, that is what I desire to
    do;
To serve Your purposes, and worship only
    You.

1150 Dave Dickerson.
Copyright © 1988 Coronation Music
Publishing/Kingsway's Thankyou Music.

YOU SHALL BE HOLY
And in everything be true,
For I, the Lord, am holy,
And My word belongs to you.

Stay in my presence,
Grow strong in My love,
With all the gifts I give you
From My kingdom here above.

We are Your children,
Abba Father, mighty God,
And growing in Your likeness,
Through grace of Jesus' blood.

Inspired by Your Spirit,
Our eternal source of power,
Release us to worship,
And to praise You every hour.

Copyright Addresses

Ateliers et Presses de Taizé, F-71250 Taizé Communauté, Cluny, France.

Karen Barrie, 511 Maple, Wilmette, Illinois 60091, USA.

Kay Chance, Glaubenszentrum 3353 Bad Gandersheim, Germany.

Christian Fellowship of Columbia, 4600 Christian Fellowship Road, Columbia, Missouri 65203, USA.

Church of England Central Board of Finance, Church House, Great Smith Street, London, SW1P 3NZ.

CopyCare, P.O. Box 77, Hailsham, East Sussex, BN27 3EF, UK.

David Higham Associates, 5-8 Lower John Street, Golden Square, London, W1R 3PE, UK.

Daybreak Music Ltd, Silverdale Road, Eastbourne, East Sussex, BN20 7AB, UK.

Timothy Dudley-Smith, 9 Ashlands, Ford, Salisbury, Wiltshire, SP4 6DY, UK.

Gabriel Music, P.O. Box 840999, Houston, Texas 77284-0999, USA.

Grace! Music, 11610 Grandview Road, Kansas City, Missouri 64137, USA.

Heart of David Music, *contact* Grace! Music.

Hi-Fye Music, 8-9 Frith Street, London, W1V 5TZ, UK.

IMP, Southend Road, Woodford Green, Essex, IG8 8HN, UK.

The Independent Music Group, Independent House, 54 Larkshall Road, Chingford, London, E4 6PD, UK.

Josef Weinberger Ltd, 12-14 Mortimer Street, London, W1N 7RD, UK.

Jubilate Hymns, 4 Thorne Park Road, Chelston, Torquay, Devon, TQ2 6RX

Kingdom Faith, Foundry Lane, Horsham, West Sussex, RH13 5PX, UK.

Kingsway's Thankyou Music, P.O. Box 75, Eastbourne, East Sussex, BN23 6NW, UK.

Melva Lea, P.O. Box 2744, Del Mar, California 92014, USA.

Mike and Claire McIntosh, Grace Church, PO Box 24000, Federal Way, Washington 98093, USA.

Len Magee Music, 71 Merridown Drive, Carrara, Queensland 4211, Australia.

Leosong Copyright, *contact* The Independent Music Group.

Make Way Music, P.O. Box 263, Croydon, Surrey, CR9 5AP, UK.

OCP Publications, 5536 N.E. Hassalo, Portland, Oregan 97213, USA.

Oxford University Press, 70 Baker Street, London, W1M 1DJ, UK.

C. Simmonds, 22 St Michael's Road, Bedford, Bedfordshire, MK40 2LT, UK.

Mary Smail, c/o Rev. Tom Smail, 366 Alexandra Road, Croydon, Surrey, CR0 6EU, UK.

Songs for Today, *contact* Windswept Pacific.

Sovereign Music UK, P.O. Box 356, Leighton Buzzard, Bedfordshire, LU7 8WP, UK.

Linda Stassen, New Songs Ministries, R.R. 1 Box 454, Erin, Tennessee 37061, USA.

Warner Chappell Music, *contact* IMP

Wild Goose Resource Group, Iona Community, Pearce Institute, 840 Govan Road, Glasgow, G51 3UU, Scotland, UK.

William Elkin Music Services, Station Road Industrial Estate, Salhouse, Norwich, Norfolk, NR13 6NY, UK.

Windswept Pacific, 27 Queensdale Place, London, W11 4SQ, UK.

Index of titles and first lines

(Titles where different from first lines are shown in *italics*)